GARDENS
ACROSS AMERICA

GARDENS ACROSS AMERICA

*The American Horticultural Society's Guide
To American Public Gardens and Arboreta
Volume II: West of the Mississippi*

THOMAS S. SPENCER AND
JOHN J. RUSSELL

TAYLOR TRADE PUBLISHING
Lanham • New York • Dallas • Boulder • Toronto • Oxford

Copyright ©2006 by Friar's Lantern
First Taylor Trade Publishing edition 2006

This Taylor Trade Publishing paperback edition of *Gardens across America* is an original publication. It is published by arrangement with the authors.

Back cover photos (top to bottom): Normandale Community College—The Japanese Garden, Bloomington, MN; Zen Garden, © The Huntington Library, Art Collections, and Botanical Gardens, San Marino, CA; The Living Desert Zoo and Gardens, Palm Desert, CA.

Published by Taylor Trade Publishing
An imprint of The Rowman & Littlefield Publishing Group, Inc.
4501 Forbes Boulevard, Suite 200
Lanham, Maryland 20706

Distributed by National Book Network

Library of Congress Cataloging-in-Publication Data

Spencer, Thomas S., 1946–
    Gardens across America : the American Horticultural Society's guide to American public gardens and arboreta / Thomas S. Spencer and John J. Russell.
        p. cm.
    Includes bibliographic references and index.
    ISBN-10: 1-58979-296-3 (pbk. : alk. paper)
    ISBN-13: 978-1-58979-296-8
    1. Gardens—United States—Guidebooks. 2. Botanical Gardens—United States—Guidebooks. 3. Arboretums—United States—Guidebooks. 4. Parks—United States—Guidebooks. 5. United States—Guidebooks. I. Russel, John J., 1945– II. Title
    SB466.U6S64   2005
    712'.5'0973—dc22   2005002525

∞™ The paper used in this publication meets the minimum requirements of American National Standard for Information Sciences—Permanence of Paper for Printed Library Materials, ANSI/NISO Z39.48–1992.
Manufactured in the United States of America.

CONTENTS

THE AMERICAN HORTICULTURAL SOCIETY

Founded in 1922, the non-profit American Horticultural Society (AHS) is one of the oldest member-based national gardening organizations in North America. The Society's membership includes more than 35,000 avid gardeners and horticultural professionals as well as numerous regional and national partner organizations. The AHS vision is to make America a nation of gardeners, a land of gardens.

The AHS headquarters at George Washington's River Farm in Alexandria, Virginia, is a national showcase for gardening and horticultural practices. The natural beauty of this 25-acre historic site along the Potomac River is enhanced by a blend of formal and naturalistic gardens, including woodlands, meadows, a water feature, an azalea garden, and award-winning children's gardens.

Through its national educational programs, awards, and publications, AHS connects people to gardening to help raise awareness of earth-friendly gardening practices, introduce children to plants, bring together leaders to address important national issues, and showcase the art and science of horticulture. Among these programs are

- The annual National Children and Youth Garden Symposium
- The National Awards program
- The AHS Plant-Heat Zone map
- The horticultural reference book series
- The SmartGarden™ earth-friendly gardening program
- Online gardening courses through the Horticultural Gardening Institute
- The Travel/Study program to visit inspiring gardens around the world
- The Horticultural Internship program
- The Great American Gardeners lecture and workshop series

Benefits of AHS membership include a subscription to the nationally acclaimed *The American Gardener* magazine, access to a toll-free gardener's hotline, participation in a free member seed exchange, free or discounted admission to many flower shows and botanical gardens, and much more.

If you care about gardening—whether it's your hobby, your passion, or your profession—you should be a member. It's not just what you'll learn that makes AHS membership so rewarding, it's what you share as part of a community of gardeners—past, present, and future. For more information about the American Horticultural Society, call (800) 777-7931, or visit the AHS website at www.ahs.org.

The AHS Mission: To open the eyes of all Americans to the vital connection between people and plants; to inspire all Americans to become responsible caretakers of the Earth; to celebrate America's diversity through the arts and sciences of horticulture; and to lead this effort by sharing the Society's unique national resources with all Americans.

FOREWORD

America's public gardens are extraordinary places. Whether small or large, whether framed by spectacular views or nestled in the fabric of the city, whether originally created as a personal garden or designed specifically for public use, each public garden is a unique expression of its region, its mission, its designers, and its caretakers.

We are so fortunate in this country to have a strong tradition of exceptional public gardens. There is no better way to experience the remarkable and varied beauty of this great land of ours—or to understand the creativity and ingenuity of its gardeners—than by visiting our public gardens.

What do public gardens offer? First and foremost, they are well-designed green spaces filled with the beauty and wonder of plants. They also offer what all good gardens offer—inspiration for the spirit and refreshment for the soul. In addition, public gardens display many design ideas that can be taken home to a personal garden or emulated in public parks, school grounds, or other municipal green spaces.

Public gardens are also important places of learning. They not only showcase a wide variety of plants suitable for home gardens in their region, but they offer opportunities to see these plants grown well using environmentally sound practices. If the public garden is also a botanic garden or arboretum, it will have collections of plants identified with informative labels and signs.

In addition, public gardens are often places of research. Public gardens test plants from different regions for adaptability. They conserve endangered plants both in the wild and in the laboratory. They evaluate the environmental effects of modern day culture, from pollution to chemical use to non-renewable resources. This research is critical to guiding the decisions and practices of home gardeners, industry leaders, and policy makers.

Many public gardens also express the character of their communities through special events and seasonal celebrations. These range from displays of spring bulbs, lilacs, and tropical flowers to chili peppers, pumpkins, and poinsettias, and from concerts and ethnic festivals to art exhibits and holiday light displays.

The America Horticultural Society believes strongly that public gardens in America are among our greatest and most underappreciated treasures. To demonstrate our support for public gardens, members of the AHS are entitled to free or discount admission to many public gardens through the AHS "Reciprocal Admissions Program." Gardens that participate in this program are indicated in this guide.

Our public gardens help to connect each one of us, no matter how old or young, to the larger world of plants and gardens. It is my hope that this book will inspire the reader to want to visit each and every one of the gardens listed. In return you will receive the precious gifts these gardens offer—peace, serenity, inspiration, and education—as well as cherished memories of visits shared with family and friends.

Katy Moss Warner
President, American Horticultural Society

EDITORS' INTRODUCTION

We believe that this book, along with its companion volume dealing with facilities east of the Mississippi, fills a need long-felt by the American garden-loving public for a comprehensive guide to public gardens and arboreta that is portable, readable, useful, attractive, and comprehensive. Our book is intended to enable the garden lover to plan more productive and enjoyable excursions by providing essential information on sites and their offerings.

It is unique in its scope, focusing on more than 450 of a total of almost 1,200 gardens and arboreta in both volumes. No other source contains detailed information on so many. We have sought to be as inclusive as possible, the thought being to permit the reader to decide not to visit a facility, which he can do only after being made aware of its existence.

Our book is "current" in that it provides complete and accurate contact data (address, telephone, facsimile, TDDY telephone, and website address) as well as information on hours and days of operation, admission fees, on-site food availability, accessibility for the disabled, parking facilities, and other such topics. It also describes the facility's collection and the facility itself, in many instances illustrating one or the other with a color photograph. These descriptions and illustrations not only help the reader to place the facility as to type, but also, along with facts about annual attendance, size, membership availability, and other factors, permit the reader to make qualitative and quantitative judgments about it. Of course, the sophisticated garden visitor knows that such a process is not without its dangers; there are hundreds of wonderful small and, sadly, sparsely attended gardens in the United States.

Finally, a few words about accuracy are in order. First, space limitations have prevented us from setting forth in as much detail as we would have liked regarding facilities and operations. For example, a garden listed as accessible to the disabled may be only partly so. Second, some attendance figures may include persons attending related facilities, such as zoos. Third, some institutions listed have not responded fully to our repeated requests for information, perhaps in a few cases resulting in publication of dated or misinterpreted information. Fourth, we have chosen to not include specific information on the scheduling and nature of temporary events and exhibits in the belief that such transitory information is most reliably gained by contacting the institution directly as close to the time of a proposed visit as possible. Finally, we have chosen not to include in the main body of the guide display and other gardens operated by commercial facilities, such as nurseries. A list of commercial facilities maintaining display gardens may be found in the Appendix.

We have made every possible effort to verify the information contained in this book, by sending each facility a questionnaire, making follow-up telephone calls, visiting websites, and checking a number of secondary sources. Nevertheless, the data in this book can be no more accurate than that which we have received (we hope no less accurate), and, therefore, when in doubt, the reader should contact the facility directly. We apologize for any inconvenience caused by errors in this book, whatever the source. We also welcome suggestions from those who use this book regarding institutions that should be added or other changes that would make future editions more useful.

John J. Russell and Thomas S. Spencer
Monkton, Maryland
May 15, 2005

HOW TO USE
THIS BOOK

We have approached questions of design and organization in this book from the point of view of the reader; ease of use and accessibility were our paramount concerns. To that end, we have tried to be consistent in format and to avoid unnecessary and annoying abbreviations as much as possible, even though to do so uses more space on the page.

The main body of the guide is organized alphabetically by state and then community. Each state listing is preceded by a map, which indicates the communities in which facilities may be found. In a few appropriate cases, we have included maps of metropolitan areas as well. The number in parentheses after a community indicates the number of facilities listed in this guide in that community; the absence of a number means that there is only one such facility listed. The maps are intended merely to indicate the approximate location of communities with gardens or arboreta, in order to assist the reader in planning excursions, not to function as a detailed road map.

Organizations are arranged alphabetically under the community in which they are located. If there is an initial "The" in an institution's name, it is ignored in determining entry order. Also, "St." is alphabetized as "Saint" and "Ft." as Fort. ("The University of Arizona Campus Arboretum" falls under U, not T. "St. John's University" sorts as "Saint John's University.")

Within entries, information always occupies the same position. Contact information immediately follows the organization name, followed by data on admission fees, attendance, year established, availability of membership, accessibility to the disabled (a "P" means partial accessibility), and parking arrangements.

Next is information on hours of operation. The data following "Open:" are the regularly scheduled hours of operation. Following "Closed:" are the exceptions to the hours shown in "Open:", such as holidays. Please note that if an institution is regularly closed on Mondays, it will be shown as "Open: Tuesday to Saturday, XX am-XX pm"; Monday would not appear under "Closed:", as it is understood in the "Open:" section.

"Facilities:" and "Activities:" have been designed to allow the reader to skim the listings for a particular piece of information without having to read the entire text. The categories in bold type are in alphabetical order followed by specific information in parentheses when appropriate. For instance, if you wish to know which gardens in a certain city have libraries, simply look under "Facilities:" in each entry. You might find, for example, "Library (12,000 volumes; non-circulating; Tues-Wed, 11am-1pm)." Finally, there is a more detailed description of the facility, designed to give the reader a "feel" for it.

The index, in addition to the formal name of each institution, includes cross references to facilitate finding the entries of organizations for which the proper name is unknown.

We encourage users of this guide to contact us with any suggestions for improving the organization and presentation of data in future editions.

(AHS RAP)

When you see this acronym/symbol after the name of a garden, it means the garden participates in the American Horticultural Society's Reciprocal Admissions Program (RAP). Through this program, American Horticultural Society (AHS) members are eligible for free or discounted admission and many other benefits at the nearly 200 participating gardens and arboreta located throughout North America.

To learn more about the RAP and the many other benefits of membership in the American Horticultural Society, see page vii or visit the AHS website at www.ahs.org.

ALASKA

•Fairbanks

Anchorage. •Palmer
Homer.

The number in parentheses following the city name indicates the number of gardens/arboreta in that municipality. If there is no number, one is understood. For example, in the text one listing would be found for Anchorage.

ANCHORAGE

ALASKA BOTANICAL GARDEN (AHS RAP)

Campbell Road (off Tudor Road), Anchorage, AK 99520
Tel: (907) 770-3692
Internet Address: http://www.alaskabg.org
Admission: Fee: adult $5.00, child $3.00, senior $3.00, family $10.00
Established: 1993
Membership: Y
Wheelchair Accessible: P
Parking: Park at Benny Benson School
Open: May 15 to September 15, Daily, 9am-9pm. September 16 to
May 14, Daily, daylight hours
Facilities: Gardens (herb, perennial, rock, wildflower); Grounds (110
acres, of which 11 are under development); Nature Trails
Activities: Education Programs; Guided Tours (additional fee)

Begun by the Alaska Horticultural Association, the gardens contain over 480 varieties of cultured plants and approximately 92 native species of plants in the Campbell Tract area. Theme gardens include the Upper Perennial Demonstration Garden, illustrating cost-effective ways of creating garden borders; the Lower Perennial Garden, presenting examples of perennials that are hardy in South Central Alaska; a rock garden, designed by the Alaska Rock Garden Society and including both shade and sunny rock gardens; a formal herb garden with raised beds; and a wildflower trail, displaying many examples of the common wildflowers native to the Anchorage area. Future plans for ABG include establishing a rose garden, children's garden, edible plant garden, and building more natural trails.

FAIRBANKS

UNIVERSITY OF ALASKA, FAIRBANKS— GEORGESON BOTANICAL GARDEN (GBG)

Agricultural & Forestry Experiment Station, 117 W. Tanana Drive, Fairbanks, AK 99775
Tel: (907) 474-1944; Fax: (907) 474-1841
Internet Address: http://www.uaf.edu/snras/gbg
Admission: Fee: adult $1.00, child free
Attendance: 30,000
Established: 1991
Membership: Y
Wheelchair Accessible: Y
Parking: Free parking.
Open: May to September, Daily, 7am-8pm
Best Time(s) of Year to Visit: mid-July to August (giant vegetables)
Facilities: Gardens (children's, flower, vegetable, hardy perennial); Grounds (5 acres); Special Collections (hardy ferns, herbs, native plants)
Activities: Classes; Education Programs; Guided Tours (June-August, Fri, 2pm; by reservation; small fee); Self-Guided Tours

Originally the demonstration flower garden at the UAF Agricultural and Forestry Experiment Station, in 1991 the facility became the Charles Georgeson Botanical Garden, dedicated to the study of propagation, cultivation, and conservation of native and introduced plant species in the subarctic north. The Garden contains annual flowers, vegetables, fruits, wildflowers, herbs, hardy perennials and native aquatic plants. Attractions include Alaskan giant vegetables in the Family Food Garden and a nature trail identifying the native flora common to Alaska's northern boreal forest.

HOMER

PRATT MUSEUM—BOTANICAL GARDEN

3779 Bartlett St., Homer, AK 99603-7597
Tel: (907) 235-8635; Fax: (907) 235-2764
Internet Address: http://www.prattmuseum.org
Admission: Fee: adult $6.00, child (<6) free, child (6-18) $3.00, senior $5.50, family $20.00
Attendance: 30,000
Membership: Y

Wheelchair Accessible: Y
Parking: Free on site, auto and RV
Open: February to mid-May, Tuesday to Sunday, noon-5pm; mid-May to mid-September, Daily, 10am-6pm; mid-September to December, Tuesday to Sunday, noon-5pm; Closed: New Year's Day, Thanksgiving Day, Christmas Day
Facilities: Garden (native plant); Herbarium; Museum; Shop (books on gardening and native plants, wildflowers)
Activities: Education Programs

A natural history museum, the Pratt features exhibits including a botanical garden and a forest nature trail. The Garden contains more than 150 local species including forget-me-nots, columbine, chocolate lilies, fireweed, cranberries, and Labrador tea. The Pratt Museum is wholly owned by the Homer Society of Natural History, a non-profit organization.

PALMER

MATANUSKA VALLEY AGRICULTURAL SHOWCASE (COLONY GARDEN OR VIC GARDEN)

723 S. Valley Way (at East Fireweed Ave.), Palmer, AK 99645
Tel: (907) 745-2880; Fax: (907) 746-4164
Internet Address: http://www.palmerchamber.org
Admission: No Charge/Donations Accepted
Attendance: 35,000
Established: 1967
Membership: Y
Wheelchair Accessible: Y
Parking: On site
Open: May to September, Daily, 9am-6pm
Best Time(s) of Year to Visit: August (blooms & giant vegetables)
Facilities: Garden (native plant, perennial, trees, giant vegetables); Grounds (1 acre)

Located next to the Palmer Visitors Center, this garden features thematic plantings featuring native flowers, annuals, perennials, giant vegetables, herbs, and fruits.

ARIZONA

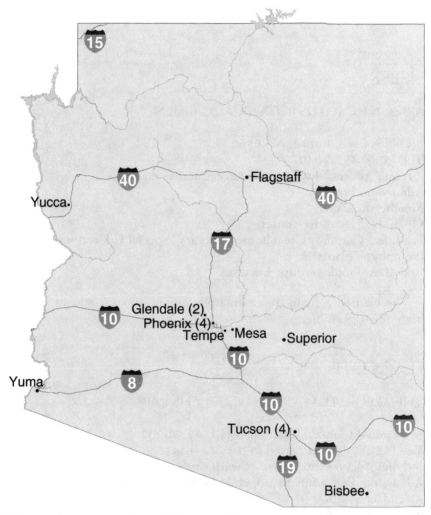

The number in parentheses following the city name indicates the number of gardens/arboreta in that municipality. If there is no number, one is understood. For example, in the text four listings would be found under Phoenix and one listing under Mesa.

BISBEE

ARIZONA CACTUS BOTANICAL GARDEN

8 Cactus Lane, Bisbee, AZ 85603
Tel: (520) 432-7040
Internet Address: http://www.arizonacactus.com
Admission: Free
Membership: Y
Open: Daily, sunrise-sunset
Facilities: Gardens; Greenhouses; Library; Special Collections
(xerophytic plants)
Activities: Guided Tours; Lectures

The Garden contains representative samples of over 800 varieties of
high desert plant life.

FLAGSTAFF

THE ARBORETUM AT FLAGSTAFF (AHS RAP)

S. Woody Mountain Road, Flagstaff, AZ 86002
Tel: (520) 774-1442; Fax: (520) 774-1441
Internet Address: http://www.thearb.org
Admission: Fee: adult $4.00, child (6-12) $1.00, senior $3.00
Attendance: 8,000
Established: 1981
Membership: Y
Wheelchair Accessible: Y
Open: April to December 15, Daily, 9am-5pm; Closed: December 16
to March 31
Facilities: Gardens (water conservation, herb, shade, butterfly);
Greenhouse; Grounds (200 acres; signs explain plants and animals);

Library (1,500 volumes); Shop; Special Collections (native plants, grasses); Visitors Center
Activities: Classes; Docent Program; Guided Tours (bird watching); Plant Sales

Located in the world's largest ponderosa pine forest at 7,150 feet above sea level, the Arboretum is dedicated to helping visitors understand the unique environment of the High Southwest.

GLENDALE

CITY OF GLENDALE—ELSIE MCCARTHY SENSORY GARDEN

7637 North 55th Ave. (at Morten Ave., south of Northern Ave.), Glendale, AZ 85301
Tel: (623) 930-2650
Internet Address: http://www.ci.glendale.az.us/Recreation/Elsie-McCarthy-Sensory-Garden
Admission: Free
Membership: N
Wheelchair Accessible: Y
Parking: Public parking lot with handicapped spots
Open: 6am-5pm
Best Time(s) of Year to Visit: October to March
Facilities: Garden (sensory)

Designed for the visually impaired, the Garden was developed to stimulate the senses of sight, sound, smell, and touch through the use of specific plants and trees for texture and scent, water features for sound, touch and sight and evening lighting for dramatic visuals. The garden contains five themed gardens: The Wisdom Garden, the Celebration Garden, the Contemplation Garden, the Reflection Garden and the Story Totem Garden, each with a unique type of water feature. The garden flora on the grounds are native to the Sonoran Desert, such as creosote, desert lavender turpentine, slipper plant, hesperaloe, prickly pear, and cactus.

CITY OF GLENDALE—XERISCAPE BOTANICAL GARDEN

5959 W. Brown St. (off 59th Ave., just south of Peoria Ave.), Glendale, AZ 85307
Tel: (623) 930-3596; Fax: (623) 842-2161; TDDY: (623) 930-2197

Internet Address:
http://www.ci.glendale.az.us/WaterConservation/xeriscapegarden.cfm
Admission: Free
Established: 1990
Wheelchair Accessible: Y
Open: Monday to Saturday, 9am-5pm; Sunday, 1pm-5pm; Closed:
Legal Holidays
Best Time(s) of Year to Visit: Spring, Fall
Facilities: Garden (xeriscape); Grounds (4 acres)
Activities: Classes (registration, (623) 930-3760); Self-Guided Tours
(audio wand may be checked out in the library)

Located on the grounds of the Glendale Public Library, the Xeriscape
Botanical Garden is considered one of the best demonstration gardens
in the Southwest. It contains over 1,000 low-water-use plants, most labeled with common and botanical names. In addition to a large cacti
section, there are many palm trees in the parking lot medians. There is
also an ethnobotanical area (plants that are edible or medicinal in purpose). Listening wands for self-guided tours and free landscaping
brochures are available inside the library. A virtual tour of the Garden
and detailed information on all the plants are available at
http://www.gc.maricopa.edu/glendalelibrary.

MESA

MESA COMMUNITY COLLEGE—ROSE GARDEN

1833 W. Southern Ave., Mesa, AZ 85202
Tel: (480) 461-7000
Internet Address:
http://www.mc.maricopa.edu/organizations/community/rosegarden/
Admission: Free
Established: 1996
Open: Daily
Best Time(s) of Year to Visit: April (peak bloom)
Facilities: Garden (Rose); Grounds (designed by LeRoy Brady)
Activities: Events Rose Show and Fall Festival (Nov)

Located on the campus of Mesa Community College, the Garden
contains more than 5,000 roses representing over 500 rose varieties. An
All-America Rose Selection, Inc. test garden, the Garden was developed

and is maintained by MCC in partnership with the Mesa-East Valley Rose Society.

PHOENIX

CITY OF PHOENIX—JAPANESE FRIENDSHIP GARDEN (RO HO EN)

Margaret T. Hance Park, 1125 North 3rd Ave., Phoenix, AZ 85003
Tel: (602) 262-6412; Fax: (602) 495-5557
Internet Address: http://www.ci.phoenix.az.us/PARKS/jfg.html
Admission: Fee: adult $1.00, child (<13) free
Attendance: 5,000
Established: 2002
Membership: Y
Wheelchair Accessible: Y
Parking: Lots located west of facility
Open: Saturday, 10am-4pm; Sunday, noon-4pm; Closed: June to August
Best Time(s) of Year to Visit: March to May
Facilities: Garden (Japanese); Grounds (3½ acres); Tea House
Activities: Events Tea Ceremony (2nd Sat in month, noon-3:45pm, reservations required); Guided Tours (groups 10+, Tues & Thurs, $3/person, schedule in advance); Self-Guided Tours (brochure available)

The Garden is a joint project of the sister cities of Phoenix, Arizona and Himeji, Japan. A delegation from Phoenix visited Japan in 1988 to view several gardens. In 1988 and 1990, a design team of landscape architects and architects from Himeji visited Phoenix to view the garden site and assist in the design. The Garden combines the knowledge and skills of both teams to create an authentic Japanese stroll garden that is adapted to the demands of a desert environment. The Garden is operated by the Phoenix Parks and Recreation Department.

DESERT BOTANICAL GARDEN (AHS RAP)

1201 N. Galvin Parkway (adjacent to Papago Park), Phoenix, AZ 85008-3490
Tel: (602) 941-1225; Fax: (602) 481-8124; TDDY: (602) 481-8143
Internet Address: http://www.dbg.org
Admission: Fee: adult $9.00, child (<3) free, child (3-12) $4.00, student $5.00, senior $8.00

Attendance: 250,000
Established: 1937
Membership: Y
Wheelchair Accessible: Y
Parking: Free on site
Open: October to April, Daily, 8am-8pm; May to September, Daily, 7am-10pm; Closed: Independence Day, Christmas Eve to Christmas Day.
Best Time(s) of Year to Visit: March to May
Facilities: Amphitheater (50 seats); Auditorium (100 seats); Food Services Patio Café (outdoor; salads, sandwiches); Gardens; Greenhouse; Grounds (145 acres); Herbarium (50,000 specimens); Library (Mon-Fri, noon-4pm, (602) 481-8133); Shops Garden Shop (plants, gifts; daily, 9am-5pm; (602) 481-8113); Special Collections (cactaceae, agavaceae, aloaceae, flora of the Sonoran Desert.); Trails (5)
Activities: Concerts; Demonstrations; Education Program (adults and children); Guided Tours Bird (7am); Garden (10:30am & 1pm, varies with season); Lectures; Workshops

A living museum featuring exotic desert plants in a Sonoran Desert setting, the Desert Botanical Garden is home to nearly 50,000 desert plants, representing 3,886 taxa in 133 plant families (nearly 70% of which are of documented, wild-collected origin). The collection is especially strong in cactaceae (1,350 taxa), agavaceae (35 taxa of yucca and 141 taxa of agave), aloaceae, and native flora of the Sonoran Desert. Other major collections include Old World succulents (1,207 taxa) and desert trees and shrubs (1,116 taxa). It is also serves as an important conservation institution with a collection of 169 rare, threatened or endangered plant species from the world's deserts, especially the southwestern U.S. and northern Mexico. The Garden offers a variety of workshops and lectures on horticulture, desert landscaping, ethnobotany, art and photography, natural crafts, and health and wellness. The Garden is accredited by the American Association of Museums.

MARICOPA COUNTY COOPERATIVE EXTENSION—
DEMONSTRATION GARDENS & LANDSCAPE
INTERPRETIVE TRAIL

4341 East Broadway Road, Phoenix, AZ 85040-8807
Tel: (602) 470-8086; Fax: (602) 470-8092
Internet Address:
http://ag.arizona.edu/maricopa/garden/html/general/intrail.htm

Admission: Free
Facilities: Gardens (annual, bulb, children's, healing, herb, native plant, rose, fruit plants/trees, turf, vegetable, wildflower, wildlife habitat); Grounds (2½ acres); Trail
Activities: Self-Guided Tours (descriptive "Trail Guide" fact sheets are available)

Situated on the grounds of the University of Arizona's Maricopa County Cooperative Extension office, exhibits focus on environmentally responsible landscaping and gardening in the low desert and include an educational trail explaining the decisions that go into developing and maintaining an effective landscape. The site is broken up into sections to illustrate a variety of components (i.e., an entryway, transition zone, wildflower meadow, native plants trail, vegetable demonstration gardens, etc.). Plantings include native and desert adapted landscape plants, desert wildflowers, antique roses, tropical and semitropical fruiting plants and trees, annual flowers, flowering bulbs, herbs, deciduous fruit trees, traditional and native seed vegetables, turf variety plots, wildlife habitat, and a children's garden. The Landscape Interpretive Trail was created and is maintained by volunteer Master Gardeners, who are on site to answer questions from the public on the 2nd and 4th Saturdays of each month from 8 am to 10 am.

VALLEY GARDEN CENTER

1809 N. 15th Ave. (1 block north of McDowell Road), Phoenix, AZ 85603
Tel: (602) 252-2120
Internet Address: http://www.phoenixbonsai.com/VGC.html
Admission: Free
Membership: Y
Open: Daily
Facilities: Gardens (rose); Grounds (3 acres); Library (1,400 volumes, available to club members)
Activities: Education Programs; Events Spring Festival (late Mar), Fall Festival (early Oct)

The Valley Garden Center is a private, non-profit organization serving ten active and nine associate horticultural clubs. Surrounding the spacious clubhouse are colorful gardens, including an All-America Rose Selections display garden containing 1,200 plants representing 110 rose varieties, a koi pond, and many mature trees.

SUPERIOR

BOYCE THOMPSON ARBORETUM STATE PARK

37615 E. U.S. Highway 60, Superior, AZ 85273
Tel: (520) 689-2723; Fax: (520) 689-5858
Internet Address: http://arboretum.ag.arizona.edu/l
Admission: Fee: adult $6.00, child (<5) free, child (5-12) $3.00
Attendance: 75,000
Established: 1924
Membership: Y
Wheelchair Accessible: Y
Open: Daily, 8am-5pm; Closed: Christmas Day.
Facilities: Arboretum; Gardens (cactus, demonstration, eucalyptus forest, herb, legume); Greenhouse; Grounds (323 acres); Library; Museum Store; Trails; Visitor Center
Activities: Events Earth Arbor Day (Apr), Fall Color Festival (Nov), Herb Festival (Apr), Landscaping Festival & Plant Sale (Spring & Fall); Guided Tours; Lectures; Temporary Exhibitions; Traveling Exhibitions

Surrounded by the Tonto National Forest, the Arboretum is the American Southwest's oldest arboretum and botanical gardens. Founded by mining magnate Colonel William Boyce, it brings together plants from the world's varied deserts and dry lands and displays them alongside examples of the native Sonoran Desert vegetation. Representatives of most of the Arboretum's living collection of over 800 species of cacti are displayed in the Cactus Garden and in the cactus greenhouse at the Smith Interpretive Center. Other exhibits include a demonstration garden presenting a series residential theme gardens featuring a variety of drought-tolerant and water-efficient plants, an herb garden, a legume garden, and an Australian eucalyptus forest. Additionally, wildflowers are found throughout the Arboretum grounds.

TEMPE

CITY OF TEMPE—XERISCAPE DEMONSTRATION GARDEN

Tempe Woman's Club Park (corner of College Ave. & Weber Drive), Tempe, AZ 85280
Tel: (480) 350-2668; Fax: (480) 350-8336; TDDY: (480) 350-8400
Internet Address: http://www.tempe.gov/water/conserve.htm

Admission: Free
Parking: On site
Open: Daily, dawn-dusk
Best Time(s) of Year to Visit: Winter to Spring
Facilities: Garden (xeriscape); Grounds (10 acres)
Activities: Classes; Demonstrations; Self-Guided Tours; Workshops

A municipal garden, the site demonstrates the proper irrigation and cultural practices associated with desert landscaping.

TUCSON

ARIZONA-SONORA DESERT MUSEUM

2021 N. Kinney Road, Tucson, AZ 85744-8918
Tel: (520) 883-1380; Fax: (520) 883-2500
Internet Address: http://www.desertmuseum.org/index.html
Admission: Fee (Nov-April): adult $12.00, child (<6) free, child (6-12) $4.00; Fee (May-Oct): adult $9.00, child $2.00
Membership: Y
Wheelchair Accessible: Y
Open: October to February, Daily, 8:30am-5pm; March to September, Daily, 7:30am-6pm; June to August, Saturday, until 10pm
Facilities: Food Services (2 restaurants); Gardens (desert, cactus); Grounds (21 acres); Shops (2)

The Arizona-Sonora Desert Museum is a zoo, natural history museum and botanical garden. In addition to featuring interpretive displays of living animals and plants in their natural desert settings, the Museum has two gardens: the Cactus Garden with over 140 species of cactus and other Sonoran Desert plants and the Desert Garden with over 160 species of plants, a butterfly garden, red garden, succulent garden, gray foliage garden, grass garden and moth garden.

CITY OF TUCSON—GENE C. REID PARK ROSE TEST GARDEN

900 S Randolph Way, Tucson, AZ 85716
Tel: (520) 791-4873; Fax: (520) 791-4008
Admission: Free
Attendance: 20,000
Established: 1960
Parking: Ninety parking spaces

Open: Daily, sunrise-sunset
Best Time(s) of Year to Visit: April to October
Facilities: Garden (rose)

Located just west of Reid Lake, the Garden, featuring 1,080 rose beds and 101 species of roses, is sponsored by the City of Tucson Parks and Recreation Department, the Rose Society of Tucson, and All-America Rose Selections, Inc.

TOHONO CHUL PARK INC.

7366 N. Paseo del Norte, Tucson, AZ 85704
Tel: (520) 742-6455; Fax: (520) 797-1213
Internet Address: http://www.tohonochulpark.org/
Admission: Fee: adult $5.00, child $2.00, student $3.00, senior $4.00; Free admission first Tuesday of each month
Attendance: 230,000
Established: 1982
Membership: Y
Wheelchair Accessible: Y
Open: Daily, 8am-5pm; Closed: Christmas Day, Independence Day, New Year's Day, Thanksgiving Day
Facilities: Art Exhibits; Food Services Restaurant (Daily, 8am-5pm); Gardens (hummingbird, Spanish Colonial, children's, ethnobotanical, demonstration); Greenhouses (10am-4pm); Grounds (49 acres; cholla forest); Library (800 volumes); Nature Trails; Nursery; Shops (2; 9:30am-5pm, Mon-Sat; 11am-5pm, Sun)
Activities: Concerts; Education Programs; Guided Tours; Lectures; Plant Sales

Tohono Chul Park is a desert preserve located in the midst of an ever-growing urban area in northwest Tucson. Its mission is to enrich people's lives by providing them the opportunity to find peace and inspiration in a place of beauty, to experience the wonders of the Sonoran Desert, and to gain knowledge of the natural and cultural heritage of this region.

TUCSON BOTANICAL GARDENS

2150 N. Alvernon Way, Tucson, AZ 85712-3199
Tel: (520) 326-9686 Ext: 10; Fax: (520) 324-0166
Internet Address: http://www.tucsonbotanical.org/
Admission: Fee: adult $5.00, child (<6) free, child (6-11) $2.50, senior $3.00

Attendance: 80,000
Established: 1968
Membership: Y
Wheelchair Accessible: Y
Open: September to May, Daily, 8:30am-4:30pm; Summer, Daily, 7:30am-4:30pm; Closed: New Year's Day, Independence Day, Thanksgiving Day, Christmas Day
Facilities: Food Services Picnic area; Gardens (see text); Greenhouse; Grounds (5 acres); Library (Mon/Wed/Fri, 1:30pm-4:30pm, non-circulating); Nursery; Shop
Activities: Education Programs; Guided Tours (Wed, Fri, Sat - 10am); Plant Sales

The Gardens feature a backyard bird garden, barrio garden (nuestro jardín), butterfly garden, cactus and succulent garden, compost demonstration area, herb garden, iris garden, Native American crops, reception garden, sensory garden, spring wildflower garden, a Tohono O'odham round house and exhibit, tropical exhibit, and xeriscape garden.

YUCCA

DESTINATION: FOREVER RANCH AND GARDENS (D:FR)

17 miles outside Yucca, AZ 86438
Box 160, 1711 Stockton Hill Road Kingman AZ 86401
Tel: (928) 766-2597
Internet Address: http://www.dfranch.com
Admission: by appointment; no fee
Established: 1999
Membership: N
Wheelchair Accessible: P
Parking: Gravel parking area
Open: by appointment
Best Time(s) of Year to Visit: September to April
Facilities: Grounds (40 acres (7 acres planted; remainder pre-existing vegetation); Special Collections (native plant; focus on cacti and succulents)
Activities: Plant Sales (at Yucca townsite location)

Situated in the southwestern foothills of the Hualapai Mountains at an altitude of 3,000 feet, Destination: Forever Ranch is dedicated to the creation of a desert botanical garden and sustainable living resource center in the Arizona desert. Occupying an ecological transition zone between three major biomes (Mojave Desert, Sonoran Desert, and Arizona Interior Chaparral/Great Basin), it offers a wide variety of scenery and a diverse population of xeriphytic flora and fauna. Currently, over 3,000 cacti, succulents, shrubs, and small trees have been planted. Most of the introductions are native plants such as ocotillo, Joshua trees, barrel cactus, and hedgehog cactus. There are also non-native specimens from dryland regions of the globe, such as Baja Mexico and the Andes Mountains.

YUMA

ARIZONA HISTORICAL SOCIETY—SANGUINETTI HOUSE AND GARDENS

240 S. Madison Ave. (just off Route I-8, Giss Parkway exit), Yuma, AZ 85364-1421
Tel: (928) 782-1841; Fax: (928) 783-0680
Internet Address: http://www.arizonahistoricalsociety.org
Admission: Fee: adult $3.00, child $2.00, senior $2.00; Free first Saturday in month
Attendance: 4,500
Established: 1963
Membership: Y
Wheelchair Accessible: P
Parking: On street and parking lot across street
Open: Tuesday to Saturday, 10am-4pm; Closed: State Holidays
Best Time(s) of Year to Visit: Winter to Spring
Facilities: Architecture Sanguinetti House (adobe residence, ca. 1870); Gardens; Library (non-circulating); Shop (books, local crafts, period gifts)
Activities: Education Programs (upon request); Guided Tours (by appointment)

Located in the historic north end of town, the Sanguinetti House Museum was constructed in the 1870s, and was purchased in 1890 by pioneer merchant E. F. Sanguinetti. He added to the home as his family grew and created an Italian oasis with a small garden and aviaries, which are maintained today. The house contains exhibits and period rooms. Sanguinetti House, the adjacent Adobe Annex, and nearby Molina Block are operated by the Rio Colorado Division of the Arizona Historical Society. The House is listed on the National Register of Historic Places.

ARKANSAS

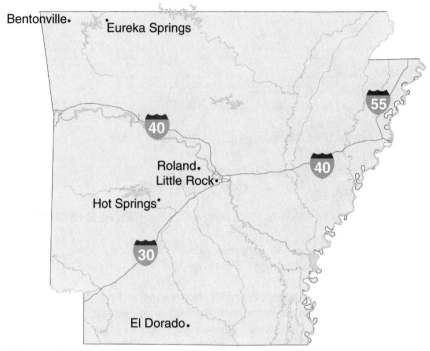

The number in parentheses following the city name indicates the number of gardens/arboreta in that municipality. If there is no number, one is understood. For example, in the text one listing would be found for Little Rock.

BENTONVILLE

PEEL MANSION MUSEUM AND GARDEN

400 S. Walton Blvd., Bentonville, AR 72712-5705
Tel: (501) 273-9664
Internet Address: http://biz.ipa.net/peel/
Admission: Fee: adult $3.00, child (6-12) $1.00
Membership: Y
Open: Tuesday to Saturday, 10am-4pm; Closed: December 23 to
January 6.
Facilities: Architecture (Italianate residence, 1875)
Activities: Flower and Garden Show (end of May)

The Gardens feature historic roses, perennials and native plants. Careful research over many months has resulted in an extensive inventory of nineteenth-century plantings. Various vignette gardens are interlaced among curvilinear walks and large shade trees.

EL DORADO

SOUTH ARKANSAS COMMUNITY COLLEGE— SOUTH ARKANSAS ARBORETUM

Mount Holly Road and Timberlane (off Rte 82B, adjacent to
El Dorado High School), El Dorado, AR 71731
Tel: (870) 862-8131 Ext. 170
Admission: Free
Parking: Free on site
Open: Daily, 8am-5pm; Closed: Holidays
Facilities: Arboretum; Grounds (17 acres); Trails (5 miles)
Activities: Guided Tours (arrange in advance); Self-Guided Tours

Operated by South Arkansas Community College, the Arboretum exhibits plants indigenous to Arkansas's Gulf Coastal Plain region and exotic species including flowering azaleas and camellias.

EUREKA SPRINGS

EUREKA SPRINGS GARDENS

Blue Spring Heritage Center, 1537 CR 210 (off Route 62, 5½ miles west of Eureka Springs), Eureka Springs, AR 72632
Tel: (479) 253-9244; Fax: (479) 253-9256
Internet Address: http://www.eurekagardens.com
Admission: Fee: adult $7.25, child (<10) free, child (10-17) $4.00
Parking: On site
Open: March 15 to Thanksgiving, 9am-6pm
Facilities: Gardens (herb, heritage, native plant, woodland); Grounds (33 acres); Trails (1+ miles); Shop (American Indian and handcrafted items unique to the Ozark Region, pottery, artwork, books, music)

Yielding over 38 million gallons of water daily, Blue Spring has been a tourist attraction since 1948. Eureka Springs Gardens were begun in 1998 and in 2003 "the rich history of the land was blended with the beauty of the Gardens to become the Blue Spring Heritage Center." In addition to woodland gardens highlighting native plants, the site offers two Native American gardens: the Medicine Wheel Garden, featuring healing herbs and native plants related to the spiritual practices of Native Americans and the Three Sister Garden, illustrating a traditional Native American practice of planting pole beans, squash and corn as an interdependent community of plants.

HOT SPRINGS

UNIVERSITY OF ARKANSAS—GARVAN WOODLAND GARDENS

550 Arkridge Road (in Hot Springs National Park), Hot Springs, AR 71913
Tel: (800) 366-4664; Fax: (501) 262-9301
Internet Address: http://www.garvangardens.org
Admission: Fee: adult $7.00, child (<6) free, child (6-12) $4.00, senior $6.00

Attendance: 75,000
Membership: Y
Wheelchair Accessible: Y
Parking: Free on site
Open: April to October, 9am-6pm; November to March, 10am-5pm;
Closed: New Year's Day, Thanksgiving Day, Christmas Day
Facilities: Amphitheater; Gardens (Bulb Meadow, Daffodil Hill,
Camellia Trail, Japanese); Grounds (210 acres); Shop; Visitor Center
Activities: Events Holiday Lights Display (mid-Nov-early Jan); Guided
Tours Groups (docent, by reservation); Self-Guided Tours

In 1956, Verna Cook Garvan began to develop the site as a garden and possible future residence. Over the next forty years, Mrs. Garvan planted thousands of specimens, which now form an impressive collection. Upon her death, Mrs. Garvan left the property to the University of Arkansas. A joint project of the University of Arkansas School of Architecture's Department of Landscape Architecture and the Division of Agriculture's Cooperative Extension Service, University of Arkansas, the gardens feature more than 128 species of ornamental and native shrubs and wildflowers, 260 varieties of flowering perennials and groundcovers, 111 different types of roses, 260 ornamental trees and more than 2,000 plantings of 160 different varieties of azaleas. The garden also contains a new pavilion designed by architect E. Fay Jones, winner of the American Institute of Architects' prestigious Gold Medal and former Dean of the University of Arkansas School of Architecture. Japanese maples and tree peonies are located in the Garden of the Pine Wind, a rock and stream garden recently ranked the top new Japanese garden in the nation. Most trails are ADA accessible with a few areas not recommended for those who have difficulty walking. There are plentiful benches and boulders placed throughout the Gardens, allowing visitors to rest, or just sit and enjoy the tranquility. Be sure to wear comfortable clothes and sturdy walking shoes.

LITTLE ROCK

STATE CAPITOL ROSE GARDENS

Arkansas State Capitol, Little Rock, AR 72201
Tel: (501) 682-6244
Internet Address: http://www.sosweb.state.ar.us/grounds.html
Admission: Free
Open: Capitol Building, Monday to Friday, 7am-5pm; Saturday to Sunday, 10am-5pm.
Facilities: Arboretum; Gardens (rose, iris); Grounds (24 acres)

Activities: Guided Tours Capitol Building (Mon-Fri, 9am-4pm, free);
Self-Guided Tours

The Capitol grounds include two rose gardens, containing approximately 1,500 roses; an iris garden; 40,000 annual bedding plants; and 350 trees (47 different species), 20 types of shrubs. A grounds brochure is available for visitors. The rose garden is accredited by All-America Rose Selections, Inc.

ROLAND

ARKANSAS ARBORETUM

Pinnacle Mountain State Park, 11901 Pinnacle Valley Road, Roland, AR 72135
Tel: (501) 868-5806; Fax: (501) 868-5018
Internet Address: pinnaclemountain@arkansas.com
Open: Daily, dawn-dusk
Facilities: Grounds Arboretum (71 acres), Park (1,800 acres); Library; Trail (1/2 mile); Visitor Center
Activities: Guided Tours

Located within the state park at the base of Pinnacle Mountain, the Arkansas Arboretum contains examples of native flora representing Arkansas's six natural divisions. Currently under development, when completed it will feature native trees and shrubs from all regions of Arkansas.

CALIFORNIA

The number in parentheses following the city name indicates the number of gardens/arboreta in that municipality. If there is no number, one is understood. For example, in the text two listings would be found under Santa Cruz and one listing under Lancaster.

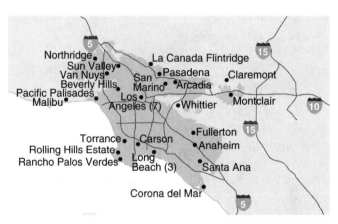

Greater Los Angeles Metropolitan area (including Anaheim, Arcadia, Beverly Hills, Carson, Claremont, Corona del Mar, Fullerton, La Canada Flintridge, Long Beach, Los Angeles, Malibu, Montclair, Northridge, Pacific Palisades, Pasadena, Rancho Palos Verdes, Rolling Hills Estate, San Marino, Santa Ana, Sun Valley, Torrence, Van Nuys, and Whittier)

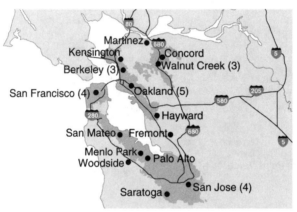

Greater San Francisco metropolitan area (including Berkeley, Concord, Fremont, Hayward, Kinsington, Martinez, Menlo Park, Oakland, Palo Alto, San Francisco, San Jose, San Mateo, Saratoga, Walnut Creek, and Woodside)

ANAHEIM

ANAHEIM'S WATERWISE GARDEN

2150 E. Katella Ave. (next to Amtrak Station), Anaheim, CA 92806
Tel: (714) 765-4256; Fax: (714) 765-4152
Internet Address: http://www.anaheim.net/utilities/water.html
Admission: Free
Established: 1998
Membership: N
Wheelchair Accessible: Y
Parking: In adjacent Anaheim Angels Stadium lot
Open: Daily, 24 hours
Facilities: Garden (xeriscape); Grounds (½ acre)
Activities: Education Programs

Bordering the Amtrak Train Station next to Anaheim Angels Stadium, the Waterwise Demonstration Garden displays 33 low-water-use plant species selected for their contrast in color, texture, and shape. The Garden also includes a water-efficient irrigation system. The Garden is sponsored by Anaheim Public Utilities.

APTOS

CABRILLO COLLEGE—ENVIRONMENTAL HORTICULTURE CENTER AND BOTANICAL GARDENS

6500 Soquel Drive, Aptos, CA 95003
Tel: (831) 479-6241
Internet Address: http://www.cabrillo.cc.ca.us/divisions/becho/hort/
Admission: Free
Facilities: Gardens (aquatic, children's, exotic foliage, native plant); Greenhouses; Grounds (11 acres); Herbarium; Shade Houses; Shop;

Special Collections (California natives, fuschia, salvia, succulents);
Visitor/Community Center
Activities: Education Programs; Lectures; Plant Sale (Spring)

Situated on the hill above the main campus at a site with spectacular views of the Monterey Bay, the Environmental Horticulture Center includes one of the largest salvia collections in the world, as well as significant collections of California natives (especially those from the Monterey Bay region), plants from the Mediterranean regions of the world, succulents, and species fuchsias. Exhibits feature specialized gardens of exotic foliage plants, gardens for children, natural habitat gardens, aquatic gardens, greenhouses, and shade houses.

ARCADIA

LOS ANGELES COUNTY ARBORETUM AND BOTANIC GARDEN (AHS RAP)

301 N. Baldwin Ave., Arcadia, CA 91007-2697
Tel: (626) 821-4623; Fax: (626) 447-3763
Internet Address: http://www.arboretum.org/
Admission: Fee: adult $6.00, child (<5) free, child (5-12) $1.50, student $4.00, senior $4.00; Free: 3rd Tuesday in month
Attendance: 250,000
Established: 1948
Membership: Y
Wheelchair Accessible: Y
Parking: Free parking
Open: Daily, 9am-4:30pm
Closed: Christmas Day
Facilities: Arboretum; Climatic Areas (Australian, African, Mediterranean, Southwestern, South American, Asiatic/North American); Food Services Peacock Café (9am-4:30pm); Gardens (aquatic, Biblical, four season, herb, native oak grove, perennial, rose, tropical forest, water conservation); Greenhouses (begonia, tropical); Grounds (127 acres); Library (30,000 volumes; Mon-Fri, 9am-5pm; Sat-Sun, 10am-1pm); Nursery; Shop (9:30am-4:30pm; 447-8751); Special Collections (acacia, aloe, cassia, eucalyptus, leptospermum, magnolia, melaleuca, senna, tabebuia, cycads); Tram (11am-3pm, $2/person)
Activities: Arts Festival; Concerts; Education Programs; Flower Shows; Guided Tours; Lectures; Temporary Exhibitions

Plant collections are arranged primarily by geographic origins. The grounds also contain several historical structures, including Native American wickiups, a reconstruction of the original (1840) adobe rancho, a Queen Anne cottage and matching Coach Barn constructed on the grounds in the 1880s, and a late nineteenth-century train depot. The Arboretum is managed jointly by the Parks and Recreation Department of Los Angeles County and by the private, non-profit California Arboretum Foundation.

AUBURN

PLACER NATURE CENTER—HISTORICAL & NATIVE PLANT GARDEN

3700 Christian Valley Road, Auburn, CA 95602
Tel: (530) 878-6053; Fax: (530) 878-6053
Internet Address: http://www.placernaturecenter.org
Admission: Free
Attendance: 8,000
Established: 1992
Membership: Y
Wheelchair Accessible: Y
Parking: Handicapped and regular parking
Open: Monday to Friday, 8am-4pm; 2nd Saturday in month, 10am-3pm
Facilities: Garden (1/2 acre, historical and native plants, iris, kitchen, Native American, drought tolerant, European, Asian, butterfly, orchard); Greenhouse; Grounds Center (40 acres); Picnic Area; Trails 1 mile
Activities: Education Programs

Located in the heart of the Sierra Nevada Foothills, the Center, an environmental education facility with exhibit hall and teaching laboratory, offers a garden featuring native fruits, vegetables and flowers, several nature trails, a courtyard with a bog and pond, and a compost education center. The Center is a community-based non-profit organization.

AVALON

WRIGLEY MEMORIAL AND BOTANICAL GARDEN

1404 Avalon Canyon Road (Catalina Island), Avalon, CA 90704
Tel: (310) 510-2288

Internet Address: http://www.catalina.com/memorial.html
Admission: Fee: adult $5.00, child-free
Established: 1935
Membership: Y
Open: Daily, 8am-5pm
Facilities: Grounds (37.85 acres)
Activities: Guided Tours

   With its commanding view of Avalon Bay, the Wrigley Memorial is the centerpiece of the Botanical Garden. It was built in 1933-34 with the goal of using as much Catalina materials as possible. The idea for a garden came from Mr. Wrigley's wife, Ada. In 1935, she supervised Pasadena horticulturist Albert Conrad, who planted the original Desert Plant Collection. Catalina Island's temperate marine climate made it possible to showcase plants from every corner of the earth. In 1969, the Wrigley Memorial Garden Foundation expanded and revitalized the garden's 37.85 acres. Along with the new plantings came a new attitude. In the same way that the Wrigley Memorial uses primarily native building materials, the Garden places a special emphasis on Catalina Island endemic plants, including the rare Catalina Ironwood. In 1996 the Wrigley Memorial Garden Foundation merged with the Catalina Island Conservancy.

BERKELEY

BERKELEY MUNICIPAL ROSE GARDEN

1200 Euclid St. (between Eunice St. & Bay View Place),
Berkeley, CA 94708
Tel: (510) 644-6530
Admission: Free
Established: 1938
Parking: On street
Open: Daily, dawn-dusk
Best Time(s) of Year to Visit: May
Facilities: Garden (rose); Grounds (3 1/2 acres)

   Situated in a ravine formed by Codornices Creek, the Garden features over 3,000 roses planted in an amphitheater consisting of six stone terraces surmounted by a rustic redwood pergola supporting a variety of climbing roses.

REGIONAL PARKS BOTANIC GARDEN

Tilden Regional Park, Wildcat Canyon Road and South Park Drive,
Berkeley, CA 94708

Tel: (510) 841-8732; Fax: (510) 848-6025
Internet Address: http://www.nativeplants.org/
Admission: No charge/donations accepted
Established: 1940
Membership: Y
Wheelchair Accessible: P
Parking: On-site parking lot and along Anza View Road
Open: Daily, 8:30am-5pm; Closed: New Year's Day, Thanksgiving Day,
Christmas Day.
Facilities: Grounds (10 acres); Special Collections (California
manzanita, wild lilac).
Activities: Classes; Guided Tours (Sat & Sun, 2pm); Lecture Series;
Plant Sale (3rd Sat in Apr)

Located in Wildcat Canyon in the heart of the North Berkeley Hills, the Garden, organized into ten major climate areas of California, features California native plants growing together as in their natural habitat in the appropriate climate area. Notable among the specimens are representatives of nearly all the state's conifers and oaks, a very good collection of wild lilacs (Ceanothus species), and probably the most complete collection of California manzanitas to be found anywhere. There are also expanding collections of Californian native bunchgrasses and aquatics, and representatives of about 300 taxa that are classified in the California Native Plant Society's landmark study, *Inventory of Rare and Endangered Vascular Plants of California.*

UNIVERSITY OF CALIFORNIA BOTANICAL GARDEN (AHS RAP)

200 Centennial Drive (Strawberry Canyon), Berkeley,
CA 94720-5045
Tel: (510) 643-2755; Fax: (510) 642-5045
Internet Address: http://botanicalgarden.berkeley.edu
Admission: Fee: adult $3.00, child (<3) free, child (3-18) $1.00,
student-free, senior $2.00; Free: Thursday
Attendance: 40,000
Established: 1890
Membership: Y
Wheelchair Accessible: Y
Parking: Adjacent parking lot
Open: Day after Labor Day to Day before Memorial Day, 9am-5pm;
Memorial Day to Labor Day, Monday to Tuesday, 9am-5pm;
Wednesday to Sunday, 9am-8pm; Closed: New Year's Eve to New
Year's Day, ML King Day, Thanksgiving Day, Christmas Eve to
Christmas Day, 1st Tuesday in month

Facilities: Amphitheater (in redwood grove); Climatic Areas (African hill, Asia, Australasia, Mediterranean/Europe, Mesoamerica, New World desert, North America, South America); Gardens (aquatic, Chinese medicinal, California cultivar, economic plant, herb, native plant, old rose, palm & cycad, perennial); Greenhouses (desert, fern and carnivorous, rainforest, tropical); Grounds (34 acres); Library (600 volumes); Shop (Daily, 10:30am-4:30pm, 642-3343)
Activities: Bird Walks; Education Programs; Guided Tours (Sat & Sun, 1:30pm); Lectures; Temporary Exhibitions

The fifth largest botanic garden in the world, the Garden contains over 13,000 taxa and over 20,000 plants. Arranged by region of origin, the Garden has outstanding collections of cacti, rhododendrons, Chinese medicinal herbs, Western herbs, southern African plants, and California natives. The five best-represented families, with the number of accessions in parentheses, are as follows: Cactus family (2,669), Lily family (1,193), Sunflower family (1,151), Heath family (897), and Orchid family (950). The remainder is distributed among the other 319 families in the collection, including approximately 500 accessions of ferns and fern allies. Special collections of Chinese medicinal herbs, plants of economic importance, Old Rose cultivars, and California native plants restricted to serpentinite substrates are also featured. Voucher specimens for many of the collections are filed in the separately administered UC and Jepson Herbaria on campus. Vouchering of woody species and other long-lived perennials is ongoing. The Garden is noted for its large number of rare and endangered species.

BEVERLY HILLS

VIRGINIA ROBINSON GARDENS

1008 Elden Way (off Crescent Drive), Beverly Hills, CA 90210
Tel: (310) 276-5367
Internet Address: http://parks.co.la.ca.us/virginia_gardens.html
Admission: Fee (by reservation only): adult $7.00, child (5-12) $2.00, student $4.00, senior $4.00
Established: 1982
Open: Tuesday to Friday, by advance reservation only
Best Time(s) of Year to Visit: April to May (peak bloom)
Facilities: Architecture (Beaux Arts residence, 1911); Gardens (formal, Italian-style, kitchen, rose, terrace); Grounds (6½ acres); Special Collections (tropical, subtropical)
Activities: Guided Tours (Tues-Thurs, 10am & 1pm; Fri, 10am; by appointment only)

The former residence of Mr. and Mrs. Harry Winchester Robinson and one of the first homes in Beverly Hills, the site contains five distinct landscapes (Italian terrace garden, formal mall garden, rose garden, kitchen garden, and Renaissance Revival pool pavilion), featuring exotic tropical and subtropical flora and connected by brick paths, fountains, and ponds. It is one of four gardens maintained by the County of Los Angeles Department of Parks and Recreation.

CARSON

CALIFORNIA STATE UNIVERSITY, DOMINGUEZ HILLS— JAPANESE FRIENDSHIP GARDEN (SHIN-WA-EN)

University Campus, 1000 E. Victoria St., Carson, CA 90747
Tel: (213) 526-3753
Internet Address:
http://www.csudh.edu/archives/csudh/japanesegarden/broch.html
Admission: Free
Established: 1978
Facilities: Garden (Japanese); Grounds (1,100 square feet, 1978 design by Yamashiro Haruo); Teahouse

Located in the atrium area of the Social and Behavioral Sciences Building, the Garden blends elements of traditional Japanese tea and dry gardens with the unique character of the Dominguez Hills, creating a miniature island landscape dominated by symbolic mountains and forests and surrounded by the sea. The teahouse, constructed of redwood and cedar, is used for tea ceremonies and other university events.

CHICO

CALIFORNIA WATER SERVICE CO.—DROUGHT TOLERANT DEMONSTRATION GARDEN

Southeast corner of East 1st & Sheridan Aves., Chico, CA 95926
Tel: (530) 895-0564; Fax: (530) 895-8492
Internet Address:
http://www.calwater.com/Conservation/chico_conv_gdn.htm
Admission: Free
Established: 1993
Wheelchair Accessible: Y
Facilities: Garden (xeriscape); Grounds (1/2 acre)

Featuring drought-tolerant plants, the Garden contains over 150 varieties of trees, shrubs, perennials, ground covers, ferns and grasses. Designated beds have been specifically planted to attract butterflies and hummingbirds, and showcase Butte County native plants, sun-loving perennials, shade-loving ferns, ground covers and a variety of grasses. A full-color drawing is displayed at the site as well as brochures naming and locating the different beds and plants.

CITRUS HEIGHTS

RUSCH BOTANICAL GARDEN

7801 Auburn Blvd., Citrus Heights, CA 95610
Tel: (916) 725-5550; Fax: (916) 725-2541
Internet Address: http://www.sunriserecreationpark.org/index.html
Open: dawn-dusk
Facilities: Gardens (2 acres)

The garden is maintained by the City of Sacramento Sunrise Recreation and Park District. It features rose, herb, citrus, and African gardens.

CLAREMONT

CLAREMONT GRADUATE UNIVERSITY—RANCHO SANTA ANA BOTANIC GARDEN (RSABG)

1500 N. College Ave. (off Foothill Blvd.), Claremont, CA 91711-3157
Tel: (909) 625-8767; Fax: (909) 626-7670
Internet Address: http://www.cgu.edu/inst/rsa/
Admission: Suggested contribution $4.00, family $8.00
Attendance: 100,000
Established: 1927
Membership: Y
Wheelchair Accessible: Y
Open: Daily, 8am-5pm; Closed: New Year's Day, Independence Day, Thanksgiving Day, Christmas Day
Best Time(s) of Year to Visit: November to March (manzanita), March to April (California wild lilac), Spring (wildflowers, perennials, shrubs)
Facilities: Grounds (86 acres); Herbarium (Mon-Fri, by appointment only); Library (77,000 volumes, Mon-Fri, by appointment only); Shop; Special Collections (California wild lilac, manzanita)
Activities: Concerts; Education Programs; Guided Tours

Rancho Santa Ana Botanic Garden is devoted to the collection, cultivation, study, and display of native California plants. Located at an elevation of 1,350 feet on the outwash plain of the San Gabriel Mountains, the Garden is laid out in three distinct areas. Indian Hill Mesa is heavily planted with mature cultivars and wild species of California native plants. The Mesa is also home to the Southern Riparian Woodland, the California Cultivar Garden, the Basketry Trail, the Oak Woodland Trail, and the Home Demonstration Garden. The East Alluvial Gardens include the Desert Garden, Coastal Dune and California Channel Islands collections. The Plant Communities, the northern 55 acres of the Garden, display in naturalistic plant associations some of the most impressive specimens in the entire collection.

CONCORD

CONTRA COSTA WATER DISTRICT— WATER EFFICIENT GARDEN

1331 Concord Ave., Concord, CA 94520
Tel: (925) 688-8321; Fax: (925) 688-8122
Internet Address: http://www.ccwater.com
Admission: Free
Established: 1991
Wheelchair Accessible: Y
Parking: On site
Open: Daily, sunrise-sunset
Facilities: Garden (xeriscape); Grounds (1 acre)
Activities: Education Programs

A demonstration garden featuring water-efficient plants, the garden is low-maintenance, and the native and exotic drought tolerant perennials and shrubs are well suited to the local climate and soil.

CORONA DEL MAR

SHERMAN LIBRARY AND GARDENS

2467 E. Coast Hwy., Corona del Mar, CA 92625
Tel: (714) 673-2261; Fax: (714) 675-5458
Internet Address: http://www.slgardens.org/
Admission: Fee: adult $3.00, child (<6) free, child (6-12) $1.00;
Mondays: Free

Attendance: 70,000
Established: 1966
Membership: Y
Wheelchair Accessible: Y
Parking: 2 lots: Dahlia & Pacific Coast Hwy. and Dahlia & 3rd Ave.
Open: Daily, 10:30am-4pm; Closed: New Year's Day, Thanksgiving Day, Christmas Day
Best Time(s) of Year to Visit: March to mid-October
Facilities: Auditorium (150 seats); Conservatory; Food Services Café (Mon-Fri, 11am-2:30pm); Garden; Gardens (desert, discovery (sensory), fern, herb, Japanese, rose, sun, shade, tea, tropical); Grounds (2.2 acres); Lath House; Library (6,000 volumes; Tues-Thurs, 9am-4:30pm)
Activities: Concerts; Education Programs; Guided Tours; Lectures; Temporary Exhibitions

The garden is designed to be a horticultural display garden, rather than a botanical garden. Areas include a cactus/succulent garden, fern grotto, herb garden, Japanese garden, rose garden, and a tropical conservatory featuring orchids, heliconias and gingers. The botanical collection is very broad with over 1,000 species and 200 genera, including plants from around the world.

DAVIS

UNIVERSITY OF CALIFORNIA, DAVIS ARBORETUM (AHS RAP)

La Rue Road, Davis, CA 95616
Tel: (530) 752-2498; Fax: (530) 752-5796
Internet Address: http://www.aes.ucdavis.edu/public/default.htm
Admission: Voluntary contribution
Established: 1936
Membership: Y
Wheelchair Accessible: Y
Parking: On campus, $3/day
Open: Daily, 24 hours
Facilities: Climatic Areas (California desert, foothill, north coast; Mediterranean climate); Gardens (demonstration flower, medicinal and culinary herb, native plant, perennial, white flower, oak grove, redwood grove); Grounds (100 acres); Herbarium; Library; Special Collections (oaks)
Activities: Guided Tours (call 530-752-4880)

Located on the campus of the University of California, Davis, the Arboretum occupies a two-mile stretch along Putah Creek. Specializing in plants adapted to a Mediterranean climate, with hot, dry summers and cool, wet winters, the Arboretum is arranged in a series of gardens that represent different geographic areas, plant groups, horticultural themes, or historical periods. The Ruth Risdon Storer Garden features flowering perennials and small shrubs that are especially well suited to Central Valley gardens. The Arboretum is a major source of horticultural information for inland California. Displays now being developed will feature plants from Australia, the Southwest U.S., Mexico, Argentina and Chile. The Early California Garden will represent a garden from the rancho period, roughly 1840-1860, when California was part of Mexico. The California Plant Communities Garden will feature compact representations of the habitat zones of the local watershed. A map is available from Arboretum Headquarters, which is located on LaRue Road just west of California Avenue.

EL CAJON

THE WATER CONSERVATION GARDEN

12122 Cuyamaca College Drive West, El Cajon, CA 92019
Tel: (619) 660-0614; Fax: (619) 660-1687
Internet Address: http://www.thegarden.org/
Admission: Free
Established: 1999
Parking: Free on site.
Open: Daily, 9am-4pm
Facilities: Amphitheater (300 seats); Garden (cactus/succulent, container, fragrance, ground cover, native plant, slope, turf, vegetable, white, xeriscape); Grounds (4½ acres, design by Jon Powell of Deneen Powell Atelier
Activities: Education Programs; Events Folk Music Festival (Summer)

Located on the campus of Cuyamaca College, the Garden is designed to demonstrate the techniques of xeriscape landscaping. The site consists of demonstration gardens, an amphitheater with seating for more than 350, and multiple educational exhibits. The Garden has over 360 trees and over 100,000 square feet of landscaping. Educational exhibits feature plants from five areas of the world with similar climates (southwestern U.S., western South America, South Africa, the Mediterranean, and Australia). The Garden is a joint project of the Grossmont-Cuyamaca Community College District and a number of sponsoring public agencies led by the San Diego County Water Authority.

ENCINITAS

QUAIL BOTANICAL GARDENS (AHS RAP)

230 Quail Gardens Drive, Encinitas, CA 92024-2707
Tel: (760) 436-3036; Fax: (760) 632-0917
Internet Address: http://www.qbgardens.com
Admission: Fee: adult $8.00, child (<3) free, child (3-12) $3.00,
student $5.00, senior $5.00; Free, first Tuesday in month
Attendance: 110,000
Established: 1958
Membership: Y
Wheelchair Accessible: Y
Parking: Free on site
Open: Daily, 9am-5pm; Closed: New Year's Day, Thanksgiving Day,
Christmas Day
Facilities: Auditorium (96 seats); Bird Sanctuary; Climatic Areas
(Africa, Cape S. Africa, Australia, Canary Islands, Central America,
New & Old World Deserts, Himalayan, Mediterranean, Arid
Madagascar, Middle East, New Zealand, Pacific, Arid S. America, S.
California, Tropical Rainforest); Concession Area; Gardens
(children's, bamboo, fire safety, herb, lawn, native plant, palm,
pinetum, subtropical fruit, walled); Gift Shop & Nursery; Grounds
(30 acres); Library (500 volumes); Special Collections (bamboo)
Activities: Arts Festival; Concert Series (Summer); Films; Guided Tours
Children (1st Tues in month, 10:30am;, General (Sat, 10am), Group
(10+, reserve 30 days in advance, fee); Lectures; Plant Sales; Temporary
Exhibitions

Quail Botanical Gardens features diverse and important plant collections, including ancient cycads, palms, flowering trees, and the largest
bamboo collection in the United States. The twenty-four gardens include
plants from all over the world. An interactive children's garden, Seeds of
Wonder, is designed to engage children 2-6 years old.

ESCONDIDO

SAN DIEGO WILD ANIMAL PARK—GARDENS

15500 San Pasqual Valley Road (Highway 78), Escondido,
CA 92027-7017
Tel: (760) 747-8702; Fax: (760) 746-7081

Internet Address: http://www.sandiegozoo.org/wap/visitor_info.html
Admission: Fee: adult $23.95, child (<3) free, child (3-11) $16.95;
Reduced fee ticket available for park and zoo
Wheelchair Accessible: Y
Parking: On site, $6.00
Open: late December to mid-June, Daily, 9am-4pm; mid-June to
early-September, Daily, 9am-8pm; early September to early
December, Daily, 9am-4pm; early December to late December,
9am-8pm (Festival of Lights)
Facilities: Arboretum (conifer); Food Services (3 restaurants);
Gardens (bonsai, cactus/succulent, epiphyllum, herb, native plant,
protea, old world succulent, xeriscape); Grounds (1,800 acre wildlife
park); Shops (6, including The Plant Trader, offering exotic & easy-
to-grow plants)
Activities: Guided Tours California Nativescapes Botanical Garden
(Mar-May, 2nd Sat in month, (760) 741-0829)

A division of the Zoological Society of San Diego, the Wild Animal
Park is also an accredited botanical garden. The botanical collection
includes some 4,000 species, with more than 260 endangered species
of aloe, cactus, euphorbia, cycads, zamia, protea, palms and agave.
Their North African cypress is one of only twelve left in the world.
Specialty gardens include the California Nativescapes Botanical Garden, representing ten of California's native plant communities and containing about 500 species of native plants; an herb garden, containing
more than 400 varieties of herbs; the Baja Garden, displaying plants
from the Baja Peninsula in Mexico; an epiphyllum garden containing
600 plants; a waterwise garden, demonstrating the use of a variety of
drought-tolerant plants and zoned irrigation systems in landscape gardening; a protea garden; an Old World succulent garden; and a bonsai
house. Additionally, the Park's conifer forest displays over 1,000 plants
representing 400 species.

FALLBROOK

FALLBROOK FIRESCAPE GARDEN

Los Jilgueros Preserve, Mission Road (north of High School),
Fallbrook, CA 92028
Tel: (760) 728-0889
Internet Address:
http://sd.znet.com/~schester/fallbrook/attractions/conservancy.html
Admission: Free.

Established: 1995
Facilities: Garden (firescape); Grounds Firescape Garden (1/2 acre),
Los Jilgueros Preserve (46 acres)
Activities: Education Programs

Located in the northwest corner of the Los Jilgueros Preserve, the Garden features over 100 varieties of fire-resistant and drought-resistant plants, with many plants identified by labels.

FOLSOM

AMERICAN RIVER WATER EDUCATION CENTER— GARDEN (ARWEC GARDEN)

7794 Folsom Dam Road (off Folsom-Auburn Road),
Folsom, CA 95630
Tel: (916) 989-7100; Fax: (916) 989-7151
Internet Address: http://www.mp.usbr.gov/arwec/
Admission: Free
Attendance: 12,000
Established: 1999
Wheelchair Accessible: N
Parking: Free parking nearby; ADA compliant
Open: Education Center, Monday to Saturday, 9am-4:30pm
Facilities: Gardens (native plant, xeriscape); Grounds (3/4 acre);
Visitor Center (open Mon–Fri)
Activities: Education Programs Reservations required (Mon-Sat
[conservation; hydro-electric production]); Guided Tours Education
Center (Mon-Fri 2:30-4:30)

Located adjacent to the Center (containing a variety of water education exhibits), the outdoor garden provides a model for a landscape that will thrive even during dry periods and highlights the beauty of the natural landscape. It is divided into two sections: a xeriscape exhibit and a native plant area. The Center is a program of the United States Bureau of Reclamation.

FORT BRAGG

MENDOCINO COAST BOTANICAL GARDENS (AHS RAP)

18220 N. Highway #1, Fort Bragg, CA 95437-8740
Tel: (707) 964-4352; Fax: (707) 964-3114
Internet Address: http://www.gardenbythesea.org/

Admission: Fee: adult $7.50, child $1.00, child, senior $6.00
Attendance: 50,000
Established: 1961
Membership: Y
Wheelchair Accessible: Y
Open: March to October, Daily, 9am-5pm; November to February, Daily, 9am-4pm; Closed: Second Saturday in September, Thanksgiving Day, Christmas Day
Facilities: Display House; Gardens (coastal bluff, dahlia, fern canyon, heather, perennial, north forest, rhododendron, rose, vegetable, woodland); Grounds (47 acres); Nursery; Picnic Area; Shop; Special Collections (Pacifica iris)
Activities: Education Programs; Guided Tours; Workshops

Fronting directly on the ocean, the site contains manicured formal gardens, a dense coastal closed-cone pine forest, fern-covered canyons, diverse plant collections, and flower-filled coastal bluffs overlooking the blue Pacific Ocean. Whale fanciers can take shelter in the Cliff House to watch winter and spring migrations, bird watchers will delight in the over 100 species of birds that live in or visit the Gardens annually. In addition, over 80 wild mushroom varieties can be found here during the winter rainy season. Retired nurseryman Ernest Schoefer and his wife, Betty, founded Mendocino Coast Botanical Gardens in 1961. By 1992, the Gardens had been purchased with grants from the California Coastal Conservancy and transferred to the Mendocino Coast Recreation and Park District. It is now operated as a public trust, non-profit membership organization.

FREMONT

ALAMEDA COUNTY WATER DISTRICT—DROUGHT TOLERANT DEMONSTRATION GARDEN (ACWD GARDEN)

43885 S. Grimmer Blvd., Fremont, CA 94538
Tel: (510) 659-1970; Fax: (510) 770-1793
Internet Address: http://www.acwd.org/waterconserv-garden.html
Admission: Free
Membership: N
Wheelchair Accessible: Y
Parking: Free on site
Facilities: Garden (xeriscape); Grounds (2,500 square feet; design by Nancy Hardesty of Hardesty Benoit Associates)
Activities: Education Programs

Situated in front of the ACWD Headquarters Building, the Garden was designed to show example of a wide variety of drought-tolerant plants and water irrigation systems. Plantings were chosen to demonstrate that color and texture need not be sacrificed when using drought tolerant plants and to provide sequential color, with flowers blooming and/or leaf color interest for almost twelve months of the year.

FRESNO

FORESTIERE UNDERGROUND GARDENS

5021 W. Shaw Ave. (east of Highway 99), Fresno, CA 93722-5026
Tel: (559) 271-0734
Internet Address: http://www.undergroundgardens.com/
Admission: Fee (reservation required): adult $9.00, child (4-12) $6.00, child (13-17) $7.00, senior $8.00
Established: 1906
Open: Fall to Spring, Saturday to Sunday, by reservation; Easter to Labor Day, Wednesday to Sunday, 10am-4pm
Facilities: Grounds (4½ acres)
Activities: Guided Tours (by reservation)

Listed on the National Register of Historic Places, the Underground Gardens were created by Baldasare Forestiere, a Sicilian immigrant. The site consists of a complex of underground caverns, grottos, patios, and garden courts encircling his underground home. While constructing his home, Forestiere found that while the hardpan surface was not suitable for agriculture, the more pliable subsurface soils would support trees and plants. Working with hand tools over the next forty years (until his death in 1946 at the age of 67), he constructed more than 90 underground rooms and 10 acres of patios, courts, archways and grottoes at a depth of ten to twenty feet below surface. Plantings include a wide variety of citrus and other fruit trees with only their crowns protruding above ground level, as well as grape arbors. After his death the site was neglected, and only a portion has been restored.

SHINZEN JAPANESE GARDEN (SHINZEN GARDEN)

Woodward Park, Audubon Drive (off Friant Road), Fresno, CA 93755-6178
Tel: (559) 226-8034
Internet Address: http://www.shinzenjapanesegarden.org

Admission: Fee (+Park Entrance Fee $3/vehicle): adult $3.00, child
(<4) free, child (4-14) $1.00, senior $1.00, family $3.00; Free
November through February
Attendance: 10,000
Established: 1981
Membership: Y
Wheelchair Accessible: Y
Open: May to September, Monday to Friday, 5pm-dusk; Saturday to
Sunday, 10am-dusk; Holidays, 10am-dusk; October to April, Saturday
to Sunday, 10am-dusk
Facilities: Architecture (Japanese teahouse, granite lanterns and
benches; double moon bridge); Garden (Japanese; grove of 82
flowering apricot trees); Grounds (5 acres, designed by landscape
architect Paul Saito in conjunction with Japanese master teahouse
designer Shiro Nakagawa)
Activities: Festivals Fall Color Festival (annual, first full weekend in
November), Spring Blossom Festival (annual, weekend nearest the
vernal equinox), Toro Nagashi (Floating Lantern) Ceremony (annual,
August); Guided Tours (call for appointment (559) 621- 2900)

Located within Fresno's Woodward Region Park, the Garden is dedicated to Fresno's Sister City, Kochi, Japan, as a symbol of friendship and
international brotherhood, and for the promotion of cultural relations between the two cities. The Garden is planned around the four seasons, with
each seasonal area containing distinctive plantings. The spring section features azaleas, camellias, crab apples, irises, flowering cherries, and plums.
The cooling waters of the koi pond are the centerpiece of the summer section. Tulip trees, Chinese pistache and tallow trees display their bright fall
colors in the autumn section, while a large waterfall, pines, and evergreens
dominate the winter section. The authentic thatched-roof teahouse was
constructed in Japan, disassembled, and then reconstructed in the Garden.

UNIVERSITY OF CALIFORNIA COOPERATIVE EXTENSION— GARDEN OF THE SUN

Discovery Center, 1944 N. Winery Ave., Fresno, CA 93702-4516
Tel: (559) 456-4151
Internet Address: http://ucce.ucdavis.edu/files/programs/890
Admission: Fee: adult $2.00, child (<3) free
Open: Monday to Saturday, 10am-4pm
Facilities: Gardens (children's, cut flower, fruit & berry, herb, no
barriers, perennial, shade, vegetable); Grounds (1 acre, design by
landscape designer Robert Truxell)

Activities: Education Programs; Guided Tours Master Gardeners on site (Mon/Wed/Fri, 9am-1pm, $4/person, or by appointment); Workshops

The garden includes an extensive orchard of fruit trees, berries, and vines; beds of vegetables, drought-tolerant perennials, and cut flower; a shade garden; an All-American Selections display garden; specialty gardens for children; a no-barriers garden designed for the physically challenged; and a compost demonstration area. Planted in a semicircle around a coastal sequoia to symbolize the rays of the sun, an herb garden features a lovely selection of lavenders and a variety of theme gardens. The Garden of the Sun was developed and is maintained by participants in the Cooperative Extension's Master Gardener Program.

FULLERTON

THE FULLERTON ARBORETUM—CALIFORNIA STATE UNIVERSITY, FULLERTON

1900 Associated Road at Yorba Linda Blvd., Fullerton, CA 92831
Tel: (714) 773-3579; Fax: (714) 449-7066
Internet Address: http://arboretum.fullerton.edu
Admission: Voluntary contribution
Attendance: 140,000
Established: 1972
Membership: Y
Wheelchair Accessible: Y
Parking: Free on site
Open: Daily, 8am-4:45pm; Closed: New Year's Day, Thanksgiving Day, Christmas Day.
Facilities: Architecture Heritage House (Victorian cottage, 1894 with entry and kitchen gardens); Climatic Areas (temperate, tropical, arid); Gardens (children's; compost demonstration; herb; historic; organic; deciduous & rare fruit orchards; rose); Grounds (26 acres); Library; Shop (Sat,10am-4pm; Sun, 1pm-4pm)
Activities: Education Programs; Guided Tours; Plant Sales (weekends); Workshops

The Arboretum displays its botanical collection in three climatic zones. The temperate climatic zone emphasizes forms from temperate areas around the world that are adaptable to the summer-dry Southern California climate. The tropical zone presents a selection of species that are adaptable to the relatively frost-free coastal plain of Southern California. The arid zone contains the most extensive collections in the garden, a natural consequence of the arboretum's emphasis on plants potentially of use in the dry Southern California environment. The central portion of the arboretum contains the cultivated collections, including historical as well as modern horticultural varieties. A rare fruit grove, created by local members of the California Rare Fruit Growers Association, is one of the more experimental of the horticultural plantings. A brochure prepared by the arboretum to help visitors take a self-guided tour is available.

GLEN ELLEN

QUARRYHILL BOTANICAL GARDEN

12825 Sonoma Highway, Glen Ellen, CA 95442
Tel: (707) 996-3166; Fax: (707) 996-3198
Internet Address: http://www.quarryhillbg.org
Admission: tours by horticultural groups only: adult $15.00, student $5.00, senior $5.00;
$10 per person for groups of 10 or more
Established: 1987
Parking: Limited parking; carpooling advised
Open: by reservation only
Best Time(s) of Year to Visit: March to October
Facilities: Grounds (60 acres); Special Collections (temperate zone east Asian plants)
Activities: Guided Tours (horticultural groups, advance reservation only)

The garden is dedicated to the preservation and procreation of rare and unusual east Asian plants, particularly from the border region between China and Tibet. The collection includes over 10,000 plants of over 300 genera.

GRANITE BAY

SAN JUAN WATER DISTRICT—WEL GARDEN

9935 Auburn Folsom Road, Granite Bay, CA 95746
Tel: (916) 791-0115; Fax: (916) 791-7361
Internet Address: http://www.sjwd.org/welgarden.htm
Admission: Free
Established: 1992
Wheelchair Accessible: P

Parking: Free on site
Open: Monday to Friday, 8:30am-5pm
Facilities: Garden (bulb, deer-resistant, fire-resistant, herb, native plant, orchard, perennial, pond, rose, rock, shade, turf substitute, water conservation); Grounds (10 acres)
Activities: Education Programs

Located behind the Water District offices, the W(ater) E(fficient) L(andscape) Garden contains drought-tolerant plants and demonstrates the use of such plants and other water management techniques to ensure efficient outdoor water consumption and fire-safe landscaping. It features an inviting entry area, parking lot landscaping, an oak tree preservation site, fire-resistant plants, a turf substitute demonstration area, a pond garden, and an orchard area that attracts butterflies and hummingbirds. The garden is supported by the U.S. Bureau of Reclamation.

HAYWARD

HAYWARD AREA RECREATIONAL DISTRICT— JAPANESE GARDENS

22373 N Third St. (off Crescent Ave.), Hayward, CA 94541
Tel: (510) 881-6715; Fax: (510) 881-6763
Internet Address: http://www.haywardrec.org
Admission: Free
Established: 1980
Parking: Free on site
Open: Daily, 10am-4pm
Facilities: Garden (Japanese); Grounds (3 acres, design by landscape architect Kimura Kimio)

The gardens contain more than 4,000 Japanese and native California trees, rocks, and plants in traditional Japanese style. The area also includes a small pond, waterfall, teahouse, and other wooden structures.

HOPLAND

FETZER VINEYARDS VISITOR CENTER—ORGANIC GARDEN

13601 Eastside Road (Route 175), Hopland, CA 95449
Tel: (707) 744-1250; Fax: (707) 744-7488
Internet Address: http://www.fetzer.com/

Open: Daily, 9am-5pm
Facilities: Gardens (organic); Grounds (5 acres); Visitor Center
Activities: Guided Tours (Apr-Oct, 4/day; Nov-May, daily, 2pm)

The organic garden at Fetzer Vineyards Visitor Center is composed of seven theme gardens, each with a different design scheme or purpose, such as wine education, food for the kitchen, or attracting beneficial insects, hummingbirds or Monarch butterflies. Each area of the garden has sensory plants to smell, taste or touch. Highlights include the Mediterranean Walk, planted in Mediterranean and California-native gray and aromatic plants underneath a canopy of pomegranates and olives; the Reserve Garden, a formal garden centered on a large, octagonal gazebo covered with wisteria and old-fashioned roses surrounded by trellised Dijon-clone Chardonnay grapes, an English-style perennial border with persimmon trees, and a 150-foot long bed of white and apricot roses; the Border of Life, featuring plants whose flowers attract birds and butterflies as well as insects beneficial to gardeners and farmers; the Mediterranean Wine Region Garden, offering in a geometric design plants such as lavender, acanthus, thyme, rosemary and santalina and punctuated by white iceberg roses; the Mulberry Wine Varietal Garden, containing fruiting mulberry trees planted around a trellis covered with 12 wine grape varietals; the Berry Area, containing a variety of berries as well as cherry tomatoes and a large bed of edible flowers like anise hyssop, nasturtiums, violas, and day lilies; the Herb Crescent, consisting of a variety of thymes, oreganos, scented geraniums, mints, tarragons and other herbs; the Mini Orchard, containing over fifty varieties of apples and pears; and the Vegetable Area, consisting of raised beds holding a variety of vegetables.

KENSINGTON

UNIVERSITY OF CALIFORNIA, BERKELEY—BLAKE GARDEN

70 Rincon Road, Kensington, CA 94707
Tel: (415) 524-2449
Internet Address: http://www-laep.ced.berkeley.edu/laep/blake.html
Admission: Free
Wheelchair Accessible: P
Parking: Free on site
Open: Monday to Friday, 8am-4:30pm; Closed: Academic Holidays, New Year's Day, Thanksgiving Day, Christmas Day
Best Time(s) of Year to Visit: Spring, Fall

Facilities: Architecture (residence, 1925 design by Walter Bliss); Gardens (formal); Greenhouse; Grounds (10.9 acres); Picnic Area
Activities: Guided Tours (groups 10+, arrange in advance)

Blake is composed of two parts, Blake House and Blake Garden. Deeded to the University in 1957, the house is now the University president's official residence. The garden serves as a teaching facility for the University's Department of Landscape Architecture, an outdoor laboratory for plant identification, planting design, problems in spatial relationships, and all phases of landscape architecture. The garden development began in 1925 when Mr. and Mrs. Anson Blake of Berkeley chose the bare site for its view, terrain, and unusual rock outcrop. The house was oriented to take advantage of the view and to shelter a portion of the garden against the strong prevailing wind. Shelter belts of laurel, cryptocarya, coast redwood, Canary Island pines, acacias and hoherias were soon planted. Miss Mable Symmes, Mrs. Blake's sister and one of the first students in the Department of Landscape Design, made the first plan for a garden to serve two houses. One of the houses was sold and is now the Carmelite Monastery, north of the redwood grove. Approximately 2,500 species and varieties obtained throughout the world were planted in the garden. Extensive collections of ferns, vines, South African bulbs, and unusual conifers were developed.

LA CANADA FLINTRIDGE

DESCANSO GARDENS (AHS RAP)

1418 Descanso Drive, La Canada Flintridge, CA 91011
Tel: (818) 949-4200; Fax: (818) 949-7982
Internet Address: http://www.DescansoGardens.org
Admission: Fee: adult $6.00, child (<5) free, child (5-12) $1.50, student $4.00, senior $4.00
Attendance: 300,000
Established: 1957
Membership: Y
Wheelchair Accessible: Y
Parking: Free on site
Open: Daily, 9am-5pm; Closed: Christmas Day
Best Time(s) of Year to Visit: Winter (camellia), mid-March to mid-May (azalea, iris, lilac), Summer (rose), Fall (fall color, Japanese Garden maples)
Facilities: Architecture Boddy House (former residence, 1937 design by architect J. E. Dolena of Beverly Hills), Mission Style Meeting Hall;

Food Services Japanese Tea House (Feb-July & Sept-Nov, Sat-Sun, 11am-4pm), Patina's Santo Lina Café (daily, 10am-3pm); Gardens (camellia forest, day lily, fern canyon, iris, Japanese, lilac, native plant, rose, topiary); Grounds (160 acres, 80 acres cultivated, 20 acres oak forest); Library; Narrow Gauge Railroad (Sat-Sun, 10am-4pm, fee); Picnic Area (9am-4:30pm); Shop (books, plants, garden-related gifts; Mon-Fri, 10am-4pm, Sat-Sun, 10am-4:45pm); Special Collections (camellia, lilac, rose); Visitor Center

Activities: Concerts Under the Oaks (summer); Dance Recitals; Education Programs; Events Arts Festival, Flower Festival (spring), Japanese Garden Festival (autumn); Films; Guided Tours Groups (arrange in advance, (818) 949-4201; Tram (Tues-Fri, 1pm, 2pm, 3pm; Sat-Sun, 11am, 1pm, 2pm, 3pm; fee); Lectures

In 1937, Manchester Boddy, publisher of the *Los Angeles Daily News*, purchased the natural "bowl" in the San Rafael Hills that provides the secluded setting for Descanso Garden. Boddy cleared the land and built an elegant two-story mansion of 22 rooms. In 1953, Boddy sold Rancho del Descanso to the County of Los Angeles. Today, in a successful public-private partnership, Descanso is operated and maintained by the non-profit Descanso Gardens Guild, Inc. The heart of Descanso Gardens is the 20-acre California live oak forest containing 35,000 camellias, the largest display of camellias in the nation. Complementing the Camellia Forest, the five-acre International Rosarium offers a significant collection of more than 3,000 old garden and modern roses arranged in more than twenty theme gardens to facilitate study. Each grouping has its own planting concept with roses of a particular type accompanied by companion plantings of flowering trees, shrubs, and perennials. Combining the elements of traditional tea, strolling and zen design, the Japanese Garden features Japanese maples, azaleas, bamboo, and other plants from Asia. Additional gardens include the California Garden, celebrating native plants, and the Lilac Garden, offering over 500 fragrant lilacs, as well as day lily and iris gardens and a fern canyon.

LAGUNA BEACH

HORTENSE MILLER GARDEN

Laguna Beach, CA 92651
Tel: (949) 499-3311 *Ext:* 426
Internet Address: http://www.hortensemillergarden.org
Admission: docent-led tour by appointment only
Established: 1959

Membership: Y
Wheelchair Accessible: N
Parking: Arrange at time of tour
Open: Wednesday & Saturday, 10am-noon, by appointment only;
Closed: National Holidays.
Facilities: Gardens (native plant, perennial, xeriscape); Grounds (2½
acres); Library (natural history, horticulture)
Activities: Guided Tours (Tues-Sat, 15 individuals/day, maximum,
(949) 497-0716)

Situated on the upper slopes of Boat Canyon overlooking the Pacific
Ocean, the garden displays more than 1,500 plant species of worldwide
origin in a natural setting, including many coastal-adapted trees. The garden is located at a private residence in a gated community. All tours are
docent-led and must be arranged in advance through the city's recreation
department—(949) 497-0716.

LANCASTER

CALIFORNIA STATE PARKS—ANTELOPE VALLEY CALIFORNIA POPPY RESERVE

15101 W. Lancaster Road (extension of Ave I), Lancaster, CA 93536
Tel: (805) 724-1180; Fax: (805) 940-7327
Internet Address: http://www.calparksmojave.com/poppy/
Admission: Fee (March 15 to May 1): $4.00/auto; Free (May to March 14)
Attendance: 62,000
Wheelchair Accessible: P
Parking: Free on site
Open: Visitor Center: March 15 to May 1, Monday to Friday, 9am-
4pm; Saturday to Sunday, 9am-5pm
Best Time(s) of Year to Visit: mid-April (call Wildflower Hotline 948-
1322)
Facilities: Grounds (1,745 acres); Trails (7 miles); Visitors Center
Activities: Nature Walks (see schedule at Visitor Center); Ranger or
Docent led walks (Sat-Sun, 11am and 1pm)

The State Reserve was established to protect and perpetuate outstanding displays of native wildflowers, particularly the California golden
poppy (Eschscholzia californica), the state flower. Other wildflowers, including coreopsis, cream cups, goldfield, lupine, and owl's clover, share
the desert grassland producing a mosaic of color and fragrance each
spring. Wildflower blooms occur from March through May with the peak

viewing period usually in mid-April. As the flowering season varies from year to year, it is suggested that you call in advance of planning your visit.

LOMPOC

LA PURISIMA MISSIONS STATE HISTORIC PARK—GARDENS

2295 Purisima Road (3 miles northeast of Lompoc on Highway 246), Lompoc, CA 93436
Tel: (805) 733-3713
Internet Address: http://www.lappurisimamission.org
Admission: Fee: $4/car, $3/senior car
Attendance: 260,000
Established: 1941
Membership: N
Wheelchair Accessible: P
Parking: On site, 100 spaces, bus & RV parking
Open: Daily, 9am-4:30pm; Closed: New Year's Day, Thanksgiving Day, Christmas Day.
Best Time(s) of Year to Visit: Spring, Fall
Facilities: Gardens (herb, native plant, vegetable); Grounds Gardens (4 acres)
Activities: Guided Tours (daily, 2pm, Groups (15+, no fee, 733-1303); Self-Guided Tours (a plant guide is available)

Misión la Purísima Concepción de María Santísima (founded 1787) is the largest, most complete and most authentic mission restoration project in the American West. The park visitor center features information, displays and artifacts. The park contains the church, shops, quarters, spring house, cemetery and mission gardens. As no records of mission gardens exist, the Civilian Conservation Corps designed a pleasing array of native and introduced plants. Paths radiate outward from the restored central fountain. Nearby, the herb garden is divided into medicinal and culinary varieties used during the mission era, and the vegetable garden displays seasonal offerings.

LONG BEACH

CALIFORNIA STATE UNIVERSITY, LONG BEACH—EARL BURNS MILLER JAPANESE GARDEN (AHS RAP)

6300 State University Drive, Long Beach, CA 90840
Tel: (562) 985-8885

Internet Address: http://www.csulb.edu/~jgarden/
Admission: Free
Established: 1981
Open: Tuesday to Friday, 8am-3:30pm; Sunday, noon-4pm; Closed:
Academic Holidays
Facilities: Gardens (Japanese, design by Edward R. Lovell); Grounds
(1.3 acres)
Activities: Education Programs; Guided Tours (groups—reservations
required); Workshops

The garden is an educational, cultural, and aesthetic resource that reflects the university's continuing interest in international education. Centered on a pond, the design was inspired by the Imperial Gardens in
Tokyo.

RANCHO LOS ALAMITOS HISTORIC RANCH AND GARDENS

6400 E. Bixby Hill Road, Long Beach, CA 90815-4706
Tel: (562) 431-3541; Fax: (562) 430-9694
Internet Address: http://www.rancholosalamitos.com
Admission: Free
Attendance: 30,000
Established: 1970
Membership: Y
Wheelchair Accessible: P
Parking: Free on site
Open: Wednesday to Sunday, 1pm-5pm
Facilities: Architecture (listed on the National Register of Historic
Places); Gardens (4 acres); Grounds (7½ acres)
Activities: Education Programs (monthly, Sun afternoon); Guided
Tours Groups (by appointment; Ranch House (last tour 4pm); Self-
Guided Tour Gardens

The existing gardens were created between 1920 and 1936, and clearly
express the personality of their creator, Florence Bixby, as she worked
with such noted designers as the Olmsted Brothers and Florence Yoch. In
developing her gardens, she attempted to "civilize" the area around the
rambling adobe ranch house in a way that complemented the home and
expressed her own taste and interests. Her gardens are notable for the
way in which they extend a modest domestic tranquility into the garden.
The restrained plant palette in combination with beautifully dimensioned
spaces give quiet strength and character to the garden. Rancho Los
Alamitos is owned by the City of Long Beach and operated by the Ran-

cho Los Alamitos Foundation, a non-profit organization, as a public-private cooperative effort under the auspices of the Department of Parks, Recreation and Marine.

RANCHO LOS CERITOS HISTORIC SITE—HISTORIC GARDEN

4600 N. Virginia Road, Long Beach, CA 90807-1916
Tel: (562) 570-1755; Fax: (562) 570-1893
Internet Address: http://www.rancholoscerritos.org
Admission: Free
Established: 1955
Membership: Y
Wheelchair Accessible: Y
Parking: Free on site, limited
Open: Wednesday to Sunday, 1pm-5pm; Closed: City holidays
Best Time(s) of Year to Visit: Spring (most colorful)
Facilities: Architecture (Monterey-colonial adobe ranch house, 1844; remodeled in Mission Revival-style, 1930); Gardens (herb, orchard, shade); Grounds (4.7 acres); Library (California history); Picnic Area; Shop
Activities: Education Programs; Guided Tours Garden (by request), House (Sat-Sun, on the hour); Self-Guided Tours

Once part of a early Spanish land grant, the 27,000 acre Rancho Los Cerritos evolved from cattle to sheep ranch to private home before becoming a city museum in 1955. John Temple planted the first formal garden in the 1840s-1850s. The current estate grounds, designed in 1931 by landscape architect Ralph D. Cornell, feature trees dating back to Temple's original gardens. Garden rooms include a small subtropical orchard, a California native plant section, and an inner courtyard with a small formal pond. The main garden focuses on a massive Moreton Bay Fig tree and its buttressing root system and includes a shade garden, a wisteria-covered arbor, and additional exotic and historic plants. The city added an herb garden with historic roses at a later date.

LOS ANGELES

CITY OF LOS ANGELES—CHAVEZ RAVINE ARBORETUM

Elysian Park, Stadium Way (near the Grace E. Simon Lodge),
Los Angeles, CA 90012

Tel: (213) 485-5054
Internet Address: http://www.laparks.org/dos/horticulture/chavez.htm
Admission: Free
Established: 1893
Wheelchair Accessible: P
Parking: Parking for 50 cars
Open: Daily, daylight hours
Facilities: Arboretum

The Arboretum was founded in 1893 by the Los Angeles Horticultural Society. Many of its original trees are still standing, with some of the trees being the oldest or largest of their kinds in California. The Arboretum is designated an Historic Cultural Monument.

CITY OF LOS ANGELES—EXPOSITION PARK ROSE GARDEN

701 State Drive, Los Angeles, CA 90037
Tel: (213) 763-0114
Internet Address:
http://www.laparks.org/rap/exporosegarden/rosegarden.htm
Admission: Free
Established: 1928
Open: March 15 to December, Daily, 9am-sunset
Facilities: Garden (rose); Grounds (7½ acres)
Activities: Events Blooming of the Roses Festival (late April)

One of the largest and most significant public display gardens in California, the Garden contains over 15,000 roses representing approximately 200 cultivars in linear beds. Designated a Los Angeles County Point of Historical Interest, it was created in 1926-28. Although the original rose bushes of 1928 have long since been replaced, a number of plantings from the 1940s and 1950s still survive. As new hybrids become available, the older bushes, particularly those that developed poorly, are removed. The site is an accredited All-America Rose Selections display garden.

THE J. PAUL GETTY MUSEUM

1200 Getty Center Drive, Los Angeles, CA 90049-1681
Tel: (310) 440-7300; Fax: (310) 440-7722; TDDY: (310) 440-7305
Internet Address: http://www.getty.edu/getty.html
Admission: Free
Attendance: 400,000

Established: 1953
Membership: N
Wheelchair Accessible: Y
Parking: On site, reservation required—$5.00
Open: Tuesday to Thursday, 10am-6pm; Friday to Saturday, 10am-9pm; Sunday, 10am-6pm.
Closed: Legal holidays
Facilities: Auditorium (250 seats); Conservation Facilities; Food Services Café (11am-3pm, indoor and outdoor dining areas), Café Espresso (carts located throughout Center), Museum Café (self service cafeteria, open until 30 minutes before closing), Restaurant; Picnic Area; Shop
Activities: Dance Recitals; Education Programs; Gallery Talks; Lectures; Performances; Temporary Exhibitions

The museum is located at the J. Paul Getty Center, a 6-building, 110-acre campus designed by Richard Meier in the foothills of the Santa Monica Mountains. The Museum offers permanent, temporary, and special exhibitions drawn from its extensive permanent collections. Meier's master plan called for developing 19 of the 24 acres as landscape or gardens. The extensive gardens, inspired by the horticultural traditions of California and the ancient Mediterranean, reiterate the Getty Center's architectural blend of tradition and innovation. Artist Robert Irwin designed the 134,00-square-foot Central Garden. Set in the natural ravine between the Museum and the Research Institute for the History of Art, the Central Garden features a cascading stream and specialty gardens selected to accentuate the interplay of light, color, and reflection. Olin Partnership (Philadelphia) was responsible for the design of the other gardens throughout the campus.

JAPANESE AMERICAN CULTURAL & COMMUNITY CENTER— JAMES IRVINE GARDEN (SERIYU-EN)

244 S. San Pedro St., Lower Level, Los Angeles, CA 90012
Tel: (323) 628-2725; Fax: (323) 617-8576
Internet Address: http://www.jaccc.org/jaccc/irvine_garden.html
Admission: Free
Established: 1978
Parking: Metered on street or commercial lots
Open: Daily, 9am-5pm; Closed: Legal holidays
Facilities: Garden (Japanese-style); Grounds Irvine Garden (8,000 square feet, design by Takeo Uesugi & Associates), JACCC Plaza (1 acre, design by Isamu Noguchi)

Located at the Japanese American Cultural & Community Center in the Little Tokyo section of Los Angeles, the James Irvine Garden, also known as Seriyu-en (Garden of the Clear Stream), received the National Landscape Award of the American Association of Nurserymen in 1981. Inspired by traditional Japanese garden design, the Garden, screened from downtown by redwoods and other trees, features a 170-foot stream. In 2000, the *Journal of Japanese Gardening* ranked the Garden as one of the ten highest-quality Japanese gardens outside of Japan, out of 300 sites surveyed. Other public facilities at the JACCC include an 880-seat theatre and the one-acre JACCC Plaza.

LUMMIS HOME AND GARDEN (EL ALISAL)

200 East Avenue 43, Los Angeles, CA 90031
Tel: (323) 222-0546; Fax: (323) 222-0771
Internet Address: http://www.socalhistory.org
Admission: Free
Established: 1898
Parking: Side street parking by entrance
Open: Friday to Sunday, 12pm-4pm
Facilities: Garden (xeriscape); Grounds (1 ½ acres)

Composed of granite boulders and concrete, El Alisal was handcrafted between 1896 and 1910 by Charles F. Lummis, the first city editor of the *Los Angeles Times*. Now a state historic monument, its plantings emphasize water conservation and low maintenance. Fall through spring, the garden is irrigated once a week for 15 minutes; during the summer watering extends to 30 minutes per week.

MILDRED E. MATHIAS BOTANICAL GARDEN—UCLA

University of California at Los Angeles, 405 Hilgard Ave. at LaConte Ave., Los Angeles, CA 90095-1606
Tel: (310) 825-3260; Fax: (310) 206-3987
Internet Address: http://www.botgard.ucla.edu/bg-home.htm
Admission: Free
Attendance: 36,000
Established: 1929
Membership: N
Wheelchair Accessible: Y
Parking: Limited on campus, obtain permit at information kiosks
Open: Spring to Fall, Monday to Friday, 8am-5pm; Saturday to Sunday, 8am-4pm; Winter, Daily, 8am-4pm; Closed: Academic holidays

Facilities: Grounds (7 acres); Library
Activities: Education Programs; Guided Tours (groups 8+, schedule in advance 206-6707)

Located on the southeastern corner of the UCLA campus, the Garden contains approximately 5,000 species in 225 families, including plant specimens from all over the world.

UCLA—HANNAH CARTER JAPANESE GARDEN

10619 Bellagio Road, Los Angeles, CA 90024
Tel: (310) 825-4574; Fax: (310) 794-8208
Internet Address: http://www.japanesegarden.ucla.edu
Admission: reservations required
Attendance: 4,000
Established: 1965
Wheelchair Accessible: N
Parking: Limited—reservations required
Open: Tuesday to Wednesday, 10am-3pm; Friday, 10am-3pm;
Administrative Office, Monday to Friday, 8am-5pm.
Facilities: Garden (Japanese, 1961 design by Nagao Sakurai); Grounds (2 acres); Japanese garden structures; Pond (koi and water lilies)
Activities: Guided Tours (reservations required); Self-Guided Tours

This Kyoto-style garden is considered to be one of the most notable Japanese gardens in the United States. Its garden structures (main gate, garden house, bridges, shrine) were built in Japan and reassembled at the Garden by Japanese artisans. Symbolic rocks, antique stone carvings, and water basins were also shipped from Japan. Other than the old native live oaks, which predate the garden, nearly all the trees and plants belong to species that are grown in Japan. Behind the teahouse is a separate Hawaiian garden, containing five species of tree ferns and 25 other fern varieties, as well as seven classes of palms, various tropical vines, and epiphytes including aroids, orchids, and bromeliads.

MALIBU

ADAMSON HOUSE/MALIBU LAGOON MUSEUM

23200 Pacific Coast Hwy., Malibu, CA 90265
Tel: (310) 456-8432
Internet Address: http://browser.to/malibumuseum

Admission: Fee $3.00
Attendance: 14,000
Established: 1982
Membership: Y
Wheelchair Accessible: Y
Parking: On site, $6.00
Open: Wednesday to Saturday, 11am-3pm; Closed: Legal holidays
Facilities: Architecture Adamson House (Moorish-Spanish Colonial-style residence, 1929 design by Stiles O. Clements); Library; Shop (books, memorabilia, unique gifts)
Activities: Education Programs; Guided Tours (last tour commences 2pm; groups 12+, reserve in advance); Lectures; Temporary Exhibitions

Situated on one of the most beautiful beach locations in Southern California with views of Malibu Lagoon, Malibu Beach and the Malibu Pier, Adamson House is famous for elaborate ceramic tile work and creative architecture. The grounds have been restored and include a rose garden, ornamental fruit trees, Chinese magnolias, shrubs, and flowers. The adjacent Malibu Lagoon Museum contains a collection depicting the history of Malibu.

MARTINEZ

JOHN MUIR NATIONAL HISTORIC SITE

4202 Alhambra Ave. (corner of Highway 4), Martinez, CA 94553-3826
Tel: (925) 228-8860; Fax: (925) 228-8192
Internet Address: http://www.nps.gov/jomu/
Admission: Fee: adult $3.00, child (<17) free
Attendance: 35,000
Established: 1964
Membership: Y
Wheelchair Accessible: Y
Parking: Small parking lot
Open: Wednesday to Sunday, 10am-5pm; Closed: New Year's Day, Thanksgiving Day, Christmas Day
Facilities: Architecture (Italianate Victorian residence); Bookstore; Mt. Wanda Area (325 acres; nature trail); Park (8.8 acres); Visitors Center
Activities: Education Programs; Nature Walks

The Site preserves the 17-room mansion where the naturalist John Muir lived from 1890 to his death in 1914 and includes a display of native plants. The Muir house and historic Martinez adobe became part of the National Park Service in 1964. In 1992, Mt. Wanda was added to the Site. The 325-acre tract of oak woodland and grassland was historically owned by the Muir family. The Park consists of three historic structures, nine acres of fruit orchards, and 326 acres of open space (Mt. Wanda).

MENLO PARK

ALLIED ARTS GUILD GARDENS

75 Arbor Road at Cambridge Ave., Menlo Park, CA 94025
Tel: (650) 322-2405
Internet Address: http://www.alliedartsguild.org
Admission: Free
Established: 1929
Parking: Lot on site, 82 spaces
Open: Monday to Saturday, 10am-5pm
Facilities: Food Services (restaurant, Mon-Sat, luncheon); Grounds
(3 ½ acres)

A site of living history, the Allied Arts Guild was originally founded in the late 1920s to support artists in a pre-industrial village setting. Today, it is still the site of artists' studios, along with shops and a restaurant. The Spanish-style architecture, dominated by the work of local artist/architect Pedro de Lemos, was primarily completed in the late 1920's. Handcrafted elements were integrated into both the buildings and the gardens in the form of indoor and outdoor frescos, tile work, and handcrafted paving and metal details. The grounds include a series of gardens that are based on the Mediterranean character of the architecture, including a rose allée, formal Moorish garden with orangerie, enclosed courtyard with fountain, blue garden with fountain, perennial gardens, and specimen trees. A significant and respectful rehabilitation was completed by the Guild in 2004. The Allied Arts Guild is owned and operated by the Woodside-Atherton Auxiliary to the Lucile Salter Packard Children's Hospital at Stanford.

SUNSET PUBLISHING CORPORATION—SUNSET GARDENS

80 Willow Road (at Middlefield Road), Menlo Park, CA 94025-3661
Tel: (415) 321-3600
Internet Address: http://www.sunsetmagazine.com/

Admission: Free
Wheelchair Accessible: Y
Parking: Free on site
Open: 9am-4:30pm; Closed: Legal holidays
Best Time(s) of Year to Visit: Spring
Facilities: Architecture (early California-style offices, 1952 design by Cliff May,); Climatic Areas (northwest; central, northern, and southern California; southwest desert); Gardens (butterfly, test); Grounds (display garden, design by by Thomas Church
Activities: Guided Tours (Mon-Fri, 10:30am & 2:30pm); Self-Guided Tours

Designed by Thomas Church, the dean of Western landscape architects, the gardens display more than 300 varieties of shrubs, trees, vines, ground covers, annuals, and perennials in distinct areas representing the major climate zones of the West. While the trees and many shrubs are permanent fixtures in the gardens, the flower beds are replanted at least three times a year to provide seasonal color. There is also a test garden for evaluating the latest plants, devices, and projects.

MISSION VIEJO

UNIVERSITY OF CALIFORNIA, IRVINE ARBORETUM AND BOTANICAL GARDEN

UCI, North Campus, Campus Drive at Jamboree Road, Mission Viejo, CA 92717-1450
Tel: (714) 824-5833; Fax: (714) 824-5833
Internet Address: http://darwin.bio.uci.edu/arboretum/
Admission: Voluntary contribution
Attendance: 14,000
Established: 1965
Membership: Y
Open: Monday to Saturday, 9am-3pm; Closed: Legal holidays
Facilities: Climatic Areas (California, South Africa); Conservation Facilities; Grounds (14 acres); Special Collections (African aloe)
Activities: Education Programs; Events Fall Art Show, Fall Orchid Festival (Nov), Winter Bulb Festival (Mar); Flower Shows Celebrate Spring (May), Winter Orchid Show (Feb); Lectures; Plant Sales

The Arboretum has focused on developing collections of plants especially suited to the Mediterranean climate characteristic of southern California, particularly from South Africa and both Alta and Baja California. Gardens include a South African bulb garden and a 1½-acre California wildflower garden. The Arboretum is managed by the School of Biological Sciences.

MONTCLAIR

CHINO BASIN WATER CONSERVATION DISTRICT—E. ROWLEY DEMONSTRATION GARDEN

4594 San Bernardino St. (between Indian Hill & Monte Vista), Montclair, CA 91763
Tel: (909) 626-2711; Fax: (909) 626-5974
Internet Address: http://www.cbwcd.org/Gardengallery.htm
Admission: Free
Established: 1991
Open: Daily, 8am-5pm
Best Time(s) of Year to Visit: March to April
Facilities: Amphitheater (60-75 seats); Garden (xeriscape); Grounds (1 ½ acres)
Activities: Self-Guided Tours (booklet available); Education Programs; Plant Sales (spring)

The CBWCD Demonstration Garden features both native and exotic low water-use plants and water conserving landscaping practices. Designed to show types of plants and design approaches for a variety of garden styles, it is divided into six sections, each modeling a different environment. Areas include a southwestern/desert garden, California native/chaparral garden, woodland garden, riparian garden, ornamental garden, and redwood forest.

MONTECITO

CASA DEL HERRERO

1387 E. Valley Road (between Hot Springs & San Ysidro Roads), Montecito, CA 93108
Tel: (805) 565-5653; Fax: (805) 969-2371
Internet Address: http://www.casadelherrero.com
Admission: Fee, reservation required, $15.00
Established: 1993
Membership: Y
Wheelchair Accessible: P
Parking: On site, limited to 8 vehicles/tour
Open: by appointment only

Facilities: Architecture (Andalusian-style country house, 1925 design by architect George Washington Smith); Gardens (7 acres, Spanish/Moorish style); Grounds (11 acres, completed 1933, design by landscape architects Ralph Stevens and Lockwood de Forest, as well as horticulturist Peter Reidel)
Activities: Guided Tours (Wed & Sat, 10am & 2pm; reservation must be made at least 30 days in advance)

The house, a fine example of Spanish Colonial Revival architecture, is noted for its extensive use of Mediterranean tile as well as splendid examples of 13th to 18th century Spanish furniture, antique architectural detail, and artwork, as well as its 7 acres of Spanish Moorish-style gardens. Listed in the National Register of Historic Places, the site is managed by the Casa del Herrero Foundation, a non-profit organization. Tour reservations are required with payment at least thirty days prior to the tour date. Children under 10 years are not permitted.

MONTECITO WATER DISTRICT—XERISCAPE DEMONSTRATION GARDEN

583 San Ysidro Road (1½ blocks from intersection of E Valley Rd.), Montecito, CA 93108
Tel: (805) 969-2271; Fax: (805) 969-7261
Internet Address: http://www.montecitowater.com/demo.htm
Admission: Free
Wheelchair Accessible: Y
Parking: Limited in District office lot
Facilities: Garden (xeriscape); Grounds (½ acre, design by Isabelle Greene)

Located adjacent to the Water District offices, the garden illustrates that an attractive landscape may be created employing native and non-native drought tolerant plants. All the plants in the garden are labeled with both their botanical and common names as well as whether they are native to the local region. The garden is a joint project of the Water District and the Montecito Community Foundation.

NORTHRIDGE

CALIFORNIA STATE UNIVERSITY-NORTHRIDGE— BOTANIC GARDEN

Lindley Ave. (across from Science Buildings), Northridge, CA 91330-8303

Tel: (818) 677-3496; Fax: (818) 677-2034
Internet Address: http://www.csun.edu
Admission: Free
Established: 1961
Membership: Y
Wheelchair Accessible: P
Parking: Fee $4.00
Open: Monday to Friday, 8am-5pm; Closed: Legal holidays
Best Time(s) of Year to Visit: March to May
Facilities: Arboretum (3 acres); Gardens (cactus, succulent, tropical,
New Zealand, California, South African); Greenhouses (5—3,400
square feet); Grounds (2 Acres)
Activities: Guided Tours by appointment (for garden clubs)

The botanical garden and greenhouses contain more than 2,000 plants.
The garden is divided into five areas, including extensive collections of
cacti and succulents and many uncommon plant specimens from around
the world. The greenhouses contain orchids, succulents, cacti, many
species of ferns, and other potted plants. Additional displays include an
arboretum featuring cone-bearing trees (magnolias, pines, redwoods,
Japanese cryptomeria, michelias, yews) and a koi pond.

OAKLAND

CITY OF OAKLAND—LAKESIDE PARK GARDEN CENTER AND DEMONSTRATION GARDENS

666 Bellevue Ave. (at Grand Ave.), Oakland, CA 94610
Tel: (510) 238-3208
Admission: Free
Wheelchair Accessible: Y
Open: May to October, Monday to Friday, 10am-3pm; Saturday to
Sunday, 10am-4pm.
New Year's Day to April, Daily, 10am-4pm
Facilities: Gardens (cactus, city, compost, fire escape, fragrance,
fuchsia, herb, iris, Japanese, moon, lily, palm, rhododendron,
vegetable); Greenhouse; Grounds (122 acres, park)
Activities: Flower Shows

Centrally located in Lakeside Park, the Garden Center presents award-
winning horticultural displays. The Center includes a Japanese garden
with a koi pond and an extensive array of herb and flower gardens. During the year, several horticulture shows are presented free of charge.

DUNSMUIR HOUSE AND GARDENS

2960 Peralta Oaks Court, Oakland, CA 94605-5320
Tel: (510) 615-5555; Fax: (510) 562-8294
Internet Address: http://www.dunsmuir.org/
Admission: Fee: adult $5.00, child free, student $4.00
Attendance: 20,000
Established: 1899
Membership: Y
Wheelchair Accessible: P
Parking: On street
Open: Grounds, Tuesday to Friday, 10am-4pm; May to September,
First Sunday in month, noon-3pm
Best Time(s) of Year to Visit: Spring to Summer
Facilities: Architecture (37-room Colonial Revival Mansion, 1888
design by J. Eugene Freeman); Grounds (40 acres; landscape design
1906 by John McLaren)
Activities: Events Annual Scottish Highland Games (mid-July, Sat-
Sun), Family Sundays (May-Sep, 1st Sun in month, tours at 1pm &
2pm), Holidays at Dunsmuir (Dec, Sat-Sun, before Christmas);
Guided Tours Docent-led Tours (Wed, 11am & noon; Sun,
noon/1pm/2pm; fee); Self-Guided Landscape Tour

Golden Gate Park's landscape architect, John McLaren, is said to have
had input in designing the Dunsmuir Gardens. A wide variety of trees, including Camperdown elms, bunya-bunya and hornbeam, still grace the
estate's gardens and expansive meadows. In addition, the original Hell-
man estate contained a golf course, formal croquet court, tennis court,
swimming pool with Mission-style bathhouse, glass conservatory with
grotto, an elaborate aviary, formal garden maze, and Japanese garden.
Dunsmuir House mansion has been designated a National Historic Site
by the United States Department of the Interior and both the mansion
and the Carriage House have been designated Historic Landmarks by the
City of Oakland.

MILLS COLLEGE—WILLIAM JOSEPH MCINNES
BOTANICAL GARDEN

5000 McArthur Blvd. (at Seminary Ave.), Oakland, CA 94613
Tel: (510) 430-2230
Internet Address: http://www.mills.edu
Admission: No charge/Donations accepted
Attendance: 500

Membership: N
Wheelchair Accessible: P
Parking: Free on site
Open: Daily, 10am-5pm
Best Time(s) of Year to Visit: April to June
Facilities: Garden (native plant); Greenhouse; Grounds (1/2 acre)
Activities: Guided Tours (arrange in advance)

Created to support the Botany, Biology and Calflora classes, the Garden is located on the Mills College Campus to the north of the Life Sciences Building. Currently being restored, it focuses on California native plants, especially those studied by former Mills Botany Professor Howard McMinn.

MORCOM ROSE GARDEN

700 Jean St. (just off Grand Ave.), Oakland, CA 94612
Tel: (512) 238-3187
Admission: Free
Wheelchair Accessible: Y
Parking: No parking on Jean Street, park on Olive Street
Open: Daily, dawn-dusk
Best Time(s) of Year to Visit: mid-May to September
Facilities: Garden (classic Italian-style rose); Grounds (8 acres)

Located in the center of the city, Morcom is Oakland's official rose garden. The garden contains over 500 All-America Rose Selection roses and a collection of historic hybrid tea roses.

OAKLAND MUSEUM OF CALIFORNIA

1000 Oak Street, Oakland, CA 94607
Tel: (510) 238-2200; Fax: (510) 238-2258; TDDY: (510) 451-3322
Internet Address: http://www.museumca.org
Admission: Fee: adult $8.00, student $5.00, senior $5.00
Attendance: 250,000
Established: 1969
Membership: Y
Wheelchair Accessible: Y
Parking: Underground parking—$1.00 per hour; on-street parking
Open: Wednesday to Saturday, 10am-5pm; Sunday, noon-5pm;
Closed: New Year's Day, Independence Day, Thanksgiving Day, Christmas Day

Facilities: Architecture (1969 design by Kevin Roche); Auditorium; Food Services Restaurant; Galleries; Gardens; Shop; Theatre
Activities: Concerts; Education Programs; Films; Gallery Talks; Guided Tours; Lectures; Performances; Temporary Exhibitions; Traveling Exhibitions

The museum features exhibits in art, history and science. Its Art Department, founded in 1916 as the Oakland Art Gallery, houses a comprehensive California regional collection. The Department also mounts temporary exhibitions, often in collaboration with other museums. Designed by Kevin Roche of Kevin Roche, John Dinkeloo & Associates, with landscape design by the late Daniel Kiley, the museum is internationally recognized as an outstanding contribution to urban design. The three-tiered building with its spacious galleries is surrounded by a landscape of terraces, patios, sculpture gardens and ponds.

OROVILLE

CHINESE TEMPLE GARDEN

1500 Broderick Street, Oroville, CA 95965-4871
Tel: (530) 538-2496
Admission: call for fees
Established: 1863
Open: Thursday to Monday, noon-4pm; Tuesday to Wednesday, 1pm-4pm; Closed: December 15 to January.
Facilities: Garden (Chinese)
Activities: Festival Chinese Tea (May)

At one point during its mining boom, Oroville was California's second largest city. The temple was built in 1863 to serve a community of 10,000 Chinese. The Chinese Garden, containing plants originating in China, is a memorial to the original families and is one of the few in the nation open to the public. The Chinese Temple is listed on the National Register of Historic Places and California Landmarks.

PACIFIC PALISADES

SELF-REALIZATION FELLOWSHIP TEMPLE AND ASHRAM CENTER LAKE SHRINE (SRF LAKE SHRINE)

17190 Sunset Blvd, Pacific Palisades, CA 90272-3099
Tel: (310) 454-4114

Internet Address: http://www.yogananda-srf.org/temples/lakeshrine/lakeshrine.html
Admission: Free
Attendance: 52,000
Established: 1950
Membership: Y
Wheelchair Accessible: Y
Parking: Free on site
Open: Tuesday to Saturday, 9:00am-4:30pm; Sunday, 12:30pm-4:30pm
Closed: Holidays
Facilities: Gandhi World Peace Memorial; Garden (meditation); Grounds (10 acres); Shop

Dedicated by Paramahansa Yogananda, the site, with its gardens and natural spring-fed lake, is home to a variety of flora and fauna, including swans, koi, and lotus flowers.

PALM DESERT

THE LIVING DESERT ZOO AND GARDENS

47-900 Portola Ave. (1½ miles south of State Highway 111), Palm Desert, CA 92260-6156
Tel: (760) 346-5694; Fax: (760) 568-9685
Internet Address: http://www.livingdesert.org/

The Living Desert Zoo and Gardens, Palm Desert, CA.

Admission: Fall to Spring Fee: adult $10.95, child (<3) free, child (3-12) $6.50, senior $9.00; Summer Fee: Adult $7.95; Child (3-12) $4.50
Attendance: 354,000
Established: 1970
Membership: Y
Wheelchair Accessible: Y
Parking: Free on site
Open: September to June 15, Daily, 9am-5pm; June 16 to August, 8am-1:30pm; Closed: Christmas Day
Best Time(s) of Year to Visit: November to April
Facilities: Children's Desert Play Park; Food Services (2, café and grill); Gardens; Grounds (200 acre, zoo and botanical garden; 1,000, acre preserve); Shops (gift, African market, garden center); Trails; Wildlife Animal Hospital; Zoo
Activities: Classes; Demonstrations Live Animal Show, Small Animal Encounter; Guided Tours; Nature Walks

Dedicated solely to interpreting and conserving the animal and plant life of the world's deserts, the Living Desert pioneered the concept of landscape immersion in botanical gardens. The botanical gardens replicate eleven different North American desert habitats and are interspersed with specialized gardens, wildlife native to each region, and displays on geology, geography, zoology, botany, history, anthropology, conservation, and ecology. There are also over 450 desert animals representing over 150 species, wilderness hiking trails, and Native American exhibits.

PALM SPRINGS

DESERT WATER AGENCY—DEMONSTRATION GARDENS

Operations Center, 1200 Gene Autry Trail South, Palm Springs, CA 92264
Tel: (760) 323-4971; Fax: (760) 325-6505
Internet Address: http://www.dwa.org
Admission: Free
Established: 1981
Membership: N
Wheelchair Accessible: Y
Parking: On site, north (visitor) parking area
Open: Daily, 24 hours
Best Time(s) of Year to Visit: Spring
Facilities: Gardens (3, xeriscape); Grounds (1½ acres)
Activities: Guided Tours (on request)

The agency's three gardens emphasize water-efficient gardening. Garden one (1½ acres) was built in 1981 to study plant performance and water needs for the Coachella Valley region. Garden two (1½ acres) was constructed in 1985 as a demonstration garden of water efficient plants. Garden three (12 acres), a water reclamation facility built in 1988, is not open to the general public; however, guided tours may be arranged by contacting the DWA in advance.

MOORTEN BOTANIC GARDEN AND CACTARIUM

1701 S. Palm Canyon Drive, Palm Springs, CA 92264-8936
Tel: (760) 327-6555
Admission: Fee: adult $2.00, child $0.75
Established: 1938
Membership: N
Open: Monday to Saturday, 9am-4:30pm; Sunday, 10am-4pm

Facilities: Greenhouse; Library (300 volumes); Nursery
Activities: Education Programs; Films; Guided Tours; Lectures;
Temporary Exhibitions; Traveling Exhibitions

Displaying more than 3,000 species of desert plants, the majority of which are cacti and succulents, the garden is arranged according to geographic regions of the world. Specimens in the garden bloom in abundance, just as they do in the wild. The garden also serves as a bird sanctuary.

PALO ALTO

ELIZABETH F. GAMBLE GARDEN CENTER

1431 Waverley St., Palo Alto, CA 94301
Tel: (650) 329-1356; Fax: (650) 329-1688
Internet Address: http://www.gamblegarden.org/
Admission: Free
Wheelchair Accessible: Y
Open: Daily, dawn-dusk
Facilities: Architecture (residence and carriage house, 1902); Gardens (cherry tree allée, rose, wisteria); Grounds (2.3 acres)
Activities: Classes; Education Programs; Guided Tours (Wed & Thurs, 8-50 people, $3.00/person, reserve one month in advance); Teas (Main House, 3rd Wed in month, paid reservation)

The restored early twentieth-century Palo Alto estate, includes a historic home, a carriage house, tea house, and grounds. The garden is divided into three sections: a formal garden, restored to reflect its turn-of-the-century origins with heirloom roses, weeping cherry allée and wisteria garden; a woodland garden, including collections of hydrangeas, camellias, Japanese maples, and a tea house; and working gardens, including annual and perennial beds, espaliered fruit trees, cutting garden, raised beds for disabled access, iris border, salvia bed, and demonstration beds. Donated to the City of Palo Alto by Mrs. Gamble, the estate is leased to the Elizabeth F. Gamble Garden Center, a non-profit foundation.

PASADENA

TOURNAMENT HOUSE/WRIGLEY GARDENS

391 S. Orange Grove Blvd., Pasadena, CA 91184
Tel: (626) 449-4100

Admission: Free
Open: Gardens, daily; Closed: New Year's Eve to New Year's Day
Facilities: Architecture (residence, 1906-1914 design by G. Lawrence
Stimson); Garden (rose); Grounds (4½ acres)
Activities: Guided Tours (Feb-Aug, Thurs, 2pm-4pm; groups of 25+
must reserve 2 weeks in advance)

Formerly the residence of chewing gum manufacturer William
Wrigley, the mansion is now the headquarters of the Tournament of
Roses. The first floor has been restored with assistance from the
Pasadena Chapter of the American Society of Interior Designers and a
local contractor. The second floor is dedicated to displays of Tourna-
ment of Roses history and memorabilia. Surrounding the house,
Wrigley Gardens features more 1,500 varieties of roses, camellias, and
annuals set among mature specimen palms.

PLACERVILLE

INSTITUTE OF FOREST GENETICS—EDDY ARBORETUM

2480 Carson Road, Placerville, CA 95667-5199
Tel: (530) 622-1225; Fax: (530) 622-2633
Internet Address: http://dendrome.ucdavis.edu/ifg
Admission: Free
Established: 1926
Open: Monday to Friday, 8am-4:30pm; Closed: Holidays
Facilities: Greenhouses; Grounds (65 acres)
Activities: Guided Tours (by appointment)

The arboretum contains one of the best-documented collections of pines
in the world, in addition to many other native and exotic conifers. The
seeds used to establish the arboretum, whether from the United States or
other countries, came almost exclusively from native stands. Seventy-eight
pine species, 24 firs, and many other conifers are included in the collection.
The trees are individually labeled with codes identifying species.

RANCHO PALOS VERDES

WAYFARERS CHAPEL

5755 Palos Verdes Drive South, Rancho Palos Verdes, CA 90275
Tel: (310) 377-1650; Fax: (310) 541-1435
Internet Address: http://www.wayfarerschapel.org

Admission: Free
Attendance: 400,000
Established: 1949
Wheelchair Accessible: Y
Parking: Free on site
Open: Daily, 8am-5pm
Facilities: Architecture chapel (1949-1951 design by Lloyd Wright, son of Frank Lloyd Wright); Gardens (rose, topiary); Grounds (3.5 acres); Reception Area; Visitors' Center (gift shop, 9am-5pm)
Activities: Self-Guided Tour (brochure available)

The Wayfarers Chapel, also known as the "glass church," is set on a knoll with a panoramic view of the Pacific Ocean and Catalina Island. Surrounded by a grove of redwood trees, the site offers beautiful gardens and lawns, including the Forest Floor Garden and Rose Garden. The Visitors Center, opened in 2001, provides information on the Chapel, gardens, and the organic architecture of Frank Lloyd Wright. The Chapel is a national memorial to Emanuel Swedenborg, 18th-century scientist and theologian.

REDLANDS

KIMBERLY CREST HOUSE AND GARDENS

1325 Prospect Dr. (2 miles south of downtown), Redlands, CA 92373-7049
Tel: (909) 792-2111; Fax: (909) 792-2111
Internet Address: http://www.kimberlycrest.org
Admission: Suggested contribution: adult $7.00, child (6-12) $3.00, student $6.00, senior $6.00; $6 per person for groups larger than ten
Attendance: 8,000
Established: 1981
Membership: Y
Parking: Parking on site
Open: September to July, Thursday to Sunday, 1pm-4pm; Closed: Easter, legal holidays
Best Time(s) of Year to Visit: March to June
Facilities: Architecture (Victorian French-chateau-style residence, 1897 with original furnishings); Gardens (Italian, eucalyptus, citrus, rose, magnolia); Grounds (6½ acres; fountains, artistic stonework); Shop

Kimberly Crest is listed in both the California and National Registers of Historic Places. The residence is surrounded by terraced formal Italian gardens, orange groves and lily ponds.

RIVERSIDE

UNIVERSITY OF CALIFORNIA, RIVERSIDE BOTANIC GARDENS (AHS RAP)

900 University Ave., Riverside, CA 92521-0101
Tel: (909) 787-4650; Fax: (909) 787-4437
Internet Address: http://cnas.ucr.edu/~cnas/facilities/botanic.html
Admission: Suggested contribution $1.00
Wheelchair Accessible: Y
Parking: Free parking
Open: 8am-5pm; Closed: New Year's Day, Independence Day,
Thanksgiving Day, Christmas Day
Facilities: Climatic Areas (California Deserts, Baja, Australian, Latin
American, South African); Gardens (orchard); Grounds (39 acres); lath
house; Special Collections (cactus, cycad, herb, iris, lilac, and rose)

The landscaped area around the campus buildings demonstrate the use
of a wide assortment of plants that grow well in the inland area of Southern
California. UCR Botanic Gardens is a living plant museum with more than
3,500 plant species from around the world. Within the garden, plants are
grouped according to either their geographic origin or general plant type.

ROHNERT PARK

SONOMA STATE UNIVERSITY—NATIVE PLANT AND BUTTERFLY GARDEN

Zelkova Drive (northeast corner of campus), Rohnert Park, CA
94928-3609
Tel: (707) 664-2103
Admission: Free
Established: 1974
Membership: N
Wheelchair Accessible: P
Parking: Parking available—$2.50
Open: Daily, dawn-dusk
Facilities: Gardens (native plant); Grounds (4 acres)

An ongoing project of the students, faculty, and grounds staff of
Sonoma State University, the Garden features a butterfly meadow and a
wide variety of other plant communities, from oak woodlands to grass-
lands, from redwood forest to chaparral. A 49-page self-guided tour book
($5) is available at the university bookstore.

ROLLING HILLS ESTATE

SOUTH COAST BOTANIC GARDEN (AHS RAP)

26300 Crenshaw Blvd. (off Pacific Coast Highway), Rolling Hills
Estate, CA 90274
Tel: (310) 544-6815; Fax: (310) 544-6820
Internet Address: http://www.palosverdes.com/botanicgardens
Admission: Fee: adult $6.00, child (<5) free, child (5-12) $1.50,
student $4.00, senior $4.00
Established: 1962
Open: Daily, 9am-5pm; Closed: Christmas Day
Facilities: Gardens (Cactus, children's, dahlia, fuchsia, herb, rose,
sensory, woodland, xeriscsape); Grounds (87 acres); Special Collections
(acacia, eucalyptus, ficus, gingko, palms, pittosporum, podocarpus)
Activities: Classes; Concerts; Education Programs; Flower Shows;
Guided Tours; Lectures; Plant Sales

Located on the Palos Verdes Peninsula, the site was an open pit mine
from 1929 to 1956 and then used as a landfill until 1965. The garden contains over 150,000 plants representing approximately 140 families, 700
genera, and 2,000 different species. Collections are arranged to present garden visitors with a variety of plant materials providing attractive textures,
shapes, and color throughout the year. Highlights include an All-America
Rose Selections display garden, containing over 1,600 plants in formal arcs
radiating outward from a central fountain; a waterwise garden, demonstrating that a colorful, attractive home garden is possible while using very little
water; a sensory garden, emphasizing scent and touch for the visually impaired; an herb garden with fragrant, medicinal, and culinary herbs; a children's garden; and cactus, dahlia and fuchsia gardens; as well as a lake,
stream and woodland walk. A Japanese garden featuring two museum-
quality stone lanterns is under development. The garden is operated the
County of Los Angeles Department of Parks and Recreation.

ROSS

MARIN ART AND GARDEN CENTER (MAAGC)

30 Sir Francis Drake Blvd., Ross, CA 94957
Tel: (415) 454-5597; Fax: (415) 454-0650
Internet Address: http://www.maagc.org/
Admission: No charge/donations accepted
Established: 1949
Membership: Y

Wheelchair Accessible: Y
Open: Daily, 24 hours
Facilities: Gardens (botanical, butterfly, memory, rose); Grounds
(10 acres); Special Collections (specimen trees)

Operated on a non-profit basis by volunteers, the Marin Art and Garden Center houses organizations and activities that support the ongoing development of the cultural and natural assets of Marin County. The Center gardens include a wide variety of specimen trees, a profusion of flowering plants, and a botanical teaching garden jointly maintained by the Garden Society of Marin, one of the Center's founding organizations, and the Marin Master Gardeners.

SACRAMENTO

CITY OF SACRAMENTO—MCKINLEY PARK ROSE GARDEN

H St. (near 33rd St.), Sacramento, CA 95819
Tel: (916) 277-6060; Fax: (916) 454-3956
Internet Address: http://www.cityofsacramento.org/parksandrecreation/recreation/rosegard
Admission: Free
Established: 1928
Open: Daily, dawn-dusk
Facilities: Gallery (Shepard Garden & Arts Center); Garden (rose);
Grounds Park (4½ acres), Rose Garden (1½ acres)

Accredited by All-America Rose Selections, the Garden contains over 1,200 rose bushes and tree roses, as well as blooming annuals. New award-winning varieties are planted in the garden each year. McKinley Park is also home to the Shepard Garden and Arts Center, which mounts floral exhibits and hand-crafted arts shows throughout the year. The Park is maintained by the City of Sacramento Parks and Recreation Department. Also of possible interest, the city's Shepard Garden and Arts Center (3330 McKinley Boulevard, 916-443-9413) mounts floral exhibits and arts shows throughout the year.

CITY OF SACRAMENTO—WPA ROCK GARDEN

William Land Park, 15th Ave. & Land Park Drive, Sacramento, CA 95814
Tel: (916) 277-6159
Admission: Free
Established: 1940

Parking: Both on-street parking and lot
Open: Daily, all hours
Facilities: Garden (rock, white); Grounds (½ acre)

Originally built under a Depression-era Works Progress Administration program, the Garden has been extensively revived and revised since 1988. The Garden features over 2,000 varieties of primarily drought-tolerant plants that thrive in a Mediterranean habitat, including many California natives. The plantings, which include an all-white border, focus on foliage, form, and flowers. Many of the plants are selected for their attractiveness to butterflies, bees, hummingbirds, and beneficial insects. A new feature is the succulent and dry garden.

SACRAMENTO SUBURBAN WATER DISTRICT— WEL DEMONSTRATION GARDEN

7800 N. Antelope Road, Sacramento, CA 95843-3928
Tel: (916) 972-7171; Fax: (916) 972-7639
Internet Address: http://www.sswd.org
Admission: Free
Established: 1998
Wheelchair Accessible: Y
Open: by appointment
Facilities: Garden (walled, xeriscape); Grounds (2 acres, design by Doug Strayer & Celine Livengood)
Activities: Education Programs; Guided Tours (by appointment); Self-Guided Tours

Located at the district's Antelope reservoir site, the (W)ater (E)fficient (L)andscape Demonstration Garden illustrates low water, low-maintenance landscaping techniques for home gardeners. Containing more than 100 plant varieties (including many that are not routinely employed in domestic landscaping), areas of interest include ornamental grasses, lawns, mature native oak trees, many types of Mediterranean plants, and a wall garden. Interpretive signs, kiosks, and exhibits on irrigation and construction techniques give visitors an opportunity to learn by example.

SAN DIEGO

BALBOA PARK

1549 El Prado, San Diego, CA 92101-1619
Tel: (619) 239-0572; Fax: (619) 231-9495

Internet Address: http://www.balboapark.org
Admission: Free
Attendance: 1,300,000
Established: 1868
Wheelchair Accessible: P
Parking: Multiple lots of varying sizes
Open: Grounds, Daily, 24 hours; Botanical Building, Monday to
Wednesday, 10am-4:30pm; Friday to Sunday, 10am-4:30pm
Best Time(s) of Year to Visit: March to June (roses)
Facilities: Gardens (Alcazar, desert, Japanese, rose, English); Grounds
(1,200 acres); Lath Structure Botanical Building (1915, design by
Carleton Winslow; open Fri-Wed, 10am-4pm—(615) 2235-1100)
Activities: Guided Tours Desert Vegetation (4th Sat in month, 10am,
meet in front of Visitors Center—(619) 235-1122), Palm Trees (2nd Sat
in month, 10am, meet in front of Visitors Center—(619) 235-1122),
Park Ranger Tours (Tues & Sun, 1pm, meet in front of Visitors Center—
(619) 235-1122), Trees (3rd Sat in month, 10am, meet in front of
Visitors Center—(619) 235-1122); Horticulture Shows San Diego
Botanical Garden Association (Casa del Prado Bldg., Room 101, free)

Home to fifteen museums, various performing arts and international
culture organizations as well as the San Diego Zoo, Balboa Park is the
largest urban cultural park in the nation. Among the 15 gardens in the
park are a replica of the gardens at the Alcazar palace in Grenada, Spain;
the Inez Grant Parker Rose Garden, an All-America Rose Selections accredited display garden containing over 1,850 roses; a desert garden featuring over 1,300 xerophytic plants; and the Japanese Friendship Garden,
a traditional dry garden (see separate listing). The Park also contains over
14,000 trees. Some the trees and the desert garden were originally
planted by Kate Olivia Sessions. The Botanical Building, one of the original 1915 Panama-California Exhibition buildings and one of the world's
largest wood lath structures, houses over 2,100 tropical plants, including
amaryllis, anthurium, cycads, gingers, orchids, palms, and tree ferns as
well as seasonal floral and plant displays, a carnivorous plant bog, and a
touch-and-smell garden. A good place to start your tour of the Park is the
Visitors Center in the House of Hospitality located at 1549 El Prado.

BALBOA PARK—JAPANESE FRIENDSHIP GARDEN
(SAN-KEI-EN) (AHS RAP)

2125 Park Blvd. (next to Spreckels Organ Pavilion),
San Diego, CA 92101
Tel: (619) 232-2780; Fax: (619) 232-0917
Internet Address: http://www.niwa.org

Admission: Fee: adult $3.00, child (<6) free, child (7-17) $2.00, student $2.00, senior $2.50; Free: Third Tuesday in month
Established: 1915
Parking: Most convenient is the Organ Pavilion Parking Structure
Open: Tuesday to Sunday, 10am-4pm
Facilities: Exhibit House; Garden (Japanese); Grounds (2½ acres); Tea Pavilion
Activities: Education Programs; Temporary Exhibitions (bonsai)

Originally built for the 1915 Panama-California Exhibition, the Japanese Friendship Garden features traditional Japanese design principles while incorporating local regional landscape and climate. Named the San-kei-en (Three Scene Garden), it offers landscaping evocative of water, pastoral, and mountain scenery. Included are a zen garden, koi pond, waterfall, and moon viewing deck. Plans are in progress to expand the garden from its present 2½ acres to 11 acres. Features to be added include a cherry blossom grove, a tea house, tea and herb farms, an orchard, a cultural and community center, waterfalls, and many additional varieties of plants and trees.

SAN DIEGO STATE UNIVERSITY—MEDITERRANEAN GARDEN

Freshman Quad (north of Faculty/Staff Center), 5500 Campanile Drive, San Diego, CA 92182-4493
Tel: (619) 594-5506; Fax: (619) 594-4938
Internet Address:
http://typhoon.sdsu.edu/Research/Projects/Garden/site/
Admission: Free
Established: 1998
Facilities: Climatic Areas (Australia, California, Chile, Mediterranean, South African Cape)

Located in the East Quad on campus, the Mediterranean Botanical Garden contains species representative of the five major Mediterranean ecosystems of the world (Mediterranean basin, southwest and southeast Australia, South Africa's Cape region, coastal California, and central Chile, habitats characterized by moist, mild winters and warm dry summers).

SAN DIEGO ZOOLOGICAL GARDENS

Balboa Park, 2920 Zoo Drive, San Diego, CA 92103
Tel: (619) 234-3153; Fax: (619) 685-3232
Internet Address: http://www.sandiegozoo.org/

Admission: Fee: adult $21.00, child (<3) $14.00, child (3-11) $8.00;
Reduced fee ticket available for park and zoo
Attendance: 3,000,000
Established: 1916
Membership: Y
Wheelchair Accessible: Y
Open: Winter, Daily, 9am-4pm; Summer, Daily, 9am-10pm
Best Time(s) of Year to Visit: May to July, October to November
Facilities: Food Services (5—restaurant, 2 cafés, grill, and deli);
Gardens (bromeliad, fern); Shops (6)
Activities: Education Programs; Guided Tours, Botanical Bus Tours
(3rd Friday in month, free)

Accredited by the American Association of Museums (AAM), the San Diego Zoo's botanical collection contains more than 20,000 accessioned specimens, representing approximately 500 total families, 5,000 genera, and 35,000 total species.. The collection includes 215 species of palms, 97 species of aloes, 625 species of orchids, 57 species of bamboo, 92 species of cycads, 49 species of erythrinas, 32 species of acacia, 47 species of ficus, and 35 species of ginger. Plants are grown to provide not only landscaping and scenery, but also to provide dietary supplements for the many animal residents.

SAN FRANCISCO

CITY OF SAN FRANCISCO—GOLDEN GATE PARK—GARDENS

Bounded by Fulton St., Stanyan St., Lincoln Way, & Great Highway,
San Francisco, CA 94117
Tel: (415) 831-2700
Admission: Free
Open: Daily
Best Time(s) of Year to Visit: February-March (Magnolia), early Spring
(Tulip), Spring (rhododendron), late March-April (Japanese Garden),
Summer (fuschias, roses), September (dahlias)
Facilities: Arboretum; Gardens (cherry tree, dahlia, ferns, fuschia,
Japanese, magnolia, redwood grove, rose, rhododendron,
Shakespeare, tulip, wildflower); Grounds (1,017 acres)

Over 3 miles long and 9 blocks wide, the whole park is garden-like; there are certain areas, however, which should be highlighted:

Camelia Planting Area (Conservatory Drive East area).
Cherry Tree Garden (east end of Park).

Conservatory of Flowers (Lincoln at 9th Avenue), see separate listing below.

Dahlia Dell (east of Conservatory), contains over 1,000 plants.

De Laveaga Dell-AIDS Memorial Grove (near Stanyan Street entrance), for information call 750-8340.

Fern Grove (south of John F. Kennedy Drive, between Marx Meadow Drive and Overlook Drive).

Fuschia Garden (Conservatory Drive East area).

Hagiwara Japanese Tea Garden (Fell & Stanyan Streets), see separate listing.

John McLaren Rhododendron Dell (off John F. Kennedy Drive opposite 7th Avenue), contains over 850 hybrid varieties.

Magnolia Garden (west of San Francisco Couth Fair Building).

Queen Wilhelmina Tulip Garden (northwest corner of Park), displays a wide variety of tulips supplemented by annual plantings.

Redwood Memorial Grove (north of John F. Kennedy Drive, opposite 18th Ave.).

Rose Garden (between Park Presidio and Kennedy Drive), an All-America Rose Selections accredited public demonstration garden containing over sixty rose beds planted with trial varieties.

Garden of Shakespeare's Flowers (west of California Academy of Sciences), founded 1928 by California Spring Blossom and Wildflower Association, features twenty plants mentioned in Shakespeare's plays.

Strybing Arboretum and Botanical Gardens (near 9th Avenue and Lincoln Way), see separate listing.

CITY OF SAN FRANCISCO—GOLDEN GATE PARK-CONSERVATORY OF FLOWERS

Golden Gate Park, Lincoln at 9th Ave., San Francisco, CA 94118
Tel: (415) 666-7001
Internet Address: http://www.conservatoryofflowers.org
Admission: Fee: adult $5.00, child (5-11) $1.50, child (12-17) $3.00, student $3.00, senior $3.00; Free first Tuesday of month
Established: 1879
Wheelchair Accessible: Y
Parking: Parking free on street, but limited
Open: Tuesday to Sunday, 9am-4:30pm
Facilities: Greenhouse (11,000 square feet); Special Collections (Madagascan flora)

Built between 1876 and 1883, the Conservatory of Flowers is one of the oldest existing public conservatories in the Western Hemisphere. A rare example of a prefabricated structure from the Victorian era, it was modeled after the Palm house at the Kew Gardens in England. The Conservatory was closed for extensive restoration from 1995 to 2003 due to severe storm damage. The renovated Conservatory contains three galleries displaying plants from the lowland tropics, highland tropics, and aquatic plants; a gallery devoted to seasonal displays in the Victorian style of potted plants; and a gallery offering changing special exhibits. Its surviving collection, totaling over 3,000 plants, features tropical palms, orchids, bromeliads, carnivorous plants, and other rare species.

CITY OF SAN FRANCISCO—GOLDEN GATE PARK-HAGIWARA TEA GARDEN

Golden Gate Park, Fell & Stanyan Sts., San Francisco, CA 94118
Tel: (415) 752-1171
Admission: Fee: adult $3.50, child $1.25, senior $1.25
Open: 9am-5pm
Facilities: Food Services (teahouse); Gardens (Japanese); Grounds (5 acres); Shop

The oldest Japanese-style garden in the United States, the Japanese Tea Garden originated in the Japanese Village exhibit of the California Midwinter International Exposition of 1894. It is a stroll-style garden, in which visitors can enjoy from the paths and bridges many different views of the ponds, flowering cherry trees, azaleas, oriental magnolias, camellias, Japanese maples, dwarf pines, cedars and cypress. A tour booklet is available ($2.00).

CITY OF SAN FRANCISCO—GOLDEN GATE PARK-STRYBING ARBORETUM AND BOTANICAL GARDENS (AHS RAP)

Golden Gate Park, 9th Ave. at Lincoln Way, San Francisco, CA 94122
Tel: (415) 661-1316; Fax: (415) 661-7427
Internet Address: http://www.strybing.org
Admission: Voluntary contribution
Attendance: 325,000
Established: 1937
Membership: Y
Wheelchair Accessible: Y
Open: Monday to Friday, 8am-4:30pm; Saturday to Sunday, 10am-5pm; Holidays, 10am-5pm
Facilities: Auditorium; Bookstore (Open daily, 10am-4pm); Climatic Areas (Mediterranean, mild temperate, and montane tropic climatic

zones); Gardens (biblical, conifer, fragrance, Japanese, magnolia, moon-viewing, perennial, primitive plant, succulent, takamine); Grounds (55 acres; 1960 master plan design by Robert Tetlow); Library Helen Crocker Russell Library of Horticulture (18,000 volumes, 10am-4pm, non-circulating)
Activities: Education Programs; Guided Tours (departing from bookstore: Mon-Fri, 1:30pm; Sat-Sun, 10:20am & 1:30pm; departing from Friend Gate: Fri & Sun, 2pm); Lectures; Temporary Exhibitions

Strybing grows and conserves over 7,000 varieties of plants from around the world, including plants that are no longer found in their native habitats.

SAN JOSE

GUADALUPE GARDENS

W. Taylor & Spring Sts. Garden Center, 715 Spring St., San Jose, CA 95161-1991
Tel: (408) 277-5904
Internet Address: http://www.grpg.org/
Established: 1995
Open: Daily, 8am-30 minutes before dusk
Facilities: Gardens (courtyard, historic orchard, rock, heritage rose); Grounds (450 acres)

A three-mile ribbon of parkland being developed along the banks of the Guadalupe River in the heart of downtown San Jose, Guadalupe River Park is the largest urban park under development in the United States. Gardens completed to date include the Heritage Rose Garden, dedicated to preserving the history of roses and containing over 5,500 plants representing over 3,450 varieties of antique roses; the Historic Orchard, a 3.3-acre orchard, planted in 1994, to showcase the fruit varieties that once made the Santa Clara Valley famous; the Courtyard Garden, featuring flowering plants and Japanese cherry trees; and the Taylor Street Rock Garden, a drought-tolerant demonstration landscape. The Guadalupe River Park & Gardens Corporation also maintains a Garden Center at 715 Spring Street which provides meeting space, a library of horticultural materials, offices, and a center for volunteer activities. When completed the Park will also include an arboretum, a wholesale nursery complex, recreational and environmental facilities, and a river walk.

JAPANESE FRIENDSHIP GARDEN (JFG)

Kelley Park, 1300 Senter Road, San Jose, CA 95112-2593
Tel: (408) 277-2757
Internet Address: http://www.sanjoseparks.org/kp/jfg.html
Admission: Free
Attendance: 200,000
Established: 1965
Membership: N
Wheelchair Accessible: P
Parking: Fee—$6 per vehicle
Open: Daily, 10am-dusk
Facilities: Garden (Japanese); Grounds (6 acres)

The JFG is a picturesque, highly manicured traditional Japanese garden patterned after the Korakuen Garden in Okayama, Japan. This peaceful setting also has scenic ponds with koi fish. Located in Kelley Park, the Garden is a joint project of the City of San Jose and its sister city, Okayama.

OVERFELT GARDENS PARK

Overfelt Gardens
Park, San Jose, CA

2145 Educational Park Drive (at McKee Road),
San Jose, CA 95133-1703
Tel: (408) 277-2757; Fax: (408) 251-2865
Internet Address: http://www.sanjoseparks.org/og
Admission: Free
Attendance: 100,000
Established: 1966
Membership: N
Wheelchair Accessible: Y
Parking: Free on site or on street
Open: Daily, 10am-sunset
Best Time(s) of Year to Visit: Fall
Closed: New Year's Day, Thanksgiving Day, Christmas Day
Best Time(s) of Year to Visit: Spring
Facilities: Architecture Overfelt House (original family farmhouse); Chinese Cultural Center; Gardens (Chinese, fragrance, iris, rose, native plant); Grounds (33 acres); Picnic Area; Wildlife Sanctuary
Activities: Guided Tours (groups, 251-3323)

Bequeathed to the City of San Jose in 1959, Overfelt Gardens Park was once a working ranch, and the original ranch house still overlooks the park. The southern eight acres of the gardens include plantings of native and exotic tree groves and open turf, a fragrance garden, rose and iris beds; the remaining 25 acres are a landscape of rolling hills, lake shores and wandering pathways. In addition to the gardens and wildlife of Overfelt Gardens, visitors can enjoy the beautiful and contemplative Chinese Cultural Garden. Impressive statuary and points of interest include the Garden's focal point, a 30-foot bronze and marble statue of the ancient Chinese philosopher Confucius overlooking a reflecting pond, Friendship Gate, and several buildings in Chinese architectural style.

SAN JOSE MUNICIPAL ROSE GARDENS

Dana & Naglee Avenues (between Bascom & Park Avenues near Route 880), San Jose, CA 95121
Tel: (408) 277-4661; Fax: (408) 298-1701; TDDY: (408) 298-9527
Internet Address: http://www.sanjoseparks.org/rg
Admission: Free
Established: 1937
Open: Daily, 8am-30 minutes before dusk
Best Time(s) of Year to Visit: April to May
Facilities: Garden (rose); Grounds garden (5½ acres), Park (10½ acres); Picnic Area
Activities: Self-Guided Tours (brochure with map available)

An All-America Rose Selections test garden, the site contains more than 3,500 roses of 189 varieties displayed in formal beds on a natural grass stage surrounded by a cathedral of redwood trees. While focusing on hybrid tea roses, floribunda, grandiflora, climbing, miniature, and polyantha roses are also represented. Many of the Garden's original features, including the reflection pool in the center of the structural entrance, garden vases, the two-tiered water fountain, miniature rose beds and arbor, have been donated through the years by the community and the Rose Society. The Garden is operated and maintained by the City of San Jose.

SAN LUIS OBISPO

CALIFORNIA POLYTECHNIC STATE UNIVERSITY, SAN LUIS OBISPO-COLLEGE OF AGRICULTURE— LEANING PINE ARBORETUM

Environmental Horticultural Science Unit (north end of Campus, top of Via Carta), San Luis Obispo, CA 93407

Tel: (805) 756-2888; Fax: (805) 756-2869
Internet Address:
http://www.calpoly.edu/~cagr/demeter/arboretum.htm
Admission: Free
Parking: Parking permit required, check at college entrance kiosk
Closed: Academic Holidays; Saturday, 9am-5pm; Monday to Friday,
8am-5pm
Facilities: Grounds (5 acres); Climatic Areas (Australia, California,
Chile, Mediterranean basin, South Africa); Arboretum
Activities: Guided Tours (groups); Plant Sales (spring)

Situated against the hills at the north end of campus in the Environmental Horticultural Science Unit, the Arboretum features Mediter-
ranean-climate plants displayed in six areas. Five are defined by geography (Australia, California, Chile, Mediterranean basin, and South
Africa); the sixth is devoted to palms. Brochures showing the layout of
the arboretum are available at the Poly Plant Shop. The Arboretum is
maintained solely by students.

SAN LUIS OBISPO BOTANICAL GARDEN

El Chorro Regional Park, U.S. Hwy #1 (between San Luis Obispo and
Morro Bay), San Luis Obispo, CA 93403
Tel: (805) 546-3501
Internet Address: http://www.slobg.org/
Admission: No charge/donations accepted
Established: 1989
Membership: Y
Wheelchair Accessible: P
Parking: $1 on May-Sept weekends & holidays
Open: Daily, dawn-dusk
Facilities: Amphitheater (seats 80); Garden Preview Garden (2 acres);
Greenhouse; Grounds (150 acres in development); Shop
Activities: Garden Festival (May); Guided Tours (2nd Sat in month,
Apr-Nov); Plant Family Camp (Aug); Plant Sales (2nd Sat in month,
Apr-Nov)

Located in El Chorro Regional Park, the Garden will eventually oc-
cupy 150 acres. A two-acre Preview Garden has been open to the public
since 1997. The Preview Garden showcases plants from Mediterranean
climate regions and gives a hint of the future in such geographical groupings as the California native garden and the winter-blooming South
African Cape garden of aloes, succulents and bulbs. Saturday at the Garden, a monthly program of docent tours, lectures, demonstrations, plant

and garden shop sales, takes place during the growing season, April through November.

SAN MARCOS

PALOMAR COLLEGE ARBORETUM

Main Campus, 1140 West Mission Road, San Marcos, CA 92069-1487
Tel: (760) 744-1150
Internet Address: http://www.palomar.edu/arboretum/pca2.html
Established: 1973
Facilities: Arboretum; Grounds (5 acres)

In 1973, a hillside on the main campus was set aside for an arboretum. Soon thereafter, many trees, palms and bamboo from around the world were planted and labeled. Currently there are plans to expand the arboretum site, which includes more than 44 undeveloped acres.

SAN MARINO

HUNTINGTON LIBRARY, ART COLLECTIONS, AND BOTANICAL GARDENS

1151 Oxford Road, San Marino, CA 91108
Tel: (626) 405-2100; Fax: (626) 405-0225
Internet Address: http://www.huntington.org
Admission: Fee: adult $12.50, child (<5) free, student $8.50, senior $10.00; Free: First Thursday in month
Attendance: 565,000
Established: 1919
Membership: Y
Wheelchair Accessible: Y
Parking: Free on site

Huntington Library, Art Collections, and Botanical Gardens, San Marino, CA. Photograph © The Huntington Library, Art Collections, and Botanical Gardens.

Open: Labor Day to Memorial Day, Tuesday to Friday, noon-4:30pm; Saturday to Sunday, 10:30am-4:30pm; June to August, Tuesday to Sunday, 10:30am-4:30pm; Closed: New Year's Day, Memorial Day, Independence Day, Labor Day, Thanksgiving Day, Christmas Eve to Christmas Day
Best Time(s) of Year to Visit: September to May

Facilities: Architecture (beaux arts mansion, 1910 design by Myron Hunt); Auditorium (500 seats); Food Services (tea room) café), Restaurant (175 seats); Galleries (three locations); Gardens (children's, desert, herb, palm, Japanese, rose, Shakespeare, subtropical); Grounds Botanical Garden (150 acres); Library (600,000 volumes and over 4 million manuscripts); Shop (books, prints, gift items); Special Collections (camellia)
Activities: Education Programs; Flower Shows; Gallery Talks; Guided Tours; Plant Sales; Temporary Exhibitions

The Huntington Library, Art Collections, and Botanical Gardens is a research and cultural center set amidst 150 acres of gardens. Three art galleries and a library showcase collections of rare books, manuscripts, and art. The Huntington Gallery, originally the Huntington residence, contains a comprehensive collection of British and French art of the 18th- and 19th-centuries, including Gainsborough's *Blue Boy* and Lawrence's *Pinkie*. The Virginia Steele Scott Gallery of American Art brings together American paintings from the 1730s to the 1930s and a permanent exhibition devoted to the work of early 20th-century Pasadena architects Charles and Henry Greene. The Arabella Huntington Memorial Collection is housed in the west wing of the Library and features Renaissance paintings and 18th-century French sculpture, tapestries, porcelain, and furniture. Changing exhibitions and traveling shows are displayed in the MaryLou and George Boone Gallery. Highlights of the Library's Collections include the Ellesmere manuscript of Chaucer's *Canterbury Tales* (c. 1410), a Gutenberg Bible on vellum (c. 1455), the double-elephant folio edition of Audubon's *Birds of America*, and an extensive collection of early editions of Shakespeare. The Botanical Gardens are an ever-changing exhibition of color and botanical diversity. Covering 150 acres, the fifteen specialized gardens are arranged within a park-like landscape of rolling lawns. Among the most remarkable are the Desert Garden, a large outdoor grouping of mature cacti and other succulents; the Japanese Garden, featuring a drum bridge and furnished Japanese house; and the Rose Garden, showing the history of the rose over 2,000 years. The camellia collection, in two gardens, is one of the largest in the country. Other important botanical attractions include the Subtropical, Herb, and Palm gardens. The new Helen and Peter Bing Children's Garden provides young children (ages 2-7) a hands-on opportunity to experience the wonders of the natural world through interactive elements that interpret earth, air, light, and water. Features of the Children's Garden include the Fog Grotto, Sonic Pool, Rainbow Room, Pebble chimes, Topiary Volcano, and Vortex.

SAN MATEO

CITY OF SAN MATEO—JAPANESE TEA GARDEN

Central Park, 50 West 5th Ave. (at El Camino Real),
San Mateo, CA 94403
Tel: (650) 522-7440; Fax: (650) 377-4645
Internet Address:
http://www.cityofsanmateo.org/dept/parks/locations/teagarden.html
Admission: Free
Open: Monday to Friday, 10am-4pm; Saturday to Sunday,
11am-4pm
Facilities: Garden (Japanese); Grounds (design by Nagao Sakurai);
Koi pond
Activities: Education Programs

Considered one of the finest tea gardens in California, the garden includes a granite pagoda (from Toyonaka, Japan), a teahouse, lanterns, and bamboo groves. It features seasonal blooms and rare plants surrounding the shore of a large central koi pond. Designed by Nagao Sakurai, the landscape architect of the Japanese Imperial Palace, the garden is a joint effort of San Mateo, its gardening community, and a sister city in Japan.

SANTA ANA

FAIRHAVEN MEMORIAL PARK AND MORTUARY

1702 E. Fairhaven Ave., Santa Ana, CA 92705
Tel: (714) 633-1442; Fax: (714) 633-5471
Internet Address: http://www.fairhavenmemorial.com
Established: 1911
Open: Monday to Friday, 8am-8pm; Saturday, 8am-6pm; Sunday,
9am-8pm
Facilities: Arboretum; Grounds (73 acres)

A member of the American Association of Botanical Gardens and Arboreta, the Cemetery's grounds contain more than 1,000 trees originating from around the world.

SANTA BARBARA

CITY OF SANTA BARBARA—A.C. POSTEL MEMORIAL ROSE GARDEN

555 Plaza Rubio (Los Olivos and Upper Laguna Sts.), Santa Barbara, CA 93103
Tel: (805) 563-5433; Fax: (805) 563-5464
Established: 1962
Facilities: Garden (rose); Grounds Park (10½ acres)

Mission Historical Park, across from Santa Barbara's Old Mission, contains the remains of the mission's outbuildings, lawn areas, and the A. C. Postell Memorial Rose Garden. Accredited by All-America Rose Selections, the garden displays over 1,900 roses representing approximately 300 varieties.

GANNA WALSKA LOTUSLAND

695 Ashley Road, Santa Barbara, CA 93108
(Mailing address, directions to tour entrance mailed with reservation confirmation.)
Tel: (805) 969-3767; Fax: (805) 969-4423
Internet Address: http://www.lotusland.org/
Admission: Fee (by tour only): adult $15.00, child (<3) free, child (3-9) $8.00
Attendance: limit of 15,000 + 5,000 4th graders
Established: 1911
Membership: Y
Parking: On-site parking
Open: mid-February to mid-November, Wednesday to Saturday, 10am & 1:30pm, by reservation only
Facilities: Gardens (aloe, blue, bromeliad, cacti/euphorbia, cycad, desert, epiphyllum, fern, fruit orchards, Japanese, rose, succulent, theatre, topiary, water); Grounds (37 acres); Library (700 volumes); Shop (plants, gifts items, books)
Activities: Education Programs; Guided Tours (reserve in advance, 969-9990); Lectures

Situated in the foothills of Montecito to the east of the city of Santa Barbara, Lotusland offers unusual and often surreal gardens containing a variety of exotic tropical and sub-tropical species ranging from desert cacti and succulents to ginger and banana trees. Originally the site of the family home and commercial nursery of Ralph Kinton Stevens, an important early nurseryman, the property passed through as series of owners before being purchased by Madame Ganna Walska in 1941. A former opera singer and socialite, the oft-married Madame Walska made extensive and dramatic changes to the grounds, redesigning most of the earlier landscaping and creating many new gardens. To accomplish this she worked with a number of landscape architects and designers, including Lockwood de Forest, Jr., Ralph T. Stevens, William Paylen, Oswald da Ros, and Charles Glass. Gardens include an aloe garden devoted to more than 130 kinds of aloes; a blue garden, featuring blue and silver-gray trees and plants; a bromeliad garden, displaying nearly 20 genera of bromeliads covering the ground and lower limbs of large coast live oaks; a cycad garden, containing over 400 mature specimens of cycads, including ten of the eleven living genera and more than half of the known species; an epiphyllum garden, offering hanging baskets of orchid cacti and gingers and ornamental and edible bananas; a topiary garden, including a large horticultural clock as well as animal and geometric shaped topiary; a water garden, presenting Indian lotus, water lilies, and papyrus, as well as bog plants; citrus and deciduous fruit orchards; plantings featuring Old World euphorbia and New World cacti; a fern garden; a Japanese-inspired garden; a parterre rose garden; a succulent garden; a theatre garden; and a desert garden, the newest garden. Since her death in 1984, the estate has been owned and operated by the Ganna Walska Lotusland Foundation. The number of visitors permitted by the County of Santa Barbara is very low and space is limited; reservations to tour Lotus Land must be made in advance.

SANTA BARBARA BOTANIC GARDEN (SBBG) (AHS RAP)

1212 Mission Canyon Road, Santa Barbara, CA 93105-2199
Tel: (805) 682-4726 Ext: 123; Fax: (805) 563-0352
Internet Address: http://www.sbbg.org
Admission: Fee: adult $6.00, child $1.00, child, student $4.00, senior $3.00
Attendance: 120,000
Established: 1926
Membership: Y
Wheelchair Accessible: Y
Parking: Free parking for 72 cars
Open: November to February, Monday to Friday, 9am-4pm; Saturday to Sunday, 9am-5pm.
March to October, Monday to Friday, 9am-5pm; Saturday to Sunday, 9am-6pm; Closed: New Year's Day, Thanksgiving Day, Christmas Eve, Christmas Day

Best Time(s) of Year to Visit: Spring
Facilities: Gardens (ground cover, native plant, perennial border,
water conservation); Grounds (78 acres); Herbarium (140,000
specimens; Mon-Fri, by appointment); Library (8,600 volumes);
Nursery; Shop Garden Growers Nursery (plants; Tues & Thurs-Sun,
10am-3pm), Garden Shop (books, gift items, natural handicrafts,
educational toys/games); Special Collections (ceanothus, fuchsia,
manzanita); Trails (5 miles)
Activities: Concerts; Education Programs (children and adults);
Guided Tours daily; Lectures

The garden features a collection of California flora presented in eight
different habitats representing various regions throughout California,
including redwood forests, oak and canyon woodlands, meadows and
deserts. In addition to intact native vegetation indigenous to Mission
Canyon, the grounds contain over 2,700 plantings representing over
1,000 taxa. Of these, about 950 are native species or subspecies and
about 70 are cultivars of native plants, some of which have been developed by the garden staff. Many rare and endangered California plants
are planted as part of the Garden's program in rare plant conservation.
Additional exhibits include a model home demonstration garden,
ground cover display bed, and perennial borders illustrating practical
and aesthetic uses of water-conserving plants in residential landscape
design.

SANTA BARBARA COUNTY COURTHOUSE—GARDENS

1120 Anacapa Street (bordered by Anacapa, Santa Barbara, Figueroa,
& Anapamu Sts.), Santa Barbara, CA 93101
Tel: (805) 681-5650; Fax: (805) 568-2459
Admission: Free
Membership: N
Wheelchair Accessible: P
Parking: Nearby municipal parking lot
Open: Daily, 8am-sunset
Facilities: Architecture Courthouse (Spanish-Moorish style, 1929);
Gardens (sunken, tropical)

Occupying a full block in downtown Santa Barbara, the historic
courthouse grounds contain a sunken tropical garden and extensive
lawns.

SANTA CRUZ

ARBORETUM, UNIVERSITY OF CALIFORNIA, SANTA CRUZ

1156 High St. (between Bay St. and West Campus entrance),
Santa Cruz, CA 95064-1077
Tel: (408) 427-2998; Fax: (408) 427-1524
Internet Address: http://www2.ucsc.edu/arboretum
Admission: Suggested contribution $3.00
Attendance: 67,000
Established: 1964
Membership: Y
Wheelchair Accessible: Y
Parking: Free on site
Open: Daily, 9am-5pm; Closed: Thanksgiving Day, Christmas Day
Best Time(s) of Year to Visit: February to April, August to October
Facilities: Gardens (aroma, Australia, basal angiosperms, California,
conifer, eucalyptus grove, Laurasian forest, New Zealand, South
Africa, South America); Greenhouses; Grounds (135 acres); Library
(Wed-Sun, 1pm-4pm, non-lending); Nursery; Shop Norrie's Gift Shop
(plants, garden-related gift items, books); Special Collections
(Australian ornamental, cactus and succulent, native plant, primitive
flowering plant, South African protea, rare fruit)
Activities: Education Programs; Events (Hummingbird Day); Guided
Tours (1st Sat in month, or by arrangement); Lectures; Performances;
Plant Sales (spring)

Situated on what is now the campus of the University of California at
Santa Cruz and what was originally part of the vast land holdings of pioneer settler Henry Cowell, the Arboretum occupies one of the most pro-
pitious horticultural sites in the world. The climatic and topographic diversity is such as to allow experimentation with almost every species that
might be grown along the coast between San Diego and Crescent City,
and the diversity of the soils—the underlying rock includes granite,
schist, limestone, and several types of sandstone—can scarcely be
matched anywhere. The Arboretum maintains a plant collection of unusual scientific interest, including world conifers, primitive angiosperms,
and plant families from Australia, New Zealand, South Africa and South
America, as well as California natives. Other plantings include a eucalyptus grove, a Laurasian forest, a redwood grove, a cactus and succulent garden, an aroma garden, a rare fruit exhibit, and a primitive flowering plant
collection. Many of these species are not available for study in other

American botanical gardens and arboreta. Additionally, the Arboretum imports, selects and breeds choice ornamental plants, especially those that exhibit drought tolerance.

UNIVERSITY OF CALIFORNIA, SANTA CRUZ—CENTER FOR AGROECOLOGY AND SUSTAINABLE FOOD SYSTEMS (CASFS/UCSC FARM & GARDEN)

Farm: near east entrance to campus, Garden: between Merrill & Stevenson Colleges, Santa Cruz, CA 95064
Tel: (831) 459-4140; Fax: (831) 459-2799
Internet Address: http://www.ucsc.edu/casfs
Admission: Free
Attendance: 5,000
Established: 1967
Membership: Y
Wheelchair Accessible: P
Parking: Parking permit or meters on weekdays, free on weekends
Open: Daily, 8am-6pm
Best Time(s) of Year to Visit: Spring to Fall
Facilities: Greenhouse; Grounds Farm (25 acres), Garden (4 acres); Visitor Center
Activities: Education Programs The Garden Classroom (children, (831) 459-2001 or www.lifelab.org); Guided Tours Groups (schedule in advance, (831) 459-3240); Produce and Flower Sales Farm Cart (at base of UCSC campus, June-Oct, Thurs & Fri, noon-6pm); Self-Guided Tours (brochure available at Farm entrance)

The center's goal is to research, develop, and advance sustainable food and agricultural systems that are environmentally sound, economically viable, socially responsible, non-exploitative, and that serve as a foundation for future generations. On the UCSC campus, the Center operates the Alan Chadwick Garden (founded 1967) and the Farm (founded 1972). Both sites are managed using organic production methods. The Garden, relying primarily on founder Alan Chadwick's "French-intensive/biodynamic method," displays a diverse collection of ornamentals, food crops, and native California species. The Farm includes raised-bed gardens, mechanically cultivated row crops, orchards, and research plots. The public is welcome to visit both facilities. The Life Lab Science Program operates a children's garden, the Garden Classroom, on the UCSC Farm.

SANTA ROSA

LUTHER BURBANK HOME & GARDENS (LBH&G)

Santa Rosa Ave. at Sonoma Ave., Santa Rosa, CA 95402
Tel: (707) 524-5445; Fax: (707) 543-3030
Internet Address: http://www.lutherburbank.org
Admission: Free
Attendance: 60,000
Established: 1979
Membership: Y
Wheelchair Accessible: Y
Parking: On-street parking
Open: Gardens, Daily, 8am-dusk
Facilities: Carriage House (April-Oct, Tues-Sun, 10am-4pm, free);
Gardens (roses, orchards, cactus, drought-tolerant, butterfly-
attracting, sensory garden, mature specimen trees); Greenhouse;
Historic or Architecturally Significant Building Burbank Home (Open
Apr-Oct, Wed-Sun, 10am-4pm; $4.00 fee); Library; Shop
Activities: Guided Tours (Apr-Oct, Tues-Sun, 10am-3:30pm, $4/adult)

The gardens are an outdoor museum that features Burbank's work and
includes many of the plants that he developed, as well as plants popular
in the last decades of the 19th century. There are also cutting gardens,
demonstration beds featuring varieties with which Burbank worked, and
fruit trees.

MATANZAS CREEK WINERY—ESTATE GARDENS

6097 Bennett Valley Road (between Kenwood and Santa Rosa), Santa
Rosa, CA 95404
Tel: (800) 590-6464; Fax: (707) 571-0156
Internet Address: http://www.matanzascreek.com
Admission: Free
Attendance: 40,000
Established: 1971
Membership: N
Wheelchair Accessible: Y
Parking: On site
Open: Daily, 10am-4:30pm
Closed: Easter Sunday, Thanksgiving Day, Christmas Day

Best Time(s) of Year to Visit: June to August
Facilities: Gardens (lavender, shade, water); Grounds (design by
Mendocino landscape designer Gary Ratway)
Activities: Events Lavender Harvest Party (last Sat in June, limited
ticket availability, call winery for details); Self-Guided Tour
(booklet available in the winery's tasting room)

Located near the city of Santa Rosa in Northern California's Sonoma
County, Matanzas Creek Winery consists of four parts: winery, vineyards, lavender field, and gardens. The estate gardens with their emphasis on native grasses and exotic perennials were designed as an integral
complement to the 4,000-plant commercial lavender field, the rolling
vineyards, and the surrounding natural terrain.

SANTA ROSA JUNIOR COLLEGE—ROSE COLLECTION

1501 Mendocino Ave., Santa Rosa, CA 95401
Tel: (707) 524-1611; Fax: (707) 527-4231
Internet Address: http://www.santarosa.edu/~dlh/roses.html
Admission: Free
Open: Daily
Facilities: Gardens (two rose); Grounds Campus (99 acres)

The college has two large rose gardens and several smaller rose displays on its Santa Rosa campus. The Mendocino Rose Garden, established at the northeast corner of the campus in the 1930s and 1940s, contains over 150 plants including 23 varieties of older roses. The Garcia
Rose Garden, located just south of Garcia Hall, presents roses interplanted with iris, surrounded by a perimeter of agapanthus and day lilies.
Also on the campus is an extensive collection of Australian native plants,
a California native plant garden, an herb garden, and more than 1,400
trees representing about 400 species.

SARATOGA

HAKONE GARDENS

21000 Big Basin Way, Saratoga, CA 95070-5755
Tel: (408) 741-4994
Internet Address: http://www.hakone.com

Admission: Free
Established: 1916
Membership: Y
Parking: On site, $7.00
Open: Monday to Friday, 10am-5pm; Saturday to Sunday, 11am-5pm;
Closed: New Year's Day, Christmas Day
Facilities: Architecture (recreation of a 19th century Kyoto tea
merchant's home and shop); Gardens (Japanese; Pond, Tea, Zen,
Kizuna-en); Grounds (15 acres); Shop (daily, 12:30pm-4:30pm)
Activities: Art Classes; Guided Tours (Apr-Sept, Sat-Sun, 1pm-4pm);
Tea Ceremony (1st Thurs in month, 1pm-4pm)

A joint project of the City of Saratoga and a community foundation,
Hakone Garden is an authentic Japanese hillside garden. Small specialty
gardens include bamboo, tea, and zen gardens.

LUTHER BURBANK'S GOLD RIDGE EXPERIMENT FARM

7781 Bodega Ave., Sebastopol, CA 95472
Tel: (707) 829-6711
Internet Address: http://www.wschs-grf.pon.net/bef.htm
Admission: No charge/donations accepted
Established: 1975
Membership: Y
Parking: Free on site
Open: Museum, Thursday to Sunday, 1pm-4pm
Facilities: Exhibits (cottage garden, grape arbor, lilacs, orchard, roses,
trees); Greenhouse; Grounds (3 acres)
Activities: Events Open House Gala (annual, during Sebastopol's
Apple Blossom Festival); Guided Tours (Apr15-Oct 15, docent-led, by
appointment, fee); Self-Guided Tours (map available)

During his career, Luther Burbank introduced over 800 varieties
of fruits, flowers, vegetables and grains. Thousands of these new hybrids, cross breeds, and selections were developed at the 15-acre Gold
Ridge Farm, which he purchased in 1885. The current site contains
a three-acre portion of the original farm, including a restoration of the
cottage headquarters and a number of Burbank's original plantings.
Listed on the National Register of Historic Places, Gold Ridge Farm
is owned and maintained by the Western Sonoma County Historical
Society.

SUN VALLEY

THEODORE PAYNE FOUNDATION FOR WILDFLOWERS AND NATIVE PLANTS (TPF)

10459 Tuxford St., Sun Valley, CA 91352
Tel: (818) 768-1802; Fax: (818) 768-1802
Internet Address: http://www.theodorepayne.org
Admission: Free
Established: 1960
Membership: Y
Wheelchair Accessible: P
Parking: Free on site
Open: Tuesday to Saturday, 8:30am-4:30pm
Closed: New Year's Day, Independence Day, Labor Day, Thanksgiving Day, Christmas Day.
Best Time(s) of Year to Visit: Spring, Fall
Facilities: Gardens (native plant, demonstration); Grounds (22 acres); Library; Picnic area; Rest rooms; Shop (horticultural books, seeds); Special Collections (California native plants and wildflowers); Trail Flower Hill
Activities: Education Programs; Guided Tours; Wildflower Hotline (Mar-May, (818) 768-3533)

The Theodore Payne Foundation for Wild Flowers and Native Plants is a nonprofit nursery, seed store, and bookstore focusing on California native plants. In addition to its nursery, the Foundation's 22-acre canyon setting includes Flower Hill (a trail winding through chapparal and wildflowers), demonstration gardens, and extensive areas of natural wildlife habitat. The site contains approximately 800 plant species, including 100 rare or endangered plants.

THOUSAND OAKS

CONEJO VALLEY BOTANIC GARDEN (AHS RAP)

350 W. Gainsborough St., Thousand Oaks, CA 91352
Tel: (805) 494-7630
Internet Address: http://conejogarden.com
Admission: Free
Established: 1973

Membership: Y
Wheelchair Accessible: N
Parking: Free on site
Open: April to September, Daily, 7am-7pm; October to March, 7am-5pm; Closed: New Year's Day, Independence Day, Thanksgiving Day, Christmas Day
Best Time(s) of Year to Visit: Spring, Fall
Facilities: Garden Center; Gardens (Australian, bird habitat, butterfly, desert, children's, herb, native plant, oak tree grove, rare fruit orchard, salvia); Grounds (33 acres); Nature Trail (½ mile)
Activities: Education Programs Kids' Adventure Garden (Sun, 11am-3pm); Guided Tours (by appointment)

The Conejo Valley Botanic Garden preserves, cultivates and displays collections of native and other water-conserving plants, so that visitors can view many plants and trees that typically thrive in the local climate.

TORRANCE

TORRANCE CULTURAL ARTS CENTER—PINE WIND JAPANESE GARDEN (SHO FU EN)

3330 Civic Center Drive, Torrance, CA 90503
Tel: (310) 781-7050
Internet Address: http://www.tcac.torrnet.com/
Admission: Free
Membership: Y
Wheelchair Accessible: P
Parking: On site
Open: Monday to Saturday, 8am-dusk; Sunday, 10am-dusk
Facilities: Amphitheater; Garden (Japanese); Grounds (10,000 square feet, design by Japanese landscape architect Takeo Uesugi)

Funded by Epson America, the Pine Wind Garden (officially known as Sho Fu En) symbolizes a bridge between two cultures. It serves not only as a reminder of the relationship between America and Japan, but also of the special partnership that Torrance shares with its sister city of Kashiwa. The garden features authentic Oriental landscaping and architecture, including a waterfall, koi pond, and stone pathways, as well as a two-tier, redwood amphitheater with seating for up to 60 people. The rest of the Arts Center includes a community meeting hall, theatre, recreation center, art gallery, and studios.

VALLEY CENTER

PIKAKE BOTANICAL GARDENS

15515 Villa Sierra Road, Valley Center,
CA 92082-7651
Tel: (760) 749-4819; Fax: (760) 749-5386
Internet Address:
http://members.home.net/artisticcreations
Admission: Voluntary contribution
Attendance: 2,000
Wheelchair Accessible: P
Parking: Lot holds 40-45 autos, no buses
Open: by appointment only
Best Time(s) of Year to Visit: May to June
Facilities: Gardens (desert, English, tropical fruit, Mediterranean,
oriental, prayer, proteaceae, rose, rainforest); Grounds (9 acres,
landscape design by Bryan Morse)
Activities: Guided Tours (reserve in advance)

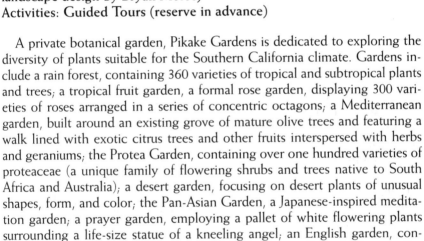

Pikake Botanical Gardens, Valley Center, CA.

A private botanical garden, Pikake Gardens is dedicated to exploring the diversity of plants suitable for the Southern California climate. Gardens include a rain forest, containing 360 varieties of tropical and subtropical plants and trees; a tropical fruit garden, a formal rose garden, displaying 300 varieties of roses arranged in a series of concentric octagons; a Mediterranean garden, built around an existing grove of mature olive trees and featuring a walk lined with exotic citrus trees and other fruits interspersed with herbs and geraniums; the Protea Garden, containing over one hundred varieties of proteaceae (a unique family of flowering shrubs and trees native to South Africa and Australia); a desert garden, focusing on desert plants of unusual shapes, form, and color; the Pan-Asian Garden, a Japanese-inspired meditation garden; a prayer garden, employing a pallet of white flowering plants surrounding a life-size statue of a kneeling angel; an English garden, containing over two hundred species of plants; an arbor walk; and a forest walk.

VAN NUYS

CITY OF LOS ANGELES DONALD C. TILLMAN WATER RECLAMATION PLANT—JAPANESE GARDEN (SUIHO-EN) (AHS RAP)

6100 Woodley Ave. (off Victory Blvd.), Van Nuys, CA 91406
Tel: (818) 756-8166; Fax: (818) 756-9648

Internet Address: http://www.thejapanesegarden.com
Admission: Fee: adult $3.00, child $2.00, senior $2.00; Open strolling, first Wednesday of each month
Attendance: 20,000
Wheelchair Accessible: Y
Parking: Gated parking lot
Open: Monday to Thursday, noon-3:15pm; by appointment; Sunday, 10am-3:15pm
Facilities: Garden (Japanese); Grounds (6½ acres, design by Kôichi Kawana)
Activities: Guided Tours (Mon-Thurs & Sat, by appointment only)

Located in the San Fernando Valley, the garden (Suiho-en) offers three distinct styles: a Zen garden, a wet strolling garden and a tea garden. Operated by the City of Los Angeles Bureau of Sanitation under the direction of the Board of Public Works, it makes use of reclaimed water from a wastewater treatment facility. The garden is authentic, but every effort has been made to assimilate it into the San Fernando Valley environment. Call to confirm the garden is open prior to visit.

WALNUT CREEK

THE GARDENS AT HEATHER FARM (AHS RAP)

1540 Marchbanks Drive, Walnut Creek, CA 94598
Tel: (925) 947-1678; Fax: (925) 947-1726
Internet Address: http://www.gardenshf.org
Admission: Free
Attendance: 30,000
Established: 1968
Membership: Y
Wheelchair Accessible: Y
Parking: Free on site
Open: Daily, dawn-dusk
Facilities: Community Building; Gardens (23; meadow, native plant, rock, rose, sensory, xeriscape); Grounds (6 acres)
Activities: Guided Tours (reserve in advance, $2.00/person)

Located in the heart of Walnut Creek and adjoining its largest park, the Gardens at Heather Farm embrace a six-acre hillside location and feature 23 demonstration gardens. Developed by volunteers, the gardens serve as a living museum, a wildlife habitat, and an outdoor classroom for public education. Specialty gardens include a meadow, sensory, rock, native plant, water-wise, and the ever-popular rose garden with 1,000 bushes representing 150 cultivars. The gardens also serve as a demonstration site for composting, water conservation, and environmentally friendly pest management methods, as well as stunning landscape techniques and designs.

LINDSAY WILDLIFE MUSEUM—NATURE GARDEN

1931 1st Ave., Walnut Creek, CA 94597-2540
Tel: (925) 935-1978; Fax: (925) 935-8015
Internet Address: http://www.wildlife-museum.org
Admission: Fee: adult $6.00, child (<3) free, child (3-16) $4.00, senior $5.00
Attendance: 112,000
Established: 1993
Wheelchair Accessible: Y
Parking: Three parking lots
Open: early September to mid-June, Tuesday to Friday, noon-5pm; Saturday to Sunday, 10am-5pm; mid-June to early September, Tuesday to Sunday, 10am-5pm; Closed: New Year's Day, Easter Sunday, Independence Day, early September, (annual maintenance), Thanksgiving Day, Christmas Day
Facilities: Exhibit Hall (8,000 square feet); Shop (books, music, clothing, jewelry, educational toys/games, bird feeders)
Activities: Education Programs

Located in Larkey Park, the Lindsay Wildlife Museum is a wildlife rehabilitation and educational center focusing on native California wildlife and natural history. The Museum's exhibit hall contains over 50 species of live, non-releasable native wild animals, a learning theatre and a discovery room with hands-on opportunities for children. Treating more than 6,000 injured and orphaned wild animals each year, its wildlife rehabilitation facility is one of the oldest and largest in the United States. Outdoor plantings represent a variety of local plant habitats, including a wildlife garden, oak woodland, meadow chaparral garden, and redwood grove.

THE RUTH BANCROFT GARDEN

1500 Bancroft Road (just north of Ygnacio Valley Road), Walnut Creek, CA 94563-3627
Tel: (925) 210-9663; Fax: (925) 944-9359
Internet Address: http://www.ruthbancroftgarden.org
Admission: Tour (by reservation only) $5.00

Established: 1972
Membership: Y
Wheelchair Accessible: Y
Parking: Parking is limited
Open: Hours vary, Call for reservation
Facilities: Garden (xeriscape); Grounds (3 acres); Special Collections (agave, African aloes, cactus, echeveria, haworthia, succulent, yucca)
Activities: Guided Tours (reservations required); Plant Sales

Begun by Mrs. Rust Bancroft and now a non-profit corporation, the Garden focuses on xeriscape landscape design. More than simply a collection, the Garden with its mature specimens serves as a paradigm of the art of xerophytic garden design. Working primarily with the dramatic forms of her beloved succulents, Mrs. Bancroft has created bold and varied compositions in which the colors, textures, and patterns of foliage provide a setting for the sparkle of floral color. The Ruth Bancroft Garden was the first in the United States to be sponsored by the Garden Conservancy.

WHITTIER

ROSE HILLS MEMORIAL PARK AND MORTUARY

3888 S. Workman Mill Road, Whittier, CA 91748
Tel: (562) 692-4766
Internet Address: http://www.rosehills.com
Admission: Free
Wheelchair Accessible: Y
Open: Daily, 8am-sunset
Best Time(s) of Year to Visit: April to October
Facilities: Gardens (Japanese, rose); Grounds Formal Garden (16 acres), Site (1,400 acres)
Activities: Concerts; Events (Annual Hispanic Celebration); Seminar (rose care)

The park is divided into two sections. The east park contains the 3.5-acre Pageant of Roses Garden, featuring more than 7,000 roses of 600 varieties including floribunda, grandiflora, hedge, hybrid tea, miniature, and tree roses. The Pageant of Roses Garden is an official display garden for both the American Rose Society and the All-America Rose Selections. In the west park a Japanese garden with meditation house is set among lakes and arched bridges.

WOODSIDE

FILOLI CENTER

86 Cañada Road, Woodside, CA 94062
Tel: (415) 364-8300; Fax: (415) 366-7836
Internet Address: http://www.filoli.org/
Admission: Fee: adult $10.00, child $1.00, student $5.00
Attendance: 58,000
Established: 1976
Membership: Y
Wheelchair Accessible: Y
Open: Tours: Mid-Feb. to October 31, Tuesday to Saturday, 10am-3:30pm; Closed: Legal Holidays
Best Time(s) of Year to Visit: Spring (wisteria bloom)
Facilities: Architecture (Georgian residence, 1915-1917 design by Willis Polk); Food Services Café (open Tues-Sat, 10am-3:30pm); Gardens (16 acres); Grounds (650 acres; gardens, 16 acres, original design by Bruce Porter and Isabella Worn); Shop
Activities: Education Programs; Guided & Self-Guided Tours; Guided Nature Hikes

Originally the residence of William B. Bourn II, Filoli is now a property of the National Trust for Historic Preservation. The garden at Filoli is a succession of separate areas or garden rooms each with a distinct character. It was designed by two native Californians: Bruce Porter, a well-known garden architect, artist and interior decorator at the turn of the century, and Isabella Worn, a celebrated floral designer and plants woman for the high society of San Francisco. The Filoli garden is considered one of the finest examples of a private estate garden representing the "Golden Age of American Gardens." The house and gardens were designed as complementary units with the north-south axis of the garden echoing the line of the house's transverse hall and the line of the existing valley.

COLORADO

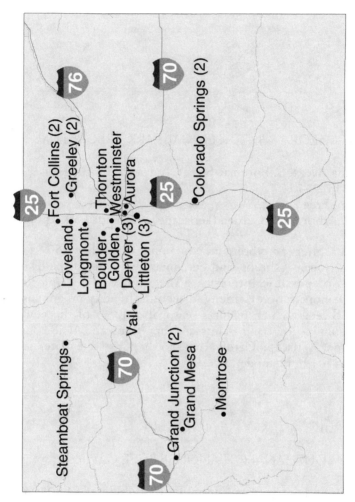

The number in parentheses following the city name indicates the number of gardens/arboreta in that municipality. If there is no number, one is understood. For example, in the text three listings would be found under Denver and one listing under Montrose.

AURORA

CITY OF AURORA—BICENTENNIAL PARK ARBORETUM

E. Alameda Ave. & S. Potomac Street, Aurora, CO 80011
Tel: (303) 739-7177
Admission: Free
Facilities: Arboretum; Garden (xeriscape); Grounds Park (34 acres)

The Park offers an arboretum containing more than 250 trees representing 85 species, shrubs, and perennials and a xeriscape display garden. Also of possible interest are the Annual Flowering Plant and Daylily Demonstration Garden (adjacent to the city greenhouse at 151 Potomac Street), which features seasonal displays of the newest varieties of annual flowering plants and day lilies and Water Conservation's Kuiper Xeriscape Garden (next to the Griswold Water Treatment Plant at 14201 E. Hampden Ave.).

BOULDER

BOULDER-DUSHANABE TEAHOUSE ROSE GARDEN

1770 13th St. (across from Central Park), Boulder, CO 80306
Tel: (303) 441-9004; Fax: (303) 492-6924
Internet Address: http://www.boulder-dushanbe.org/teahouse.html
Admission: Free
Established: 1998
Membership: N
Wheelchair Accessible: Y
Parking: On street
Open: Daily, sunrise-sunset
Best Time(s) of Year to Visit: May to June
Facilities: Food Services (teahouse restaurant); Garden (rose, 1998 design by Eve Reshetnik and Mikl Brawner); Shop

The Boulder-Dushanbe Teahouse Rose Garden is the result of a very successful collaboration between several groups. The city of Dushanbe, capital of Tajikistan, sent the intricately carved, painted, and tiled choihona (traditional teahouse) as a gift to its sister city, suggesting that a rose garden was its traditional setting. The City of Boulder provided the site and construction assistance, and continues to be responsible for irrigation. The Boulder Valley Rose Society recommended two of its members to design the garden, purchased the roses, planted them, and remains responsible for maintaining the garden. A local nursery, Harlequin's Gardens, obtained the roses, donated materials and some labor, and continues to provides pest management oversight. The private company that operates the restaurant at the Teahouse pays for maintenance of the Rose Garden. In the Tajik tradition, the Garden appears "unplanned," a celebration of color and fragrance. Containing over 49 varieties of roses chosen for their hardiness, disease resistance, and bloom sequence, the Garden functions as both a setting for the teahouse and as the Rose Society's hardy rose demonstration garden.

COLORADO SPRINGS

CITY OF COLORADO SPRINGS—MONUMENT VALLEY PARK

170 W. Cache La Poudre Blvd. (Monroe to Kiowa Sts., along Monument Creek), Colorado Springs, CO 80904
Tel: (719) 385-5940; Fax: (719) 578-6934
Internet Address: http://www.springsgov.com
Admission: Free
Established: 1904
Facilities: Garden Center (578-6654 or amarshall@ci.colospgs.co.us); Gardens; Greenhouses; Trails (4½ miles)
Activities: Classes; Education Programs

One of the city's oldest, the long, slender park follows Monument Creek through downtown Colorado Springs. The Park offers formal zinnia, begonia, tulip, and rose gardens; the Horticultural Art Society Demonstration Garden featuring an All-America Selections display garden and a xeriscape exhibit, an arboretum containing native trees and shrubs, a horticulture education center, and a production greenhouse complex.

COLORADO SPRINGS UTILITIES—XERISCAPE DEMONSTRATION GARDEN (XDG)

Mesa Water Treatment Plant, 2855 Mesa Road,
Colorado Springs, CO 80904

Tel: (719) 668-4555
Internet Address: http://www.csu.org/xeri
Admission: Free
Attendance: 30,000
Established: 1991
Wheelchair Accessible: P
Parking: Parking available at facility
Best Time(s) of Year to Visit: June to October
Facilities: Garden (xeriscape); Grounds (1½ acres)
Activities: Education Programs; Guided Tours (by appointment)

The garden contains a wide variety of drought-tolerant plant species displayed in moderate, low, very low, and no-water zones. Included are 64 species of trees; 126 species of shrubs; 340 species of perennial flowers, ground covers, vines, and ornamental grasses; and 12 types of turf. Native Colorado plants are represented by 71 species.

DENVER

DENVER BOTANIC GARDENS (AHS RAP)

1005 York St., Denver, CO 80206-3799
Tel: (720) 865-3544; Fax: (720) 865-3713
Internet Address: http://www.botanicgardens.org/
Admission: Fee (May-September): adult $8.50, child (<4) free, child (4-15) $5.00, student $5.00, senior $5.50; Fee (Winter): Adult $7.50, Child $4.00, Senior $4.00
Attendance: 340,000
Established: 1951
Membership: Y
Wheelchair Accessible: P
Parking: Free on site
Open: May to September 15, Saturday to Tuesday, 9am-8pm; Wednesday to Friday, 9am-5pm; September 16 to April, Daily, 9am-5pm; Closed: Thanksgiving Day, Christmas Day.
Facilities: Auditorium (350 seats); Conservatory Boettcher Memorial Conservatory (13,000 square feet, tropical); Gardens (30; children's, cutting, French kitchen, herb, Japanese, Mediterranean, Monet, perennial, plains, rock alpine, romantic, sensory, shade, Victorian, xeriscape); Greenhouses (14,000 square feet); Grounds (23 acres); Library (23,5000 volumes; Sat-Thurs, 9am-5pm); Shop (Mon-Fri, 10am-4pm; Sat-Sun, 9am-5pm)

Activities: Concerts; Education Programs; Events (plant and art society shows and sales); Guided Tours; Performances; Plant Sales

Denver Botanic Gardens is home to 17,000 plant species, 20,680 fungi specimens, and many gardens featuring plants from all over the world that grow well in Colorado's unique climate. Highlights include Boettcher Memorial Conservatory, containing tropical plants; an extensive, classic Herb Garden; the Laura Smith Porter Plains Garden, a native prairie environment; Mile High Garden, designed by Tom Peace, a well-known local designer and author of the book *Sunbelt Gardening*; the Monet Garden, representing the elements of design and plants that became signature motifs of Claude Monet's garden at Giverny; Shady Lane, designed by Marcia Tatroe, author of *Perennials for Dummies*; Shofu-en, a Japanese garden, designed by Kochi Kawana; the rock alpine garden, containing over 4,000 kinds of montane and alpine plants from the world's high places; the WaterSmart Garden, designed by Lauren Springer, author of *The Undaunted Garden*; and the xeriscape garden, featuring an immense display of hardy western American dryland plants. The Denver Botanic Garden also operates the Chatfield Nature Preserve in Littleton and an Alpine Unit near Idaho Springs in the Mount Evans area.

DENVER WATER DEPARTMENT—XERISCAPE GARDEN

1600 West 12th Ave., Denver, CO 80204
Tel: (303) 628-6000; Fax: (303) 628-6349
Internet Address: http://www.denverwater.org
Admission: Free
Established: 1981
Membership: N
Wheelchair Accessible: Y
Parking: In front of the administration building
Open: Monday to Friday, 7am-5pm; Saturday to Sunday, 7am-5pm, use speakerbox at gate
Facilities: Garden (xeriscape); Grounds (1 acre)
Activities: Guided Tours (schedule in advance)

The original xeriscape demonstration garden in Colorado, the Garden surrounds the Denver Water Department's offices. It contains approximately 200 species of drought-tolerant plants from the Rocky Mountains, Great Plains, and other semi-arid habitats, and examples of eight different types of turf. All plants and turf types are labeled. A self-guided tour brochure may be obtained at the entrance to the garden. On weekends, visitors must use the speakerbox at the gate to gain permission to enter.

UNIVERSITY OF DENVER—CHESTER M. ALTER ARBORETUM

2467 Vine St., Denver, CO 80208
Tel: (303) 871-2871; Fax: (303) 871-3471
Internet Address: http://www.du.edu/biology/arboretum
Admission: No charge/donations accepted
Wheelchair Accessible: Y
Parking: On street parking around campus
Facilities: Arboretum

The university has designated its University Park campus the Chester M. Alter Arboretum. In addition to over 150 tree species, the campus offers the Harper Humanities Garden, a pastoral oasis in the heart of campus. The arboretum is a member of the American Association of Botanical Gardens and Arboreta.

FORT COLLINS

CITY OF FORT COLLINS—THE GARDENS ON SPRING CREEK

2145 S. Centre Ave. (1/2 mile south of University Park Holiday Inn), Fort Collins, CO 80526
Tel: (970) 221-6881; Fax: (970) 221-6586
Internet Address: http://fcgov.com/horticulture
Admission: Voluntary contribution
Attendance: 15,000
Established: 2002
Membership: Y
Wheelchair Accessible: Y
Parking: Free on site
Open: September to April, Monday to Friday, 10am-5pm; May to August, Monday to Friday, 10am-4pm.
Best Time(s) of Year to Visit: May to August
Facilities: Climatic Areas (foothills, meadow, riparian, wetland); Conservatory; Gardens (children's, experiential, four seasons, fruit/vegetable, meditation, Mediterranean, native plant, perennial, permaculture, rock, rose, water, wildlife habitat, xeriscape); Greenhouse (1,400 square feet); Grounds (18 acres, design by EDAW, Inc.; 4 acres natural); Visitor Center

In contrast to a traditional botanic garden, the Gardens on Spring Creek offer programming that emphasizes not only the end result of the botanical display, but also the process of growing plants, through active public involvement. It places less emphasis on science and research and more on applied horticulture, including environmental horticulture and food crops.

COLORADO STATE UNIVERSITY—HORTICULTURAL TRIAL GARDENS (PERC)

630 W. Lake St. (adjacent to the CSU campus), Fort Collins, CO 80523
Tel: (970) 491-7179; Fax: (970) 491-7745
Internet Address: http://www.hla@colostate.edu
Admission: Free
Membership: N
Wheelchair Accessible: P
Parking: Limited parking at 630 W. Lake
Open: daylight hours
Facilities: Gardens; Grounds Annual Trial Garden (2.8 acres), Research Center (14 acres); Plant Environmental Research Center (arboretum, perennial garden, turf plots, vegetable research plots)
Activities: Guided Tours (on request)

Designated an All-American Selections Trial Garden, the trial gardens at CSU present a challenging environment for the plants, gardens, and growers alike. The environmental conditions are characterized by high altitude (approx. 5,000 ft.), intense solar radiation, drying winds, severe hail storms, extreme fluctuations between day and night temperatures, season-long need for irrigation, and heavy clay soils. The site features shade and sun annuals and all-season beds. Additionally, the Plant Environmental Research Center, located at 650 W. Lake, has 750 different taxa of herbaceous perennials growing in its demonstration/research garden, which was started in 1980.

GOLDEN

JEFFERSON COUNTY SHERIFF'S COMPLEX—ROSE GARDEN

200 Jefferson County Parkway, Golden, CO 80401
Tel: (303) 271-5477
Internet Address:
http://www.co.jefferson.co.us/ext/dpt/officials/sheriff/roses.htm
Admission: Free
Established: 1993

Parking: Free on site
Facilities: Garden (rose)

Located at the northeast corner of the county complex in Golden, the Garden contains over 2,500 roses representing over 400 varieties, including hybrid tea, floribunda, grandiflora, miniature, shrub, old garden, climbing, David Austin English and Dr. Griffin Buck hardy roses, as well as nearly 2,500 perennials and shrubs. Accredited by All-America Rose Selections, it is the only public rose garden in the United States to be planted at a jail and maintained by inmates. The roses are labeled by name and there are usually inmate workers available to answer your questions. The garden is a cooperative project of the Jefferson County Sheriff's Office, the Denver Rose Society, and the CSU Cooperative Extension of Jefferson County.

GRAND JUNCTION

COLORADO STATE UNIVERSITY TRI RIVER AREA COOPERATIVE EXTENSION—DEMONSTRATION GARDENS

Mesa County Office, 2775 Route 50, Grand Junction, CO 81503
Tel: (970) 244-1834; Fax: (970) 244-1700
Internet Address: http://www.colostate.edu/Depts/CoopExt/
TRA/PLANTS/demogardens/demo.htm
Admission: Free
Parking: Free on site
Facilities: Gardens (ornamental grass, perennial, plant select, rose, xeriscape); Grounds (design by Mark Gibbons of Landscape Specialties, Grand Junction)
Activities: Self-Guided Tour (map available on site)

Located at the County Extension office near the fairgrounds, the demonstration gardens include two rose gardens, featuring old garden, hardy shrub, miniature, and species roses; the Plant Select Garden, a joint project of Denver Botanic Gardens and Colorado State University designed to identify and publicize the plants best suited for the climate of the High Plains and Intermountain regions; two xeriscape gardens; a perennial garden; and an ornamental grass garden.

WESTERN COLORADO BOTANICAL GARDENS (AHS RAP)

655 Struthers St. (end of S. 7th Street), Grand Junction, CO 81501
Tel: (970) 245-8565; Fax: (970) 245-9001

Internet Address: http://www.wcbotanic.org/
Admission: Fee: adult $3.00, child (<5) free, child (5-12) $1.50,
student $2.00, senior $2.00
Membership: Y
Open: April to October, Tuesday to Sunday, 10am-5pm; November to
March, Tuesday to Sunday, 10am-4:30pm
Facilities: Butterfly House; Gardens (children's, Japanese, native, rose,
sensory); Greenhouse (4,000 square feet); Grounds (12.3 acres)
Activities: Education Programs; Guided Tours (reserve 2 weeks in
advance, $2.00/person, 245-3288); Lectures; Workshops

Located on the banks of the Colorado River, the Gardens include a
greenhouse with over 600 tropical plants; a butterfly house containing
200 North American native butterflies of 24 species; Ann's Garden featuring over 32 varieties of hybrid dahlias; and the Weddle Native Garden,
depicting the ecosystems of 13 geological elevation zones that surround
the Grand Valley.

GRAND MESA

GRAND MESA NATIONAL FOREST VISITOR'S CENTER—
DEMONSTRATION GARDENS

Trickle Park Road, across from Cobbett Lake, Grand Mesa,
CO 81416
Tel: (970) 242-8211; TDDY: (970) 874-6660
Internet Address: http://www.fs.fed.us/r2/gmug/
Admission: Free
Established: 2001
Membership: N
Wheelchair Accessible: Y
Parking: Two parking lots
Open: Memorial Day to September, Daily, 9am-5pm
Best Time(s) of Year to Visit: August
Facilities: Gardens (native plant); Picnic Area; Visitor Center

Located adjacent to the Visitor's Center atop the Grand Mesa at an
altitude of over 10,000 feet, the Demonstration Gardens feature native
plants in meadow, bog, and woodland habitats. The Gardens are a
joint project of the United States Forest Service, the Colorado Sate
University Cooperative Extension Master Gardener program, the Colorado Native Plant Society, Colorado University, and the Scenic By-
ways Committee.

GREELEY

CENTENNIAL VILLAGE MUSEUM—GARDENS

1475 A St., Greeley, CO 80631
Tel: (970) 350-9220; Fax: (970) 350-9570
Internet Address: http://www.greeleymuseum.com
Admission: Fee: adult $5.00, child (6-11) $3.00, senior $4.00; Free:
selected Saturdays
Attendance: 15,000
Established: 1976
Membership: Y
Wheelchair Accessible: N
Parking: Free on site, ample
Open: mid- April to mid-October, Tues-Sat, 10am-4pm
Best Time(s) of Year to Visit: mid-April to mid-October (garden in
bloom)
Facilities: Architecture (30 historic structures); Gardens (day lily, herb,
native plant, Victorian); Grounds (5½ acres); Shop Selma's Store (350-
9224)
Activities: Guided Tours (group, schedule in advance)

   Located on the north side of Greeley, the Village features structures
depicting the architecture, lifestyle and people of the Colorado High
Plains between 1860 and 1920. Gardens on site include a Victorian setting, a formal herb garden, an American Hemerocallis Society display
garden, and a natural area managed by the Audubon Society.

HOUSTON GARDENS

515 23rd Ave. (at 4th St.), Greeley, CO 80634
Tel: (970) 353-4837
Admission: Voluntary contribution
Attendance: 1,500
Membership: N
Parking: Parking on-site
Open: May to October, Tuesday to Saturday, 8:30-4:30
Best Time(s) of Year to Visit: June to August
Facilities: Gardens (day lily); Grounds (4 acres—nature, representing
4 of 5 life zones in Colorado)

   Greeley was founded in 1870 as Union Colony, a cooperative agricultural enterprise organized by Nathan Meeker, agricultural editor of

the *New York Tribune*, with the support of Horace Greeley, journalist-politician. The gardens were developed to commemorate the Union Colony pioneers and their work in the greening of the "Great American Desert." There is an American Hemerocallis Society display garden on site.

LITTLETON

CITY OF LITTLETON—WAR MEMORIAL ROSE GARDEN

5804 S. Bemis St. (directly west of Sterne Park), Littleton, CO 80120
Tel: (303) 721-8478; Fax: (303) 798-3030
Internet Address: http://www.sspr.org
Admission: Free
Established: 1968
Membership: N
Wheelchair Accessible: Y
Parking: Free on site
Open: Daily, dawn-dusk
Facilities: Gardens (rose); Grounds (2 acres); Picnic Area

Honoring American soldiers who died in World Wars I and II, the Garden contains approximately 800 hybrid teas, florabundas, polyanthas, and miniature roses in twenty beds arranged in a formal circular design around an antique, stone fountain. An additional collection of 49 Old Garden Roses are arranged in beds near the gazebo. Accredited by All-America Rose Selections, the Garden was created by the Arapahoe Rose Society. The Garden is owned by the City of Littleton and managed by the South Suburban Parks and Recreation District.

DENVER BOTANIC GARDENS—CHATFIELD NATURE PRESERVE

8500 Deer Creek Canyon Road, Littleton, CO 80123
Tel: (303) 973-3705; Fax: (303) 973-1979
Internet Address: http://www.botanicgardens.org/chatfld/htm
Admission: Fee—$5.00 per passenger vehicle; Free: first Friday in month
Wheelchair Accessible: P
Open: Daily, 9am-5pm
Closed: Legal holidays

Facilities: Arboretum; Garden (xeriscape); Grounds (700 acres); Restored 19th-century Farmstead
Activities: Education Programs; Guided Tours (reserve in advance)

A 19th century farmstead has been restored to present an authentic view of pioneer life on the Colorado High Plains. Exhibits include a 2½-acre xeriscape garden containing over 150 labeled plant species.

HUDSON GARDENS

6115 South Santa Fe Drive (one mile south of West Bowles),
Littleton, CO 80120
Tel: (303) 797-8565
Internet Address: http://www.hudsongardens.org
Admission: Fee: adult $4.00, child (<3) free, child (4-12) $2.00, senior $3.00; Free Nov-April
Established: 1996
Membership: Y
Open: Daily, 9am-5pm
Facilities: Gardens (16; butterfly, conifer grove, cottage, cutting, deciduous woodland, demonstration, fragrance, perennial, prairie/grass, rock, rose, water, wetland, wildflower); Grounds (30 acres, design by landscape architect Doug Rockne of Littleton); Shop (gardening tools, seeds, books, gifts, garden ornaments)
Activities: Classes; Concerts (summer); Education Programs; Events 4th of July, Mother's Day Brunch, Scarecrow Festival, Supper with Santa; Guided Tours; Performances

Comprised entirely of plants, flowers and trees that grow in the dry Colorado climate, Hudson Gardens is a classic regional display garden. Presented in one continuous, contiguous flow, its sixteen distinct gardens include a cottage garden surrounding the former Hudson residence; a fragrance garden; a two-acre oval garden; a rose garden, displaying roses in historical sequence; a cutting garden; a butterfly bank garden; a rock garden; a water garden; a secret garden; a native wildflower garden; a cascade area; a conifer grove with 40 types of conifers; deciduous woodlands; wetlands; and a prairie grass garden, featuring historic grasses and native plants; shrubs and trees. There are also six changing demonstration gardens highlighting the latest in annuals, herbs, perennials, vegetables, and aquatic plants. The gardens are maintained by the Hudson Foundation in partnership with the South Suburban Park and Recreation District.

LONGMONT

CITY OF LONGMONT—XERISCAPE DEMONSTRATION GARDEN

Sunset Park, 1900 Longs Peak Ave., Longmont, CO 80501
Tel: (303) 651-8446; Fax: (303) 651-8348
Admission: Free
Attendance: 1,000
Established: 1995
Membership: N
Wheelchair Accessible: P
Parking: Parking available adjacent to the garden
Open: 24 hours per day
Best Time(s) of Year to Visit: Summer
Facilities: Garden (xeriscape)

Located across from the swimming pool, the Garden contains 80 varieties of drought-tolerant trees, shrubs, and perennials. Interpretive materials and plant lists are available.

There is an additional xeriscape demonstration garden at 310 Quail Road in Longmont.

LOVELAND

CITY OF LOVELAND—JEFF PETERSON XERISCAPE GARDEN

1st St. & Washington Ave. (near the Civic Center Complex), Loveland, CO 80537
Tel: (970) 962-3000; Fax: (970) 962-2903
Internet Address: http://www.ci.loveland.co.us/WP/xeriscape.htm
Admission: Free
Established: 1997
Facilities: Gardens (bulb, floral, ornamental, grass, turf grass, herb, native plant, perennial,, shade, wildlife, xeriscape)

Occupying a narrow space one block long, between the street and an irrigation ditch, the Garden contains over 3,390 plantings representing 99 species. The Garden is a joint project of the Parks & Recreation Department, Water & Power Department, and the Northern Colorado Water Conservancy District. Visitors can obtain a plant list at the Parks and Recreation Office.

MONTROSE

MONTROSE BOTANIC GARDEN

Pavilion Drive, Montrose, CO 81420
Tel: (970) 249-9055
Admission: No charge/donations accepted
Established: 1995
Membership: Y
Wheelchair Accessible: Y
Parking: On site and on street
Open: Daily, 24 hours
Facilities: Gardens (xeriscape); Grounds (3 acres)

Conceived as a demonstration garden, Montrose Botanic Garden is a project of the Montrose Botanical Society. There are currently three gardens at the site, the Entry Garden, the Promenade, and a xeriscape demonstration garden. Twelve additional gardens are planned.

STEAMBOAT SPRINGS

YAMPA RIVER BOTANIC PARK ASSOCIATION

Off Highway 40 at Trafalger, Steamboat Springs, CO 80477-6269
Tel: (970) 879-4300; Fax: (970) 870-0173
Internet Address: http://www.steamboat springs.net
Admission: No charge/donations accepted
Attendance: 15,000
Established: 1997
Membership: Y
Wheelchair Accessible: Y
Parking: Parking for 200 cars
Open: Daily, dawn-dusk
Facilities: Gardens 5 acres (50; annual, bulb, butterfly, day lily, hummingbird, medicinal & culinary herb, iris, native plant, medicinal, color, pioneer, rock, rose, September, sunshine, water, xeriscape)
Activities: Concerts (12:15 Thursdays, June-August)

Yampa River Botanic Park Association, Steamboat Springs, CO

Located between the Old Town and the Ski Mountain, at an altitude of 6,820 feet, the Yampa River Botanic Park offers a unique and challenging environment. The park features many high-altitude plants. Topography was built to yield various exposures to the sun, thereby creating microclimates for some fifty gardens. Also of possible interest is the xeriscape demonstration garden featuring high-altitude perennials on the Yampa River Core Trail near Fletcher Park.

THORNTON

CITY OF THORNTON—XERISCAPE DEMONSTRATION GARDEN

Thornton Recreation Center, 11151 Colorado Blvd.,
Thornton, CO 80229
Tel: (303) 255-7636
Internet Address: http://cityofthornton.net/
Established: 1997
Membership: N
Wheelchair Accessible: Y
Open: dawn to dusk
Facilities: Garden (xeriscape—three separate water use zones);
Grounds (½ acre)
Activities: Self-Guided Tour (brochure available)

Located south of the Thornton Recreation Center's main parking lot at 110th and Colorado Boulevard, the Garden contains 125 species of drought tolerant trees, shrubs, perennials, and grasses. All plants are labeled with information panels.

VAIL

BETTY FORD ALPINE GARDENS (AHS RAP)

Ford Park, Vail, CO 81657
Tel: (970) 476-0103; Fax: (970) 476-1685
Internet Address:
http://www.bettyfordalpinegardens.org
Admission: No charge/donations accepted
Attendance: 100,000
Established: 1987
Membership: Y
Wheelchair Accessible: Y
Parking: Main Vail parking structure or Ford Park
Open: Snowmelt to Snowfall, Daily, dawn-dusk
Facilities: Gardens (alpine, children's, meditation, perennial, rock, xeriscape); Grounds (3 acres); Shop

Betty Ford Alpine
Gardens, Vail, CO

Activities: Children's Programs Kids Amphitheater (Wed, 10:30am); Guided Tours (Mon/Thurs/Sat, 10:30am, main gate); Horticulture Therapy Program Schoolhouse Garden

At an altitude of 8,200 feet one of the highest alpine gardens in the world, the Betty Ford Alpine Gardens are best known for their brilliant display of alpine flowers. At the main entrance gate, the Alpine Tundra Garden demonstrates the ecological processes in the evolution of mountain tundra with plantings drawn both from the Rocky Mountains and from around the world. Beginning in the Kids Amphitheater, where stones mark the summer and winter solstices, the Children's Garden simulates a hike up the local mountain range passing through montane, subalpine, and alpine life zones. Home to the Gardens Horticultural Therapy Program, the Schoolhouse Garden features handicapped accessible beds containing a growing collection of herbal and useful plants from mountain cultures around the world. While hardly an English perennial border, the Mountain Perennial Garden translates the English gardening tradition into a sunken garden, demonstrating with over 1,000 varieties of both traditional and unusual taxa the wide variety of perennials, including alpines, that will grow in the mountain landscape. Inspired by the gardening traditions of the Far East, the Mountain Meditation Garden offers a place of quiet contemplation focusing on the spiritual aspects of mountain, waterfall, stream, rock, and specimen plants. The Alpine Rock Garden recreates alpine environments and a collection of plant communities found in the North American Rocky Mountains.

WESTMINSTER

BUTTERFLY PAVILION AND INSECT CENTER—GARDENS

6252 West 104th Ave., Westminster, CO 80020
Tel: (303) 469-5441; Fax: (303) 469-5442
Internet Address: http://www.bbutterflies.org
Admission: Fee: adult $7.95, child $4.95, senior $5.95
Attendance: 250,000
Established: 1995
Membership: Y
Wheelchair Accessible: Y
Parking: Free on site
Open: Labor Day to Memorial Day, Daily, 9am-5pm; Memorial Day to Labor Day, Daily, 9am-6pm
Facilities: Conservatory (7,200 square feet, tropical rain forest); Gardens (annual, cactus/succulent, perennial, vegetable); Grounds (10

acres); Trail Big Dry Creek Nature Trail (shortgrass prairie & riparian ecosystems)
Activities: Education Programs

The first stand-alone non-profit insect zoo in the nation, the Center is an educational facility for the study of insects and other invertebrates. Housing over 1,000 butterflies representing more than 50 species, the conservatory features tropical foliage and flowering plants. Designed with the idea of educating the public on the importance of preserving habitats, the gardens at the Center contain over 200 different species of plants whose life cycles are intimately intertwined with butterflies. Gardens include perennial gardens with butterfly nectar and host plants, an annual garden with plants that are butterfly nectar sources, a cactus and succulent garden, and a vegetable garden. The nature trail illustrates two significant Colorado ecosystems—the short grass prairie and riparian ecosystems.

Hawaii

Haena. **Kauai**

Koloa. Poipu (2)   **Oahu**

.Haleiwa
Wahiawa.
Aiea. .Kaneohe (2)
Honolulu (5). .Koko Crater

Maui

Wailuku..Kahului (2)
Kula (3). .Keanae (2)
Hana (2)

Hawaii

.Papaikou

Captain Cook.

The number in parentheses following the city name indicates the number of gardens/arboreta in that municipality. If there is no number, one is understood. For example, in the text five listings would be found under Honolulu and one listing under Captain Cook.

Island of Hawaii

CAPTAIN COOK

BISHOP MUSEUM—AMY B. H. GREENWELL ETHNOBOTANICAL GARDENS

82-6188 Mamalahoa Highway, Captain Cook, HI 96817
Tel: (808) 323-3318
Internet Address: http://www.bishopmuseum.org/greenwell/
Admission: Fee: adult $14.95, child (<4) free, child (4-12) $11.95, senior $11.95
Wheelchair Accessible: P
Parking: Ample parking
Open: 9am-5pm; Closed: Christmas Day
Facilities: Grounds (12 acres); Herbarium; Special Collections (native plants, Polynesian introduced plants, crop plants)

The Amy B. H. Greenwell Ethnobotanical Gardens supports native Hawaiian cultural traditions of land use and plants and conserves the plant resources of traditional Hawaiian cultural activities. The landscape plan reflects four vegetation zones used by prehistoric Hawaiians in Kona, and includes a five-acre archaeological remnant of the Kona Field System. The gardens feature 250 types of plants used by Hawaiians, including native and Polynesian introduced plants.

PAPAIKOU

HAWAII TROPICAL BOTANIC GARDEN

27-717 Old Mamalahoa Highway (RR143-A) (8½ miles north of Hilo), Papaikou, HI 96781
Tel: (808) 964-5233; Fax: (808) 964-1338
Internet Address: http://htbg.com/
Admission: Fee: adult $15.00, child (<6) free, child (6-16) $5.00
Established: 1984
Parking: Free parking
Open: Daily, 8:30am-5pm; Closed: New Year's Day, Thanksgiving Day, Christmas Day

Facilities: Gardens; Grounds (17 acres); Shop; Special Collections (aroid, bromeliad, ginger, heliconia, maranta, orchid, palm)

The Hawaii Tropical Botanical Garden is a museum of living plants, including palms, heliconias, gingers, bromeliads, and many rare and exotic species from all parts of the tropical world. Over 2,000 species, representing more than 125 families and 750 genera, are found in the garden. The 40-acre Onomea Valley is a natural greenhouse, protected from buffeting tradewinds and blessed with fertile volcanic soil. Created as a nature preserve to protect the beauty and harmony of the rain forest, plants are placed in a naturalized setting among pools, streams, and cascading waterfalls. Some of the Garden's mango and coconut palm trees are over 100 years old.

Island of Kauai

HAENA

NATIONAL TROPICAL BOTANICAL GARDEN— LIMAHULI GARDEN AND PRESERVE

560 Kuhio Hwy., Haena, HI 96766
Tel: (808) 826-1053
Internet Address: http://www.ntbg.org/limahuli.html
Admission: Self-Guided Tour Fee $10.00
Membership: Y
Open: Tuesday to Friday, 9:30am-4pm; Sunday, 9:30am-4pm; Closed: Thanksgiving Day, Christmas Day
Facilities: Garden (15 acres); Grounds (1,000 acres, 985 acre forest); Shop; Visitor Center
Activities: Education Programs; Guided Tours ($15/person, reservations required); Self-Guided Tours

Located on Kauai's wet north shore, Limahuli Garden and Preserve is situated in a verdant tropical valley covering three distinct ecological zones. The collections of Limahuli Garden emphasize rare and endangered plants of Hawaii, plants of ethnobotanical value, and the preservation of natural ecosystems. In 1997, Limahuli Garden was selected by the American Horticultural Society as the best natural botanical garden in the U.S., noting its research, teaching and educational programs have demonstrated the best sound environmental practices of water, soil, and rare plant conservation in an overall garden design.

KOLOA

OUTRIGGER KIAHUNA PLANTATION RESORT— MOIR PA'U A LAKA CACTUS AND FLOWER GARDEN

2253 Poipu Road, Koloa, HI 96756-9534
Tel: (808) 742-6411
Admission: Free
Established: 1932
Membership: N
Wheelchair Accessible: N
Parking: Free on site
Open: Daily, 8:30am-4:30pm
Facilities: Grounds (35 acres); Special Collections (aloe, cactus, succulent)
Activities: Guided Tours (Tues, 9am; Thurs, 4pm);
Self-Guided Tour

The resort property was originally the estate of Hector Moir and Alexandra Knudsen. A wedding gift from the bride's father, the couple moved into the lava stone manor house, now the main lobby of the resort, upon their wedding in 1930. Mrs. Knudsen started the gardens as a hobby and soon discovered that cactus and succulents thrived in the area's arid setting. In 1954, the Moirs officially opened the gardens to the public. Set among lily ponds and lagoons, the grounds feature landscaped tropical gardens containing cactus, succulents, orchids, bomeliads, and other plants and trees, including wiliwili, hau, coconut, and plumeria.

POIPU

NATIONAL TROPICAL BOTANICAL GARDEN— ALLERTON GARDEN

4425 Lawai Road (10 miles from Lihue), Poipu, HI 96756
Tel: (808) 742-2623
Internet Address: http://www.ntbg.org/allerton.html
Admission: Fee $30.00
Open: Monday to Saturday, 9am-2pm
Facilities: Architecture (former private estate); Garden (tropical); Grounds (100 acres); Palmetum; Special Collections (bamboo)

Activities: Guided Tours (Tues-Sat, 9am/10am/1pm/2pm; reservations required, $30/person)

Located in Lawai-kai Valley adjacent to the McBryde Garden, Allerton Garden was imagined first by Hawaii's Queen Emma in the late 19th century and then by Alexander McBryde at the turn of the 20th century. But it was Robert and John Gregg Allerton, beginning in 1938, who successfully transformed their vision into a physical landscape replete with gravity-fed fountains, pools, statuary, and other surprise features hidden among the lush tropical foliage. The Bill and Jean Lane Visitor Center (directly across from Spouting Horn in Poipu, Kauai) is the check-in point for tours of the McBryde Garden and the Allerton Garden. Robert Allerton's Illinois residence is also listed; see University of Illinois at Urbana-Champaign—Robert Allerton Park.

NATIONAL TROPICAL BOTANICAL GARDEN— MCBRYDE GARDEN AND HEADQUARTERS

4425 Lawai Road, Poipu, HI 96756
Tel: (808) 642-2623; Fax: (808) 332-9765
Internet Address: http://www.ntbg.org
Admission: by reservation only $15.00
Established: 1964
Membership: Y
Open: 9:30am-4:00pm; Closed: Thanksgiving Day, Christmas Day
Facilities: Conservation Center; Garden (largest ex situ collection of native Hawaiian flora); Grounds (252 acres); Herbarium (27,000 dried plant specimens); Library (8,000 volumes, use by appointment); Shop (in Visitor Center); Visitor Center (Mon-Sat, 8:30am-5pm).
Activities: Guided Tours (Mon-Sat, 9am & 1pm, reserve in advance, $30/person); Lectures; Self-guided Tours (trams leave every hour on the half hour [last at 2:30pm])

Located in the Lawai Valley on the south shore of Kaua'i, McBryde Garden is home to major research and conservation collections and specimen plants, including the world's largest collection of threatened and endangered plants of Hawaii. The National Tropical Botanical Garden headquarters and science, conservation, and education facilities are located at this site. The Bill and Jean Lane Visitor Center (directly across from Spouting Horn in Poipu, Kauai) is the check-in point for tours of the McBryde Garden and the Allerton Garden.

Island of Maui

HANA

HANA MAUI BOTANICAL GARDENS

470 Ulaino Road, Hana, HI 96713
Tel: (808) 248-7725; Fax: (808) 248-7725
Admission: Fee: adult $3.00, child-free
Attendance: 3,000
Established: 1987
Membership: N
Wheelchair Accessible: N
Parking: ½ acre paved lot
Open: Daily, 9am-5pm
Facilities: Grounds (10 acres); Special Collections
(native Hawaiian and Polynesian introduced plants)
Activities: Self-Guided Tour

Hana Maui Botanical Gardens, Hana, HI. Breadfruit.

The garden features native Hawaiian and Polynesian-introduced plant species as well as displaying tropical fruit and flowers from other areas.

NATIONAL TROPICAL BOTANICAL GARDEN— KAHANU GARDEN

Ula'ino Road (off Route 360 at Mile Marker 31), Hana, HI 96765
Tel: (808) 248-8912
Internet Address: http://www.ntbg.org/kahanu.html
Admission: Self-Guided Tour: $10.00
Open: Monday to Friday, 10am-2pm
Facilities: Architecture Pi'ilanihale Heiau (Polynesian religious structure); Garden; Grounds (122 acres); Special Collections (breadfruit, Polynesian crops)
Activities: Guided Tours (by reservation); Self-Guided Tours

Fringed by a vast native pandanus forest, Kahanu Garden is located on the Hana coast, along the far eastern shore of the Hawaiian island of Maui. It features plant collections from the Pacific Islands, concentrating on plants of value to the people of Polynesia, Micronesia, and Melanesia.

Kahanu Garden contains the largest known collection of breadfruit with cultivars from over 17 Pacific island groups and Indonesia, the Philippines, and the Seychelles. The massive Pi'ilanihale Heiau, a structure made out of lava rock, is believed to be the largest ancient place of worship in Polynesia.

KAHULUI

KAHULUI PUBLIC LIBRARY—COURTYARD GARDEN

90 School St., Kahului, HI 96732
Tel: (808) 873-3097
Admission: Free
Membership: N
Wheelchair Accessible: Y
Parking: Parking free and plentiful
Open: Tuesday, 1pm-8pm; Wednesday to Saturday, 10am-5pm
Facilities: Garden (native plant)

Featuring over 20 endemic and indigenous Hawaiian plants, the Garden was created and is maintained by the Native Hawaiian Plant Society in order to foster public awareness of these rare and fast-disappearing plants.

MAUI NUI BOTANICAL GARDEN

150 Kanaloa Ave., Kahului, HI 96733
Tel: (808) 249-2798; Fax: (808) 249-0325
Internet Address: http://mnbg.org/
Admission: Voluntary contribution
Wheelchair Accessible: Y
Parking: Street parking and stadium parking lot
Open: Monday to Friday, 9am-4pm; Saturday, 9am-2:30pm;
Closed: Legal holidays
Facilities: Greenhouse; Grounds (7 acres); Special Collections (native and Polynesian introduced plants; coastal and dry forest)
Activities: Classes; Education Programs; Guided Tours for groups (by request; $10 per person); Plant Sales

Started by Rene Sylva in 1976, the garden is devoted exclusively to coastal and dry forest native Hawaiian and Polynesian introduced plants.

KEANAE

GARDEN OF EDEN ARBORETUM AND BOTANICAL GARDEN (GARDEN OF EDEN)

10600 Hana Highway, Keanae, HI 96768
Tel: (808) 572-9899
Internet Address: http://www.mauigardenofeden.com
Admission: Fee: adult $7.50, child-free
Attendance: 50,000
Established: 1976
Membership: N
Wheelchair Accessible: P
Open: Daily, 8am-3pm
Facilities: Grounds (26 acres); Special Collections (Ti plants, palms, exotic fruits, hardwoods)

Created by Alan Bradbury, Maui's first ISA certified arborist and landscape designer, the arboretum features nature trails offering panoramic ocean views set among over 500 botanically labeled native Hawaiian trees, flowers and foliage, as well as plants and trees gathered from the south Pacific region and tropical rain forests around the world.

KEANAE ARBORETUM

Hana Highway at Mile Post 16, Keanae, HI 96799
Tel: (808) 984-8106; Fax: (808) 984-8111
Admission: Free
Membership: N
Wheelchair Accessible: N
Parking: Very limited parking
Open: daylight hours

The Arboretum, containing over 150 varieties of tropical plants, shrubs, and trees, is divided into three sections: cultivated Hawaiian plants, introduced tropical trees, and native forest trees. Also on the grounds are several functioning taro paddies. There are no facilities on the grounds.

KULA

ENCHANTING FLORAL GARDENS OF KULA

Highway 37 (across from the 10-mile marker), Kula, HI 96790
Tel: (808) 878-2531; Fax: (808) 878-1805
Internet Address: http://www.flowersofmaui.net
Admission: Fee: adult $5.00, child (6-11) $1.00
Membership: N
Wheelchair Accessible: Y
Parking: On site
Open: Daily, 9am-5pm
Best Time(s) of Year to Visit: April to May
Facilities: Gardens (8 acres); Picnic Area

Located on the slopes of Mount Haleakala, the gardens contains over 2,000 varieties of tropical and semitropical flowers and plants from around the world.

KULA BOTANICAL GARDENS

638 Kekaulike Ave. (Route 377) (just north of Waipoli Road), Kula, HI 96790
Tel: (808) 878-1715
Admission: Fee: adult $5.00, child (<6) free, child (6-12) $1.00
Attendance: 28,000
Membership: Y
Wheelchair Accessible: Y
Parking: Free on site
Open: Daily, 9am-4pm
Facilities: Gardens (native plant, orchid); Grounds (9 acres); Shop (Hawaiian made items, snacks); Special Collections (protea)
Activities: Guided Tours (12+, on request); Self-Guided Tours

Located at the 3,300 foot elevation on the slopes of Haleakala, Maui's dormant volcano, Kula Botanical Gardens features nearly 2,000 types of exotic and native Hawaiian plant life sited among streams, waterfalls, an aviary, and a koi pond. Specimens include collections of proteas, orchids, and bromeliads, as well as native plants.

UNIVERSITY OF HAWAII-CTAHR-MAUI AGRICULTURAL RESEARCH CENTER— ROSE GARDEN

424 Mauna Place Kula, HI 96790
Tel: (808) 878-1213; Fax: (808) 878-6804
Admission: Free
Attendance: 200
Membership: N
Wheelchair Accessible: P
Parking: Limited parking in lot
Open: Monday to Thursday, 7am-3:30pm; Closed:
Legal holidays
Best Time(s) of Year to Visit: December to March
Facilities: Garden (rose—34 varieties; 550 plants; AAS winners);
Greenhouses (3,200 square ft.); Grounds Research Station
(20 acres-planted with protea)
Activities: Agricultural research (tomato)

The Kula station has participated as a demonstration garden for the All-America Rose Selection by displaying their yearly rose winners.

WAILUKU

KEPANIWAI HERITAGE GARDEN

Route 30 (near Kahului Airport & Iao Valley State Park),
Wailuku, HI 96700
Admission: Free
Open: Daily, 7am-7pm
Facilities: Gardens (Japanese)

Located in north central Maui, this county park is dedicated to Hawaiian immigrants from Japan, China, Polynesia, and the Philippines. The grounds feature plants instrumental to the growth of Hawaiian horticulture set among small buildings and monuments.

Island of Oahu

AIEA

HONOLULU BOARD OF WATER SUPPLY— HALAWA XERISCAPE GARDEN

Halawa Industrial Park, 99-1268 Iwaena St., Aiea, HI 96701
Tel: (808) 527-6113
Internet Address:
http://www.lava.net/bws/fa_conserv/fa01_ct01_mainpage.htm
Admission: Free
Parking: Small lot across from garden
Open: Wednesday, 10am-2pm; Saturday, 10am-2pm
Facilities: Garden (xeriscape); Grounds (3 acres)
Activities: Classes (xeriscaping); Education Programs; Guided Tours
(arrange in advance); Plant Sale (annual); Self-Guided Tours

This demonstration garden highlights over 300 varieties of water conserving plants, water saving irrigation systems, mulches, and other water saving landscape ideas. Plantings feature tropical plants that are unique to Hawaii including Hibiscus Brackenridge, the Hawaii state flower. A self-guided tour brochure is available. A project of the Honolulu Board of Water Supply, the garden is located just outside Honolulu at the end of the Halawa Valley.

HALEIWA

WAIMEA VALLEY AUDUBON CENTER—WAIMEA ARBORETUM AND BOTANICAL GARDEN

59-864 Kamehameha Highway, Haleiwa, HI 96712-9406
Tel: (808) 638-9199; Fax: (808) 638-9197
Admission: Fee: adult $8.00, child (<4) free, child (4-12) $5.00; Last hour: adult $5.00, child (4-12) $3.00
Attendance: 190,000
Established: 1973
Membership: Y
Wheelchair Accessible: Y
Parking: Fee on site, $2/auto
Open: Daily, 9:30am-5pm

Facilities: Arboretum; Botanical Garden; Food Services Country
Kitchen (snacks), Pikake Pavilion (cafeteria & restaurant, 400 seats);
Grounds Cultivated (150 acres), Valley (1,875 acres); Library (2,000
volumes, upon request, non-circulating); Shop (nature store); Special
Collections (erythrina, ginger, heliconia, hibiscus)
Activities: Education Programs (children); Guided Tours (Sun &
Tues, 2pm)

Located on the north shore of Oahu, Waimea Arboretum and Botanical Garden consists of 35 major botanical collections situated in a narrow
valley extending from sea level to 1,000 feet. The focus of the collections
is the flora of threatened tropical island ecosystems including Hawaii,
Guam, the Ogasawara Islands, and the Mascarenes. Together, the gardens
feature over 5,000 taxa of tropical plants, all of them carefully documented and tracked. Since 2003, the National Audubon Society under an
agreement with the City and County of Honolulu has managed, operated, and safeguarded the cultural, botanical, and ecological resources of
Waimea Valley.

HONOLULU

THE CONTEMPORARY MUSEUM AND GARDEN (TCM)

2411 Makiki Heights Drive, Honolulu, HI 96822
Tel: (808) 526-0232; Fax: (808) 536-5973; TDDY: (808) 643-8833
Internet Address: http://www.tcmhi.org
Admission: Fee: adult $5.00, child free, student $3.00, senior $3.00;
Free: Third Thursday in month
Attendance: 40,000
Established: 1961
Membership: Y
Wheelchair Accessible: Y
Parking: Limited free parking on site
Open: Tuesday to Saturday, 10am-4pm; Sunday, noon-4pm; Closed:
Legal holidays
Facilities: Architecture Original Facility (Cooke-Spalding House, 1920
design by Hart Wood), Renovation (adapted to museum use by CJS
Group Architects); Food Services Café (Tues-Sat, 11am-3pm; Sun,
noon-3pm); Galleries (6); Grounds (3.5 acres, gardens designed by
Rev. K.H. Inagaki & restored by J.C. Hubbard); Sculpture Garden;
Shop (books, jewelry, small sculptural objects, crafts)
Activities: Gallery Talks; Guided Tours (Tues-Sun, 1:30pm);
Permanent Exhibits; Temporary Exhibitions; Traveling Exhibitions

The Contemporary Museum, located on a 3.5-acre site in Honolulu's scenic Makiki Heights, is a cultural oasis combining exhibitions of contemporary art with the natural beauty of Hawaii. The Museum's gardens were originally created between 1928 and 1941 by Reverend K. H. Inagaki, a Honolulu minister with a special interest in landscape design. Transforming the hillside into sloping lawns and a secluded garden ravine that was named Nu'umealani, or Heavenly Terraces, Reverend Inagaki's intention was to create a retreat in which to meditate and experience the harmony of nature. In 1979-80 the gardens were revamped and restored under the supervision of Honolulu landscape architect James C. Hubbard. With the subsequent addition of selected pieces of sculpture from the permanent collection, the garden provides both a natural setting for works of art and a quiet place for contemplation and renewal.

HONOLULU BOTANICAL GARDENS— FOSTER BOTANICAL GARDEN

50 N. Vineyard Blvd., Honolulu, HI 96817
Tel: (808) 522-7066
Internet Address: http://www.co.honolulu.hi.us/parks/hbg/fbg.htm
Admission: Fee: adult $5.00, child (<6) free, child (6-12) $1.00;
Hawaii residents $3.00
Attendance: 75,000
Established: 1931
Open: Daily, 9am-4pm; Closed: New Year's Day, Christmas Day
Facilities: Grounds (20 acres)
Activities: Guided Tours (Mon-Fri, 1pm; reservations recommended);
Plant Sales (annual)

The oldest of the five Honolulu Botanical Gardens, Foster Botanical Garden displays a mature and impressive collection of tropical plants, including some that were planted in the 1850s by Dr. William Hillebrand. Highlights include the Lyon Orchid Collection, a collection of Old and New World orchid species; a hybrid orchid display; an economic garden; the Prehistoric Glen, a collection of primitive plants from around the world; and a palm collection.

HONOLULU BOTANICAL GARDENS—LILI'UOKALANI BOTANICAL GARDEN

114 N. Kuakini St. (near School St.), Honolulu, HI 96817
Tel: (808) 522-7060

Internet Address: http://www.co.honolulu.hi.us/parks/hbg/#liliuokalani
Admission: Free
Parking: Free on site
Open: Daily, 9am-4pm; Closed: New Year's Day, Christmas Day
Facilities: Grounds (7½ acres); Picnic Area; Special Collections (native plants)

Once the property and favorite picnic grounds of Queen Liliuokalani, the last reigning monarch of Hawaii. the site was bequeathed to the City and County of Honolulu to be used for the public's enjoyment. The Garden features native Hawaiian plants in a naturalistic setting that includes a stream and waterfall. Located near Foster Botanical Garden, the Garden is one of five gardens making up the Honolulu Botanical Gardens.

NATIONAL MEMORIAL CEMETERY OF THE PACIFIC—GARDENS

Punchbowl Crater, 2177 Puowaina Drive, Honolulu, HI 96813
Tel: (808) 566-1430; Fax: (808) 532-3756
Internet Address: http://www.cem.va.gov/nchp/nmcp.htm
Admission: Free
Attendance: 5,000,000
Parking: Limited on site.
Open: March to September, Daily, 8am-6:30pm; October to February, Daily, 8am-5:30pm
Facilities: Gardens (rock); Grounds Cemetery (111½ acres), Gardens (7 acres); Special Collections (endangered Hawaiian native plants)
Activities: Guided Tours Cemetery (led by American Legion volunteers, (808) 946-6383)

Located in Punchbowl Crater, the Memorial Parks is the final resting place for more than 38,000 casualties of World War II, the Korean Conflict, and Vietnam. Constructed in 1990, the Gardens feature native Hawaiian endangered species.

UNIVERSITY OF HAWAII AT MANOA—HAROLD L. LYON ARBORETUM (AHSRAP)

3860 Manoa Road, Honolulu, HI 96822-1180
Tel: (808) 988-0456; Tel: (808) 988-0462
Internet Address: http://www.lyonarboretum.com
Admission: Fee: adult $7.00, child (<13) $3, student $5.00, senior $4.00

Attendance: 28,000
Established: 1918
Membership: Y
Wheelchair Accessible: Y
Open: Monday to Saturday, 9am-4pm; Closed: Public Holidays
Facilities: Arboretum; Garden, Greenhouses; Grounds (194 acres);
Herbarium; Library; Shop
Activities: Education Programs (adults, undergraduate/graduate
students and children); Guided Tours (1st Fri & 3rd Wed of month,
1pm; 3rd Sat of month, 10am; reservations required); Lectures; Self-
Guided Tours (map available at the Reception Center); Temporary
Exhibitions

Lyon Arboretum was established in 1918 by the Hawaiian Sugar
Planters Association to demonstrate the value of watershed restoration,
test tree species for reforestation, and collect plants of economic value. In
1953, it became part of the University of Hawaii and its emphasis shifted
from forestry to horticulture with nearly 2,000 ornamental and economically useful plants having been introduced to the grounds in the last 30
years. An active research facility and academic resource, as well as a public tropical garden, its extensive tropical plant collection emphasizes native Hawaiian species, tropical palms, aroids, ti, taro, heliconia and ginger. Plantings include an Hawaiian native garden, the Beatrice H. Krauss
Hawaiian Ethnobotanical Garden, and an herb garden.

KANEOHE

HONOLULU BOTANICAL GARDENS—HO'OMALUHIA BOTANIC GARDEN

45-680 Luluku Road, Kaneohe, HI 96744
Tel: (808) 233-7323
Internet Address: http://www.co.honolulu.hi.us/parks/hbg/hmbg.htm
Admission: Free
Attendance: 83,368
Established: 1982
Open: Daily, 9am-4pm; Closed: New Year's Day, Christmas Day
Facilities: Camping Sites (permit required); Grounds (400 acres);
Picnic Area; Special Collections (aroid, heliconia, tropical tree)
Activities: Guided Tours (Sat, 10am; Sun, 1pm; reserve in advance)

Ho'omaluhia features geographical groupings of plantings from the
major tropical regions around the world with a special emphasis on native

Hawaiian plants. The garden also includes ethnobotanical exhibits. The Garden is one of five Honolulu Botanical Gardens.

SENATOR FONG'S PLANTATION AND GARDENS

47-285 Pulama Road, Kaneohe, HI 96744-5026
Tel: (808) 239-6755; Fax: (808) 239-6469
Internet Address: http://www.fonggarden.com
Admission: Fee: adult $10.00, child $6.00, senior $8.00; Group discounts
Attendance: 100,000
Parking: Parking available
Open: Daily, 10am-4pm; Closed: New Year's Day, Christmas Day
Facilities: Food Services; Grounds (725 acres); Shop; Visitor Center
Activities: Tram Tours

The site includes tropical forests, flower gardens and fields, producing 100 varieties of fruits and nuts.

KOKO CRATER

HONOLULU BOTANICAL GARDENS—KOKO CRATER BOTANIC GARDEN

Inside of Koko Crater (east end of Oahu), Koko Crater, HI 96700
Tel: (808) 522-7066
Internet Address: http://www.co.honolulu.hi.us/parks/hbg/kcbg.htm
Admission: Free
Attendance: 8,000
Established: 1958
Open: Daily, 9am-4pm; Closed: New Year's Day, Christmas Day
Facilities: Gardens; Grounds (60 acres); Trail (2 miles)
Activities: Guided Tours Group (by appointment, 522-7060); Self-Guided Tour

One of five Honolulu Botanical Gardens, Koko Crater Botanical Garden is located inside of the crater. A hot, dry site, its collections feature drought-tolerant plants that are adaptable to this environment and to water conservation techniques. The collections include African plants, cacti, alluaudias, aloes, baobabs, euphorbias, sansevierias, adeniums, native erythrinas (wiliwili), dryland palms and bougainvillea. The four major collections arranged by geographical areas are the Americas,

Hawaii, Madagascar, and Africa. Long-range plans for Koko Crater Botanical Garden focus on the continued cultivation of rare and endangered dryland plants. The Dean Conklin Plumeria Grove, a collection of hundreds of plumeria cultivars, lines the road into the main crater. The Grove is owned and managed by the City and County of Honolulu, Parks and Recreation Department. Koko Crater Botanical Garden is under development; comfort stations and other visitor accommodations are not available.

WAHIAWA

HONOLULU BOTANICAL GARDENS—WAHIAWA GARDEN

1396 California Ave., Wahiawa, HI 96786
Tel: (808) 621-7321
Internet Address: http://www.co.honolulu.hi.us/parks/hbg/wbg.htm
Admission: Free
Attendance: 5,000
Established: 1950
Open: Daily, 9am-4pm; Closed: New Year's Day, Christmas Day
Facilities: Grounds (27 acres)
Activities: Guided Tours (arrange in advance, 621-7321); Plant Sale (annual)

Developed on a high plateau in central Oahu as an experimental arboretum by sugar planters in the 1920s, this tropical rain forest garden provides a cooler, moister environment than the other four Honolulu Botanical Gardens. Collections include native Hawaiian plants, palms, aroids, tree ferns, heliconias, calatheas, and epiphytic plants.

IDAHO

The number in parentheses following the city name indicates the number of gardens/arboreta in that municipality. If there is no number, one is understood. For example, in the text two listings would be found under Moscow and one under Boise.

BOISE

IDAHO BOTANICAL GARDENS

2355 Old Penitentiary Road, Boise, ID 83712-8252
Tel: (208) 343-8649; Fax: (208) 343-3601
Internet Address: http://www.idahobotanicalgarden.org
Admission: Fee (April to October): adult $4.00, child (<6) free, child
(6-12) $3.00, senior $3.00; Fee (November to March): adult $3.00,
child (<6) free, child (6-12) $2.00, senior $2.00
Established: 1983
Membership: Y
Wheelchair Accessible: P
Parking: Parking available in close proximity to gardens
Open: April, Monday to Friday, 9am-5pm; Saturday to Sunday, 10am-
6pm; May to September, Monday to Thursday, 9am-5pm; Friday, 9am-
8pm; Saturday to Sunday, 10am-6pm; October, Monday to Friday,
9am-5pm; Saturday to Sunday, 10am-6pm; November, Monday to
Friday, 9am-5pm; Saturday to Sunday, noon-4pm; December to
January, Monday to Friday, 9am-5pm; February to March, Monday to
Friday, 9am-5pm; Saturday to Sunday, noon-4pm
Best Time(s) of Year to Visit: May to October (Cactus Garden, Peony
Garden)
Facilities: Gardens (13; alpine, butterfly/hummingbird, cactus,
children's, contemporary English, herb, iris, meditation, native plant,
peony, rose, water); Grounds (50 acres)
Activities: Concerts (Summer, Thurs evenings); Education Programs;
Festival Winter Garden Aglow (December, daily, 6pm-9pm, holiday
lights); Plant Sale (spring)

The garden occupies land that originally served as the farm and nursery
for the Idaho State Penitentiary, the Old Penitentiary, now a museum, shut
its doors in 1973. Among the twelve theme gardens are a contemporary
English garden, designed by landscape architect John Brooks; an iris garden,
focusing on Dykes Medal Iris varieties; a rose garden, featuring heirloom
and other old-style roses in a perennial setting; and a peony garden, con-

taining 21 varieties of hybrid peony. Ground breaking for the first phase of a new Lewis and Clark Native Plant Garden is scheduled for April 2004. The garden will feature plants described by Lewis and Clark that were found on their expedition, and will include rest and interpretive areas.

KETCHUM

SAWTOOTH BOTANICAL GARDEN

3 Gimlet Road (at intersection with Route 75), Ketchum, ID 83353
Tel: (208) 726-9358; Fax: (208) 726-5435
Internet Address: http://www.sbgarden.org
Admission: Free
Attendance: 6,800
Established: 1997
Membership: Y
Wheelchair Accessible: P
Parking: Parking on site
Open: 9am-dark
Best Time(s) of Year to Visit: June to September
Facilities: Gardens (native and drought-tolerant plants); Greenhouse (1,550 square feet); Grounds (5 acres)
Activities: Education Programs; Guided Tours

Formerly known as the Sawtooth Community Garden, the site features native flora of the Wood River valley in both natural and ornamental settings. Additionally, there is a greenhouse displaying a variety of flowering perennials, herbs, and vines.

MOSCOW

UNIVERSITY OF IDAHO ABORETUM AND BOTANICAL GARDEN

South of President's Residence, Nez Perce Dr., North of Pelouse River Drive West, Moscow, ID 83844
Tel: (208) 885-5978; Fax: (208) 885-5748
Internet Address: http://www.uidaho.edu/arboretum/
Admission: Free
Established: 1982
Membership: Y
Wheelchair Accessible: P
Parking: Free parking
Open: daylight hours

Best Time(s) of Year to Visit: late Spring to Fall
Facilities: Arboreta (55 acres); Gardens (10 acres)

With plantings begun in 1982 and still under development, the University of Idaho Arboretum and Botanical Garden site extends southward from the President's residence on Nez Perce Drive to Palouse River Drive West along the east and south sides of the UI Golf Course. Plants are displayed in geographical blocks by plant origin with the southernmost area designated for display gardens. Currently under development are numerous designated groves and plantings, including the Centennial Oak Grove, Asian and European lilacs, Western North American conifers, planting of aspens, red and sugar maples, Ginkgo and Asian derived crab apples. At present, space devoted among sections includes: Asian section, 11 acres; European section, 4.5 acres; eastern North American section, 10 acres; western North American section, 26 acres; and display gardens, 10 acres. A parking area at the southern end is accessible from Palouse River Drive West.

UNIVERSITY OF IDAHO—CHARLES HUSTON SHATTUCK ARBORETUM

Central Campus, Arboretum Hill, Moscow, ID 83843-4193
Tel: (208) 885-6250
Internet Address: http://www.uidaho.edu?Uicommunications
Admission: Free
Facilities: Arboretum (14 acres)

With planting begun on Arboretum Hill in 1910, the Charles Houston Shattuck Arboretum contains one of western North America's oldest university woody plant collections, including some of the finest old specimen trees in the Northern Rocky Mountain area (i.e., giant sequoia, California incense cedar, American beech, Canadian hemlock, and Scotch maple).

POCATELLO

IDAHO STATE UNIVERSITY—IDAHO STATE ARBORETUM TREE WALK

Idaho Museum of Natural History, 5th Ave. and E. Dillon St., Pocatello, ID 83209-8096
Tel: (208) 236-3317; Fax: (208) 282-5893
Internet Address: http://imnh.isu.edu or http://www.isu.edu/departments/isutour/tree-wal

Admission: No charge/donations accepted (arboretum); Fee (Museum)
Attendance: 250
Established: 1991
Wheelchair Accessible: Y
Parking: Designated museum parking spaces, request free pass
Open: Tree Walk, Daily, 24 hours; Museum, Monday, 4pm-8pm;
Tuesday to Friday, 10am-5pm; Saturday, noon-5pm; Closed: Museum:
legal holidays
Best Time(s) of Year to Visit: Spring, Fall
Facilities: Arboretum; Grounds (6 acres)
Activities: Self-Guided Tour (brochure & audio recording available at
museum)

Located on the campus of Idaho State University, the fifty trees that
make up the Tree Walk are part of a 6-acre green courtyard featuring native and non-native trees, shrubs, and plants adjacent to the Idaho Museum of Natural History. The Arboretum is a unit of the Idaho Museum
of Natural History.

REXBURG

BRIGHAM YOUNG UNIVERSITY-IDAHO—THOMAS RICKS DEMONSTRATION GARDEN

500 S. Center St., Rexburg, ID 83460
Tel: (208) 496-2018
Internet Address: http://www.byui.edu/horticulture/
demonstration_gardens.htm
Admission: Free
Established: 1977
Facilities: Gardens (perennial, rose, shade, sunken bowl , trial,
vegetable, water, wedding, woodland pond); Greenhouses (6);
Grounds (10 acres); Picnic Area
Activities: Plant Sales (weekly)

Located on the south side of the college campus off the Taylor/Ben-
son parking lot, the garden includes three water features, a picnic
structure, reception area, test gardens, fruit tree orchard, a rose garden
offering over 50 varieties of roses, a shade garden, other flower beds,
and a native plant garden. The trial gardens, containing over 250 varieties of annuals and 100 varieties of perennials, include an All-
American Selections garden. The entire garden has been designed,
constructed, and is maintained by the faculty, staff and students of the
Horticulture Department.

IOWA

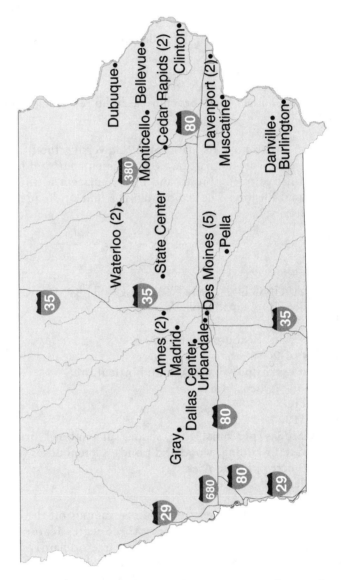

The number in parentheses following the city name indicates the number of gardens/arboreta in that municipality. If there is no number, one is understood. For example, in the text five listings would be found under Des Moines and one under Pella

AMES

IOWA STATE UNIVERSITY—DEPARTMENT OF HORTICULTURE GREENHOUSES

Horticulture Building (off Osborne Drive), Ames, IA 50011
Tel: (515) 294-2751; Fax: (515) 294-0730
Internet Address: http://www.hort.iastate.edu/facilities/index.php
Admission: Free
Established: 1915
Parking: Memorial Union Parking Ramp
Open: Monday to Thursday, 8am-4:30pm; Friday, 8am-1pm;
Closed: Major holidays
Best Time(s) of Year to Visit: October to November, January to May
Facilities: Conservatory (tropical, subtropical); Greenhouses (26,700 square feet)
Activities: Guided Tours (groups 10+, schedule in advance)

The greenhouses are attached to the Horticulture Building and support activities related to specific courses, research projects, extension demonstrations, and departmental functions. A conservatory, consisting of two houses with benches, contains about 380 species of tropical and subtropical plants organized and labeled in family groups. Between these two houses is a conservatory where plants are grown in a natural setting with ponds and waterfalls.

REIMAN GARDENS—IOWA STATE UNIVERSITY

1407 Elwood Drive (just south of ISU Jack Trice Stadium),
Ames, IA 50011
Tel: (515) 294-2710; Fax: (515) 294-4817
Internet Address: http://www.reimangardens.iastate.edu
Admission: Fee: adult $7.00, child (<3) free, child (4-17) $4.00, student-free, senior $6.00

Attendance: 150,000
Established: 1995
Membership: Y
Wheelchair Accessible: Y
Parking: Free on site
Open: April to October, Tuesday to Sunday, 9am-4:30pm
Facilities: Butterfly House; Conservatory (5,000 square feet); Gardens 14 acres (annual, children's, dwarf conifer, fragrance, hardwood forest, herb, peony, rose, trial, vegetable, wetland); Greenhouses; Grounds (14 acres); Learning Center (Mon-Fri, 8am-5pm); Library
Activities: Education Programs; Guided Tours (by appointment); Lecture Series; Plant Sales

Reiman Gardens celebrate the natural and botanical diversity of Iowa, as well as the gardening and horticultural traditions of ISU. Plantings include over 25,000 annuals, 300 trees, and over 100 different herbaceous perennials. The rose garden, accredited by All-America Rose Selections as a test garden, contains modern garden roses (hybrid teas, floribundas, and grandifloras), antique roses, and an assortment of Griffith Buck roses.

BELLEVUE

BELLEVUE STATE PARK—BELLEVUE BUTTERFLY GARDEN

24668 Highway 52, Bellevue, IA 52031
Tel: (563) 872-4019; Fax: (563) 872-4773
Internet Address: http://www.state.ia.us/parks/bttrfly.htm
Admission: Free
Established: 1985
Membership: N
Wheelchair Accessible: P
Parking: Gravel parking lot 1/2 mile from garden
Open: Daily, 4am-10:30pm
Best Time(s) of Year to Visit: August to early September
Facilities: Garden (butterfly); Grounds Bellevue State Park (780 acres), Butterfly Garden (1 acre); Trails (2 miles); Visitor Center South Bluff Nature Center
Activities: Education Programs

Located just south of the picturesque town of Bellevue in two separate tracts, the park offers spectacular views of the river, the wildlife, and a butterfly garden. The Butterfly Garden is designed specifically to attract butterflies by providing nectar plants for adults and host plants for caterpillars.

Some 60 species of butterflies are expected each year. Surrounding the garden are cottonwoods, wild cherry, hackberry and willows, which also serve as host plants for the butterflies. Adjacent to the garden is a three-acre prairie site and wildlife food plots.

BURLINGTON

CITY OF BURLINGTON—CRAPO PARK ARBORETUM

Great River Road, 2900 South Main, Burlington, IA 52601
Tel: (319) 753-8140; Fax: (319) 753-8101
Admission: Free
Established: 1895
Wheelchair Accessible: P
Parking: Ample on-street parking
Open: Daily, 5am-11pm
Facilities: Arboretum; Band Shell; Electric Fountain; Grounds Park (85 acres, 1895 by the landscape engineering firm of Earnshaw and Punshon of Cincinnati, Ohio); Log Cabin Museum; Shakespeare Garden

Containing over 200 species of trees, Crapo Park also offers numerous plantings of perennial and annual flowers. A comprehensive listing of trees in the arboretum is available in front of the Schnedier House in the Park. The park was designed by the firm of Earnshaw and Punshon of Cincinnati.

CEDAR RAPIDS

BRUCEMORE—GARDENS

2160 Linden Drive, S.E., Cedar Rapids, IA 52403
Tel: (319) 362-7375; Fax: (319) 362-9481
Internet Address: http://www.brucemore.org
Admission: Fee (Mansion Tour): adult $7.00, student $3.00; Free (Grounds)
Attendance: 40,000
Established: 1981
Membership: Y
Wheelchair Accessible: Y
Parking: On site, near Visitor Center & Mansion
Open: Grounds, Monday to Saturday, 9am-4pm; Sunday, noon-4pm
Facilities: Architecture (Queen Ann-style residence, 1884-86); Gardens (cutting, formal); Greenhouse (Lord & Burnham, ca. 1915); Grounds (26 acres)

Activities: Guided Tours mansion (Tues-Sat, 10am-3pm; Sun, noon-3pm; on the hour)

Brucemore, a National Trust Historic Site since 1981, is a Queen Anne-style mansion situated in a park-like setting in the heart of Cedar Rapids, Iowa. Today, Brucemore consists of 26 acres and 8 buildings, including the mansion, greenhouse, carriage house, Garden House, Bookbindery-Squash Court, duplex, pool house, and chicken coop. Brucemore's natural space consists of more than the gardens. Between 1906 and 1927, the landscape architect O. C. Simonds, a founder of the Prairie School of landscape design, played an active role in the development of the grounds. Among Simonds' recommendations were the use of local plantings, water features, and the construction of outdoor "rooms" within a landscape. These "rooms" were three-dimensional spaces made up of the lawn as a base plane, shrubs as a vertical, and sky and tree canopy as the overhead plane. The formal garden, best described as a large-scale cottage garden, features geometric beds and borders planted in a naturalistic style. Cutting gardens, located behind the carriage house, are the source of cut flower materials for in-house use. The greenhouse grows over 125 varieties of annual and perennial plants every spring to fill the gardens and containers throughout the estate.

CITY OF CEDAR RAPIDS—NOELRIDGE PARK GARDENS

4900 Council St. NE, Cedar Rapids, IA 52403
Tel: (319) 286-5760; Fax: (319) 398-5045
Admission: Free
Established: 1975
Open: April to October, 6am-10pm (Park); 7am-3:30pm (Greenhouse)
Best Time(s) of Year to Visit: July to October
Facilities: Gardens (7 acres—annuals, herbs, perennials—1,400 varieties); Greenhouses

A large multipurpose park, Noelridge includes an All-American Selections display garden, other test gardens, and greenhouses.

CLINTON

BICKELHAUPT ARBORETUM

340 South 14th St. (off Bluff Blvd.), Clinton, IA 52732-5432
Tel: (319) 242-4771; Fax: (319) 242-4771

Internet Address: http://www.bickarb.org/
Admission: Free
Attendance: 15,000
Established: 1970
Wheelchair Accessible: Y
Parking: Parking available—handicapped and regular
Open: Daily, dawn-dusk
Best Time(s) of Year to Visit: April (daffodils), April to May (flowering trees), October (fall foliage)
Facilities: Arboretum; Gardens (herb, medicinal plant, shade, shrub rose); Grounds (14 acres); Library (lending); Special Collections (arborvitae, dwarf & rare conifers, day lily, flowering trees, hosta, lilac, native plants/grasses, perennial, viburnum); Visitor Center
Activities: Education Programs; Guided Tours (groups, reserve in advance)

The Arboretum was a gift to the public by Robert and Frances Bickel-haupt. The area surrounding their home has been turned into an outdoor museum of select, labeled trees, shrubs, ground covers, perennials, and annual flowers. Highlights include the Heartland Collection of Garden Conifers and a pinetum (600 plants); an extensive collection of flowering trees, including crab apples (23 kinds), magnolias (10 kinds), redbud, and silverbell; over 300 different varieties of ornamental shrubs (including a lilac collection of more than 40 varieties); prairie restoration and gardens featuring native plants and grasses; a shade garden containing over 200 hosta cultivars, a medicinal and culinary herb garden, as well as other shade-loving plants; a day lily collection, featuring all the Stout Medal winners; and a shrub rose collection, focusing on plants that do not need spraying, winter protection, and other special care.

DALLAS CENTER

THE BRENTON ARBORETUM (AHS RAP)

2629 Palo Circle, Dallas Center, IA 50063
Tel: (515) 992-4211; Fax: (515) 992-3303
Internet Address: http://www.thebrentonarboretum.com/
Admission: No charge/donations accepted
Established: 1996
Membership: N
Parking: Four parking lots
Open: February to December, Wednesday to Sunday, 10 am-8pm or sunset

Facilities: Arboretum; Grounds (121 acres); Trails 5
Activities: Education Programs (for adults and children); Guided Tours

Located approximately twenty miles west of Des Moines, the arboretum consists of relatively young plantings set in large groupings of singular species on scenic, rolling prairie land with a pond, streams, and wetlands. It features over 1,800 woody plants, including almost all Iowa native trees and shrubs, a select number of exotic trees, as well as wildflowers and native grasses. Each tree is tagged with its common name, scientific name, and the date of planting. An informational brochure, giving basic arboretum facts, a foldout map indicating driving routes, and walking trails is available.

DANVILLE

THE SECRET GARDEN

10182 Danville Road (County Road X31), Danville, IA 52623
Tel: (319) 392-8288
Internet Address: http://www.the-secret-garden.net
Admission: Free
Membership: N
Wheelchair Accessible: P
Parking: Free on site
Open: April to December, Daily, 8am-8pm
Best Time(s) of Year to Visit: April to October
Facilities: Architecture (1846, peg and post barn); Gardens (theme gardens, including cutting gardens & herb garden); Grounds (6 acres); Shop (dried flowers)
Activities: Guided Tours (by appointment, fee)

A mid-19th-century farm, the Secret Garden features native flowers and natural grasses, theme gardens, and field-grown perennials.

DAVENPORT

CITY OF DAVENPORT—STAMPE LILAC GARDEN (DUCK CREEK LILAC GARDEN)

Duck Creek Park, 3300 E. Locust St., Davenport, IA 52803
Tel: (563) 326-7812; Fax: (563) 326-7815
Admission: Free
Membership: N

Wheelchair Accessible: Y
Parking: On site with handicapped access
Open: Daily, sunrise-sunset
Best Time(s) of Year to Visit: April to May
Facilities: Gardens (lilac); Grounds Garden (½ acre)
Activities: Plant Sales (Mother's Day Plant Sale)

With over 250 lilac bushes representing over 50 varieties, the Garden boasts the Quad Cities' largest collection of lilacs, plus many other perennials and annuals. Beginning in early April, flower enthusiasts can see narcissi, daffodils, crocus, and young blooming lilacs. In mid-April, hyacinths, tulips and crab apples will begin to bloom. The garden is maintained by the Davenport Horticultural Society (contact 326-7812).

VANDER VEER BOTANICAL PARK (AHS RAP)

215 W. Central Park Ave. (between Brady and Harrison Sts.),
Davenport, IA 52803
Tel: (563) 326-7818; Fax: (563) 326-7955
Internet Address: http://www.cityofdavenportiowa.com/leisure/parks/
botanical.htm
Admission: Free (Park); Fee (Conservatory): adult $1.00, child (<17) free; Free (Conservatory): Tuesday.
Attendance: 25,000
Established: 1888
Membership: Y
Wheelchair Accessible: Y
Parking: Two vehicle entrances off W. Central Park Avenue
Open: Grounds, Daily, sunrise-½ hour after sunset; Conservatory, Tuesday to Sunday, 10am-4pm.
Facilities: Conservatory; Gardens (children's, flower, hosta, rose, sculpture, vegetable); Grounds park (33 acres with lagoon, Grand Allée, Stone Fountain, historical structures; original design by Olaf Benson); Shop (garden-related gifts)
Activities: Education Programs; Flower Shows Azalea (mid-January-Valentines Day, Chrysanthemum (October-Thanksgiving), Easter Lily (mid-February-April), Holiday Show (post-Thanksgiving-mid-January), Hydrangea & Fuschia (May), Tropicals, Outdoor, Rose (June-September); Guided Tours (groups, reserve in advance, (563) 323-3298); Plant Sales (May)

Vander Veer Botanical Park features a conservatory surrounded by an All-America Rose Selections display garden containing 1,800 roses representing approximately 145 varieties; an All-American Selections flower and vegetable display garden; the Hosta Glade; and other specialty gardens. The Conservatory has a permanent collection of over 15,000 plants and is famous for its year-round displays of ornamental plants, a tradition since the construction of the original conservatory in 1897.

DES MOINES

BETTER HOMES & GARDENS—TEST GARDENS

1716 Locust St. (between Grand & Locust Sts.), Des Moines, IA 50309-3023
Tel: (515) 284-3994
Internet Address: http://www.bhg.com
Admission: Free
Established: 1998
Open: May to Oct, Friday, noon-2pm
Facilities: Gardens (clay, dwarf conifer, ornamental grass, herb, perennial border, rock, rose, shade, sun, vegetable, wildflower meadow); Grounds (½ acre)
Activities: Guided Tours (groups 8+, by appointment)

Located on half a city block outside the headquarters of the Meredith Corporation (publisher of *Better Homes & Gardens*), the Test Garden consists of 22 formal and informal garden rooms and beds, containing 2,500 trees, shrubs and perennial plants, 17,000 bulbs, hundreds of annuals, paths, ponds, and garden structures. A rose garden features a collection of hardy landscape roses that need no spraying. Because the Test Garden serves as the magazine's photographic studio, many of its elements are transitory, created to illustrate a particular assignment and removed after photographing.

CITY OF DES MOINES—LILAC ARBORETUM

Ewing Park, 1900 McKinley Ave. (at Indianola), Des Moines, IA 50316
Tel: (515) 237-1386; Fax: (515) 237-1407
Internet Address: http://www.ci.des-moines.ia.us/departments/PR/home%20page.htm
Admission: Free
Established: 1943
Parking: Free on site
Open: Daily, 6am-sunset
Best Time(s) of Year to Visit: mid-April to mid-May
Facilities: Arboretum

The Lilac Arboretum contains over 1,400 plants representing 120 varieties.

DES MOINES BOTANICAL CENTER (AHS RAP)

Robert D. Ray Drive, Des Moines, IA 50316-2854
Tel: (515) 961-2323
Internet Address: http://www.botanicalcenter.com/
Admission: Fee: adult $4.00, child $2.00, student $2.00, senior $2.00
Attendance: 250,000
Established: 1979
Membership: Y
Wheelchair Accessible: Y
Parking: 180 parking spaces
Open: 10am-6pm; Closed: New Year's Day, Thanksgiving Day, Christmas Day
Facilities: Botanic Gardens; Exhibition Area; Food Services Garden Café; Gardens (perennial); Grounds (14.4 acres); Library (500 volumes, non-circulating); Reading Room; Shop; Special Collections (bonsai, cactus/succulent, orchid)
Activities: Education Programs (adults and children); Flower Shows (11/year); Guided Tours (groups, Mon-Fri, 10am-4pm, reserve at least 7 days in advance); Lectures; Temporary Exhibitions; Workshops

Operated by the Des Moines Water Works, the Des Moines Botanical Center contains one of the largest collections of ornamental and native plants in the Midwest. More than 1,000 species and varieties of tropical, sub-tropical, and xerophytic plants, as well as seasonal flower shows are on display beneath its plexiglass dome (150 feet in diameter and 80 feet in height). The Hirsch/Ladany Bonsai collection is held to be one of the best bonsai collections in the United States. Outside gardens feature herbaceous perennials.

DES MOINES WATER WORKS—ARIE DEN BOER ARBORETUM

Water Works Park, 408 Fleur Drive, Des Moines, IA 50321
Tel: (515) 283-8791
Internet Address: http://www.dmww.com
Admission: Free
Attendance: 10,000
Wheelchair Accessible: P
Open: Daily, 6am-10pm

Best Time(s) of Year to Visit: last week of April to 1st week of May
(crab apples)
Facilities: Grounds Water Works Park (1,500 acres)

The Des Moines Water Works operates Water Works Park, about 1500
acres of land near downtown Des Moines. The Arboretum contains an
extensive collection of flowering crab apples (approximately 300 varieties) gathered by the late Arie den Boer, a renowned horticulturist.

TERRACE HILL HISTORIC SITE- GARDEN

2300 Grand Ave., Des Moines, IA 50312
Tel: (515) 281-3604; Fax: (515) 281-7267
Internet Address: http://www.terracehill.org/
Admission: Fee: adult $5.00, child $2.00
Attendance: 18,000
Established: 1971
Membership: Y
Wheelchair Accessible: Y
Parking: On street
Open: March to December, Tuesday to Saturday, 10am-1:30pm
Closed: Legal holidays
Best Time(s) of Year to Visit: Spring to Summer
Facilities: Architecture (Second Empire residence, 1869 design by
architect William Boyington of Chicago); Garden (Victorian); Grounds
(8 acres)
Activities: Guided Tours (Mar-Dec, Tues-Sat, 10am-1:30pm; groups
10+, reserve in advance)

Terrace Hill was built by Iowa's first millionaire, Benjamin F. Allen.
Since 1971, Terrace Hill has been the official residence of the Governor
of Iowa. The grounds feature a recreated Victorian formal garden.

DUBUQUE

DUBUQUE ARBORETUM AND BOTANICAL GARDEN

3800 Arboretum Drive (Marshall Park at
32nd St.), Dubuque, IA 52001-1030
Tel: (563) 556-2100; Fax: (563) 556-2443 Dubuque Arboretum and
Internet Address: Botanical Garden, Dubuque, IA.
http://www.dbq.com/arboretum/

Admission: Free
Attendance: 65,000
Established: 1980
Membership: Y
Wheelchair Accessible: P
Parking: On site, 2 hard-surface lots
Open: Arbor Day to October, Daily, 8am-sunset; November to April, Monday to Friday, 9am-5pm; Saturday, 9am-1pm; Closed: New Year's Day, Thanksgiving Day, Christmas Day.
Best Time(s) of Year to Visit: May to October
Facilities: Arboretum; Gardens (herb, hosta, Japanese, knot, prairie, rose, shade, vegetable, water, woodland); Greenhouse; Grounds (52 acres); Home Gardening Learning Center; Library (9am-sunset); Shop (9am-sunset); Special Collections (dahlia, dwarf conifer, hosta, iris, lily); Visitors Center
Activities: Concerts Sunday Dinner Concerts; Education Programs

The Dubuque Arboretum boasts the largest public hosta garden in the country (13,000 plants representing 700 varieties), as well as a nationally recognized dwarf conifer collection (450 specimens), an All-American Selection display garden, and a seed-saver display garden. Its rose garden, containing over 800 roses, has received 12 consecutive All-America Rose Selections Committee awards. A Japanese garden and English formal garden are under construction. Dubuque is the only all-volunteer arboretum and botanical garden in the U.S., with over 375 participants.

GRAY

HERITAGE ROSE GARDEN

Main St (between 1st & 2nd), Gray, IA 50110
Tel: (712) 563-2742
Internet Address:
http://www.auduboncounty.com/tourism/attractions.htm
Admission: Donations accepted
Attendance: 1,000
Established: 1995
Membership: N
Wheelchair Accessible: Y
Parking: On street
Best Time(s) of Year to Visit: June to August
Facilities: Garden (children's, rose); Grounds (½ acre)
Activities: Guided Tours (reserve in advance)

Featuring over 225 old fashioned, Canadian Explorer, and Buck roses, this charming country garden includes arbors, arches, a fountain, benches, an angel standing watch over the children's garden, and as its focus point, the historic 15-foot-tall steeple and bell from the town's first church. The garden was developed and is maintained by volunteers.

MADRID

IOWA ARBORETUM (AHS RAP)

1875 Peach Ave., Madrid, IA 50156-7571
Tel: (515) 795-3216; Fax: (515) 795-2619
Internet Address: http://www.iowaarboretum.com
Admission: Fee: adult $2.00, child (<12) free
Attendance: 35,000
Membership: Y
Wheelchair Accessible: Y
Parking: Free paved lot on site
Open: Grounds, Daily, sunrise-sunset
Facilities: Gardens (butterfly, dwarf conifer, herb, hosta, perennial, shade); Greenhouse; Grounds Gardens & Horticulture Display (40 acres), Native Timber (350 acres), Restored Prairie (4 acres); Shop (books, garden tools, clothes, holiday decorations); Trails (3, ½ mile each)
Activities: Guided Tours (by appointment, $2/person)

Located in scenic, rural Boone County, the Iowa Arboretum offers the largest and most diverse display of plants that can be grown in Iowa. Forty acres have been developed as a "Library of Living Plants" showcasing hundreds of trees, shrubs and flowers in eighteen plant collections including hostas, perennials, dwarf conifers, ornamental grasses, herbs, nut trees, children's garden, butterfly garden, and Buck roses. Self-guided nature trails run through the 330-acre forest preserve featuring century-old oak trees, scenic overlooks, deep ravines, and streams. The arboretum is a non-profit, privately funded facility.

MONTICELLO

RIVERSIDE GARDENS

3rd St. & Route 151, Monticello, IA 52310
Tel: (319) 465-3898
Internet Address:
http://www.monticello.ia.us/RecTourism/default.html#Riverside

Admission: No charge/donations accepted
Established: 1988
Parking: 2 small lots on site and on street
Open: Garden, Daily, dawn-dusk; Visitor Center: Memorial Day to Labor Day, Daily, 11am-3pm.
Best Time(s) of Year to Visit: Memorial Day to Fall
Facilities: Gardens (38); Grounds; Picnic Area; Visitor Center
Activities: Education Programs; Events Garden Club Garden Walk & Tour (July, 2nd Sunday, fee); Teas

Located on the north side of Monticello at the site of the city's first stagecoach stop along the Old Military Trail, the grounds feature more than 30 flower beds. The gardens are a showcase for the diversity of flowers available for today's gardens, including a wide variety of annuals, perennials and hostas; a heritage garden with historic plants; wetland and restored prairie areas; and nature trails. The visitor/nature center offers information on horticulture, a display of the 1900-era city botanical gardens, early garden history and catalogues, and early Iowa farming information.

MUSCATINE

MUSCATINE ART CENTER

1314 Mulberry Ave., Muscatine, IA 52761
Tel: (563) 263-8282; Fax: (563) 263-4702
Internet Address: http://www.muscatineartcenter.org
Admission: Free
Attendance: 12,000
Established: 1965
Membership: Y
Wheelchair Accessible: Y
Parking: On street and Cedar St. parking lot
Open: Tuesday to Wednesday, 10am-5pm; Thursday, 10am-5pm and 7pm-9pm; Friday, 10am-5pm; Saturday to Sunday, 1pm-5pm; Closed: Legal holidays
Facilities: Architecture (Edwardian mansion, 1908); Auditorium; Classrooms; Gallery; Gardens (Japanese); Grounds (4 acres); Library (1,000 volumes, non-circulating)
Activities: Concerts; Education Programs (adults and children); Films; Gallery Talks; Guided Tours (groups, schedule in advance); Lectures; Permanent Exhibits; Temporary Exhibitions (change every 6-8 weeks)

The Art Center complex includes the Edwardian Musser Mansion and the Stanley Gallery, which presents changing exhibitions and provides space for studio art classes. The grounds of the Muscatine Art Center include a "Japanese Garden" with pagodas, small pools, waterfalls and native Iowa wildflowers. Originally installed in 1929, the garden underwent extensive renovation in 1990. In addition, an enclosed courtyard has been developed for outdoor sculpture.

PELLA

PELLA HISTORICAL VILLAGE AND SCHOLTE GARDENS

507 Franklin St., Pella, IA 50219
Tel: (515) 628-4311; Fax: (515) 628-9192
Internet Address: http://www.pellatuliptime.com/
Admission: Fee: adult $7.00, child (K-12) $1.00
Open: Museum: January to February, Thursday to Saturday, 11am-4pm; March to December, Monday to Friday, 9am-5pm; Saturday, 10am-3pm
Facilities: Architecture (21 historic buildings); Gardens
Activities: Education Programs; Flower Shows Fall Festival (September), Tulip Time (May/June); Guided Tours Garden Tour & Tea (June/July)

Celebrating its Dutch heritage, the museum complex consists of 21 buildings situated in a courtyard laced with red brick walkways and beautiful flower gardens, featuring over 28,000 tulips, as well as annuals, perennials and flowering shrubs. Nearby, the home of Pella's founder, Dominie Scholte is located along Pella's central square. Behind the house, Scholte Gardens contain over 40,000 tulips supplemented by annual flowers in the fall and summer months. There is also a sunken garden three blocks north of the square on Main Street.

STATE CENTER

IOWA ROSE SOCIETY GARDEN

300 3rd St., S.E. (Old U.S. Route 30), State Center, IA 50247
Tel: (641) 483-2559
Internet Address: http://www.midiowaenterprise.com
Admission: Free
Wheelchair Accessible: Y

Parking: Roadside
Open: May to November, Daily
Facilities: Garden (rose); Grounds (1 acre)
Activities: Events Rose Festival (3rd weekend in June)

The garden features over 4,000 roses representing both old and new rose varieties. Garden is lighted from 8pm to 11pm.

URBANDALE

LIVING HISTORY FARMS

2600 NW 111th St., Urbandale, IA 50322
Tel: (515) 278-2400; Fax: (515) 278-9808
Internet Address: http://www.lhf.org
Admission: Fee, 1-Day Pass: adult $10.00, child (4-12) $6.00, senior $9.00; 2-day Pass: adult-$15, child-$9, senior-$13.50
Attendance: 110,000
Established: 1916
Membership: Y
Wheelchair Accessible: Y
Open: May to 1st Sunday in October, Daily, 9am-5pm
Facilities: Exhibition Areas Farm (ca. 1850), Farm (ca. 1900), Henry A. Wallace Crop Center, Indian Village (ca. 1700), Town (ca. 1875); Gardens (Native American, heritage vegetable, nature trail, 100-year crop walk); Grounds (600 acres); Shop (recreated general store [1878])
Activities: Demonstrations; Education Programs

Living History Farms presents the history of Iowa agriculture and society spanning 300 years, from an Iowa Indian Village, through an oxen-powered 40-acre pioneer farm of 1850, a rural community of 1875, and a horse-powered 120-acre farm of 1900, to a multimedia exhibit on twentieth-century agriculture. On-site interpreters at each exhibition area perform seasonal activities and demonstrations.

WATERLOO

CEDAR VALLEY ARBORETUM AND BOTANIC GARDEN (CVABG) (AHS RAP)

Orange Road (east of Hawkeye Community College),
Waterloo, IA 50704

Tel: (319) 226-4966
Internet Address: http://www.cedarnet.org/gardens/
Admission: Suggested contribution $3.00
Attendance: 12,000
Established: 1997
Membership: Y
Wheelchair Accessible: P
Open: Monday to Saturday, 10am-5pm; 1pm-4pm
Best Time(s) of Year to Visit: June to September
Facilities: Gardens (children's, community, enabling, rose, herb, hosta, prairie); Grounds (75 acres)

Currently under development, Cedar Valley features botanic gardens, natural prairie, fountains, ponds, trails, and an arboretum. The Enabling Garden, designed by Gene Rothert, is now open.

UNIVERSITY OF NORTHERN IOWA— BOTANICAL CENTER

1227 West 27th Street, Waterloo, IA 50614-0421
Tel: (319) 273-2247; Fax: (319) 273-7223
Internet Address: http://www.bio.uni.edu/botanicalcenter/
Open: Monday to Friday, 7:30am-4pm
Facilities: Greenhouse
Activities: Education Programs

The UNI Biology Botanical Center greenhouse contains a teaching collection that includes a diversity of species that range from ancient tree ferns and cycads to a large number of economically important varieties from around the world. Exhibits include a tropical room containing approximately 250 plants from tropical ecosystems; a desert room containing arid climate plants including New and Old World succulents; and an aquatic Learning Center featuring a hydroponics display, a large stone waterfall, a spillway, a fast moving stream, a peat bog, and a variety of other aquatic environments; and a propagation room.

KANSAS

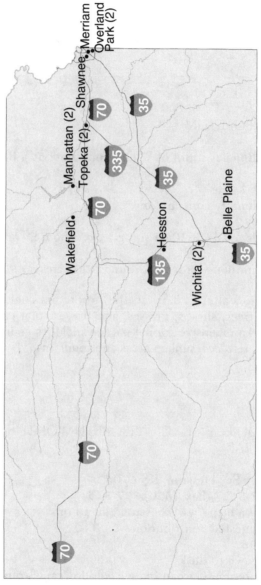

The number in parentheses following the city name indicates the number of gardens/arboreta in that municipality. If there is no number, one is understood. For example, in the text two listings would be found under Wichita and one listing under Hesston.

BELLE PLAINE

BARTLETT ARBORETUM

301 N. Line (20 miles south of Wichita on Route 55), Belle Plaine, KS
67013
Tel: (316) 488-3451
Admission: Voluntary contribution
Established: 1910
Open: Grounds, Daily, 8:30am-sunset; Greenhouse, Daily, 9:30am-
11am
Facilities: Arboretum; Gardens; Grounds (20 acres)

Begun by Dr. Walter E. Bartlett, the Arboretum contains native and
exotic mature trees, shrubs, grasses, and flowers that can tolerate the
local climate. An extensive formal garden includes courtyards, hedge-
bordered beds, terraces, sunken areas and fountains.

HESSTON

HESSTON COLLEGE—DYCK ARBORETUM OF THE
PLAINS (AHS RAP)

177 W. Hickory St., Hesston, KS 67062
Tel: (620) 327-8127; Fax: (620) 327-3151
Internet Address: http://www.hesston.edu/arbor/
Admission: Suggested contribution $2.00
Established: 1982
Open: Daily, dawn to dusk
Facilities: Arboretum; Garden (native wildflower); Grounds (13 acres)

The focus of the arboretum is on trees, shrubs, grasses, flowering perennials, and annuals native to Kansas. Some attention is also directed to horticultural plants that are adaptable to the south central Kansas environment. The Great Plains Wildflower Garden maintains five planting beds,

each dedicated to a different region of the Great Plains and containing only taxa native to that region. The Prairie Window, an 18-acre expansion of the Arboreta, is being planned. This project will focus on the presentation and interpretation of the three major native ecosystems present in Kansas.

MANHATTAN

CITY OF MANHATTAN—CITY PARK ROSE GARDEN (BERRY GARDEN)

Poyntz Ave. & 11th St., Manhattan, KS 66502
Tel: (785) 587-2757; Fax: (785) 587-2727
Internet Address: http://www.ci.manhattan.ks.us/Parks/City.asp
Admission: Free
Established: 1930
Membership: N
Wheelchair Accessible: P
Parking: Street parking and small lots
Open: Daily, 6am-11pm
Facilities: Garden (roses with ornamental fountain); Grounds City Park (45 acres); Picnic Area

A multipurpose site, City Park includes a rose garden. It was established as a WPA project during the Depression. City Park also features an historic log cabin museum.

KANSAS STATE UNIVERSITY GARDENS (KSU GARDENS)

1500 Denison Avenue, north of Claflin Road, Manhattan, KS 66502
Tel: (785) 532-3271;
Fax: (785) 532-3273
Internet Address:
http://www.ksu.edu/gardens
Admission: Free
Attendance: 13,500
Membership: Y
Wheelchair Accessible: Y

Kansas State University Gardens, Manhattan, KS

Parking: On site, vehicles must be registered in visitor center
Open: Gardens: March to November, Daily, dawn-midnight
Facilities: Conservatory (Victorian-style 1907; Mar-Nov, Mon-Fri, 10am-4pm); Gardens (adaptive/native plant, butterfly, cottage);

Grounds (19 acres; 4 acres completed, 15 acres under construction);
Insect Zoo (M/W/F, 10am-4pm; Sat, 11am-2pm); Shop; Special
Collections (day lily, iris, rose); Visitor Center (Mar-Nov, Mon-Fri,
10am-4pm), Quinlan Visitor Center (former stone dairy Barn)
Activities: Education Programs; Flower Shows; Guided Tours (arrange
in advance); Plant Sales (iris, last Sat in July); Self-Guided Tours
Campus Tree Walk (brochure available)

Located on the main campus of KSU, the University Gardens is a 19-
acre horticulture display garden that is designed to show landscape and
tested ornamental plant material in different aesthetic settings. A 19th-
century conservatory is the focal point of the extensive garden and landscape plantings. Approximately 300 species of plants are grown in the
Conservatory's desert, tropical and semi-tropical ecological regions.
North of the Conservatory, the day lily collection (more than 250 cultivars, including All-American Hemerocallis Society Stout Silver Medal
winners) and the iris collection (175 different varieties) are located in the
Conservatory Garden. The rose collection (over 300 plants) is located directly east of the Conservatory. Three specialty gardens (cottage, butterfly, and native/adaptive plants) are located in the Visitor Center Garden,
situated south of the Conservatory and west of the Visitor Center. The
University Gardens is in the second stage of a three-phase development
plan. Alumni, children's, sensory, and woodland gardens; hosta and
peony collections; and a wetland ecological zone are planned.

MERRIAM

HELEN CUDDY MEMORIAL ROSE GARDEN AND ARBORETUM

Antioch Park, 6501 Antioch Road, Merriam, KS 66202
Tel: (913) 831-3355; Fax: (913) 831-3311
Internet Address: http://www.jcprd.com/pages/02_parks/index.html
Admission: Free
Parking: In front of rose garden, 20 spaces
Open: March to October, Daily, 5am-11pm; November to February,
Daily, 7:30am-8pm
Best Time(s) of Year to Visit: May to September
Facilities: Arboretum; Gardens (iris, perennial, rose); Grounds Park
(44 acres)

Situated in Antioch Park, the rose garden is part of the Memorial Arboretum, which features 625 rose bushes and a cascading fountain, an iris
garden and a mixed bed of colorful flowers. A perennial bed, also inside

the arboretum, is planted with lamb's ear, hibiscus, crocus, grape hyacinths and different kinds of grasses.

OVERLAND PARK

CITY OF OVERLAND PARK—DEANA ROSE CHILDREN'S FARMSTEAD DEMONSTRATION GARDENS

13800 Switzer Road (at 137th), Overland Park, KS 66212
Tel: (913) 897-2360
Internet Address: http://www.opkansas.org/_Vis/Farmstead/index.cfm
Established: 1978
Open: April to May, Daily, 9am-5pm; June to early September, Daily,
9am-8pm; early September to October, Daily, 9am-5pm
Facilities: Food Services Concession Stand (sandwiches, snacks);
Gardens (butterfly, heirloom, herb, perennial, shade, vegetable);
Grounds Park (12 acres)
Activities: Guided Tours

Created and maintained by the Johnson County Extension Master
Gardeners, the site offers an heirloom garden, a butterfly garden, a vegetable garden, a shade garden, and winding brick walkways. Exhibits include new recommended varieties of vegetables and perennials, low-water maintenance flowers, herbs, and ground covers.

CITY OF OVERLAND PARK—OVERLAND PARK ARBORETUM AND BOTANICAL GARDEN

179th at Antioch Sts., Overland Park, KS 66212
Tel: (800) 262-7275
Internet Address: http://www.opprf.org/
Membership: Y
Parking: Parking available
Open: Grounds: April to October, Daily, 8am-7:30pm; November to
March, Daily, 8am-5pm; Visitor Center: April to October, Daily,
10am-7:30pm; November to March, Daily, 10am-5pm; Closed: New
Year's Day, Thanksgiving Day, Christmas Day
Facilities: Arboretum; Education and Visitors Center (8,000 square
feet); Gardens (children's, native plant, water, woodland); Grounds
(300 acres); Picnic Areas; Trails (5 miles)

Managed by the City of Overland Park, the Arboretum and Botanical
Garden is in the midst of a 20-year development plan. About 85% of the

land will be dedicated to the preservation and restoration of the eight natural ecosystems present on the site. The remaining portion includes traditional botanical gardens, the visitor center, and maintenance facilities, as well as a planned 16,000 square-foot conservatory. Within the park over 75 species of trees have been identified.

SHAWNEE

OLD SHAWNEE TOWN—GARDENS

11501 W. 57th St. at Cody St., Shawnee, KS 66203
Tel: (913) 248-2360; Fax: (913) 248-2363
Internet Address: http://www.cityofshawnee.org/parks/
OldShawneeTown/oldshawneetown.htm
Admission: Fee: adult $1.00, child (<6) free, child (6-12) $0.50
Established: 1966
Open: February to 2nd week in December, Tuesday to Saturday, noon-5pm; Closed: New Year's Day, ML King Day, President's Day, Memorial Day, Independence Day, Labor Day, Thanksgiving Day, Christmas Day
Facilities: Architecture (17 historic or replica structures); Gardens (heirloom, herb); Shop
Activities: Guided Tours

A project of the Shawnee Historical and the City of Shawnee Department of Parks and Recreation, Old Shawnee Town features a combination of original historic structures and replicas of buildings from the late 1800's to early 1900's, as well as two gardens. The Heirloom Garden, maintained by volunteers from the Shawnee Master Gardeners, represents a typical garden of the Victorian era, planted with flowers and herbs commonly found in the Midwest. The Herb Garden, maintained by the Johnson County Kansas State Research and Extension Master Gardeners, displays culinary and medicinal herbs and plants used in making dyes.

TOPEKA

CITY OF TOPEKA—E. F. A. REINISCH MEMORIAL ROSE AND DORAN ROCK GARDEN

Gage Park, 4320 West 10th Ave., Topeka, KS 66604-0000
Tel: (785) 368-3838
Internet Address: http://www.topeka.org
Admission: Free

Established: 1930
Wheelchair Accessible: Y
Parking: Parking lot north of garden
Open: 6am-11pm
Best Time(s) of Year to Visit: late May to early June (roses), early
September to mid-September (roses)
Facilities: Gardens (rock, rose); Grounds Park (160 acres, partially
designed by landscape architect George Kessler)

An All-America Rose Selections test garden, the Rose Garden contains over 6,500 plants representing 400 varieties. Visitors may also view possible upcoming releases in the Logan Test Garden. Immediately adjacent are the Doran Rock Garden and annual plantings around the reflecting pool. The garden is located in George Park, which also features a zoological park, a mini-train, a historic carousel, an aquatic center, and a center for the performing arts.

CITY OF TOPEKA—WARD-MEADE PARK BOTANICAL GARDENS

124 N.W. Filmore, Topeka, KS 66606
Tel: (785) 368-3888; Fax: (785) 368-3890
Internet Address: http://www.topeka.org
Admission: Free
Membership: N
Wheelchair Accessible: P
Parking: Parking at 1st and Clay
Open: Daily, 8am-dusk
Best Time(s) of Year to Visit: Spring to Fall
Facilities: Architecture (19th-century buildings; one on National
Register); Gardens (2.5 acres); Grounds (6 acres)
Activities: Self-Guided Tour

This history park features a Victorian mansion and Prairie Crossing Town Square (a grouping of 19th-century buildings), as well as a botanical garden. The Gardens contain 550 varieties of trees and shrubs, as well as over 6,000 annuals in thirty beds.

WAKEFIELD

KANSAS LANDSCAPE ARBORETUM

488 Utah Road, Wakefield, KS 67487
Tel: (785) 461-5760; Fax: (785) 461-5116

Internet Address:
http://www.mrk.usace.army.mil/Milford/land_arbor.htm
Admission: No charge/donations accepted
Established: 1972
Membership: Y
Wheelchair Accessible: P
Parking: On site
Open: Daily, dawn-dusk
Facilities: Arboretum; Bird Sanctuary; Grounds (193 acres); Nature
Center; Trails
Activities: Guided Tours (schedule in advance)

The arboretum contains over 1,000 species of exotic and native woody plants, including a large flowering crab apple tree collection (170 trees, representing over 50 varieties). Winding roads connect tree collections, three nature trails for walking, a bird sanctuary, and a pond oasis. Another area of interest is a historic farmhouse with a garden area, which may be reserved for picnics and family events. The Arboretum is located next to Milford Lake on land leased from the U.S. Army Corps of Engineers. It is a non-profit corporation supported solely by contributions and memberships.

WICHITA

BOTANICA, THE WICHITA GARDENS (AHS RAP)

Sim Park, 701 Amidon at Murdoch, Wichita, KS 67203-3162
Tel: (316) 264-9799; Fax: (316) 264-0587
Internet Address: http://www.botanica.org
Admission: Fee: adult $6.00, child (<5) free, child (6+) and senior $5.00, family $12.00
Attendance: 105,000
Established: 1985
Membership: Y
Wheelchair Accessible: Y
Parking: On site, next to entrance
Open: November to March, Monday to Friday, 9am-5pm; April to May, Monday to Saturday, 9am-5pm; Sunday, 1pm-5pm; June to September, Monday, 9am-5pm; Tuesday, 9am- 8pm; Wednesday to Saturday, 9am-5pm; Sunday, 1pm-5pm; October, Monday to Saturday, 9am-5pm; Sunday, 1pm-5pm; Closed: New Year's Day, Thanksgiving Weekend, Christmas Day

Best Time(s) of Year to Visit: April to May (tulip,), April to Frost (herb, perennial, wildflower), June to July (day lily, lily), Summer (annual, rose), May to June (iris, peony)
Facilities: Auditorium (300 seats); Butterfly House (2,880 square feet; June-Sept, Mon-Sat, 9am-5pm; Sun, 1pm-5pm); Food Services (Catered lunch, Wed, 11am-1pm); Gardens (24 themed gardens; annual, aquatic, butterfly, day lily, native, perennial, pinetum, rock, Shakespeare, rose, sensory, wildflower, woodland, xeriscape); Greenhouse; Grounds (10 acres); Library Frank Good Library (3,500 volumes); Shops Butterfly Shop (June-Sept), Hollyhocks (gifts, garden-related items); Special Collections (juniper, peony)
Activities: Education Programs (children); Guided Tours (groups 12+, reserve in advance); Lectures (Wed, 12:15pm, free); Workshops (teachers)

Botanica offers visitors a wide variety of gardening displays including a teaching garden providing examples of creative garden structure and walkway designs, as well as flora that grow well in the Great Plains region; a rose garden, showcasing more than 350 bushes; a butterfly garden drawing both native and migratory butterflies to its flowering and food plants; a pinetum featuring varieties not common to the Great Plains; a Shakespearean Garden displaying many of the flowers and herbs mentioned in Shakespeare's writings, as well as other popular Elizabethan plants; meadow and woodland wildflower gardens; a sensory garden; and a xeriscape garden. The entry gardens feature changing displays of seasonal flowers, flowering trees, and shrubs.

SEDGWICK COUNTY EXTENSION ARBORETUM AND DEMONSTRATION GARDEN (AHS RAP)

7001 W. 21st North at Ridge Road, Wichita, KS 67205-1759
Tel: (316) 722-7721; Fax: (316) 722-7727
Internet Address: http://www.sedgwickcountyextension.com
Admission: Free
Established: 2003
Membership: Y
Wheelchair Accessible: P
Parking: On site
Open: Grounds, Daily, dawn-dusk; Office, Mon-Fri, 8am-5pm.
Facilities: Arboretum; Gardens (access, container, herb, raised bed, vegetable)
Activities: Education Programs; Workshops

The extension maintains an arboretum containing 195 trees representing 97 species as well as horticulture demonstration gardens. The planting of trees adapted to south central Kansas on the grounds of the Sedgwick County Extension Center began in 1994 and the grounds were dedicated as an arboretum in 2003. The Demonstration Gardens, created and maintained by extension master gardeners, include a formal herb garden, as well as demonstrations of raised beds, wheel chair accessible beds, and container gardens.

LOUISIANA

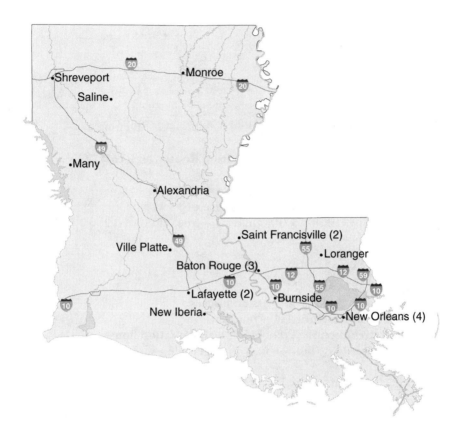

As this book was going into production in September 2005, Louisiana was just recovering from the ravages of hurricane Katrina. Because the condition of the public gardens in these states won't be known for quite some time, it is advisable to call them first before planning a visit.

The number in parentheses following the city name indicates the number of gardens/arboreta in that municipality. If there is no number, one is understood. For example, in the text three listings would be found under Baton Rouge and one listing under Ville Platte.

ALEXANDRIA

HISTORIC KENT PLANTATION HOUSE—GARDENS

3601 Bayou Rapides Road (½ mile from Routes 165/167/71),
Alexandria, LA 71303
Tel: (318) 487-5998; Fax: (318) 441-4154
Internet Address: http://www.kenthouse.org
Admission: Fee: adult $5.00, child (<6) free, child (6-12) $2.00,
senior $4.00
Attendance: 10,000
Membership: Y
Wheelchair Accessible: N
Parking: Ample parking for cars and buses
Open: Monday to Saturday, 9am-5pm
Facilities: Architecture (French colonial plantation house,
ca. 1796); Gardens (herb, parterre, vegetable); Grounds
(4 acres)
Activities: Funeral Festival (October); Guided Tours (groups 10+,
$4/person); Plant Sales (herbs, spring & fall)

In addition to an authentic Creole plantation house built prior to the
Louisiana Purchase, the site offers outbuildings including a milk house,
carriage house, kitchen, two slave cabins, sugar house, barn, blacksmith
shop, a kitchen dependency, an herb and vegetable garden, a parterre
garden, and a cemetery. Kent House is listed on the National Register of
Historic Places.

AVERY ISLAND

JUNGLE GARDENS

Avery Island Road (off Route 329), Avery Island, LA 70513
Tel: (318) 369-6243

Internet Address: http://www.tabasco.com/html/historian_averyvisit.html
Admission: Fee
Established: 1936
Membership: N
Wheelchair Accessible: Y
Parking: Free on site
Open: Daily, 9am-5pm
Best Time(s) of Year to Visit: March to July (nesting season)
Facilities: Bird Sanctuary; Gardens (Chinese, palm, sunken); Grounds
(250 acres); Picnic Area; Shop; Visitors Center
Activities: Guided Tours

The gardens, begun by Edward Avery McIlhenny of Tabasco fame, features thousands of camellias representing approximately 600 varieties, thousands of azaleas of many varieties, a palm collection, bamboo, and iris, as well as many rare and unusual plants. Also a bird sanctuary, it is home to over 20,000 heron and snowy egrets.

BATON ROUGE

LAURENS HENRY COHN, SR. MEMORIAL PLANT ARBORETUM

12056 Foster Road, Baton Rouge, LA 70811
Tel: (225) 775-1006; Fax: (225) 775-1006
Internet Address: http://www.brec.org/nature/arboretum.htm
Admission: Free
Attendance: 13,000
Established: 1965
Wheelchair Accessible: Y
Parking: Paved parking on grounds
Open: Daily, 8am-4:45pm; Closed: Major holidays
Best Time(s) of Year to Visit: April-June and October-December
Facilities: Arboretum; Classrooms; Conservatory 3,000 square. Feet
(tropicals); Grounds (16 acres); Library; Museum Sharecroppers
Museum; Special Collections (camellia, conifer/evergreen, crape
myrtle, Japanese maple, day lily, ginger, banana, native fern)
Activities: Guided Tours (arrange in advance, maximum group size 14
people); Lectures; Seed Exchange Program; Self-Guided Tours
(pamphlet available)

The arboretum contains over 250 labeled trees and shrubs, greenhouses filled with orchids and other tropicals, an herb/fragrance garden, and the Sharecroppers' Museum. Major plant collections include Japanese maples, camellias, evergreens/conifers, and crape myrtles. The Arboretum is maintained by BREC, the Recreation and Park Commission for the Parish of East Baton Rouge.

LOUISIANA STATE UNIVERSITY—BURDEN CENTER

Burden Research Station, 4560 Essen Lane, Baton Rouge,
LA 70809-3424
Tel: (225) 765-3990; Fax: (225) 763-3993
Internet Address: http://www.lsuagcenter.com/inst/research/
stations/burden/
Admission: Free. (Fee for museum)
Open: Daily, 8:30am-5pm
Facilities: Gardens (semi-formal; annual, perennial, rose, trial);
Grounds Center (425 acres, 150 acres of forest), Windrush Gardens
(25 acres), Plant Trial Gardens (5,000 square feet), Orangerie (1,242
square feet); Rural Life Museum (20 buildings on 5 acres; open daily,
8:30am-5pm; closed major holidays)

The Burden Center is on the grounds of the old Windrush Plantation, which was donated to LSU in the 1990s. The Center focuses on research projects relating to fruit and vegetable crops, ornamentals and nursury production, and turfgrass. The gardens of the old Burden plantation home, Windrush Gardens is a part of this agricultural research center. The gardens, featuring native plants and classical statuary, are segmented by great walls of hedges and trees, winding paths, and open areas. The facility also features an approved AARS Public Garden, consisting of 1,500 rose plants, representing 150 varieties and annual and perennial trial gardens in raised beds. The Burden Center is also home to the Steele Burden Memorial Orangerie, containing temporary and permanent displays of tropical and subtropical plants. Finally, adjacent to Windrush Gardens is the LSU Rural Life Museum, a 20-building complex depicting life on a typical 19th-century working plantation.

LOUISIANA STATE UNIVERSITY—HILLTOP ARBORETUM

11855 Highland Road, Baton Rouge, LA 70810-4808
Tel: (225) 767-6916; Fax: (225) 768-7740
Internet Address: http://www.lsu.edu/hilltop
Admission: Free
Attendance: 5,000
Established: 1981
Membership: Y
Wheelchair Accessible: P

Parking: On site 25 car lot, bus parking available
Open: Daily, sunrise-sunset
Facilities: Arboretum; Building (7,000 square feet); Grounds
(14 acres); Shop
Activities: Guided Tours (Tues, 8am-3:30pm, reservations suggested,
769-2363); Self-Guided Tours

Hilltop Arboretum, a part of the School of Landscape Architecture, features an extensive collection of Louisiana native trees, shrubs, and plants.

BURNSIDE

HOUMAS HOUSE PLANTATION AND GARDENS

40136 Highway 942, Burnside, LA 70725
Tel: (504) 891-9494
Internet Address: http://www.houmashouse.com/
Admission: Fee (house tour additional) $10.00
Established: 1940
Wheelchair Accessible: Y
Open: 9am-5pm
Closed: New Year's Day, Thanksgiving Day, Christmas Day
Best Time(s) of Year to Visit: March (azalea)
Facilities: Architecture (Greek Revival Mansion, 1840); Gardens
(boxwood, camellia, wisteria arbor)
Activities: Guided Tours (on the hour and half-hour)

Situated in a park-like setting of 200-year-old live oaks, Houmas House is listed on the National Register of Historic Places. The Plantation was the nation's leading sugar cane producer, producing 20 million pounds of sugar per year in the late 19th century. The formal boxwood gardens contain sweet olive, magnolia grandiflora, Lady Banksia roses, angel's trumpets, banana shrub and plumbago. In fall and winter, the camellia garden features sasanquas and japonicas and in spring is underplanted with thousands of tulips. A 180-foot wisteria arbor supports three different varieties of wisteria. Massive Formosa azaleas bloom in March.

LAFAYETTE

ACADIAN VILLAGE AND GARDENS

200 Greenleaf Drive, Lafayette, LA 70506-7400
Tel: (800) 962-9133

Internet Address: http://www.acadianvillage.org
Admission: Fee: adult $7.00, student $3.00, senior $6.00
Established: 1976
Open: Daily, 10am-5pm; Closed: New Year's Day, Mardi Gras, Easter, Thanksgiving Day, Christmas Eve, Christmas Day.
Best Time(s) of Year to Visit: Spring to Fall
Facilities: Gardens and Woodlands (10 acres)

The village depicts 19th-century Cajun (Acadian) society. Most of the buildings are authentic and have been moved to this location. The village is a project of the Lafayette Association for Retarded Citizens.

UNIVERSITY OF LOUISIANA AT LAFAYETTE— IRA S. NELSON HORTICULTURE CENTER

2206 Johnston St., Lafayette, LA 70503-2016
Tel: (337) 482-5339
Established: 1960
Open: Academic Year, Monday to Friday, 7am-4pm
Facilities: Conservatory; Greenhouses; Special Collections (holly)

The center includes a number of greenhouses containing bromeliads, orchids, tropical foliage plants, cacti and orchids; an amaryllis house; and a conservatory featuring large specimen plants and water gardens. The University served as the primary test site of Chinese hollies following their introduction into the United States and the campus retains an extensive holly collection.

LORANGER

ZEMURRAY GARDENS

23115 Zemurray Gardens Drive (Highway 40), Loranger, LA 70446
Tel: (985) 878-2284
Admission: Fee: adult $4.00, child (1-12) $3.00, senior $3.00
Attendance: 3,000
Membership: N
Wheelchair Accessible: N
Parking: Parking lot
Open: mid-March to mid-April, Daily, 10am-6pm

Best Time(s) of Year to Visit: Spring
Facilities: Picnic Area
Activities: Self-Guided Tours

This privately operated garden features azaleas, camellias, iris, dogwood, and honeysuckle surrounding a 20-acre lake.

MANY

HODGES GARDENS, PARK AND WILDERNESS AREA

Highway 171 South (between Shreveport & Lake Charles),
Many, LA 71449
Tel: (318) 586-3523; Fax: (318) 586-7111
Internet Address: http://www.hodgespark.com
Admission: Fee (spring/summer): adult $6.50, child free, student
$3.00, senior $5.50
Established: 1956
Open: Daily, 8am-5pm; Closed: Christmas Eve, Christmas Day
Best Time(s) of Year to Visit: February (camellia, daffodil, iris,
tulip), March (anemone, old rose, pansy, wisteria), mid-March to
early April (dogwood), April (azalea), May (magnolia), Summer
(hydrangea, day lily, water lily), Fall (chrysanthemum, rose, fall
foliage)
Facilities: Conservatory; Gardens (formal, herb, rock, rose);
Greenhouses; Grounds Gardens (70 acres), Site (4,700 acres); Picnic
Grounds; Wildlife Refuge
Activities: Christmas Lights Festival (December 1-December 23,
6pm-10pm)

In the early 1940's, A. J. Hodges, a pioneer conservationist, began a vast reforestation effort in west central Louisiana, including a 4,700-acre experimental arboretum. Recognizing the potential of an abandoned stone quarry discovered on the site, Mr. Hodges and his wife, Nona Trigg Hodges, created a unique scenic garden utilizing the natural rock formations. Centered on the quarry, Hodges Gardens offers 70 acres of landscaped gardens, including an All-America Rose Selections display garden, as well as a conservatory and greenhouses housing exotic tropicals. Hodges Gardens is now owned and operated by the nonprofit A. J. and Nona Trigg Hodges Foundation.

MONROE

THE BIEDENHARN MUSEUM—ELSONG GARDENS AND CONSERVATORY (AHS RAP)

2006 Riverside Drive, Monroe, LA 71201
Tel: (318) 387-5281; Fax: (318) 387-8253
Internet Address: http://www.bmuseum.org/
Admission: Voluntary contribution
Attendance: 30,000
Established: 1971
Wheelchair Accessible: Y
Parking: Parking lots across street
Open: Monday to Saturday, 10am-5pm; 2pm-5pm;
Closed: New Year's Day, Easter, Thanksgiving Day, Christmas Eve to Christmas Day
Facilities: Auditorium (50 seats); Conservatory (3,000 square feet); Gardens (Biblical, formal, oriental); Library (2,000 volumes)
Activities: Garden Symposia (April); Guided Tours (on the hour; groups of 10+, reservation required); Lectures (garden topics)

Built in 1914 by Joseph Biedenharn, the first bottler of Coca-Cola, the house is now a museum of rare manuscripts, Bibles, and musical instruments. Surrounding the residence, ELsong Gardens (named for Biedenharn's daughter, contralto Emy-Lou Biedenharn) contain several thousand flowering plants, as well as seven water features and sculpture from around the world. The Conservatory, patterned after English glass houses, and is home to hundreds of tropical and semi-tropical plants.

NEW IBERIA

SHADOWS-ON-THE-TECHE—GARDENS

317 East Main St. (intersection of State Routes 182 & 14), New Iberia, LA 70560-3728
Tel: (337) 369-6446; Fax: (337) 365-5213
Internet Address: http://www.shadowsontheteche.org/
Admission: Fee: adult $7.00, child (<6) free, child (6-11) $4.00, senior $6.25
Attendance: 26,000

Established: 1961
Membership: Y
Wheelchair Accessible: Y
Parking: On street & lot at Shadows Visitor Center (320 E. Main St.)
Open: Daily, 9am-4:30pm; Closed: New Year's Day, Easter,
Thanksgiving Day, Christmas Eve to Christmas Day
Facilities: Architecture (Plantation House, 1831-34); Grounds (2½ acres)
Activities: Guided Tours (9am-4:30pm); Lectures

A property of the National Trust for Historic Preservation, Shadows-on-the-Teche was constructed between 1831 and 1834 by sugar planter David Weeks and his wife. Four generations of the Weeks family lived at the Shadows from 1834 until 1958, when the property was given to the National Trust by William Weeks Hall, the great-grandson of the builder and final family owner. Today the Shadows has been carefully restored with original furnishings to present a picture of life on a Southern plantation in the antebellum period. However, the landscape has not been restored to a particular style or period, but reflects an increasing emphasis on the aesthetic rather than the functional over four generations. Weeks Hall, who had trained as a painter at the Pennsylvania Academy of Fine Arts, created a 20th-century ornamental garden evocative of the property's 19th-century legacy. The landscaped gardens feature ancient live oak trees, Spanish moss, azaleas, camellias, crepe myrtles, magnolias, gingers and garden statuary.

NEW ORLEANS

BEAUREGARD KEYES HOUSE AND GARDEN

1113 Chartres St., New Orleans,
LA 70116-2504
Tel: (504) 523-7257
Admission: Fee: adult $5.00, child free,
child (6-12) $2.00, student $4.00,
senior $4.00
Attendance: 7,500
Established: 1970
Membership: N
Wheelchair Accessible: N
Open: Monday to Saturday, 10am-3pm; Closed: Legal holidays
Best Time(s) of Year to Visit: January to October

Beauregard Keyes House and
Garden, New Orleans, LA.
French parterre in springtime.

Facilities: Architecture (Raised center hall, Federal style residence, 1826 design by architect François Correjalles)
Activities: Guided Tours (on the hour)

Built in 1826 by Joseph LeCarpentier, this national landmark was the former residence of Confederate General P. G. T. Beauregard and later novelist Frances Parkingson Keyes. The formal garden has been restored to the style of the 1840's.

HERMANN-GRIMA HISTORIC HOUSE GARDEN

820 St. Louis St., New Orleans, LA 70112
Tel: (504) 525-5661; Fax: (504) 568-5661
Internet Address: http://www.HGCHH.org
Admission: Fee: adult $6.00, child (<8) free, child and student $5.00, senior $5.00
Attendance: 20,000
Parking: Parking garage nearby
Open: Monday to Saturday, 10am-4pm; Closed: Legal Holidays, Lundi Mardi Gras to Mardi Gras
Facilities: Architecture (Federal-style mansion, 1831; open hearth kitchen; slave room); Shop (in restored 19th-century stable)
Activities: Guided Tours (10am, 11am, noon, 1:30pm, 2:30pm, 3:30pm)

The courtyard of this French Quarter national historic landmark, contains flagstone parterres featuring perennials and annuals documented to mid-19th-century New Orleans.

LONGUE VUE HOUSE AND GARDENS (AHS RAP)

7 Bamboo Road (off Metairie Road), New Orleans, LA 70124-1065
Tel: (504) 488-5488; Fax: (504) 486-7015
Internet Address: http://www.longuevue.com
Admission: Gardens: adult $10.00, child $5.00, student $5.00
Attendance: 52,000
Established: 1968
Membership: Y
Wheelchair Accessible: Y
Open: Monday to Saturday, 10am-4:30pm; Sunday, 1pm-5pm; Closed: Most holidays
Facilities: Architecture (Greek Revival-style mansion, 1939-42 design by William & Henry Platt); Auditorium (80 seats); Gardens (formal,

Spanish, English; design by landscape architect Ellen Biddle Shipman);
Grounds (8 acres); Library (100 volumes, for research); Shop
Activities: Films; Gallery Talks; Guided Tours (Tours in English,
Spanish, French, Italian, Japanese, German); Lectures; Permanent
Exhibits; Temporary Exhibitions

The former home of the philanthropic Stern family, the 20th-century
mansion and surrounding gardens comprise one of America's great urban
estates. Inspired by the Alhambra and Generalife gardens in Granada,
Spain, the outdoor design is centered on the Spanish Court, a large formal garden with fountains and mosaic walkways. A series of smaller Spanish and English gardens flank the Spanish Court and include indigenous
flora such as live oaks, magnolias, azaleas, crape myrtles and roses. Other
features include 23 fountains, a giant sundial, a bamboo tunnel and a
maze. Longue Vue is listed on the National Register of Historic Places.

NEW ORLEANS BOTANICAL GARDEN

Victory Ave. in New Orleans City Park (behind the New Orleans
Museum of Art), New Orleans, LA 70124-4608
Tel: (504) 483-9386; Fax: (504) 483-9485
Internet Address:
http://www.neworleanscitypark.com/garden/index.html
Admission: Fee: adult $5.00, child (<5) free, child (5-12) $2.00
Established: 1936
Membership: Y
Wheelchair Accessible: Y
Parking: Free parking
Open: Tuesday to Sunday, 10am-4:30pm
Facilities: Grounds (13 acres); Train Garden (highlights New Orleans
neighborhoods and architecture)
Activities: Guided Tours (Tues-Sun, 10am-3pm, groups 20+,
$8/person, reserve 2 weeks in advance)

Located in City Park, the fifth largest urban park in the nation, the
New Orleans Botanical Garden has its roots in the Great Depression
as a project of the Works Progress Administration (WPA). Originally
known as the City Park Rose Garden, the garden opened in 1936 as
New Orleans' first public classical garden combining both art and nature. Designed for everyone in New Orleans to enjoy, it is one of the
few remaining examples of public garden design from the WPA and
Art Deco Period, remaining today as a showcase of three notable tal-
ents: New Orleans architect Richard Koch, landscape architect

William Wierdon, and artist Enrique Alferez. Reborn as the New Orleans Botanical Garden in the early 1980s, today's garden contains over 2,000 varieties of plants from all over the world set among the nation's largest stand of mature live oaks. The site contains several theme gardens containing aquatics, ornamental trees and shrubs, perennials, and a conservatory containing the Living Fossils exhibit of prehistoric plants and a tropical rain forest. The garden also encompasses the Garden Study Center, the Pavilion of the Two Sisters, and the newly rebuilt Lath House.

SAINT FRANCISVILLE

AFTON VILLA GARDENS

9247 U.S. Route 61 (4 miles north of Saint Francisville),
Saint Francisville, LA 70775
Tel: (504) 635-6773
Admission: Fee
Open: May 1 to July 1, Daily, 9am-4:30pm; October 1 to
December 1, Daily, 9am-4:30pm
Facilities: Grounds Gardens (10 acres), Parkland (30 acres)

Once the premier residence in the region, Afton Villa, a 40 room Gothic-Revival mansion that took eight years to build (1849-57), was totally destroyed by fire in 1963. However the extensive formal gardens and pleasure ground which surrounded the plantation house have been preserved. Inspired by the work of Vita Sackville-West at Sissinghurst Castle in England, the current owners integrated the extant architectural elements of the plantation with formal gardens and landscaped parkland. A long oak-alley with numerous native plants lines the entrance to the site. Among the plants represented are camellias, sweet olive, magnolia fuscata, flowering seasonal bulbs (including over 80,000 daffodils), hydrangeas and azaleas. Other native plants include tulip tree, winter honeysuckle, cowcumber, wild ferns, Silverbell tree and Grancy Greybeard.

ROSEDOWN PLANTATION AND HISTORIC GARDENS

12501 Highway 10 (intersection of U.S. Rte 61 & LA Rte 10),
Saint Francisville, LA 70775
Tel: (504) 635-3332
Admission: Fee: adult $10.00, child (6-17) $4.00, senior $8.00
Open: Daily, 9am-5pm

Facilities: Architecture (plantation house, 1835); Gardens (flower, herb, medicinal, parterre); Greenhouse; Grounds Gardens (28 acres); Shop

Wealthy cotton planter Daniel Turnbull built Rosedown in 1835. His wife, Martha Barrow Turnbull, conceived formal gardens that in fruition were recognized as one of the 19th century's most famous horticultural collections. In the 1960s it was restored under the direction of Ralph Gunn of Houston using Martha Turnbull's garden journal. Today, it is one of the nation's most important historical gardens, containing many trees and shrubs from the original plantings, including live oaks, azaleas, and camellias.

SALINE

BRIARWOOD: CAROLINE DORMON NATURE PRESERVE

216 Caroline Dormon Road (2 miles south of Saline), Saline, LA 71070
Tel: (318) 576-3379
Internet Address: http://www.cp-tel.net/dormon
Admission: Fee $5.00
Attendance: 3,000
Established: 1972
Membership: Y
Wheelchair Accessible: P
Open: March to May, August & November, Saturday, 9am-5pm; Sunday, noon-5pm
Facilities: Garden (native plant); Grounds (125 acres); Trails
Activities: Guided Tours (groups 5+, by appointment)

Briarwood, a botanical and wildlife sanctuary, is the former home of conservationist and author Caroline Dormon. Dormon, the first woman employed in forestry in the United States, was primarily responsible for the establishment of the 600,000-acre Kisatchie National Forest. The Preserve, crisscrossed with trails, contains pine forests and native Southeastern wildflowers including a Louisiana iris bog.

SHREVEPORT

THE GARDENS OF THE AMERICAN ROSE CENTER (AHS RAP)

8877 Jefferson Paige Road, Shreveport, LA 71119
Tel: (318) 938-5402; Fax: (318) 938-5405

Internet Address: http://www.ars.org/
Admission: Fee: adult $4.00, child (<12) free, senior $3.00
Attendance: 80,000
Established: 1972
Membership: Y
Parking: Parking for busses and 200 cars
Open: April to October, Daily, 9am-6pm
Best Time(s) of Year to Visit: April-May to Oct-Dec
Facilities: Chapel; Fountain; Gardens (68, rose); Grounds Gardens
(42 acres), Site (118 acres); Japanese Tea Garden; Shop
Activities: Education Programs; Festival Christmas in Roseland
(late Nov-December, $10/auto); Workshops

The gardens of the American Rose Center serve as the national head-quarters of the American Rose Society. The Center's 68 individual gardens contain over 20,000 roses representing over 450 varieties, including floribundas, hybrid teas, grandifloras, and miniatures. The focus of the gardens is the Windsound Carillon surrounded by All-America Rose Selections winners. Founded in 1892, the American Rose Society is a national organization with over 24,000 members and over 380 local chapters and affiliates throughout the country.

VILLE PLATTE

LOUISIANA ARBORETUM STATE PRESERVATION AREA

Chicot State Park, 4213 Chicot Park Road (State Route 3042),
Ville Platte, LA 70586
Tel: (888) 677-6100
Internet Address: http://www.crt.state.la.us/crt/parks/arbor/arbor2.htm
Admission: Free
Established: 1961
Open: Daily, 8am-5pm
Facilities: Arboretum; Grounds (300 acres); Herbarium; Outdoor
Classroom; Trails.
Activities: Guided Tours (groups 10+, by appointment)

The Louisiana State Arboretum in Ville Platte, a state preservation area is an excellent example of a mature beech-magnolia forest, containing centuries-old giant beech, magnolia, oak, and ash trees. Atypical of the terrain in the Louisiana prairie land, the topography of the

Arboretum is varied and dramatic. The landscape ranges from nearly flat to relatively steep slopes along the terrace ridges. Due to this great variation in topography, almost every type of Louisiana vegetation, except coastal marsh and prairie, is represented on the site. Trees, shrubs and flowers are labeled for observation along an extensive network of trails.

MINNESOTA

The number in parentheses following the city name indicates the number of gardens/arboreta in that municipality. If there is no number, one is understood. For example, in the text two listings would be found under Minneapolis and one listing under Baxter.

BAXTER

NORTHLAND ARBORETUM

1350 Excelsior Road North, Baxter, MN 56425
Tel: (218) 829-8770
Admission: Fee: adult $3.00, child $1.00, family $5.00
Attendance: 4,000
Established: 1974
Membership: Y
Parking: Parking at Visitor Center
Open: Summer, Daily, 8am-sundown; Fall to Spring, Daily, 8am-10pm.
Facilities: Gardens (gazebo, Minnesota Monet area, memorial, natural areas); Grounds (540 acres); Picnic Area; Trails (12 miles—varied terrain)
Activities: Education Programs (natural history, birding, landscaping, gardening)

The arboretum contains jack pine savanna, marsh and prairie.

BLOOMINGTON

NORMANDALE COMMUNITY COLLEGE— THE JAPANESE GARDEN

Corner of France Ave. & 98th Street,
Bloomington, MN 55431
Tel: (952) 487-8101
Attendance: 2,000
Established: 1976
Wheelchair Accessible: Y
Parking: Free parking adjacent to garden
Open: June to September
Best Time(s) of Year to Visit: Spring to Fall

Normandale Community College, The Japanese Garden Bloomington, MN.

Facilities: Garden (Japanese, design by garden architect Takao
Watanabe of Tokyo)
Activities: Self-Guided Tours

The first authentic Japanese garden in the upper Midwest, Japanese
Garden, is located at the Northeast corner of the campus. Designed by
Takeo Watanabe, the garden features rustic buildings, imported lanterns,
and a waterfall. It is a subtle blend of water, rock, and plant textures.

CHASKA

UNIVERSITY OF MINNESOTA—MINNESOTA LANDSCAPE ARBORETUM (AHS RAP)

3675 Arboretum Drive, Chaska, MN 55318
Tel: (952) 443-1412; Fax: (612) 443-2521
Internet Address: http://www.arboretum.umn.edu/
Admission: Fee: adult $7.00, child (<15) free; Groups $5.00 per person
Attendance: 260,000
Established: 1958
Membership: Y
Wheelchair Accessible: Y
Parking: Free parking
Open: March to October, Daily, 8am-8pm; November to February,
Daily, 8am-5:30pm; Closed: Thanksgiving Day, Christmas Day
Best Time(s) of Year to Visit: Spring to Fall
Facilities: Food Services Tearoom (cafeteria-style lunches);
Gardens/Collections (annual, home demonstration, dwarf conifer,
herb, hosta glade, Japanese, perennial, prairie, rose, wildflower, shade
tree, peeper meadow, rain, crab apple, hedge, native tree); Grounds
(1,000 acres); Library (15,000 volumes, non-circulating); Shop
(books, cards, gift items)
Activities: Education Programs (adults, undergraduates and children);
Films; Guided Tours General (Tues-Sat, 10:30am, free), Groups (Tues-
Fri, reserve in advance, $2/person), Tram Tour (Tues-Sun, $2/person,
443-1411); Hobby Workshops; Lectures

The arboretum features 1,000 acres of natural woodlands, wetlands,
prairie, collections featuring northern-hardy plants, and 32 spectacular
annual and perennial display gardens. Highlights include the Pamela J.
Wilson Rose Garden, an All-America Rose Selections accredited display
garden; the Garden of Pure Water (Seisui tei), a Japanese-style garden
designed by Koichi Kawana and featuring cold-hardy azaleas and pines

set among Japanese artifacts; the Clotilde Irvine Sensory Garden; numerous perennial gardens; a hosta glade; dahlia, day lily, lily, and chrysanthemum collections; a shade tree exhibit; and a prairie. Enjoy miles of hiking trails in summer and cross-country ski trails in winter through northern woodlands, native prairie and natural marshes. In spring, summer and fall, take a guided tram tour around a beautiful three-mile drive, or join a free volunteer-guided walking tour through the many display gardens.

COLLEGEVILLE

ST. JOHN'S UNIVERSITY—ST. JOHN'S ARBORETUM

Saint John's University, Collegeville, MN 56321
Tel: (320) 363-3163; Fax: (320) 363-3202
Internet Address: http://www.csbsju.edu/arboretum
Admission: No charge/donations accepted
Membership: Y
Wheelchair Accessible: Y
Open: Daily
Facilities: Arboretum (2,500 acres of native habitats, including prairie, lakes, wetlands, savanna, hardwood forests); Herbarium
Activities: Guided Tours

The St. John's 2,480-acre campus includes prairie, oak savanna, wetlands, and forest habitats. The first three, now rare in Minnesota, are the subject of the St. John's Habitat Restoration Project. A restored 50-acre prairie, containing over 90 species of prairie grasses and flowers, is located east of the entrance road to the University and north of East Gemini Lake. A 35-acre oak savanna represents the transition stage between the Big Woods of the east and the prairies of the west. A 60-acre wetland was restored with the construction of two dams on the north fork of the Watab river. Forest habitats include extensive hardwoods on over 1,700 acres and 125 acres of conifer plantations. The entire campus was dedicated as a natural arboretum in 1997.

DULUTH

CITY OF DULUTH—LEIF ERICKSON ROSE GARDEN

1301 London Road (at 13th Ave. East), Duluth, MN 55805
Tel: (218) 723-3425
Facilities: Gardens (rose, herb); Grounds (2½ acres)

Overlooking Lake Superior and Duluth's famous Lift Bridge, the garden offers over 3,000 rose bushes representing approximately 99 varieties, as well as an herb garden, a fountain and a marble gazebo.

GLENSHEEN HISTORIC ESTATE—GARDENS

3300 London Road, Duluth, MN 55804
Tel: (888) 454-4536; Fax: (218) 726-8911
Internet Address: http://www.glensheen.org
Admission: Grounds Pass $5.00
Attendance: 85,000
Established: 1979
Membership: Y
Wheelchair Accessible: Y
Parking: Surface lot adjacent to estate, handicapped spaces
Open: May to October, Daily, 9:30am-4pm; November to April, Saturday to Sunday, 11am-2pm; Closed: New Year's Day, Easter, Thanksgiving Day, Christmas Day.
Best Time(s) of Year to Visit: July to August
Facilities: Architecture (neo-Jacobean Mansion, 1905-8); Grounds (7½ acres, formal gardens and landscaped areas); Shop
Activities: Concerts (July); Education Programs (adults, undergraduate/graduate students and children); Events Festival of Fine Art and Craft (Aug); Guided Tours House (fee, adult $11, family $33)

Built by mining millionaire Chester A. Congdon, Glensheen features gently sloping terrain with formal gardens. In 1968, Glensheen was given to the University of Minnesota and was opened to the public as a museum in 1979.

MANKATO

R. D. HUBBARD HOUSE—PALMER CENTENNIAL GARDEN

606 South Broad St., Mankato, MN 56001-3817
Tel: (507) 345-5566
Internet Address: http://www.rootsweb.com/~mnbechs
Admission: Free (gardens); small fee for house
Membership: Y
Wheelchair Accessible: Y
Parking: On-street parking
Open: (House) May to early September, Saturday to Sunday, 1pm-4pm; Gardens, dawn-dusk

Facilities: Architecture (Victorian mansion, 1871; carriage house, 1890); Gardens (Victorian)
Activities: Guided Tours (by appointment)

The oldest remaining example of a Victorian mansion in the area, the 18-room Hubbard House went through several expansions and renovations. The house, carriage house, and grounds, restored to their 1905 appearance, include Victorian gardens. Owned by City of Mankato and operated by the Blue Earth County Historical Society, the site is listed on the National Register of Historic Places.

MINNEAPOLIS

CITY OF MINNEAPOLIS—LYNDALE PARK GARDENS

1500 E. Lake Harriet Pkwy. (adjacent to Roseway Road), Minneapolis MN 56303
Tel: (612) 370-4900; Fax: (612) 370-4831
Internet Address: http://www.minneapolisparks.org
Admission: Free
Established: 1908
Wheelchair Accessible: Y
Parking: Automated parking pay stations
Open: Daily, 7:30am-10pm
Best Time(s) of Year to Visit: mid-April to May (Rock Garden), May to Frost (Perennial Garden), mid-June to late September (Rose Garden)
Facilities: Bird Sanctuary; Gardens (perennial, rock, rose); Grounds Park (50 acres), Bird Sanctuary (17 acres)
Activities: Guided Tours (schedule 3 weeks in advance, (612) 313-7726)

Located on the northeast shore of Lake Harriet, Lyndale Park Gardens encompasses four distinct gardens: the Rose Garden, the Annual/Perennial Garden, the Peace (Rock) Garden, and the Perennial Trial Garden. The second oldest public rose garden in the United States (begun in 1907-8) and an accredited All-America Rose Selections display and test garden, the Rose Garden contains over 2,400 roses representing over 300 varieties in 85 beds. Situated between two fountains, the formal Annual/Perennial Garden offers 300 types of perennials and annuals displayed in 2 long perennial borders and 6 annual beds. The meandering Perennial Trial Garden, maintained by volunteers from the Men's Garden Club of Minneapolis, features perennials that are being tested over several seasons for hardiness, disease resistance and other attributes. The Peace (Rock) Garden, redesigned and rebuilt by artist Betty Ann Addison between 1983 and 2000, displays a selection of hardy alpine plants and dwarf conifers. Immediately adjacent to the Peace Garden is the Thomas Sadler Roberts Bird Sanctuary.

ELOISE BUTLER WILDFLOWER GARDEN AND BIRD SANCTUARY

1 Theodore Wirth Parkway at Glenwood Ave., Minneapolis, MN 55409
Tel: (612) 370-4903; Fax: (612) 370-4831
Admission: Free
Attendance: 45,000
Established: 1907
Membership: Y
Wheelchair Accessible: N
Open: April 15 to October 15, Daily, 7:30am-dusk
Facilities: Library (100 volumes, on premises use); Nature Center; Trail 2/3 mile
Activities: Permanent Exhibits; Temporary Exhibitions

The nation's oldest public wildflower garden, the Garden was established in 1907 by transplanted Easterner Eloise Butler, who feared the city would eventually gobble up the local flora and fauna. The garden has over 400 species of wildflowers in three habitats: prairie, woodland, and bog.

NORTHFIELD

CARLETON COLLEGE—COWLING ARBORETUM AND JAPANESE GARDEN

Parr House (Arboretum Headquarters), North College St. (Route 19), Northfield, MN 55057
Tel: (507) 646-5413
Internet Address: http://webapps.acs.carleton.edu/campus/arb & acs.carleton.edu/campus/j
Open: Spring to Fall, Daily, 7am-10pm
Facilities: Arboretum; Gardens (Japanese, wildflower); Grounds Arboretum (880 acres), Japanese Garden (1974-76 design by David Slawson)
Activities: Education Programs

Situated on a natural border between prairie and forest, Cowling Arboretum features a variety of distinct habitats (floodplain/successional floodplain forest, upland/successional upland forest, oak savanna, prairie, and wetland areas), as well as a wildflower garden. The Arboretum is divided by Highway 19 into two areas. The "Upper Arb" (south of the highway) has greater trail density and generally smaller natural areas. In contrast the "Lower Arb" (lower because it contains the low-lying flood-plain of the Cannon River) has populations of rare plants and animals and larger areas of natural communities. Located behind Watson Hall, Carleton's Japanese garden, the Garden of Quiet Listening (Jo Ryo En), is a dry landscape garden (kare-sansui). It features a stream of dark, flat stones emptying into a lake of white gravel, surrounded by large rocks, two stone lanterns, low shrubs, ground cover, and trees carefully arranged to simulate a microcosm of hills and mountains. In 2000, the *Journal of Japanese Gardening* ranked the Garden as one of the 10 highest-quality gardens outside of Japan, out of 300 sites surveyed.

SAINT CLOUD

CITY OF SAINT CLOUD—MUNSINGER GARDENS (AHS RAP)

Riverside Drive South and Michigan Ave, Saint Cloud, MN 56303
Tel: (320) 255-7238
Internet Address: http://ci.stcloud.mn.us/Web/departments/Parks/
Gardens/mgcg%20home%20pa
Admission: Free
Established: 1915
Open: Spring to Fall, Daily, 7am-10pm
Facilities: Gardens (lily pond, rock)

Originally (ca.1880) the site of a sawmill, now the site of the Munsinger Gardens, the land was acquired by the City of Saint Cloud in 1915. The original greenhouse, rock garden, lily pond and fountain were constructed during the Depression under the Works Progress Administration. The Gardens feature shade-loving plants, including a wide variety of hostas and ferns. At the corner of Killian Boulevard and 14th Street is the Clemens Rose Gardens, featuring over 1,100 rose bushes. (See next entry.)

CITY OF SAINT CLOUD—CLEMENS ROSE GARDENS

Killian Blvd and 13th St., Saint Cloud, MN 56303
Tel: (320) 255-7238
Internet Address: http://ci.stcloud.mn.us/Web/departments/Parks/
Gardens/mgcg%20home%20pa
Admission: Free
Established: 1985
Open: Spring to Fall, 7am-10pm
Best Time(s) of Year to Visit: June to September (rose)
Facilities: Gardens (formal, rose); Shop (garden gifts, shop)

The site contains two gardens, the Formal Garden and the Virginia Clemens Rose Garden. With over 1,100 roses, representing over 70 varieties, it is one of the largest public rose gardens in Minnesota.

SAINT PAUL

MARJORIE MCNEELY CONSERVATORY AND COMO ORDWAY JAPANESE GARDEN (AHS RAP)

Como Park, 1325 Aida Place (intersection of Estabrook and Lexington), Saint Paul, MN 55103
Tel: (612) 487-8200; Fax: (612) 489-8960
Internet Address: http://www.comozooconservatory.org
Admission: Fee: adult $1.00, child (<6) free, child (6-12) $0.50, senior $0.50
Attendance: 407,000
Established: 1915
Membership: Y
Wheelchair Accessible: Y
Parking: On street and nearby lot
Open: Conservatory: April to September, Daily, 10am-6pm; October to March, Daily, 10am-4pm; Japan Garden: May to September, Daily, 10am-6pm
Facilities: Conservatory (Victorian-style, 1913); Gardens (Japanese); Grounds Como Park (450 acres); Shop; Special Collections (bonsai, bromeliad, fern, orchid, palm)
Activities: Sunken Garden Flower Shows Spring Flowering Bulbs (mid-March-mid-May), Roses, Geraniums & Annuals (mid-May-Sept), Chrysanthemums (Oct-Nov), Poinsettias (Dec), Azaleas & Cyclamen (Jan-early March); Guided Tours; Lectures; Permanent Exhibits; Workshops

Termed the "jewel in the crown of Como Park," the Victorian-style Conservatory houses a variety of plants, flowers and cultural activities. The central Palm Dome displays a growing collection of understory palms, as well as orchids and bromeliads. The North Wing displays plants that have a connection with humans, such as food, spice, or fibers and also connections that are spiritual, cultural or social in nature. The Fern Room is home to ferns from throughout the tropics. A new fern room, orchid house, and bonsai gallery were scheduled to open in 2005. In addition to the permanent exhibits, the Conservatory presents five floral display shows in the Sunken Garden (South Wing)

during the year. Accessed through the Conservatory, the Como Ord-
way Memorial Japanese Garden is landscaped in the Sansui mountain
and water style and features a Japanese Tea House. The Conservatory
is listed on the National Register of Historic Places.

UNIVERSITY OF MINNESOTA, ST. PAUL—DEPARTMENT OF HORTICULTURAL SCIENCE DISPLAY AND TRIAL GARDEN

Gortner & Folwell Aves., Saint Paul, MN 55108
Tel: (612) 624-4242; Fax: (612) 624-4941
Internet Address: http://www.sustland.umn.edu/design/dtgarden.html
Admission: Free
Established: 1977
Parking: Limited in immediate area
Facilities: Gardens (annual, native plant, perennial, prairie, shade, sun,
sustainable, texture, turf, water, woodland); Grounds (3 acres)
Activities: Education Programs

Located at the north end of the St. Paul campus, between the major
cluster of campus buildings and the Minnesota Agricultural Experiment
Station fields, the Garden functions primarily as a learning laboratory
for horticulture and landscape architecture students. It is divided into
15 sections including sun and shade perennial gardens, annual and
perennial trial areas, a woodland garden, a prairie garden, a sustainable
garden, an All-American Selections display garden, a water garden, a
texture garden, and a turf identification area. In addition to plant displays, the site offers a variety of demonstration landscape features, such
as decks, patios, water features, fences, walls, seating, walkways, a pergola, and a kiosk.

WAYZATA

THREE RIVERS PARK DISTRICT—NOERENBERG GARDENS

2840 North Shore Drive (junction of County Roads 51 & 84),
Wayzata, MN 55391
Tel: (763) 559-6700; Fax: (763) 559-3287; TDDY: (763) 559-6719
Internet Address: http://www.threeriversparkdistrict.org
Admission: Free
Established: 1972
Wheelchair Accessible: Y
Parking: Paved parking lot on site

Open: May to October 15, Daily, 8am-sunset
Facilities: Gardens (formal); Special Collections (day lily)
Activities: Guided Tours (by reservation)

Located on the north shore of Lake Minnetonka on Crystal Bay, Noerenberg Gardens is the former estate of Frederick Noerenberg. The gardens include a wide variety of unusual annuals and perennials, an assortment of grasses, a large day lily collection, an azalea collection, and a grape arbor. The park features accessible brick pathways and an ornamental boathouse/gazebo overlooking the lake. The site is maintained by the Three Rivers Park District.

MISSOURI

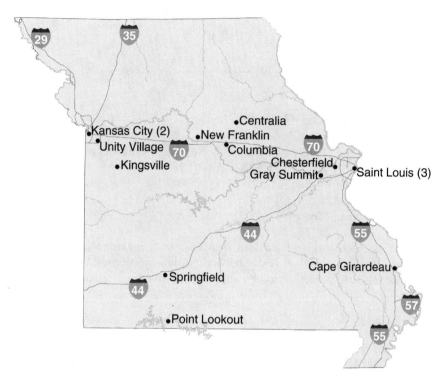

The number in parentheses following the city name indicates the number of gardens/arboreta in that municipality. If there is no number, one is understood. For example, in the text three listings would be found under Saint Louis and one listing under Chesterfield.

CAPE GIRARDEAU

CAPAHA PARK ROSE GARDEN

Corner of Perry Avenue and Parkview St., Cape Girardeau, MO 63701
Tel: (573) 335-4124; Fax: (573) 335-5126
Admission: Free
Established: 1953
Facilities: Garden (rose)

One of three rose test gardens in Missouri, the garden is a nationally accredited Rose Display Testing Garden. The garden contains 42 rose beds which are jointly tended by the city and five local garden clubs.

CENTRALIA

CENTRALIA HISTORICAL SOCIETY—CHANCE GARDENS

319 E. Sneed St., Centralia, MO 65240-1341
Tel: (573) 682-5513; Fax: (573) 682-2953
Admission: Free
Attendance: 10,000
Established: 1936
Membership: N
Wheelchair Accessible: P
Open: dawn to dusk
Facilities: Architecture (Victorian residence, 1904); Gardens (seasonal beds, rose, koi/lily pond); Grounds (½ acre, 1935 design by Maude Dawson Taylor, a Kansas City architect)

Adjacent to the Historical Society museum, Chance Gardens contains seasonal beds of mixed tulips followed by summer perennials and annuals, shrubs, rocks, water and winding paths. The Museum was originally the home of industrialist and inventor Albert Bishop Chance, who began the garden as a hobby in 1935. There is also a more recent rose garden to the east of the Museum. Both house and garden are listed on the National Register of Historic Places.

CHESTERFIELD

SOPHIA M. SACHS BUTTERFLY HOUSE AND EDUCATION CENTER

Faust Park, 15193 Olive Blvd., Chesterfield, MO 63017
Tel: (636) 530-0076; Fax: (636) 530-1516
Internet Address: http://www.butterflyhouse.org
Admission: Fee: adult $6.00, child (<4) free, child (4-12) $4.00, senior $4.50
Attendance: 175,000
Established: 1995
Membership: Y
Wheelchair Accessible: Y
Parking: Free on site, 250 spaces
Open: day after Labor Day to day before Memorial Day, Tuesday to Sunday, 9am-4pm.
Memorial Day to Labor Day, Daily, 9am-5pm; Closed: New Year's Day, Thanksgiving Day, Christmas Day
Facilities: Conservatory (8,000 square feet); Garden (native butterfly); Shop Madame Butterfly Gift Shop; Visitor Center
Activities: Education Programs; Temporary Exhibitions

The heart of the Butterfly House is its tropical conservatory housing more than a thousand tropical butterflies representing as many as 60 butterfly species and 150 tropical plant species. Outside, the Native Habitat is a "backyard" demonstration garden displaying plants that were carefully selected to provide habitat for the animals in Faust Park and to serve as host plants for caterpillars and nectar sources for butterflies. The Butterfly House is a division of the Missouri Botanical Garden (see separate listing under St. Louis).

COLUMBIA

UNIVERSITY OF MISSOURI—BOTANIC GARDEN (AHS RAP)

University Campus, Columbia, MO 65211
Tel: (573) 882-4240; Fax: (573) 884-3032

Admission: Voluntary contribution
Membership: Y
Wheelchair Accessible: P
Parking: Metered and garage parking
Open: Daily, sunrise-sunset
Best Time(s) of Year to Visit: Spring to Fall
Facilities: Gardens (perennial, rose, annual, bulb, day lily, hydrangea, and butterfly gardens; ornamental trees and shrubs); Museums (art and archeology, anthropology)

The University of Missouri Botanic Garden consists of the MU Columbia campus containing 650 varieties of plants and more than 6,000 landscape trees. The University is an accredited member of the American Association of Botanical Gardens and Arboreta and received the 2000 National Grand Award by the Professional Grounds Management Society and *Landscape Management Magazine* in the college and university category.

GRAY SUMMIT

SHAW NATURE RESERVE

Highway 100 and Interstate 44 (Exit 253), Gray Summit, MO 63039-0038
Tel: (636) 451-3512
Internet Address: http://www.mobot.org/MOBOT/naturereserve
Admission: Fee: adult $3.00, child (<13) free, senior $2.00
Attendance: 55,000
Established: 1925
Membership: Y
Wheelchair Accessible: P
Parking: Several lots on site
Open: Daily, 7am-½ hour after sunset; Closed: 1st weekend in December
Facilities: Architecture Joseph H. Bascom House (brick residence, 1879; exhibits); Gardens Whitmire Wildflower Garden (5 acres); Grounds Pinetum (55 acres), Prairie (150 acres), Total (2,500 acres), Wetland (20 acres); Trails (14 miles); Visitor Center (Mon-Fri, 8am-4:30pm; Sat-Sun, 9am-5pm)
Activities: Education Programs

Shaw Nature Reserve, an extension of the Missouri Botanic Garden, includes a full array of natural Ozark Border habitats (bottom land forest, upland oak-hickory forest, bluffs, glades, tall grass prairie, savanna, and marsh wetlands) and managed plant collections (The Pinetum, and the Whitmire Wildflower Garden). Near the entrance to the Reserve, the Pinetum displays an extensive collection of native and exotic conifers set around a three-acre lake in a landscape reminiscent of 19th-century English design. Included in the collection are Norway spruce, bald cypress and white pine with accent plantings of dogwood, redbud, and magnolia. In the spring, thousands of daffodils grace the meadows. The Whitmire Wildflower Garden contains hundreds of Missouri-native and other wildflower species grouped by natural habitat. The collection includes plant species of limestone glade, pine savanna, prairie, meadow, woodland and wetland communities. There is also a showy display of wildflowers suited for home landscaping. Missouri Botanic Garden's main facility is listed under St. Louis.

KANSAS CITY

CITY OF KANSAS CITY—LAURA CONYERS SMITH MUNICIPAL ROSE GARDEN

Jacob L. Loose Memorial Park, 52nd St. & Pennsylvania,
Kansas City, MO 64112
Tel: (816) 784-5300; Fax: (816) 513-7719
Internet Address:
http://www.kcmo.org/parks.nsf/web/loose?opendocument
Established: 1939
Parking: Free on site
Open: Daily, 7:30-4pm
Best Time(s) of Year to Visit: June to September
Facilities: Gardens (rose, fragrance, hostas); Grounds Loose Park
(74 acres), Rose Garden (2½ acres, 1937 design by landscape architect
Sidney J. Hare); Picnic Area
Activities: Guided Tours

An accredited All-America Rose Selections display garden, the Laura Conyers Smith Rose Garden contains over 4,000 roses (including miniatures, hybrid teas, grandifloras, florabundas, and heritage roses) representing nearly 150 varieties. Planted in a circular plan centering on a fountain, the roses are complemented by limestone and wooden pergolas, statuary, walkways and verandas. In addition to the Municipal Rose Garden, Loose Park features an All-American Selections display garden, scenic walking paths, a wading pool, a lily pond, a small lake, and a duck island. The Rose Garden is maintained by the Kansas City Rose Society in partnership with the Kansas City, Missouri Parks and Recreation Department.

LINDA HALL LIBRARY OF SCIENCE ENGINEERING AND TECHNOLOGY—ARBORETUM

5109 Cherry St., Kansas City, MO 64110-2498
Tel: (816) 363-4600; Fax: (816) 926-8790
Internet Address: http://www.lhl.lib.mo.us/
Admission: Free
Established: 1949
Open: Monday, 9am-8:30pm; Tuesday to Friday, 9am-5pm; Saturday, 10am-4pm
Best Time(s) of Year to Visit: late April to May (tree peonies); May to June, roses
Facilities: Arboretum; Architecture (Art Deco library); Gardens (butterfly, dwarf conifer, herb, wildflower); Grounds (14 acres); Special Collections (iris, tree peonies)
Activities: Guided Tours (by prior arrangement)

Situated on the University of Missouri, Kansas City Volker Campus, but not affiliated with the University, Linda Hall Library is an independent research library specializing in science and technology. The Library grounds contain an arboretum with over 450 trees representing 58 genera and 165 species, one of the largest collections of tree peonies in the Midwest, antique shrub roses, and an area of natural prairie featuring over 50 species of indigenous perennials. One section of the grounds is planted with zinnias, marigolds, shasta daisies, Mexican sunflowers, parsley and fennel in order to attract butterflies by providing nectar and habitat. A guide to the arboretum and gardens may be purchased ($5.00) inside the library at the front desk.

KINGSVILLE

POWELL GARDENS (AHS RAP)

1609 N.W. U.S. Highway 50, Kingsville, MO 64061
Tel: (816) 697-2600; Fax: (816) 697-3576
Internet Address: http://www.powellgardens.org/
Admission: Fee (April-October): adult $7.00, child (5-12) $3.00, senior $6.00; Fee (November-March): adult $6.00, child (5-12) $2.00, senior $5.00
Established: 1988
Parking: Fee (November-March): $4.50/$1.50/$3.50
Open: April to October, Daily, 9am-6pm; November to March, Daily, 9am-5pm; Closed: New Year's Day, Thanksgiving Day, Christmas Day

Facilities: Conservatory; Food Services Café Thyme (Wed-Sun, 11am-2pm); Gardens (dogwood walk, iris, perennial, rock, seasonal display, shade, wildflower); Greenhouses (5; 15,000 square feet); Grounds (915 acres); Picnic Area; Shop: The Gifted Gardener; Visitor Education Center
Activities: Classes; Education Programs; Field Trips; Guided Tours (Apr-Oct, $4/person)

This new botanical garden surrounding a twelve-acre lake features plantings in a variety of settings. At the Visitor Center, seasonal display beds present changing exhibits. A large perennial garden (over 3 acres in size) contains approximately 1,200 cultivars of perennials, including over 350 varieties of day lilies. A large shade garden, the Rock and Waterfall Garden, includes 700 azaleas, as well as big-leaf type magnolias and other unique shrubs, including collections of clethras, enkianthus, Chinese allspice, striped-bark maples, and a trial area for big leaf (blue) hydrangeas. The Island Garden presents two acres of native and exotic water plants, including water lilies of all types, as well as native marsh and bog plants. The Meadow features native prairie grasses and wildflowers. One hundred sixty-eight iris varieties that have received the American Iris Society's Award of Merit highlight the collection on Iris Hill, which also contains over 240 other varieties, some "Old Favorites" and many new ones. In the display conservatory 150 types of orchid as well as other tropical plants may be found.

NEW FRANKLIN

UNIVERSITY OF MISSOURI—HORTICULTURE AND AGROFORESTRY RESEARCH CENTER

10 Research Center Road, New Franklin, MO 65274
Tel: (660) 848-2268; Fax: (660) 848-2144
Internet Address: http://www.aes.missouri.edu/harc/
Admission: Free
Open: Monday to Friday, 8am-5pm
Facilities: Architecture Thomas Hickman House (brick house, 1819); Gardens (display, historic); Grounds (540 acres)
Activities: Education Programs; Guided Tours (arrange in advance)

An interdisciplinary plant science center that conducts research and education programs, the center also supports University Extension programs such as field days and workshops for the general public. A self-guided driving tour and interpretive trails highlight the center's cultural features, natural resources, and research activities. Display gardens feature both perennial and annual flowering plants especially suited to Missouri's growing conditions. The Thomas Hickman House, among the oldest standing brick houses west of the Mississippi River, houses permanent educational displays of local archeological, geological, and historical interest. Adjacent period gardens reproduce an early nineteenth-century landscape. Additionally, a small-scale reconstruction of Missouri's first botanical garden built by John Hardeman in Old Franklin in 1820 ties the center to its local cultural heritage. Hardeman, a horticulturist, collected plants from around the world for his 10-acre gardens, which were destroyed by floodwaters in 1826.

POINT LOOKOUT

COLLEGE OF THE OZARKS—GREENHOUSES AND ARBORETUM

Highway V & Highway 65 (2 miles south of Branson, MO), Point Lookout, MO 65726
Tel: (417) 334-6411
Internet Address: http://www.CofO.edu
Admission: Free
Attendance: 30,000
Established: 1906
Membership: N
Wheelchair Accessible: P
Parking: Free on campus
Open: Monday to Friday, 8am-5pm; Saturday, 8am-4pm
Best Time(s) of Year to Visit: April to October
Facilities: Arboretum; Greenhouses (5, 2,000 square feet each); Grounds Arboretum (7 acres)
Activities: Plant Sales (greenhouse)

The college was founded in 1906 as an agricultural school to give worthy students an education, especially those without sufficient means. While maintaining its agricultural heritage, in 1965 it expanded to a full four-year college. The Greenhouses, located east of Edwards Mill, are home to the Clint McDade orchid collection. Mr. McDade, one of the school's first students, donated the nucleus of the collection, which today numbers more than 7,000 plants.

SAINT LOUIS

CITY OF ST. LOUIS—THE JEWEL BOX CONSERVATORY AND GARDENS

Forest Park, Wells & McKinley Drives (east of the St. Louis Zoo), Saint Louis, MO 63122
Tel: (314) 531-0080; Fax: (314) 535-3901
Internet Address: http://stlouis.missouri.org/citygov/parks/jewelbox/
Admission: Fee-$1.00; Free: Mon & Tues, 9am-noon
Established: 1936
Wheelchair Accessible: Y
Parking: On street
Open: Daily, 9am-5pm

City of St. Louis—The Jewel Box Conservatory and Gardens, Saint Louis, MO. Thomas J. Sieve photograph.

Facilities: Conservatory (Art Deco-style, 1936 design by William Becker); Gardens; Grounds Conservatory (17 acres), Forest Park (1,371 acres)
Activities: Flower Shows (Spring, Easter, Mother's Day, Summer, Fall Chrysanthemum, Christmas)

A striking Art Deco-style conservatory listed in the National Register of Historic Places, The Jewel Box, houses tropical trees, foliage plants, flowers, water falls and fountains, as well as presenting six seasonal floral displays exhibits throughout the year. It is surrounded by rose gardens, lily ponds, statuary, and monuments. Located in the city's largest park, site of the 1904 World's Fair, the Jewel Box is operated by the City's Department of Parks, Recreation and Forestry.

CITY OF ST. LOUIS—TOWER GROVE PARK

Bounded by Magnolia Ave, Grand Ave., Arsenal St. & Kingshighway, Saint Louis, MO 63116-1901
Tel: (314) 771-2679
Internet Address: http://stlouis.missouri.org/parks/tower-grove
Admission: Free
Established: 1872
Facilities: Conservatory Piper Palm House (1878); Food Services Palm House Café Madeleine (Mar-Nov, 10am-3pm); Grounds (289 acres); Picnic Area

Activities: Concerts Music Pavilion; Guided Tours; Lectures Series; Performances

Henry Shaw, the founder of the Missouri Botanical Gardens, gave this pleasure park to the City of St. Louis in 1868. Designated a National Historic Landmark, Tower Grove is a 19th-century Victorian walking park featuring fanciful pavilions, palm house, lily ponds, romantic ruins, and sculpture interspersed among lawns, flowers, and over 8,000 trees and shrubs.

MISSOURI BOTANICAL GARDEN (SHAW'S GARDEN) (AHS RAP)

4344 Shaw Blvd., Saint Louis, MO 63110
Tel: (314) 577-9400; Fax: (314) 577-9595
Internet Address: http://www.mobot.org
Admission: Fee: adult $7.00, child (<13) free, senior $5.00; Fee (St. Louis residents): Adult $3, Senior $1.50
Attendance: 857,789
Established: 1859
Membership: Y
Wheelchair Accessible: Y
Parking: Free on site
Open: Grounds: Memorial Day to Labor Day, Monday to Tuesday, 9am-8pm; Wednesday, 7am-8pm; Thursday to Friday, 9am-5pm; Saturday, 7am-5pm; Sunday, 9am-5pm; Grounds: Labor Day to Memorial Day, Monday to Tuesday, 9am-5pm; Wednesday, 7am-5pm; Thursday to Friday, 9am-5pm; Saturday, 7am-5pm; Sunday, 9am-5pm; Closed: Christmas Day
Best Time(s) of Year to Visit: April to October (peak bloom & color)
Facilities: Auditorium (400 seats); Classrooms; Conservatory Climatron (½ acre, geodesic dome), Linnean House (1882), Shoenberg Temperate House; Food Services Garden Café; Gallery Spink Gallery; Gardens (over 30; aquatic, azalea, boxwood, bulb, Chinese, dwarf conifer, day lily, residential display, English woodland, German, herb, hosta, iris, Japanese, magnolia, maze, perennial, rock, rose, scented, dry streambed, Victorian); Grounds (79 acres); Herbarium Monsanto Center; Library Monsanto Center (118,000 volumes; Mon-Fri, 8:30am-5:30pm); Shop Garden Gate Shop (plants, books, garden accessories), Little Shop Around the Corner (resale, antiques); Special Collections (azalea, bulbs, day lilies, hosta, iris, tropicals); Visitor Center Ridgway Center
Activities: Education Programs (adults, college students and children); Flower Shows; Guided Tours (daily, 1pm); Lectures; Plant Sales (by plant societies)

Founded by English immigrant Henry Shaw in 1859, the Missouri Botanical Garden, a National Historic Landmark, is one of the oldest botanical gardens in the United States. The Gardens are home to three conservatories, over 30 different gardens, a world famous Botanical Research Center, an active Education Division, and much more. The main visitors' center and entrance, the Ridgway Center, contains the Garden Gate Shop, the Garden Cafe, educational facilities, art exhibits, and the Spink Gallery, which features a display of ceramics. The stunning Climatron Conservatory has become a symbol of the Missouri Botanical Garden. Inspired by the designs of R. Buckminster Fuller. its geodesic dome shelters some 1,200 species of plants, including orchids, epiphytes, bananas, cacao, and coffee trees in a natural, tropical setting. Complementing the Climatron, the Shoenberg Temperate House displays plants unique to the temperate regions of the world: Africa, Australia, Japan, Korea, China, South America, the Mediterranean Sea basin, coastal California, and the southeastern United States. A third conservatory, the Linnean House (the oldest continuously operating greenhouse conservatory in the United States) contains the Garden's camellia collection. The William T. Kemper Center for Home Gardening features twenty-three distinct residential-scale gardens contained in a spectacularly engineered eight-acre design and an 8,000 square-foot pavilion which contains displays, a reference library, a demonstration potting room, a greenhouse, the Plant Doctor clinic, a working beehive, and a demonstration kitchen. Its Japanese garden, Seiwa-en, is the largest stroll garden in the Western Hemisphere and was ranked in 2000 by the *Journal of Japanese Gardening* as one of the ten highest-quality Japanese gardens outside of Japan. Other exterior highlights include a Victorian area, recreating features built by Shaw in the original Garden and in the park of his country residence, Tower Grove; the boxwood garden, a formal, oval boxwood parterre accented with colorful flowers and ground cover; an informal English-style mature woodland garden; the Grigg Nanjing Friendship Garden, a Chinese garden featuring an authentic pavilion, bridge, and moon gate, accented by traditional stones, carvings, water features, and plantings; two rose gardens, an All-American Selections test garden and a formal, old-fashioned splendor with fences and arbors; an American Hemerocallis Society display garden; an iris garden; a hosta garden; a scented garden; an herb garden; an azalea-rhododendron garden; and a magnolia walk. The Shaw Nature Reserve (see separate listing) of the Missouri Botanical Garden, a second facility encompassing 2,500 acres of natural Ozark landscape and managed plant collections, is located in Gray Summit, approximately 35 miles west of St. Louis. The Sophia M. Sachs Butterfly House and Education Center (see separate listing), a division of the Missouri Botanical Garden in Chesterfield, features an 8,000 square-foot glass conservatory where visitors mingle with more than 60 species of butterflies in free flight. The Garden's Gateway Center for Resource Efficiency, located in midtown St. Louis at the EarthWays Home in Grand Center, helps promote conservation and sustainable living through tours and education programs.

SPRINGFIELD

CITY OF SPRINGFIELD—JAPANESE STROLL GARDEN

Nathaniel Greene Park, 2400 S. Scenic, Springfield, MO 65807
Tel: (417) 864-1049; Fax: (417) 837-5811
Internet Address: http://www.ci.springfield.mo.us/community/japanese_stroll_garden.html
Admission: Fee: adult $3.00, child (<13) free
Established: 1985
Parking: Free on site
Open: April to October, Thursday to Monday, 9am-7:30pm
Facilities: Garden (Japanese); Grounds Garden (7½ acres), Greene Park (59 acres); Picnic Area
Activities: Events Japanese Fall Festival (1st weekend after Labor Day)

A traditional Japanese landscape design, the stroll garden offers flowering trees and shrubs surrounding a pond and enhanced by architectural features including stepping stones, lanterns, moon bridge, and a teahouse. The Garden has been developed by the Parks Department with assistance from Springfield's Japanese Sister City of Isesaki, Japan, and the Botanical Society of Southwest Missouri.

UNITY VILLAGE

UNITY ROSE GARDEN

1901 N.W. Blue Pkwy. (Route 350 & Colburn Road), Unity Village, MO 64065-0001
Tel: (816) 524-3550
Established: 1951
Best Time(s) of Year to Visit: May to June (rose garden)
Facilities: Gardens (meditation, rose); Grounds (1,400 acres)

Home of a Christian religious movement, Unity Village compound is landscaped with Mediterranean-style grounds containing fountains, a rose garden (800 rose bushes of 40 varieties), two meditation gardens, and woodlands with walking paths and ponds that surround a natural preserve and nature prairie.

MONTANA

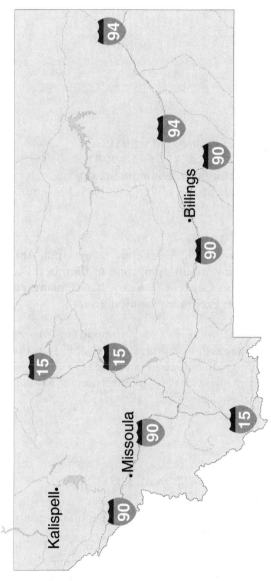

The number in parentheses following the city name indicates the number of gardens/arboreta in that municipality. If there is no number, one is understood. For example, in the text one listing would be found under Missoula.

BILLINGS

ZOO MONTANA

2100 S. Shiloh Road, Billings, MT 59106
Tel: (406) 652-8100; Fax: (406) 652-9281
Internet Address: http://www.zoomontana.org
Admission: Fee: adult $6.00, child (3-15) $3.00, senior $4.00
Established: 1994
Membership: Y
Parking: Parking for 300 cars
Open: November to March, Weekends, 10am-3pm; April to May,
Wednesday to Sunday, 10am-4pm; June to October, Daily, 10am-4pm.
Facilities: Arboretum; Gardens (sensory, native plant, xeriscape)
Activities: Education Programs; Guided Tours

A zoological and botanical park specializing in northern latitude
species, Zoo Montana's horticultural displays fall into three categories: a
sensory garden, the native riparian ecosystem within and around the zoo,
and presentation of plants native to the animals' natural habitats within
and around animal enclosures.

KALISPELL

CONRAD MANSION NATIONAL HISTORIC
SITE MUSEUM—GARDEN

4th St. East, Kalispell, MT 59903
Tel: (406) 755-2166; Fax: (406) 756-2176
Internet Address: http://www.conradmansion.com
Admission: Fee: adult $8.00, child (<12) $3.00, senior $7.00
Established: 1976
Membership: Y
Wheelchair Accessible: P

Parking: Neighborhood on street
Open: May 15 to October 15, Tuesday to Sunday, 10am-5:30pm
Best Time(s) of Year to Visit: Summer
Facilities: Architecture (Arts & Crafts-style shingle residence, 1895 design by Spokane architect Kirtland Cutter); Gardens (annual, perennial); Grounds; Shop (Victoriana)
Activities: Christmas Bazaar (October); Guided Tours (groups, arrange in advance)

Listed on the National Register of Historic Places, this turn-of-the-century residence was built by Charles E. Conrad, founder of Kalispell. In 1974, his youngest daughter, Alicia Conrad Campbell, gave the site to the city of Kalispell in memory of her pioneer parents. Original family furnishings are located throughout the 26 rooms of the Norman-style interior. The home today sits on three landscaped acres, surrounded by a dry stone fence with iron gates. Six large annual flower beds and extensive ever-blooming perennial beds provide constant color during the summer season, with pruned hedges, evergreens, and spacious lawns serving as a lush background. On two weekends each year (in May and July/August), the Museum offers special tours of the private hillside garden of Louis A. Bibler, a long-time champion of the Conrad Mansion.

MISSOULA

CITY OF MISSOULA—STATE VETERAN'S MEMORIAL ROSE GARDEN

700 Brooks St. at Blaine St., Missoula, MT 59801
Tel: (406) 523-2751; Fax: (406) 523-2765
Admission: Free
Established: 1946
Facilities: Garden (rose)

The garden contains more than 2,500 rose bushes maintained as a memorial to Montanans who served in the United States military during wartime in the 20th century.

NEBRASKA

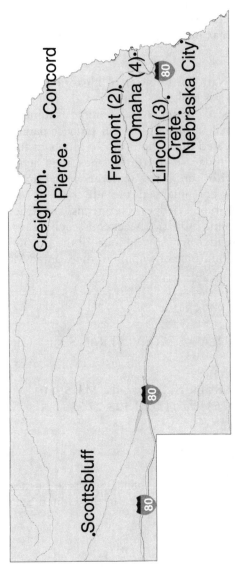

The number in parentheses following the city name indicates the number of gardens/arboreta in that municipality. If there is no number, one is understood. For example, in the text four listings would be found under Omaha and one listing under Crete.

CONCORD

UNIVERSITY OF NEBRASKA-LINCOLN—NORTHEAST ARBORETUM

UNL Haskell Agriculture Laboratory, Highway 20 (1½ miles east), Concord, NE 68726-2859
Tel: (402) 584-2261; Fax: (402) 584-2859
Admission: Free
Attendance: 80
Membership: Y
Wheelchair Accessible: N
Parking: Paved lot on site
Open: Daily, 8am-5pm
Best Time(s) of Year to Visit: June to October
Facilities: Arboretum

The goal of this young arboretum near Concord is to evaluate trees and shrubs for their adaptability to northeast Nebraska, and to be an outdoor classroom where these plants may be researched, studied and observed. The arboretum is an affiliate of the Nebraska Statewide Arboretum.

CREIGHTON

CITY OF CREIGHTON—BRUCE PARK ARBORETUM

1205 Main Street, Creighton, NE 68726
Tel: (402) 582-4866
Internet Address: http://www.arboretum.unl.edu
Admission: Free
Established: 1992
Membership: Y
Wheelchair Accessible: Y
Parking: On street
Facilities: Arboretum; Gardens (butterfly, native grass); Grounds; Picnic Area

Bruce Park offers 175 different species of labeled woody plants, including an oak collection and serves as an informal laboratory to test the adaptability of plants to northeast Nebraska. The arboretum is an affiliate site of the Nebraska Statewide Arboretum.

CRETE

DOANE COLLEGE—OSTERHOUT ARBORETUM

1014 Boswell Ave., Crete, NE 68333
Tel: (402) 826-2161
Internet Address: http://www.doane.edu
Admission: No charge/voluntary contribution
Established: 1872
Membership: N
Wheelchair Accessible: P
Parking: Free on site
Open: Campus, Daily, 24 hours
Facilities: Gardens (azalea, rose); Grounds Campus (300 acres)
Activities: Self-Guided Tour (brochure available featuring a Spring & Summer Walk)

The Doane College campus provides a setting for more than 160 species of trees and shrubs, and a wide variety of flowering plants and bushes, including Exbury azalea, star magnolia, and flowering dogwood. Most of the campus landscape design plan is reminiscent of the English Cottage style with winding paths through century-old tree groves, naturalized areas of day lilies, daffodils, peonies and manicured flower beds, including an All-America Rose Selections test garden. Thomas Doane, an acquaintance of J. Sterling Morton, founded the college in 1872, and was responsible for the earliest plantings on the young college's barren hilltop site. Doane, a horticulturist by avocation, corresponded with Morton on several occasions regarding tree species, and also worked closely with local nurseryman Ezra F. Stephens on the forestation of the campus. The Arboretum is an affiliate of the Nebraska Statewide Arboretum.

FREMONT

LOUIS E. MAY MUSEUM—GARDENS

1643 North Nye Avenue, Fremont, NE 68025-0766
Tel: (402) 721-4515
Admission: Fee: adult $2.50, child $0.50

Attendance: 5,000
Established: 1970
Wheelchair Accessible: Y
Parking: Free on site, 25 spaces and on street
Open: April, Wednesday to Saturday, 1:30pm-4:30pm; May to
August, Wednesday to Sunday, 1:30pm-4:30pm; September to
November, Wednesday to Saturday, 1:30pm-4:30pm; December,
Wednesday to Sunday, 1:30pm-4:30pm; Closed: Legal holidays
Facilities: Arboretum; Architecture (Greek revival residence, 1874);
Gardens (rose, Victorian); Grounds (2 acres)
Activities: Plant Sales (annual, May)

Administered by the Dodge County Historical Society, the May Museum is a twenty-five room mansion built in 1874 by Fremont's first mayor, Theron Nye. The historic home is surrounded by lush lawns, beautiful trees, an old-fashioned formal rose garden and a Victorian flower garden. The Museum is an affiliate of the Nebraska Statewide Arboretum.

MIDLAND LUTHERAN COLLEGE HERITAGE ARBORETUM

900 N. Clarkson, Fremont, NE 68025
Tel: (800) 642-8382; Fax: (402) 727-6223
Internet Address: http://www.mlc.edu/links/arboretum.html
Admission: No charge/donations accepted
Attendance: 2,500
Established: 1996
Membership: Y
Wheelchair Accessible: Y
Parking: Visitor parking lot near Anderson Complex
Open: Grounds, Daily, 8am-8pm; Offices, Monday to Friday,
8am-4:30pm, except holidays
Best Time(s) of Year to Visit: April to June, September to October
Facilities: Arboretum; Grounds Campus (40 acres, of which 35 are
designated the arboretum)
Activities: Guided Tours (arrange in advance); Self-Guided Tours

The arboretum, encompassing most of the main campus of Midland Lutheran College, focuses on the use in landscaping of trees and plants from Nebraska. Most of the 500 trees are labeled and located along the sidewalks of the campus, which is very flat with little or no noticeable change in grade. The majority of trees currently listed under the arboretum description were planted about 1986. A brochure listing the trees is available at the campus reception center. The Arboretum is an affiliate of the Nebraska Statewide Arboretum.

LINCOLN

CITY OF LINCOLN—ANTELOPE PARK GARDENS

Municipal Rose Garden: 27th & C Sts.
Sunken Garden: SW corner of 27th & D Sts., Lincoln, NE 68500
Tel: (402) 441-7847; Fax: (402) 441-8706
Internet Address: http://www.ci.lincoln.ne.us/city/parks
Facilities: Garden (rose); Grounds Sunken Garden (1½ acres)

Situated along Antelope Creek, Antelope Park features two gardens. Begun as a WPA project during the Great Depression, Sunken Gardens of Lincoln offers a beautifully landscaped and terraced kaleidoscope of brilliantly colored flowers and plants centered on lily ponds and fountains. The Municipal Rose Garden is an accredited All-America Rose Selections display garden.

FOLSOM CHILDREN'S ZOO AND BOTANICAL GARDENS

1222 S. 27th St. (27th and B), Lincoln, NE 68502
Tel: (402) 475-6741
Internet Address: http://www.lincolnzoo.org/
Open: April 15 to October 15, Monday to Tuesday, 10am-5pm;
Wednesday, 10am-8pm; Thursday to Sunday, 10am-5pm
Facilities: Arboretum; Education Center; Gardens (aquatic, butterfly, children's, herb, prairie); Grounds (17 acres); Special Collection (cactus/succulent)
Activities: Education Programs

Located in Antelope Park, the site includes many examples of mature shade and ornamental trees, including ginkgo, tamarix and hophornbeam. The zoo also maintains an enclosed free-flight butterfly pavilion, a cactus/succulent collection, and an aquatic plant collection, as well as many flowering shrubs, evergreens and perennials. An heirloom garden, xeriscape, and a topiary garden are also being established. The zoo is an affiliate partner site of the Nebraska Statewide Arboretum.

UNIVERSITY OF NEBRASKA-LINCOLN—BOTANICAL GARDENS AND ARBORETUM (UNLBGA)

East Campus: 35th and Holdrege Sts., City Campus: 14th and R Sts., Lincoln, NE 68588
Tel: (402) 472-2679
Internet Address: http://bga.unl.edu/about.cfm

Admission: Free
Open: Daily, dawn-dusk
Facilities: Arboretum; Gardens
Activities: Guided Tours (groups, arrange in advance); Self-Guided
Tour (brochure available); Workshops

Spread over two campuses, UNLBGA plantings appear in a wide variety
of sites and settings. In addition to the specific gardens mentioned below,
special collections of plants are incorporated throughout the landscape. On
the East Campus, the Earl G. Maxwell Arboretum offers a great diversity of
plant species with collections of trees, shrubs, vines and perennial plants,
prairie (including a display of native wildflowers and grasses at its north
end), and trial sites for new cultivars. Special collections at Maxwell Arboretum include oak, hosta (over 80 cultivars), lilac, viburnum, and vine. Also on
East Campus are the Yeutter Garden, containing a grass lawn bounded by
colorful perennials, shrub roses, and conifers; Pfister Iris Garden, Fleming
Slope featuring perennial foliage and flowers; the Old Mall, consisting of
trees, shrubs, and herbaceous designs; the Porch and Old Rose Collection, a
replica of a 19th-century house porch landscaped with plants of the period.
The traditional entrance to the University of Nebraska-Lincoln City Campus is through the elegant arches of the Garden Gates. The Gates frame
Love Garden, an expanse of lawn bordered by perennial flower beds and
backed by Love Library. Originally, a formal rose garden, with clipped eu-
onymus and juniper hedges and beds of red roses surrounding a large lawn,
it was renovated in 1981. The new design produced greater interest by using
diverse plants to provide more seasonal change and contrast in size and textures; the perennial beds soften the edges of the paired walks leading to the
library, while dwarf yew hedges recall the formality of the old garden.
Among the other ULBGA sites to be found on the City Campus are Cather
Garden, paying tribute in an urban setting to the prairie landscape described
by Willa Cather with a collection of native grasses, wildflowers, shrubs and
trees; Sheldon Garden, a formal display area presenting contemporary
sculpture against a backdrop of mature trees, water gardens and native plant
displays; Donaldson Garden, featuring exotic trees, conifers, and oaks; and
Andrews and Burnett Gardens, offering spring bulbs and summer blooms.
UNLBGA is a member of the Nebraska Statewide Arboretum and is administered by the Department of Landscape Services.

NEBRASKA CITY

ARBOR LODGE STATE HISTORICAL PARK

2300 2nd Avenue, Nebraska City, NE 68410
Tel: (402) 873-3000

Internet Address: http://www.nebraskacity.com
Admission: Free (fee charged for house tour)
Open: April 15 to October 24
Facilities: Arboretum; Garden (formal Italian); Grounds (65 acres)

Once home to J. Sterling Morton, the father of Arbor Day, the landscape surrounding this stately mansion includes some of original plantings of white pine, chestnuts and catalpa. Joy Morton, oldest of the Mortons' four sons and founder of the Morton Salt Company completed the 52-room residence and the Italian terraced garden in 1903. A one-half mile tree trail winds through an arboretum which encompasses the entire park and features over 250 varieties of trees and shrubs. Efforts are underway to restore this historic landscape to its original design. The site is an affiliate of the Nebraska Statewide Arboretum.

OMAHA

CITY OF OMAHA—MEMORIAL PARK ROSE GARDEN

6005 Underwood Ave. (58th St. and Underwood Ave.),
Omaha, NE 68132
Tel: (402) 444-5900
Facilities: Garden (rose); Grounds Park (67 acres)

An accredited All-American Rose Selections display garden, the Memorial Park Rose Garden is dedicated to veterans who served in World War II. The formal plantings consist of over 1,000 rose bushes.

GIRLS AND BOYS TOWN ROSE GARDEN

138th St, and W. Dodge Road, Omaha, NE 68010
Tel: (402) 498-1140
Internet Address: http://www.ffbh.boystown.org/home.htm
Facilities: Gardens (rose)

The Girls and Boys Town Rose Garden dates back to the 1930s. Father Flanagan encouraged the establishment of gardens on the campus as a way of having the Girls and Boys Town students engage in a positive outdoor activity. Today, as in the past, the hundreds of rose bushes are tended by students interested in horticulture. The garden consists of 48 beds containing over 1,500 roses of various colors. The garden is an All-American Rose Selection Committee test site.

JOSLYN CASTLE INSTITUTE FOR SUSTAINABLE COMMUNITIES—GROUNDS

3902 Davenport, Omaha, NE 68131
Tel: (402) 595-2199; Fax: (402) 584-1007
Internet Address: http://www.unl.edu/JCI
Admission: Fee: adult $6.00, child $3.00
Attendance: 10,000
Membership: Y
Wheelchair Accessible: Y
Parking: Parking lot on east side of estate
Open: 1st & 3rd Sundays in month, 1pm-4pm; and by appointment
Facilities: Architecture (Scottish Baronial-style residence, 1902 design by Omaha architect John A. MacDonald); Conservatory (documented design by Jens Jensen); Grounds (5½ acres; 2 award-winning trees: English Oak & Ginko)
Activities: Guided Tours (by appointment)

Originally a private residence, since 1996 the four story, 35-room residence and park-like grounds have served as the headquarters of the Institute for Sustainable Communities, a unit of the University of Nebraska College of Architecture. The Castle is an excellent example of the Scottish Baronial architectural style, a revival or picturesque style popular in the late 19th and early 20th centuries in Britain and the Commonwealth, but rarely employed in the United States. The interior retains all of its original intergrity. Of great significance is the attached conservatory; designed by landscape architect Jens Jensen, it is one of a very few surviving examples of his residential work. A portion of the grounds, which are currently undergoing a complete restoration, may also have been designed by Jensen. The site is listed on the National Register of Historic Places and is the first historic landmark site of the Nebraska Statewide Arboretum.

LAURITZEN GARDENS: OMAHA'S BOTANICAL CENTER (OMAHA BOTANICAL GARDEN)

100 Bancroft St. (at 1st St.) (just north of the Henry Doorly Zoo), Omaha, NE 68108
Tel: (402) 346-4002; Fax: (402) 345-7310
Internet Address: http://www.omahabotanicalgardens.org
Admission: Fee: adult $6.00, child (<6) free, child (6-12) $3.00
Attendance: 100,000
Established: 1982
Membership: Y

Wheelchair Accessible: Y
Parking: Free on site, ample, also bus parking
Open: Daily, 9am-5pm; Closed: New Year's Day, Thanksgiving Day, Christmas Day
Facilities: Arboretum/Bird Sanctuary (4 acres); Auditorium; Classrooms; Conservatory Floral Display Hall (5,000 square feet); Food Services (café; daily, 10am-2pm); Gardens (children's, herb, rose, shade, spring, Victorian, woodland); Grounds (120 acres); Library; Shop (gifts, scents, garden tools and books; daily, 9am-5pm); Visitor Center
Activities: Education Programs; Guided Tours (schedule in advance); Tram Service ($2)

Lauritzen Gardens offers many unique outdoor garden areas. The Parking Garden and the Arrival Garden feature annual and perennial flowers. The Festival Garden, with colorful annual plantings and open expanses of lawn, is the site of several annual events. The Victorian Garden, featuring perennials and architectural remnants, combines characteristics of both English and Victorian gardens. The Spring Flowering Walk signals the beginning of the season with thousands of blooming bulbs. The Song of the Lark Meadow is reminiscent of Nebraska's prairies and is filled with wildflowers. The Rose Garden, with over 2,000 roses, creates a colorful formal display, highlighted by a large armillary sphere and other architectural features. The Arboretum and Bird Sanctuary contains seven regional plant communities and demonstrates how to attract and identify Midwestern birds. The Children's Garden, offering a butterfly garden, a sunflower house, a maze and an animal garden, encourages youth to learn about nature. The Herb Garden, under a prairie-style arbor, is comprised of ten thematic planting beds. The Shade Garden contains hundreds of hosta and a garden gazebo. A woodland trail, leading to hilltop overlooks, winds through a native hardwood community. The Garden in the Glen is a calming peaceful space with a stream, pools, and small waterfalls. The Floral Display Hall in the Visitors Center features changing exhibits, including a spring flower show, a fall chrysanthemum show, and a holiday poinsettia show.

PIERCE

GILMAN PARK ARBORETUM

Mill Street (1 block north of Main Street), Pierce, NE 68767
Tel: (402) 329-4873; Fax: (402) 329-4035
Internet Address: http://www.piercenebraska.info/arboretum
Admission: Voluntary contribution
Attendance: 3,000
Established: 1993

Membership: N
Wheelchair Accessible: Y
Parking: Large gravel parking lot
Open: Daily, all hours
Best Time(s) of Year to Visit: April to October
Facilities: Arboretum (includes "Millenium Group" of famous and historic trees); Architecture (one of two remaining rigid-connected lattice pony truss bridges in Neb.); Gardens (xeriscape, butterfly, wildflower, wetland, lake); Grounds (14 acres)
Activities: Guided Tours (for groups—with reservation)

Surrounding Bill Cox Memorial Lake, the arboretum is served by a 1.2-mile paved path. There are over 220 different species or cultivars of woody plants present, along with landscape gardens containing over 1,200 plants representing 80 varieties of perennials and grasses. A trail guide brochure containing information on over 80 plants is available on site. A project of the Pierce Tree Board, the Arboretum Committee, and the city of Pierce, the Arboretum is an affiliate of the Nebraska Statewide Arboretum.

SCOTTSBLUFF

UNIVERSITY OF NEBRASKA-LINCOLN—D. A. MURPHY PANHANDLE ARBORETUM

UNL Panhandle Research and Extension Center, 4502 Avenue I (Highway 71), Scottsbluff, NE 69361-4939
Tel: (308) 632-1230
Internet Address: http://www.panhandle.unl.edu/arboretum/arbor.htm
Parking: East and south of the University of NE Complex
Facilities: Arboretum; Grounds (40 acres); Special Collections (ground cover, iris)
Activities: Education Programs; Guided Tours

The D. A. Murphy Arboretum consists of landscaped grounds and research/demonstration plots at the University of Nebraska Panhandle Research and Extension Center and adjacent State Office Complex. Emphasis is placed on horticulture and landscape education, demonstration and beautification with a mix of both high- and low-maintenance landscapes. Collections reflect the diversity of plant material and plant communities that can thrive in western Nebraska, including both native and adapted plant materials. Exhibits include a ground cover collection, the Trails West Iris Collection with over 135 varieties of iris, a xeriscape demonstration area, and a native grass prairie. The Arboretum is an affiliate of the Nebraska Statewide Arboretum.

NEVADA

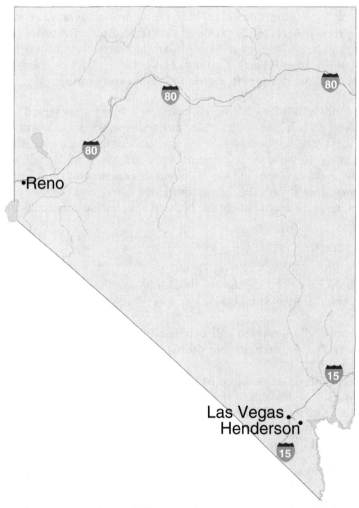

The number in parentheses following the city name indicates the number of gardens/arboreta in that municipality. If there is no number, one is understood. For example, in the text one listing would be found under Las Vegas.

HENDERSON

ETHEL M. CHOCOLATE FACTORY—
BOTANICAL CACTUS GARDEN

2 Cactus Drive, Henderson, NV 89014
Tel: (888) 627-0990; Fax: (702) 451-8379
Internet Address: http://www.ethelm.com
Admission: Free
Attendance: 750,000
Established: 1980
Membership: N
Wheelchair Accessible: Y
Parking: Free on site
Open: Daily, 8:30am-7pm
Facilities: Gardens (cactus); Grounds (3.2 acres); Shop (cactus, candy)
Activities: Self-Guided Tours (groups 10+, reserve in advance, (702) 435-2641)

Founded in 1981 by Forrest Mars, Sr., retired CEO of Mars Incorporated, this luxury chocolate manufactory also offers a botanical garden containing over 350 rare and exotic species of cacti.

LAS VEGAS

LAS VEGAS VALLEY WATER DISTRICT—
DESERT DEMONSTRATION GARDENS

3701 West Alta Drive (near Valley View Blvd.), Las Vegas, NV 89153
Tel: (702) 258-3205
Internet Address: http://www.lvvwd.com/conservation/ddg/ddg.html
Admission: Free
Established: 1982
Wheelchair Accessible: Y

Open: Daily, 8am-5pm; Closed: Legal Holidays
Facilities: Garden (xeriscape; cactus, cottage, courtyard, fruit &
vegetable, herb, native wash, oriental, rock, terraced); Grounds (2½
acres); Visitor Center
Activities: Classes; Guided Tours; Workshops

Created by the Las Vegas Valley Water District, the Gardens are dedicated to water conservation through education and demonstration of
water-efficient landscaping. The gardens feature more than 300 species of
desert-compatible vegetation in 11 themed gardens. Brochures are free
and available at the Desert Demonstration Gardens Visitor Center.
LVVWD is developing a new demonstration garden at Las Vegas Springs
Preserve.

RENO

WILBUR D. MAY ARBORETUM AND BOTANICAL GARDEN

1595 N. Sierra St., Reno, NV 89503-1716
Tel: (702) 785-4153; Fax: (702) 785-4707
Internet Address: http://www.maycenter.com/
Admission: Free
Open: Daily, sunrise-sunset
Best Time(s) of Year to Visit: Spring (flowering shrubs, roses), May to
September (annuals, perennials)
Facilities: Arboretum; Gardens (annual, English country, perennial,
songbird, wetland); Grounds (12 acres)
Activities: Guided Tours (groups, by appointment)

Wilbur D. May Arboretum and Botanical Garden's primary purpose is
to research and demonstrate the botanical possibilities of the high desert
environment. Situated in a transitional zone between the Sierra Nevada
Mountains and the Great Basin Desert at an elevation of 4,600 feet, it is
challenged by a rugged climate with daily temperature variations of 50°
or more, an average annual precipitation of 7 inches, and a growing season of less than 100 days. The arboretum contains groves of trees, wetland habitats, outdoor courtyards, and secluded gardens. Gardens include
Burke Garden, styled after an English country garden, featuring blooming
perennials shaded by several graceful elms; Honey's Garden, consisting
primarily of yellow and white flowering shrubs and roses; Dixie's Plaza
Garden, a colorful display of perennials and annuals; and Songbird Garden, attracting many native birds with its aromatic flowers, nesting sites,
nutritious seeds and colorful fruits. Self-guided tour maps are available.

Located in Rancho San Rafael Regional Park, the Wilbur D. May Center, which also includes a museum and a family discovery park, is owned and operated by the Washoe County Parks & Recreation Department. Garden Court, located in the museum's north wing, may also be of interest. This indoor tropical retreat is accented by a palm-fringed waterfall and two ponds stocked with koi and goldfish, and eight planting beds featuring exotic plants and flowers. Garden Court displays are changed quarterly with plants that reflect the change of seasons.

New Mexico

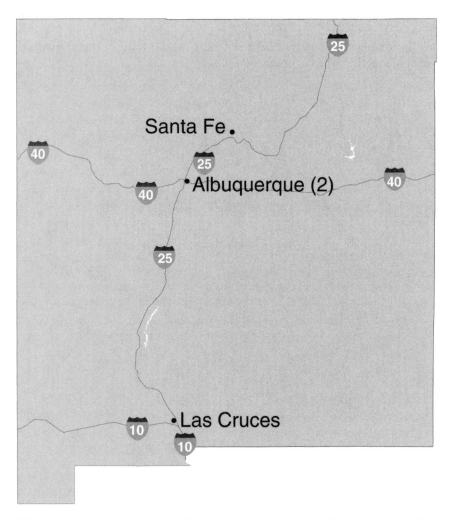

The number in parentheses following the city name indicates the number of gardens/arboreta in that municipality. If there is no number, one is understood. For example, in the text two listings would be found under Albuquerque and one under Santa Fe.

ALBUQUERQUE

ALBUQUERQUE BIOLOGICAL PARK—RIO GRANDE BOTANIC GARDEN

2601 Central Ave. NW, Albuquerque, NM 87102
Tel: (505) 764-6200;
Fax: (505) 848-7192; TDDY: (505) 764-6297
Internet Address: http://www.cabq.gov/biopark/garden/index.html
Admission: fee (gardens & aquarium): adult $7.00, child (3-12) $3.00, senior $3.00
Established: 1996
Open: 9am-5pm; June to August, Saturday to Sunday, 9am-6pm;
Closed: New Year's Day, Thanksgiving Day, Christmas Day
Facilities: Conservatories (2; 10,000 square feet); Food Services Shark Reef Café (Tues-Sun, 9am-5pm; 848-7182); Gardens (native plant, rose, Spanish/Moorish, xeriscape); Grounds (16 acres); Shop
Activities: Education Programs; Guided Tours; Lecture Series BioPark Brown Bag (1 Thurs & 1 Sat/month, lunchtime; 764-6214)

A core facility of Albuquerque Biological Park, the Rio Grande Botanic Garden includes a state-of-the-art conservatory, formal theme gardens and a demonstration garden. Showcasing plants of the southwest and other climates, the Garden contains 11,000 plant specimens comprising 1,450 species. The Conservatory houses two collections: the Desert Pavilion, a collection of 900 species featuring plants from the lower Chihuahuan and Sonoran Deserts (including unique species from Baja California in a naturalized setting); and the Mediterranean Pavilion, a collection of more than 100 species, including many exotic species from around the world. The formal gardens offer variants on the walled garden with traditional Spanish/Moorish and English landscape design in tile, ironwork, plantings and water features, as well as a ceremonial rose garden.

ALBUQUERQUE ROSE GARDEN

Wyoming Regional Library, 8205 Apache Ave., N.E. (between Inez &
Utah), Albuquerque, NM 87110
Tel: (505) 856-0595
Admission: Free
Established: 1961
Facilities: Garden (rose)

Originally established in 1961 by the Albuquerque Rose Society, the
Garden was redesigned by Campbell, Okuma and Perkins Associates
and replanted with new roses in 1993. Accredited by All-America Rose
Selections, the new garden contains 1,203 bushes representing 493
cultivars of 26 classes of roses. The general plan is for hybrid teas on
the northeast, old garden roses and floribundas on the east, hybrid ru-
gosas along the south library wall, polyanthas and miniatures in raised
beds on the northwest, and hybrid musks in shady spots along the
north wall and adjacent to the west entrance. A small collection of
newer ground cover roses occupies the western most garden strip between parking lot and street. Climbing and rambling roses stretch
along the 70 ft. long pergola on the northeast, the steel trellises that
comprise the north wall of the shade structure, and four large arches in
the east garden. While located on the grounds of the Wyoming Regional Library, all garden maintenance is provided by members of the
Albuquerque Rose Society.

LAS CRUCES

NEW MEXICO STATE UNIVERSITY—CHILE PEPPER INSTITUTE DEMONSTRATION GARDEN

West end of Campus (Fabian Garcia Science Center),
Las Cruces, NM 88003
Tel: (505) 646-3028
Internet Address: http://www.chilepepperinstitute.org
Admission: Call for fees; Free to educational groups
Attendance: 150
Established: 1992
Membership: Y
Wheelchair Accessible: N
Parking: Very limited
Open: June to October, Daily, 9am-3pm

Facilities: Garden (chiles)
Activities: Guided Tours (arrange in advance)

The Demonstration Garden includes more than 150 different varieties of chile from all of the main species of Capsicum. (The genus Capsicum includes all the peppers from the mildest bell to the hottest habanero.) The Garden is intended to show a few of the different pod shapes, sizes and colors.

SANTA FE

EL ZAGUAN—GARDEN

545 Canyon Road, Santa Fe, NM 87504-2535
Tel: (505) 983-2567
Admission: Free
Open: Garden, Monday to Saturday, 9am-5pm; Office & Exhibit Area, Monday to Friday, 9am-noon & 1:30pm-5pm
Facilities: Architecture (Spanish pueblo-style/territorial-style residence, 1850/1875; restoration directed by Kate M. Chapman); Gardens (Historic, sensory)
Activities: Guided Tours Sensory Garden Tour (Thurs, 1pm, reservations required)

Long regarded as one of New Mexico's showplaces, El Zaguan (The Passageway), was originally the home of James L. Johnson, one of the first Yankee merchants to settle permanently in Santa Fe. Today El Zaguan houses the office of the Historic Santa Fe Foundation, an exhibit area, and private apartments. Reportedly laid out in the 1880's by writer and archaeologist Adolph Bandelier, the garden is similar to the one that may have been planted originally by Mrs. Johnson.

North Dakota

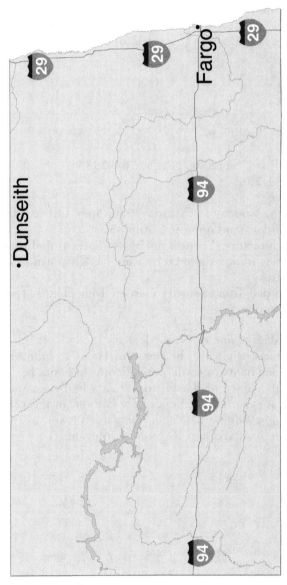

The number in parentheses following the city name indicates the number of gardens/arboreta in that municipality. If there is no number, one is understood. For example, in the text one listing would be ound under Fargo.

DUNSEITH

INTERNATIONAL PEACE GARDEN

Highway 281 (15 miles north of Dunseith straddling the U.S.-Canadian border), Dunseith, ND 58329
Tel: (701) 263-4390; Fax: (701) 263-3169
Internet Address: http://www.peacegarden.com/
Admission: Fee $10 per car
Attendance: 200,000
Established: 1932
Membership: Y
Wheelchair Accessible: Y
Parking: Paved parking lots
Open: mid-May to mid-September, Daily, 9am-7pm
Facilities: Arboretum; Food Services Garden Café; Gardens (formal, floral clock, annuals, perennials, wildflowers); Greenhouses; Grounds (2,369 acres); Interpretive Center; Shop (souvenirs)
Activities: Guided Tours (on request)

International Peace Garden, Dunseith, ND

Straddling the U.S.-Canadian border between North Dakota and Manitoba, the International Peace Garden was created as a symbol of the history of amicable relations between the two countries. The site offers colorful gardens, landscapes and wilderness areas. The formal gardens feature flower beds with annually-changing designs complemented by a floral clock, water, fountains, trees and shrubs. The Civilian Conservation Corps constructed many of the original buildings, roads, and bridges during the 1930s. The International Peace Garden is an Affiliated Area of the National Park Service—a designation given to very few non-government parks.

FARGO

NORTH DAKOTA STATE UNIVERSITY—TRIAL GARDENS

1300 18th St. North, Fargo, ND 58105
Tel: (701) 231-7971; Fax: (701) 231-8474
Internet Address: http://www.ag.ndsu.nodak.edu/plantsci/
Admission: Free
Attendance: 300
Membership: N
Wheelchair Accessible: P
Parking: Limited parking
Best Time(s) of Year to Visit: Summer
Facilities: Gardens (flower, day lily, perennials, iris, turf, ornamental grasses)
Activities: Guided Tours (on request)

Located on the western part of the NDSU campus, the trial garden at NDSU is an official All-America Selections display garden and is open to the public throughout the growing season. Also on display are over 300 perennials that are evaluated over the season for bloom, vigor, winter hardiness, and general overall quality. The day lily bed, containing over 1,000 day lilies, is designated as an official American Hemerocallis Society display garden. The majority of the day lilies are historic (pre-1970). The gardens are being moved to a new location; the move was to be completed by 2005.

OKLAHOMA

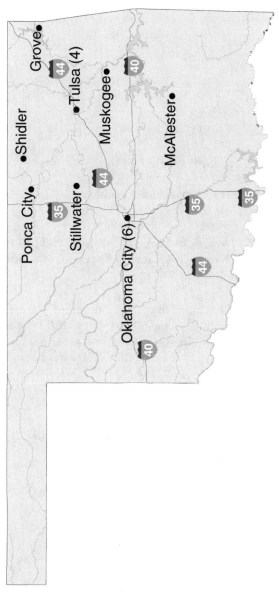

The number in parentheses following the city name indicates the number of gardens/arboreta in that municipality. If there is no number, one is understood. For example, in the text six listings would be found under Oklahoma City and one under Stillwater.

GROVE

LENDONWOOD GARDENS

1310 West 13th St., Grove, OK 74344
Tel: (918) 786-2938
Internet Address: http://www.lendonwood.org
Admission: Fee: adult $5.00, child (<13) free
Open: Daily, dawn-dusk
Facilities: Garden (American backyard, display, English terrace, Japanese, oriental); Grounds (3 acres); Special Collections (azalea, false cypress, rhododendron)

The gardens contain more than 1,400 different plants, including over 500 rhododendrons, 500 varieties of day lilies, 120 bonsai trees, 75 varieties of Japanese maples, 70 varieties of hostas, and 25 varieties of dogwood. Lendonwood is an affiliate of the Oklahoma Botanical Garden and Arboretum.

MCALESTER

ARDENEUM OF OKLAHOMA

501 North 5th St. (next to Puterbaugh House), McAlester, OK 74501
Tel: (918) 423-8555
Admission: Free
Membership: N
Facilities: Gardens (butterfly)
Activities: Guided Tours (by appointment)

Located just north of downtown, the site is the former Garrard estate. Combining the qualities of an arboretum, garden, and museum, the Ardeneum of Oklahoma offers landscaped gardens set in a former rock quarry and historical artifacts.

MUSKOGEE

CITY OF MUSKOGEE—HONOR HEIGHTS PARK

Honor Heights Drive, Muskogee, OK 74401
Tel: (918) 684-6302; Fax: (918) 684-6211
Internet Address: http://www.muskogeeparks.com
Admission: Free
Attendance: 1,000,000
Established: 1909
Membership: N
Wheelchair Accessible: P
Parking: Four parking lots; numerous pull-offs
Open: Daily, dawn to dusk
Best Time(s) of Year to Visit: April (azaleas), December (Garden of Lights)
Facilities: Amphitheater; Arboretum C. Clay Harrell Arboretum
(1992); Gardens (azalea, rose); Grounds gardens (40 acres; seven
lakes; waterfall), park (122 acres); Special Collections (dogwood,
native tree, rose); Trail Stem Beach (1 mile)
Activities: Festival Azalea Festival (April), Garden of Lights (1.2
million lights; Thanksgiving-New Year's Day, opens 5:30pm)

Honor Heights Park boasts over 25,000 azaleas representing over 600 varieties; the J. E. Conard Rose Garden, an All-American Rose Selections certified garden containing 3,500 bushes; the C. Clay Harrell Arboretum, a collection of over 300 commonly used landscape trees suitable for Oklahoma; a synoptic dogwood collection with 60 varieties; and the Oklahoma Grove, displaying 139 of 162 native trees. Much of the landscaping was done by Englishman George Palmer, the Park's first superintendent according to a design by landscape architect Myron West of Chicago in 1919. Practically all of the present azalea beds and the rose garden were planted and manicured in the 1950s under the direction of Arthur Johnson, the second park superintendent. The Park is also home to the Five Civilized Tribes Museum containing antiquities and artwork of the Five Civilized Tribes. Honor Heights is an affiliate of the Oklahoma Botanical Garden and Arboretum and is one of two gardens in Oklahoma recognized by the American Society of Landscape Architects.

OKLAHOMA CITY

CITY OF OKLAHOMA CITY—WILL ROGERS PARK AND HORTICULTURAL GARDEN

3500 NW 36th Street, Oklahoma City, OK 73112
Tel: (405) 946-2739; Fax: (405) 951-0142
Internet Address: http://www.okc.gov
Admission: Free
Attendance: 25,000
Wheelchair Accessible: P
Parking: On site, 2 large paved lots
Open: Gardens, Daily, 7am-4pm; Exhibition Center, Monday to Friday,
8:30am-4:30pm
Best Time(s) of Year to Visit: April to October
Facilities: Amphitheater; Arboretum (15 acres, 3-4,000 trees);
Conservatory Ed Lycan Conservatory (ca. 1924, Lord & Burnham);
Garden (canna, day lily, herb, iris, rose, xeriscape); Grounds Park (130
acres), Rose Garden (2 acres)
Activities: Classes; Guided Tours; Plant Sales; Self-Guided Tours
(brochure available in the Garden Exhibition Center and Ed Lycan
Conservatory)

Will Rogers Park contains the Charles E. Sparks Rose Garden, an All-American Rose Selection garden with 3,000 roses representing 250 varieties and an American Hemerocallis Society display garden. The Ed Lycan Conservatory houses one of the largest cacti and succulent collections in the world. Originating in the 1930s, the Arboretum contains more than 600 species of trees and plants that grow throughout Oklahoma, including species prized for their timber, valued as sources of food and medicine, or treasured simply for their beauty. The Park is an affiliate of the Oklahoma Botanical Garden and Arboretum.

COLES GARDEN

1415 Northeast 63rd St. (across from National Cowboy Museum),
Oklahoma City, OK 73111
Tel: (803) 345-5576; Fax: (405) 478-4513
Internet Address: http://www.Colesgarden.com
Admission: Fee: adult $5.00, child (<11) free
Membership: Y
Wheelchair Accessible: N
Parking: Free on site

Open: Monday to Saturday, 9am-5pm; Closed: New Year's Day, Thanksgiving Day, Christmas Day.
Facilities: Gardens; Grounds (15 acres); Shop (souvenirs)
Activities: Guided Tours (20+, by appointment, no charge)

Located across the street from the National Cowboy and Western Heritage Museum, Coles Garden features monumental bronze sculptures and antiquities, including an East Indian wishing swing (circa 1900) and teak horses from Queen Victoria's Jubilee (circa 1897). The garden contains a wide variety of plants and trees, and a 75-foot-wide waterfall generated between two ponds stocked with koi.

HARN HOMESTEAD MUSEUM—GARDENS

313 Northeast 16th St., Oklahoma City, OK 73104
Tel: (405) 235-4058; Fax: (405) 235-4041
Internet Address: http://www.harnhomestead.com
Admission: Fee $5.00
Attendance: 25,000
Membership: Y
Wheelchair Accessible: Y
Open: Spring to Summer, Tuesday to Friday, 10am-4pm; Sunday, 1pm-5pm; Fall to Winter, Tuesday to Friday, 10am-4pm; Closed: August.
Facilities: Architecture (Victorian farmhouse, 1904); Gardens (historic; herb, kitchen); Grounds (9½ acres)
Activities: Guided Tours; Special Programs

The site includes the Harn Homestead, a pre-statehood farmhouse furnished by the families of the 1889er Society; a stone and cedar barn with exhibits typical of the period; the Shepherd House (1890); a one-room school (1897); and a 1900 working farm. Plantings include an herb garden surrounding the storm cellar and a family garden. The Homestead is listed on the National Register of Historic Places.

MYRIAD BOTANICAL GARDENS (CRYSTAL BRIDGE) (AHS RAP)

100 Myriad Gardens (corner of Reno & Robinson Sts.), Oklahoma City, OK 73102
Tel: (405) 297-3995; Fax: (405) 297-3620
Internet Address: http://www.myriadgardens.com
Admission: Fee (Conservatory): adult $6.00, child (<4) free, child (4-12) $3.00, student $5.00, senior $5.00; Free (Grounds)
Attendance: 100,000

Established: 1988
Membership: Y
Wheelchair Accessible: Y
Parking: Free parking
Open: Gardens, Daily, 7am-11pm; Conservatory, Monday to
Saturday, 9am-6pm; Sunday, noon-6pm; Closed: New Year's Day,
Thanksgiving Day, Christmas Day
Best Time(s) of Year to Visit: April-June to September-January
Facilities: Amphitheater; Conservatory Crystal Bridge Tropical
Conservatory (1988 design by Conklin Rossant Architects of New
York; 12,320 square feet/60 feet high); Grounds (17 acres); Shop;
Sunken Lake
Activities: Festival Festival of the Arts (Spring), Independence Day
Celebration (July 4th); Guided Tours (by appointment); Performances
Theatre at Twilight; Plant Sale (annual, Spring)

Located in downtown Oklahoma City, Myriad Botanical Gardens offers an extensive permanent collection and special exhibits. The centerpiece of the garden is the Crystal Bridge Tropical Conservatory, containing humid tropic, arid tropic, and Mediterranean habitats. The
Conservatory houses over 100 palms, as well as large orchid, palm, ginger, begonia, euphorbia and bromeliad collection. Exterior plantings, including over 300 varieties of trees, shrubs and ground covers, feature native plants and non-native plants that thrive in Oklahoma's climate.
Myriad Gardens is an affiliate of the Oklahoma Botanical Garden and Arboretum.

NATIONAL COWBOY AND WESTERN HERITAGE MUSEUM—GARDENS

1700 NE 63rd St., Oklahoma City, OK 73111-7997
Tel: (405) 478-2250
Internet Address: http://www.nationalcowboymuseum.org
Admission: Fee: adult $8.50, child (<6) free, child (6-12) $4.00,
senior $7.00
Established: 1975
Membership: Y
Wheelchair Accessible: Y
Parking: Free on site
Open: Daily, 9am-5pm; Closed: New Year's Day, Thanksgiving, Christmas
Facilities: Food Services Persimmon Hill Restaurant (11am-2:30pm;
snacks & desserts, 2:30pm-4pm), Gardens (4, water features); Grounds
(18 acres); Museum; Shop; Special Collections (desert plants)

The grounds of the National Cowboy and Western Heritage Museum offer four distinct garden areas featuring native plants, plants indigenous to the deserts of the American West, and flower beds complemented by water features, sculpture, and natural areas.

OMNIPLEX GARDENS AND GREENHOUSE

Kirkpatrick Center Museum Complex, 2100 Northeast 52nd,
Oklahoma City, OK 73111
Tel: (405) 602-6664; Fax: (405) 602-3768
Internet Address: http://www.omniplex.org/
Admission: Fee: adult $7.50, child (3-12) $6.00, senior $6.00
Attendance: 350,000
Established: 1978
Membership: Y
Wheelchair Accessible: Y
Open: Monday to Friday, 9am-5pm; Saturday, 9am-6pm; Sunday,
11am-6pm; Closed: Thanksgiving Day; Christmas Day
Facilities: Food Services LeMel's Café; Gardens (children's,
contemporary, formal, herb, Japanese, orchard, rose, terrace, tropical,
vegetable, water); Picnic Area
Activities: Education Programs

Described as an amusement park for the mind, Omniplex houses 5 museums, attractions, and more than 300 interactive exhibits. The gardens and greenhouse complex offers a variety of formal and informal gardens, demonstration gardens, and tropical and production greenhouses. The Omniplex Gardens and Greenhouse is an affiliate of the Oklahoma Botanical Garden and Arboretum.

PONCA CITY

CITY OF PONCA CITY—CANN MEMORIAL GARDEN CENTER

1500 E. Grand at 14th St. (junction of Route 77 & Grand Ave.),
Ponca City, OK 74600
Tel: (580) 767-0427; Fax: (580) 767-0471
Internet Address: http://www.poncacity.com
Admission: Free
Facilities: Gardens; Grounds (10 acres)
Activities: Festival Ponca City Herb Festival (annual);
Seminars; Workshops

The formal gardens contain several hundred varieties of annuals and perennials, herbs, and water plants complemented by a gazebo, park benches, and a large tree-shaded patio. The grounds also contain over 70 species of trees. During the week from 7:00am to 3:30pm a garden employee is present to answer any questions concerning the plant material in the garden. Elsie Cann Brown, daughter of L. A. and Mary Cann, donated the gardens to Ponca City. The Cann Memorial Gardens is an affiliate of the Oklahoma Botanical Garden and Arboretum.

SHIDLER

BIVIN GARDEN

Between Shidler and Ponca City on Route 11, Shidler, OK 74652
Tel: (918) 793-4011; Fax: (918) 793-4021
Internet Address: http://www.thebivingarden.com/
Admission: Fee $2.00
Open: May to September, Saturday to Sunday, or by appointment
Best Time(s) of Year to Visit: mid-June to mid-July
Facilities: Gardens (rock, water); Grounds (6 acres)

The garden features spacious lawns, 40 flower beds, four rock gardens, ornamental ponds, aviaries, and hundreds of trees and shrubs

STILLWATER

OKLAHOMA STATE UNIVERSITY—OKLAHOMA BOTANICAL GARDEN AND ARBORETUM (AHS RAP)

3425 West Virginia Ave. (just west of the OSU campus), Stillwater, OK 74078
Tel: (405) 744-6460; Fax: (405) 744-9709
Internet Address:
http://home.okstate.edu/Okstate/dasnr/hort/hortlahome.nsf/toc/obga
Open: Monday to Friday, 8am-5pm
Facilities: Arboretum; Gardens (annual, butterfly, display, herb, Japanese, native plant, perennial, research, rock, water); Grounds (100 acres), Nursery Research (60 acres), Oklahoma Gardening Studio Gardens (3 acres), Turf Center (37 acres)
Activities: Flower Shows Spring Garden Show (annual); Guided Tours (groups, by appointment); Workshops

The Headquarters Garden features over 1,000 species of herbaceous and woody plants. Display gardens include annuals and perennials, water garden, rock garden, miniature railroad garden, native plant garden, Japanese tea garden, and 7 to 8 yearly theme gardens. It also includes the Oklahoma Gardening studio set (produced by the Oklahoma Cooperative Extension Service), the turf and nursery research centers, and Centennial Grove (an annex of the main Arboretum). The studio gardens cover 3 acres including vegetable, herb, annual and perennial gardens, a fruit orchard, formal and water gardens, a compost demonstration site and a hobby greenhouse. (The studio gardens are closed to visitors on Tuesday for filming.) The gardens at OSU serve as the headquarters for the Oklahoma Botanical Garden and Arboretum, a statewide network of affiliated gardens and arboreta.

TULSA

CITY OF TULSA—WOODWARD PARK (AHS RAP)

21st St. South & Peoria Ave., Tulsa, OK 74114
Tel: (918) 596-7275
Internet Address: http://www.CityofTulsa.org
Admission: Free
Wheelchair Accessible: Y
Parking: On site, spaces for 300 autos
Open: Woodward Park, Daily, 6am-11pm; Tulsa Garden Center, Monday to Friday, 9am-4pm
Facilities: Arboretum; Architecture Tulsa Garden Center (Italian Renaissance-style villa, 1919-21 design by Tulsa architect Noble B. Flemming); Conservatory & Display Greenhouse (Victorian-style, 1923, Lord & Burnham); Gardens (azalea, herb, rock, rose, sunken); Grounds Arboretum (3½ acres), Woodward Park (45 acres); Shop Garden Ding-bats (garden accessories, gifts)

The Woodward Park complex encompasses several areas, including an urban forest with ponds and streams, the Municipal Rose Garden, and the Tulsa Garden Center. Plantings include the 5-acre Municipal Rose Garden, containing over 9,000 plants representing over 250 varieties; an azalea garden containing 17,000 plants; a formal English-style herb garden, featuring culinary herbs; an All-American Rose Selection Test Garden; an arboretum, displaying trees and shrubs that do well in the Tulsa area; a rock garden; a sunken garden, and a 200-plant iris display bed. Its conservatory is a Victorian-style structure housing rotating displays and permanent collections of cacti, succulents, and tropical plants found in major rain forest regions of the world. The Tulsa Garden Center, located in the Park at 2435 S. Peoria

(746-5125), is home to over 35 affiliated organizations. The Center presents a monthly lecture series, landscape classes, horticulture shows, flower shows, and plant sales. The Tulsa Garden Center and the Horticulture Section of Tulsa Parks work together to stimulate and develop interest and appreciation for horticulture and for preservation and development of the park.

GILCREASE MUSEUM

1400 Gilcrease Museum Road, Tulsa, OK 74127-2100
Tel: (918) 596-2700; Fax: (918) 596-2770
Internet Address: http://www.gilcrease.org
Admission: Suggested contribution $3.00, family $5.00
Attendance: 135,000
Established: 1949
Membership: Y
Wheelchair Accessible: Y
Parking: Free on site
Open: Tuesday to Sunday, 10am-4pm; Closed: Christmas Day
Facilities: Auditorium (220 seat); Food Services Rendezvous Restaurant (Tues-Sun, 11am-2pm); Gardens (historic theme gardens; colonial, pioneer, pre-Columbian, rock, Victorian); Grounds (460 acres), Gardens (23 acres); Library (111,000 volumes, by appointment); Reading Room; Shop (prints, reproductions jewelry, pottery)
Activities: Education Programs (adults, undergraduate students and children); Films; Gallery Talks; Guided Tours (daily, 2pm; Gardens, by appointment two weeks in advance, 596-2705); Lectures; Temporary Exhibitions

The Gilcrease collection, amassed by Tulsa oilman Thomas Gilcrease, was one of the first major collectors of Western American art. Thomas Gilcrease's home is located on the grounds, as are historic theme gardens, natural meadows and woodlands, and Stuart Park. Using the Gilcrease collections as a guide, the Horticulture Section of the City of Tulsa's Park and Recreation Department have developed five theme gardens intended to complement the museum's collection. The theme gardens include a pre-Columbian garden, featuring plants which were either cultivated or gathered by the ancient Osage for food and fiber, or ceremonial and medicinal purposes; a colonial garden, displaying plants from the colonial period, such as culinary herbs and a variety of annuals, set in a parterre design typical of the 1700s; a Victorian garden, containing permanent and seasonal plants typical of the period from 1837 to 1901; a pioneer garden, recreating a typical homestead of the mid-1800s; and a rock garden, employing native sandstone boulders and ground hugging plants. Stuart

Park, a second-growth woodland of varying terrain containing native plants and trees, may be accessed only by prior arrangement.

THE PHILBROOK MUSEUM OF ART

2727 S. Rockford Road (1 block east of Peoria Ave. at 27th Place), Tulsa, OK 74114-4104
Tel: (800) 324-7941; Fax: (918) 743-4230; TDDY: (918) 749-7941
Internet Address: http://www.philbrook.org
Admission: Fee: adult $7.50, child (<2) free, student $5.50, senior $5.50
Attendance: 120,000
Established: 1938
Membership: Y
Wheelchair Accessible: Y
Parking: Free on site
Open: Tuesday to Wednesday, 10am-5pm; Thursday, 10am-8pm; Friday to Sunday, 10am-5pm; Closed: Major holidays
Facilities: Architecture (Italianate villa, 1927 designed by Edward Buehler Delk); Auditorium (250 seats); Building (175,000 square feet); Food Services La Villa Restaurant (Tues-Sun, 11am-2pm; also Thurs, 5am-7pm); Galleries (30); Grounds (23 acres, designed by landscape architect Herbert Hare, Kansas City, MO); Library (18,000 volumes, non-circulating); Sculpture Garden; Shop (art-related books, gifts, souvenirs)
Activities: Concerts (Summer, in gardens); Education Programs (adults and children); Films (Summer, in gardens); Gallery Talks; Guided Tours (daily, 10:30am & 2pm; reserve 2 weeks in advance to schedule a tour); Lectures; Self-Guided Tours (audio guide available at visitor services); Temporary Exhibitions (3-4 major traveling shows/year); Traveling Exhibitions

The unusual combination of a historical home, art collections, and gardens, Philbrook was donated in 1938 by Waite and Genevieve Phillips as the city's first art museum. Philbrook's grounds consist of Italian-inspired formal gardens, natural woods, and sweeping lawns. The Gardens have recently undergone a $7 million renovation and enhancement project including the addition of a new south garden featuring a children's maze and a sensory garden.

TULSA ZOO AND LIVING MUSEUM

6421 East 36th St. North, Mohawk Park, Tulsa, OK 74114
Tel: (918) 669-6602; Fax: (918) 669-6260

Internet Address: http://www.tulsazoo.org/
Admission: Fee: adult $6.00, child (<3) free, child (3-11) $3.00, senior $4.00
Attendance: 525,000
Established: 1927
Membership: Y
Wheelchair Accessible: Y
Parking: Free on site, 250 spaces
Open: Daily, 9am-5pm; Closed: Christmas Day
Best Time(s) of Year to Visit: March to mid-June, September to October
Facilities: Gardens (wildlife habitat); Grounds (83 acres); Picnic Area

In addition to plantings in animal exhibits replicating geographical regions of the world, there are extensive plantings throughout the zoo for botanical interest and general public enjoyment. Owned by the City of Tulsa and part of the Tulsa Parks Department, the Tulsa Zoo is accredited by the American Association of Zoos and Aquariums and the American Association of Museums. The zoo is an affiliate garden of the Oklahoma Botanical Garden and Arboretum.

OREGON

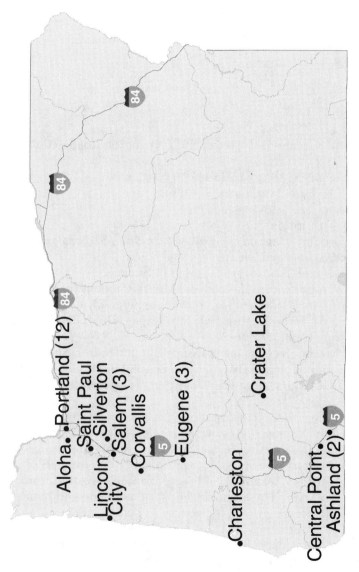

The number in parentheses following the city name indicates the number of gardens/arboreta in that municipality. If there is no number, one is understood. For example, in the text twelve listings would be found under Portland and one under Silverton.

ALOHA

JENKINS ESTATE

8005 S.W. Grabhorn Road (off SW Farmington Road), Aloha, OR 97006
Tel: (503) 642-3855; Fax: (503) 591-1028
Internet Address: http://www.thprd.org
Established: 1975
Parking: Free lot on site
Open: Grounds, Monday to Friday, 8am-5pm; Saturday to Sunday, restricted to engaged events
Best Time(s) of Year to Visit: Spring to Summer
Facilities: Architecture (farmhouse, 1880); Gardens (herb, perennial, primrose path, rhododendron, rock, rose pergola); Greenhouse; Grounds (68 acres, English-style landscape), Rhododendron Garden (1.6 acres); Trail (2.7 miles)
Activities: Concert (Summer); Events Rhododendron Show (April); Guided Tours Building (Mon-Fri, by appointment only); Plant Sales; Self-Guided Tours (Mon-Fri, 9am-4pm); Temporary Exhibitions

Located on the northwest slope of Cooper Mountain overlooking the Tualatin Valley, the estate is an elegant country farm, complete with a farmhouse, teahouse, water tower, greenhouse and gardens. The original gardens on the estate were planned by the gardener for the Prime Minister of Canada and were planted in a traditional English picturesque style. The grounds consist of wooded, wild natural growth areas in the perimeter which give way to cultivated plants, and a tamed landscape of ornamental trees, shrubs, flowers and winding gravel pathways. Gardens include a 1½-acre rhododendron garden containing more than 700 plants representing over 600 varieties, a ½-acre perennial garden, rock gardens, an herb garden, a primrose path, and a rose pergola. The herb garden includes a Braille section containing scented geraniums, lambs ears, lavender, rosemary, chives and thyme. The site is maintained by the Tualitan Hills Parks and Recreation District. Trail maps are available.

ASHLAND

CITY OF ASHLAND—LITHIA PARK

Ashland Plaza (near Oregon Shakespeare Festival theatres),
Ashland, OR 97520
Tel: (541) 488-5340; Fax: (541) 488-5314
Internet Address: http://www.mind.net/InfoStructure+LithiaPark/
lithiapk/lphp.htm
Admission: Free
Attendance: 500,000
Established: 1916
Wheelchair Accessible: P
Parking: Parking lots along Winburn Way in park
Open: Daily, 5am-11:30pm
Best Time(s) of Year to Visit: Spring, Fall
Facilities: Gardens (Japanese, rose); Grounds (93 acres; in part
designed by John McLaren, long time superintendent of Golden Gate
Park in San Francisco); Picnic Area; Trail (2 miles)
Activities: Guided Tours (May-Sep, Wed & Fri, 10am)

Situated adjacent to downtown Ashland, Lithia Park follows Ashland
Creek upstream through riparian woodlands. Flower beds, open grassy
slopes, and formal plantings blend with native trees and shrubs. It includes
a Japanese-style garden; a formal rose garden; a fine collection of conifers,
including the coast redwood, the giant sequoia, and the dawn redwood; a
collection of maples; groves of sycamore trees; two landscaped ponds; and
numerous secluded spots. The Park is listed on the National Register of
Historic Places as an outstanding example of distinctive American landscape architecture.

CITY OF ASHLAND—NORTH MOUNTAIN PARK
NATURE CENTER

620 North Mountain Ave. at Hersey St., Ashland, OR 97520
Tel: (541) 488-6606; Fax: (541) 488-6607
Internet Address: http://www.ashland.or.us
Admission: Free
Facilities: Gardens (habitat, herb, native plant); Grounds Nature
Center (15 acres), Park (40 acres); Picnic Area
Activities: Education Programs; Guided Tours (Summer, 1/month)

The Nature Center maintains three demonstration gardens. The Habitat Garden offers three areas, each designed to attract a specific class of

fauna: a butterfly garden, an amphibian/reptile garden, and a bird buffet. The Native Plant Garden features plant species native to the Rogue Valley and the surrounding mountains. The Herb Garden contains culinary and traditional medicinal herbs. The Nature Center is a division of the Ashland Parks and Recreation Department.

CENTRAL POINT

SOUTHERN OREGON RESEARCH AND EXTENSION CENTER— CLAIRE HANLEY ARBORETUM AND DEMONSTRATION GARDENS

569 Hanley Road, Central Point, OR 97502
Tel: (541) 776-7371; Fax: (541) 776-7373
Internet Address: http://extension.oregonstate.edu/sorec/mg/
Established: 1995
Open: Daily, dawn-dusk
Facilities: Arboretum; Gardens (grass, herb, kitchen, orchard, rose, shade perennial, sun perennial, xeriscape); Greenhouse; Picnic Area
Activities: Self-Guided Tours

The Demonstration Gardens, surrounding the grounds at the OSU Extension and Research buildings, were developed and are maintained with the assistance or the Jackson County Master Gardener Association. Occupying the site of the old Claire Hanley Arboretum, they consist of a variety of theme gardens, fruit orchards, cane fruits, and grape vineyards. Gardens include the Wanda Hauser Herb and Rose Garden, displaying herbs and a sampling of "Old Rose" varieties considered to be herbal; a culinary herb garden; sun and shade perennial gardens; a kitchen garden, an ornamental grass garden, a waterwise garden, and a mulch demonstration area. A variety of mature specialty trees remain from the original arboretum, which was planted in the 1960's by the Hanley sisters and supported by many local garden clubs of the day.

CHARLESTON

SHORE ACRES STATE PARK—BOTANICAL GARDENS

13030 Cape Arago Hwy. (off Route 101, 13 miles southwest of Coos Bay), Charleston, OR 97420
Tel: (800) 551-6949
Internet Address: http://www.oregonstateparks.org/park_97.php

Admission: Fee: $3/vehicle
Open: Daily, 8am-dusk
Best Time(s) of Year to Visit: late February to March (spring bulbs & daffodils), March to April (tulips), April to May (azaleas & rhododendrons), May to September (annuals & perennials), June to September (roses), August to mid-October (dahlias)
Facilities: Gardens (formal, oriental, rose); Grounds (743 acres), Formal Gardens (7 acres); Picnic Area; Shop
Activities: Festival Holiday Lights & Open House at Shore Acres (Thanksgiving-New Year's Day)

Once the estate of pioneer timber baron Louis Simpson, Shore Acres was purchased for use as a public park by the state of Oregon in 1942. The site features lushly planted gardens with plants and flowers from all over the world, including a formal garden, an oriental-style pond, and two rose gardens with 900 rose bushes, including an All-American Rose Selection display. The Friends of Shore Acres sponsor a variety of horticultural and cultural events at the garden throughout the year.

CORVALLIS

CITY OF CORVALLIS—CORVALLIS ROSE GARDEN

Avery Park, 2245 N.W. 11th St., Corvallis, OR 97330
Tel: (541) 766-6918; Fax: (541) 754-1701
Internet Address: http://www.ci.corvallis.or.us/pr/parksinfo.html
Admission: Free
Open: Daily, 6:30am-10pm
Facilities: Gardens (rhododendron, rose, wildflower); Grounds Park (75 acres)

The rose gardens contain 1,200 bushes representing 250 varieties set in an East and West garden, a Memorial Garden and an Old Rose Garden. There are also a rhododendron garden and wildflower plantings in the park.

CRATER LAKE

CRATER LAKE NATIONAL PARK—CASTLE CREST WILDFLOWER GARDEN

Steel Information Center, Route 62, Crater Lake, OR 97604
Tel: (541) 594-3000; Fax: (541) 594-3010

Internet Address: http://www.nps.gov/crla
Admission: Fee; Free: Nov-May
Attendance: 500,000
Established: 1902
Membership: N
Wheelchair Accessible: N
Parking: Lot at Steel Information Center; Rim Road: late June to mid-October, Daily
Best Time(s) of Year to Visit: August (wildflowers)
Facilities: Food Services Rim Village (cafeteria, 9am-6pm); Garden (wildflowers); Grounds Crater Lake National Park (249 square miles); Shop Rim Village (9am-6pm); Trail (½ mile); Visitor Center Steel Information Center (daily, 9am-5pm)

The nation's fifth oldest national park, Crater Lake National Park is managed by the National Park Service as a wilderness preserve. A ½-mile trail, beginning at the Steel Information Center, leads to the Castle Crest Wildflower Garden. Please note that due to snow cover much of the Park, including the Rim Drive, is not accessible from mid-October to late June.

EUGENE

CITY OF EUGENE—GEORGE E. OWEN MEMORIAL ROSE GARDEN

300 North Jefferson Ave. (north end of street, by the river),
Eugene, OR 97402
Tel: (541) 682-4800
Admission: Free
Attendance: 100,000
Established: 1950
Open: Daily, 6am-11pm.
Facilities: Garden (rose); Grounds (9 acres)

Situated along the Willamette River, the land was once the property of lumberman and philanthropist George Owen. Owen donated the land to the city of Eugene, which began planting roses there in 1950. An accredited All-American Rose Selections garden, it features over 4,500 rose bushes. The garden also contains the 1860 Black Republican Cherry Tree. Designated an Oregon heritage tree, it is believed to be the largest cherry tree in the state.

CITY OF EUGENE—HENDRICKS PARK RHODODENDRON GARDEN

2200 Summit Ave. (at Skyline Drive) (off Fairmont Blvd.),
Eugene, OR 97401
Tel: (541) 682-4800
Internet Address:
http://www.ci.eugene.or.us/pw/parks/Hendricks/index.htm
Admission: Free
Established: 1951
Open: Daily, 6am-11pm
Best Time(s) of Year to Visit: April to May (rhododendron bloom)
Facilities: Gardens (native plant, rhododendron); Grounds Garden (12 acres), Park (78 acres); Trails
Activities: Guided Tours (early April-mid May, Sunday, 1pm, main entrance, free), groups (by appointment)

Located atop the forested ridgeline of southeast Eugene, Hendricks Park overlooks the Willamette River and the City of Eugene. The primarily forested parkland contains Douglas fir trees over two hundred years old and a rich selection of forest flora, including ferns, trilliums and other wild flowers. The Rhododendron Garden, a joint effort of the American Rhododendron Society and the Eugene Parks Department begun 1951, features more than 6,000 rhododendrons and other ornamental plants, including azaleas, magnolias, and viburnum under a canopy of Oregon white oaks. In 2002 work was begun on a native plant garden. Functioning as a living bridge between the Rhododendron Garden to the north and the forested area to the south, the Garden features the native plants of the southern Willamette Valley displayed in a variety of settings, including natural, semi-natural and garden styles.

MOUNT PISGAH ARBORETUM

39401 Frank Parish Road (5 miles SE of Eugene, off Seavey Loop Road),
Eugene, OR 97405
Tel: (541) 741-4110; Fax: (541) 747-3817
Internet Address: http://www.efn.org/~mtpisgah/
Admission: No charge/donations accepted
Attendance: 177,000
Established: 1973
Membership: Y
Wheelchair Accessible: Y

Open: Daily, dawn-dusk
Facilities: Arboretum; Gardens (rhododendron, water, wildflower);
Grounds (208 acres); Library (100 volumes); Picnic Areas; Shop;
Trails (7 miles); Visitor's Center
Activities: Education Programs (adult & children); Festivals Mushroom
Festival (Oct), Spring Wildflower Festival (May); Guided Tours (747-
1504); Plant Sale (May); Workshops

Located within the greater Howard Buford Recreation Area (a Lane
County Park), the Arboretum contains diverse terrain and ecological habitats, including river meadow and oak savanna, a water garden, lower valleys and slopes, upper valleys and forested hillsides and an upper plateau.
It features a mixture of native and introduced trees, shrubs, wildflowers,
cryptogams and other species (67 families, 231 genera, and 339 taxa).

LINCOLN CITY

THE CONNIE HANSEN GARDEN

1931 NW 33rd St., Lincoln City, OR 97367
Tel: (541) 994-6338
Internet Address: http://www.conniehansengarden.com
Admission: No charge/donations accepted
Attendance: 5,000
Established: 1994
Membership: Y
Wheelchair Accessible: Y
Parking: 12 spaces, 1 handicapped and on 34th St.
Open: Grounds, Daily, 9am-5pm; Garden House: January to February,
Tues, 10am-2pm; Garden House: March to December, Tues & Sat,
10am-2pm
Best Time(s) of Year to Visit: late Spring to early Summer
Facilities: Gallery/Classroom; Grounds (1+ acres); Library; Shop (gifts)
Activities: Classes; Education Programs; Guided Tours (schedule in
advance)

Formerly the private garden of Constance P. Hansen, a respected
member of the national and regional horticultural community, the Garden is owned and operated by The Connie Hansen Garden Conservancy,
an all-volunteer, non-profit organization. A little over an acre in size the
Garden is composed of species that thrive in cool, wet coastal climates. It
contains more than one hundred rhododendrons (species and hybrids),
several species of dogwoods, magnolias, Japanese maples, numerous

spring flowering trees, viburnums, hostas, and heathers, as well as numerous species of iris, primula, and geranium.

PORTLAND

THE BERRY BOTANIC GARDEN

11505 S.W. Summerville Ave. (near Lewis & Clark College), Portland, OR 97219-8309
Tel: (503) 636-4112; Fax: (503) 636-7496
Internet Address: http://www.berrybot.org/
Admission: Fee (appointment required): adult $5.00, child (<12) free
Attendance: 3,000
Established: 1978
Membership: Y
Wheelchair Accessible: Y
Open: Garden, Daily, dawn-dusk, appointment required;
Office, 9am-4:30pm.
Best Time(s) of Year to Visit: March to May
Facilities: Architecture (traditional 1½-story frame residence, 1938 design by architect Reuben T. Sinex); Gardens (fern, native plant, rhododendron forest, rock, water); Grounds (6½ acres); Herbarium; Library (1,000 volumes); Special Collections (primula, rhododendron, alpine, native plant)
Activities: Classes; Education Programs; Guided Tours (by appointment); Plant & Seed Sales (Apr & Sept); Seed Exchanges; Symposia; Workshops

Originally the private garden of noted horticulturist Rae Selling Berry (1881-1976), the site was purchased by the Friends of the Berry Botanic Garden, a non-profit corporation, in 1978. Through her financial support of botanical expeditions, she obtained seed from many of the noted British plant explorers: Kingdon-Ward, Ludlow and Sherriff, and Joseph Rock. Few other gardens matched her collection of species rhododendrons. Perhaps no garden outside the British Isles rivaled her primula collection. Her own treks with fellow plant enthusiasts to the mountains of the American West, British Columbia, and Alaska helped her build a fine collection of alpine plants. While maintaining her collection, the Garden has grown from the treasured acquisitions of a skilled plantswoman collected for her own pleasure, to a respected botanic garden replete with education, conservation, and research programs. Major collections include rhododendrons, primulas, native plants, and alpine plants. Unusual perennials, woodland plants, specimen shrubs, and trees are displayed in a rhododendron forest, a fern garden, and a half-acre rock garden and along a native plant trail. The plantings around the residence were designed by landscape architect John Grant of Seattle, but Rae Berry arranged the placement of major areas of the garden. Self-guided tour sheets, "Pick of the Month" and Continuing the Legacy" are available at the visitors center in the main building. Please note that the garden's zoning variance only allows for visitation by appointment and does not allow signs to be posted on the main streets. Call for an appointment and directions before visiting.

BISHOP'S CLOSE—ELK ROCK GARDENS

11800 S.W. Military Lane, Portland, OR 97219-8436
Tel: (503) 636-5613; Fax: (503) 636-5616
Admission: Suggested contribution $5.00
Attendance: 3,000
Established: 1917
Membership: Y
Wheelchair Accessible: P
Parking: Free on site, 10 spaces
Open: Daily, 8am-5pm; Closed: Some holidays
Facilities: Architecture (Scottish manorhouse-style residence, 1914-16 design by D. E. Lawrence); Gardens (English-style); Grounds (6 acres, 1914 design by John Olmsted of Olmsted & Son, New York, NY)
Activities: Guided Tours Garden (by appointment, (503) 222-4114); Self-Guided Tours (brochure available)

Located on a high bluff on the western bank of the Willamette River about two miles north of Lake Oswego, Elk Rock grounds house the offices of the Bishop of the Episcopal Diocese of Oregon. Formerly the Peter Kerr estate, the property was donated by his heirs to the Episcopal Diocese of Oregon with the agreement that the gardens would be open to the public. Elk Rock Gardens are noted for their many varieties of magnolias, as well as for outstanding examples of other native and exotic plants.

CITY OF PORTLAND—CRYSTAL SPRINGS RHODODENDRON GARDEN

SE 28th & Woodstock Blvd. on 28th, Portland, OR 97202
Tel: (503) 771-8386; TDDY: (503) 823-2223
Internet Address:
http://www.portlandparks.org/Parks/CrysSpringRhodGar.htm

Admission: Fee (March-Labor Day, Thurs-Mon): adult $3.00, child
(<12) free; Free (September-March & March-Labor Day,
Tues-Wed)
Established: 1950
Membership: Y
Parking: Limited parking
Open: Daily, dawn-dusk
Best Time(s) of Year to Visit: Spring
Facilities: Grounds (7-acre woodland setting); Special Collections
(rhododendron, azalea, magnolia, ericacious plants)
Activities: Events (Early Show, 1st Sat in April; Mother's Day Weekend)

Located in the Eastmoreland neighborhood of southeast Portland,
Crystal Springs contains more than 2,500 species of hybrid rhododendrons, azaleas, magnolias and related plants. Surrounded almost entirely
by water, it is set in a grove of mature trees and features three waterfalls
and a high fountain. The original garden, on what is now called the "Island," was designed by Mrs. Ruth Hansen. The later portion of the Garden, known as the "Peninsula," was designed by Wallace K. Huntington
in 1977. The garden is jointly maintained by the Portland chapter of the
American Rhododendron Society, Portland's Master Gardener program,
the Friends of Crystal Spring Rhododendron Garden, and Portland Parks
and Recreation Staff.

CITY OF PORTLAND—HOYT ARBORETUM (AHS RAP)

Washington Park, 4000 S.W. Fairview Blvd., Portland,
OR 97221-2706
Tel: (503) 228-8733; Fax: (503) 823-4213
Internet Address:
http://www.parks.ci.portland.or.us/Parks/HoytArboretum.htm
Admission: Voluntary contribution
Attendance: 300,000
Established: 1928
Membership: Y
Wheelchair Accessible: Y
Parking: Parking at Visitors' Center
Open: Park, Daily, 6am-10pm; Visitors Center, Daily, 9am-4pm
(except Thanksgiving); Closed: New Year's Day, Christmas Day
Facilities: Arboretum; Grounds (175 acres); Library; Picnic Area;
Trails (10 miles, 2 miles wheelchair accessible); Visitors Center
Activities: Education Programs; Guided Tours (April-Oct, Sat & Sun,
2pm); Lectures; Plant Sale; Seed Exchange; Workshops

Formerly the site of the Multnomah County Poor Farm, the first trees were planted in Hoyt Arboretum in 1931. The Arboretum displays more than 900 species of trees and shrubs from around the world, arranged in family groups including one of the largest collections of distinct species of gymnosperms (conifers) in the United States.

CITY OF PORTLAND—INTERNATIONAL ROSE TEST GARDEN

Washington Park, 400 S.W. Kingston Ave., Portland, OR 97201
Tel: (503) 823-3636
Internet Address: http://www.parks.ci.portland.or.us/Parks/
IntRoseTestGarden.htm
Established: 1917
Wheelchair Accessible: P
Parking: Greater availability of parking space in evening
Open: Daily, 7am-9pm
Best Time(s) of Year to Visit: June to September
Facilities: Amphitheater; Garden (rose); Grounds (5.12 acres); Shop
Washington Park Rose Garden Store (227-7033)
Activities: Concerts (summer); Guided Tours modest fee (reserve one
month in advance)

Tucked among the Japanese Garden, Hoyt Arboretum, the zoo and the rest of Washington Park, Portland's International Rose Test Garden is the oldest official, continuously operated public rose test garden in the United States. Today, it displays more than 8,000 plantings of 550 varieties, including hybrid teas, floribundas, grandifloras, and climbing roses. Individual gardens within the confines of the International Rose Test Garden include the Gold Medal Garden, commemorating 50 years of awards in Portland; the Royal Rosarian Garden, featuring old rose favorites; the miniature rose test garden; and the Shakespearean Garden, an informal garden of graceful trees, lawn, brick walks, and hundreds of annuals and perennials.

CITY OF PORTLAND—LADD'S ADDITION
ROSE GARDENS

S.E. 16th and Harrison, Portland, OR 97201
Tel: (503) 823-3636
Admission: Free
Established: 1891
Wheelchair Accessible: N
Open: Daily, 5am-midnight

Best Time(s) of Year to Visit: early June to September
Facilities: Gardens (rose); Grounds (2.5 acres)

The Ladd's Addition gardens are located in Portland's oldest planned community. Inspired by Pierre L'Enfant's plan for the nation's capital, William S. Ladd created a diagonal street system surrounding a central park. Also included were four diamond-shaped parks located on the points of the compass. In 1909, Portland's first parks director, Emanuel Mische designed a formal landscape plan for the gardens in Ladd's Addition. He planted camelias, perennials and a lawn area in the central circle and numerous rose varieties in the four diamonds, creating a stunning stained glass effect. Today, the gardens contain over 3,000 roses representing 60 varieties, including many cultivars popular in the early 20th century.

CITY OF PORTLAND—LEACH BOTANICAL GARDEN

6704 S.E. 122nd St., Portland, OR 97236-5037
Tel: (503) 761-9503; TDDY: (503) 823-2223
Admission: Free
Established: 1972
Wheelchair Accessible: P
Open: Tuesday to Saturday, 9am-4pm; Sunday, 1pm-4pm; Closed: Some Holidays.
Facilities: Architecture (historic manor house); Grounds (9 acres); Shop; Special Collections (Leach collection, Northwest native plants)
Activities: Curator's Tour (1st Wed in month, 2pm); English Teas; Guided Tours (March-Nov, Sat, 10am and Wed, 2pm); Plant Sales; Self-Guided Tour

Located in a woodland hollow carved by Johnson Creek in southeast Portland, the Leach Botanical Garden contains more than 2,000 species, hybrids, and cultivars (including Northwest native species and Leach original collection). Formerly the residence of John and Lilla Leach, the displays native and exotic plants may be enjoyed on a self-guided tour that winds about the Manor House and down along the creek.

CITY OF PORTLAND—PENINSULA PARK SUNKEN ROSE GARDEN

N. Ainsworth (between Kerby and Albina Sts.), Portland, OR 97201
Tel: (503) 823-3636; TDDY: (503) 823-2223
Established: 1913
Wheelchair Accessible: N

Parking: Street parking
Open: Daily, 5am-midnight
Best Time(s) of Year to Visit: June to September
Facilities: Architecture Historic Bandstand (1913); Athletic
Facilities; Garden (rose); Grounds Garden (2 acres), Peninsula Park
(17 acres)

Planned by architects Ellis Lawrence and Ormand R. Bean, the gardens
were created as part of Portland's 1912 "City Beautiful" movement. The
traditional rose gardens contain almost 9,000 roses representing 65 varieties in a distinct early 20th-century design. The octagonal bandstand
overlooking the rose garden is a National Heritage historical structure
and has been designated a Portland Historic Landmark.

THE GARDEN OF AWAKENING ORCHIDS (LAN SU YUAN)

N.W. Everett St. & Third Avenue, Portland, OR 97209
Tel: (503) 228-8131
Internet Address: http://www.portlandchinesegarden.org/home
Admission: Fee: adult $7.00, child (<6) free, student $5.50,
senior $6.00
Established: 2000
Membership: Y
Wheelchair Accessible: P
Open: April to October, Daily, 9am-6pm; November to March, Daily,
10am-5pm
Facilities: Garden (Chinese, Suzhou-syle); Grounds (one city block);
Shop; Teahouse
Activities: Classes; Concerts; Guided Tours Groups (arrange 2 weeks
in advance; Individuals (daily, noon & 1pm, no reservation required);
Temporary Exhibitions

Occupying an entire city block, Lan Su Yuan (Garden of Awakening
Orchids) is the largest Suzhou-style (17th-century) garden outside
China. Within its enclosing walls, it features serpentine walkways,
ponds, bridges, open colonnades, rock groupings, delicate trees and
shrubs, lattice screens, and pavilions. In addition, the garden is home to
more than 500 varieties of plants and trees. Designed by the garden bureau of the City of Suzhou, People's Republic of China in conjunction
with the American architectural firm of Robertson, Merryman, Barnes,
the garden is managed by a non-profit corporation, Portland Classical
Chinese Garden.

JAPANESE GARDENS

Washington Park, 611 S.W. Kingston Ave., Portland, OR 97201
Tel: (503) 223-4070; Fax: (508) 223-8303
Internet Address: http://www.japanesegarden.com
Admission: Fee: adult $6.50, child (<6) free, student $4.00,
senior $5.00
Attendance: 140,000
Established: 1963
Membership: Y
Wheelchair Accessible: P
Parking: Designated in lower lot
Open: April to September, Daily, 10am-7pm (Mon, 12-7); October to
March, Daily, 10am-4pm (Mon, 12-4); Closed: New Year's Day,
Thanksgiving Day, Christmas Day
Best Time(s) of Year to Visit: March-June to November
Facilities: Gardens (Japanese, flat, strolling pond, tea, natural, sand and
stone, designed by Professor Takuma Tono); Grounds (5½ acres);
Pavilion; Shop (223-5055); Visitors Center
Activities: Demonstrations (ikebana flower arranging); Education
Programs; Guided Tours (223-9233 [April—October]); Lectures;
Performances; Readings; Workshops

Located just above the International Rose Test Gardens, the Japanese Gardens are held to be some of the finest outside of Japan. (In 2000, the *Journal of Japanese Gardening* ranked the Gardens as one of the ten highest-quality Japanese gardens outside of Japan, out of 300 sites surveyed.) Five styles of Japanese Gardens are presented: the Flat Garden (Hiraniwa), a simple, irregularly shaped garden of white sand, moss, grass, and evergreen plantings; the Strolling Pond Garden (Chisen Kaiyou Skiki), a rock and water garden consisting of two large ponds connected by a stream and a winding path; the Tea Garden (Rojiniwa), composed of inner and outer gardens containing symbolically placed elements and a ceremonial teahouse; the Natural Garden (Shukeiyen), plantings complemented by a series of cascading waterfalls, a pond, and a temple-style gate; and the Sand and Stone Garden (Seki Tei), a meticulous arrangement of rocks and raked sand within a walled enclosure. A garden map is provided with admission and more extensive guides to the flora and cultural context of the gardens are available on site. The Japanese Garden Society, a non-profit organization, operates the gardens.

LEWIS AND CLARK COLLEGE—ESTATE GARDENS AND ARBORETUM

0615 S.W. Palantine Hill Road, Portland, OR 97219-7899
Tel: (503) 768-7850
Internet Address: http://www.lclark.edu
Admission: Free
Established: 1991
Facilities: Arboretum; Architecture Myron Frank Manor House
(Tudor-style mansion, 1924-25 design by architect Herman
Brookman); Garden (rose); Grounds Arboretum (65 acres), Campus
(130 acres)

Situated in a wooded residential area six miles from downtown Portland, the College occupies the grounds of the former "Fir Acres" estate, with its landmark manor house, cottage-style gatehouse, conservatory, formal garden mall, and rose garden. Today the Frank Manor House, listed in the National Register of Historic Places, serves as the administrative core of the College. The Estate Gardens include four terraces sloping down from the manor house to the rose garden with views eastward to the Willamette Valley and the white cone of Mt. Hood. The campus arboretum is predominantly populated with maples and cedars.

THE NATIONAL SANCTUARY OF OUR SORROWFUL MOTHER— THE GROTTO (GROTTO)

Sandy Blvd and N.E. 85th Avenue, Portland, OR 97220
Tel: (503) 254-7371; Fax: (503) 254-7948
Internet Address: http://www.thegrotto.org
Admission: Fee (Upper Level Gardens): adult $3.00, child (<6) free, child (6-11) $2.50, senior $2.50; Free (Plaza Level Gardens)
Attendance: 200,000
Established: 1924
Membership: N
Parking: Paved lot on site
Open: Daily, 9am-varies by season; Closed: Thanksgiving Day, Christmas Day
Best Time(s) of Year to Visit: Spring (rhododendron), Summer (rose garden)
Facilities: Gardens; Grounds (62 acres); Shop
Activities: Events (Christmas Festival of Lights, Mother's Day Brunch, Blessing of the Animals, International Freedom Sunday); Guided Tours; Religious Services; Temporary Exhibitions

A Catholic Shrine staffed by the Order of Servants of Mary, the Grotto contains carefully landscaped grounds, an award-winning rose garden, and the Marguerite M. Casey Peace Garden, which begins as a winding, foliage-shaded path that gradually expands to a fully open park-like setting.

SAINT PAUL

CECIL AND MOLLY SMITH GARDEN

5065 Ray Bell Road, 3.5 m. S of Newburg (off Champoeg Road, west of Route 219), Saint Paul, OR 97137
Tel: (503) 223-8225
Internet Address: http://www.rhodies.org
Admission: Fee $3.00; Free: American Rhododendron Society members
Established: 1952
Wheelchair Accessible: P
Parking: Paved parking lot
Open: Spring, 10am-3pm
Best Time(s) of Year to Visit: (Spring)
Facilities: Garden (rhododendron); Grounds (5½ acres)
Activities: Guided Tours (group schedule in advance; contact tour chairman, Anya Averill); Plant Sales (Spring)

Begun by Cecil Smith, a rhododendron aficionado and hybridizer, in 1951, the Garden was purchased by the Portland chapter of the American Rhododendron Society in 1983 and is now open to the public on selected days during the spring. Situated on sloping ground under a canopy of Douglas fir and ornamental deciduous trees, the rhododendrons are complemented by a collection of companion plants, some rare and unusual, including anemone deltoidea, erythronium revolutum, hardy cyclamen, numerous species and hybrid primulas, and at least seven species of trillium. An open house schedule is available on the Portland chapter website. Groups may be accommodated at other times by special arrangements with the garden chair.

SALEM

CITY OF SALEM—BUSH'S PASTURE PARK

600 Mission St., S.E., Mission, High and Leffelle S.E., Salem, OR 97302
Tel: (503) 588-2410; Fax: (503) 378-6447
Facilities: Architecture Bush House Museum (Italianate Victorian house, 1878; 1100 Mission S.E.); Art Center Bush Barn Art Center

(1100 Mission S.E.); Conservatory/Greenhouse; Gardens (herb, rose, tulip beds); Grounds (89 acres)

Located just south of the central business district in downtown Salem, Bush's Pasture Park boasts a delicious mix of open spaces, natural groves of old oak trees, an orchard with fruit and flowering trees, gardens and a Victorian greenhouse. The rose garden, dating from the late 1950s, contains over 2,000 roses, including extensive older hybrid tea plantings, as well as the Mrs. A. R. Tartar Old Rose Collection. Other plantings include tulip beds, a small herb garden, and a wildflower garden area. Also located in the park are the Bush House Museum and the Bush Barn Art Center housing two galleries featuring the work of local artists.

DEEPWOOD ESTATE AND GARDENS

1116 Mission St., S.E., Salem, OR 97302
Tel: (503) 363-1825
Admission: Fee (House): adult $4.00, child (<6) free, child or student $3.00, senior $3.00; Free: Grounds
Attendance: 5,000
Established: 1974
Membership: Y
Wheelchair Accessible: Y
Parking: 1 block south at 12th & Lee Sts. (near garden) 75 spaces
Open: Grounds, Daily, dawn-dusk; House: May to September, Sunday to Friday, noon-5pm; House: October to April, Wednesday to Thursday, noon-5pm; Saturday, noon-5pm; Closed: Legal holidays
Facilities: Architecture (Queen Anne-style residence, 1894 design by architect W. C. Knighton); Gardens (formal English-style, boxwood, perennial border, shade, spring); Greenhouse; Grounds Gardens (2½ acres, 1929 design by landscape architects Elizabeth Lord & Edith Schryver), Site (4 acres); Trail
Activities: Guided Tours House (hourly)

Located east of Bush's Pasture Park, Deepwood Estate consists of a Victorian mansion with carriage house, formal landscaped gardens, an open meadow and a wooded area. The third owners of the home, Clifford and Alice Brown, developed the landscaped English-style gardens formally designed by the Northwest's first female landscape architecture firm, Lord-Schryver. Listed on the National Register of Historic Places, Deepwood Estate was acquired by the City of Salem in the early 1970's and is managed by Friends of Deepwood.

MISSION MILL VILLAGE—GARDENS

1313 Mill St. S.E., Salem, OR 97301
Tel: (503) 585-7012
Internet Address: http://www.missionmill.org
Admission: Fee: adult $7.00, child (<6) free, child (6-18) $4.00,
senior $6.00
Established: 1964
Membership: Y
Parking: 250 parking spaces
Open: Monday to Saturday, 10am-5pm; Closed: Legal holidays
Facilities: Gardens (dye, herb, pioneer)

Mission Mill is primarily a missionary and industrial history museum
with numerous restored buildings; there are also gardens on the site.

SILVERTON

THE OREGON GARDEN (AHS RAP)

879 W. Main St., Silverton, OR 97381
Tel: (877) 674-2733; Fax: (503) 874-8200
Internet Address: http://www.oregongarden.org
Admission: Fee (May-Sept): adult $8.00, child (<8) free, child (8-17)
$6.00, senior $7.00; Fee (Oct-April): adult $5.00, senior $4.00,
student $4.00
Established: 2001
Membership: Y
Wheelchair Accessible: Y
Parking: Free on site
Open: May to September, Wednesday to Monday, 10am-6pm;
October to April, Wednesday to Monday, 10am-4pm
Facilities: Architecture The Gordon House (residence, 1963
Usonian design by Frank Lloyd Wright, completed by Burton
Goodrich); Food Services Café on the Green; Gardens 20 specialty
gardens (children's, conifer, water); Grounds Current (80 acres),
Planned (240 acres); Shop
Activities: Classes; Concert Series (summer); Education Programs

The Oregon Garden, a public display garden and botanical complex, is
currently under construction. Phase I, which encompasses 80 acres (of an
ultimate planned size of 240 acres), is now open to the public. Exhibits

include a wetlands, composed of 16 ponds; water garden; woodland garden; conifer garden, containing Japanese maples, heaths, and alpines, as wells as conifers; children's garden with animal topiaries, oddly named plants, and a dinosaur dig; The Oregon Way, featuring plants from the state of Oregon; *Sunset Magazine*'s Top 100 "Best of the West" Garden; and an oak grove. The Oregon Garden is a joint project of the Oregon Garden Foundation, the City of Silverton, and the Oregon Association of Nurserymen.

SOUTH DAKOTA

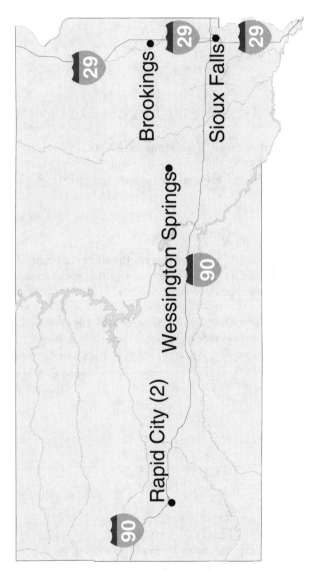

The number in parentheses following the city name indicates the number of gardens/arboreta in that municipality. If there is no number, one is understood. For example, in the text two listings would be found under Rapid City and one under Sioux Falls.

BROOKINGS

SOUTH DAKOTA STATE UNIVERSITY—MCCRORY GARDENS

6th Street & 22nd Avenue, Brookings, SD 57007
Tel: (605) 688-5136
Internet Address: http://www.sdstate.edu/~wmcg/http/mccrory.html
Admission: Free
Established: 1966
Parking: Free on site
Open: Daily, dawn-dusk
Facilities: Arboretum; Gardens (chrysanthemum, cottage, daylily, display, hosta, children's maze, peonies, prairie, rock, rose, sensory, woodland); Grounds Arboretum (45 acres), Gardens (20 acres)

Consisting of formal display gardens and the South Dakota State Arboretum, McCrory Gardens' primary emphasis is on the selection, evaluation, and display of ornamental plants suited to South Dakota's climate. The Gardens are an All-American Selections (AAS) display site. The arboretum features collections of 60 species of trees and shrubs.

RAPID CITY

THE JOURNEY MUSEUM (AHS RAP)

222 New York Street, Rapid City, SD 57701
Tel: (605) 394-6923; Fax: (605) 394-6940
Internet Address: http://www.journeymuseum.org
Admission: Fee: adult $6.50, child free, student $4.00, senior $5.00, family $13.00
Established: 1997
Membership: Y
Wheelchair Accessible: Y

Open: June to October 15, Monday to Saturday, 9am-8pm; Sunday, 10am-6pm; October 16 to May, Monday to Saturday, 10am-4pm; Sunday, 11am-4pm; Closed: Thanksgiving Day, Christmas Day, 2 weeks in January
Facilities: Galleries; Grounds (7 acres, landscaped with traditional American plants); Shop; Theatre
Activities: Demonstrations; Films; Guided Tours; Lectures; Performances; Traveling Exhibitions

This $13 million facility is a multi-media journey through time, using sight, sound, and touch to tell the story of the Black Hills. Included within the 48,000 square feet of The Journey are four separate museum collections featuring exhibits on geology, paleontology, archaeology, Sioux Indian art and culture, and pioneer history, as well as a fine art gallery and gift shop. The Journey captures and preserves the spirit not only of western South Dakota, but also of the entire frontier period of this country's history. Utilizing over 300 large sandstone boulders selected for their unique shapes and patterns, the grounds at the Museum emphasize the importance of plants to the Native Americans of the Great Plains and especially western South Dakota. Most of the selected plant material has significant medicinal, spiritual, or practical meaning to the Native Americans. The paths are designed to meander and angle around and between the rocks and beds in the manner of the trails in the Black Hills giving the visitor some sense of how portions of the landscape might have looked 200 years ago. The Journey Museum and Garden is a member of American Association of Botanical Gardens and Arboreta and the South Dakota Statewide Arboretum.

RAPID CITY MEMORIAL ROSE GARDEN
(CIVIC CENTER ROSE GARDEN)

Rushmore Plaza Civic Center, 444 Mount Rushmore Road, Rapid City, SD 57701
Tel: (605) 394-4175; Fax: (605) 394-5307
Admission: Free
Attendance: 10,000
Established: 1985
Wheelchair Accessible: Y
Parking: West of gardens
Open: Daily, 24 hours
Best Time(s) of Year to Visit: late June to early October
Facilities: Garden (rose)

Accredited by All-American Rose Selections, the Civic Center Rose Garden contains 1,000 roses representing over 100 varieties.

SIOUX FALLS

CITY OF SIOUX FALLS—SHOTO-TEIEN JAPANESE GARDENS

Terrace Park, W. 2nd St. at Grange Ave. (near Covell Lake), Sioux Falls, SD 57103
Tel: (605) 367-8222
Admission: Free
Established: 1925
Membership: N
Wheelchair Accessible: Y
Parking: North of gardens, near Aquatic Center
Open: Daily, 8am-10pm
Best Time(s) of Year to Visit: May to July
Facilities: Garden (Japanese, 1929-1936 original design; 1990 restoration by Dr. Koichi Kawana); Grounds (1 acre)

Located in Terrace Park, Shoto-teien Japanese Garden is a restoration of an old grotto-style garden built in the 1920s. It features an array of flowering trees and shrubs, pagodas, and lanterns in a lake-side setting. The Parks and Recreation Department also offers formal flower gardens in McKennan Park (1500 S. 3rd Ave. 26th St. & 4th Ave) and Tuthill Park (S. Cliff Ave. & Big Sioux River).

WESSINGTON SPRINGS

SHAKESPEARE GARDEN SOCIETY

501 Alene Ave. N., Wessington Springs, SD 57382
Tel: (605) 539-1529
Internet Address:
http://www.shakespearegarden.org
Admission: No charge/donations accepted
Attendance: 2,000
Membership: Y
Wheelchair Accessible: N
Parking: On-street parking

Shakespeare Garden Society, Wessington Springs, SD

Open: garden, daylight hours; cottage to Summer, 1pm-5pm
Facilities: Architecture (replica of Anne Hathaway's thatched cottage);
Garden (Shakespeare, arbor, goldfish pond, 30 flower beds)
Activities: Guided Tours (for groups with reservations)

The Anne Hathaway Cottage at Wessington Springs is the only structure in the Midwest that features a thatched roof. A master thatcher from Washington State undertook the project in 1995. The Shakespeare Garden and Anne Hathaway Cottage is listed in the National Register of Historic Places. In 1926, Mrs. Emma Shay, a teacher at Wessington Springs Seminary, traveled through England to increase her knowledge and ability to teach English literature. Upon her return, efforts began toward the construction of the Shakespeare Garden, and by the end of 1928 it was a noted attraction with many visitors. Anne Hathaway Cottage was built by Professor Shay and Mrs. Shay when they retired in 1932.

TEXAS

The number in parentheses following the city name indicates the number of gardens/arboreta in that municipality. If there is no number, one is understood. For example, in the text five listings would be found under Housten and one under Corpus Christi.

AMARILLO

AMARILLO BOTANICAL GARDENS

1400 Streit Drive (adjacent to the Amarillo Medical Center), Amarillo, TX 79106-3526
Tel: (806) 352-6513; Fax: (806) 352-6227
Internet Address: http://www.amarillobotanicalgardens.org
Membership: Y
Wheelchair Accessible: Y
Parking: Adjacent to facility, includes handicapped spaces
Open: Grounds, Daily; Indoor Exhibits, Tuesday to Friday, 10am-5pm; Saturday to Sunday, 1pm-5pm; Closed: Selected holidays
Best Time(s) of Year to Visit: Spring to Fall
Facilities: Gallery; Gardens (sensory); Greenhouse; Grounds Garden (2 acres), Medical Center Park (51 acres); Library (1,600 volumes)
Activities: Education Programs

Located on the grounds of the Harrington Medical Center Complex, Amarillo Botanical Gardens is dedicated to the art, knowledge, enjoyment and science of horticulture and provides educational programs for all populations. The site features sensory, butterfly/hummingbird, and other demonstration gardens.

ATHENS

EAST TEXAS ARBORETUM AND BOTANICAL SOCIETY

1601 Patterson Road (near Route 175), Athens, TX 75751
Tel: (903) 675-5630; Fax: (903) 675-1618
Internet Address: http://www.eastexasarboretum.org/
Admission: Free
Established: 1993
Parking: Free on site

Open: Daily, 8am-5pm
Facilities: Arboretum; Gardens (herb); Grounds (100 acres); Nature Trail
Activities: Education Programs; Events (Spring Fair); Workshops

The arboretum displays and interprets the natural environment of the plant communities of East Texas on a site that features a variety of environments, including dry pasture, intermittent seasonal marshes, and permanent wetlands. There is also an herb garden containing over 1,000 plants representing 54 kinds of medicinal, fragrant, and culinary herbs.

AUSTIN

LADY BIRD JOHNSON WILDFLOWER CENTER (AHS RAP)

4801 La Crosse Ave., Austin, TX 78739-1702
Tel: (512) 292-4300; Fax: (512) 292-4627
Internet Address: http://www.wildflower.org/
Admission: Fee: adult $5.00, child (<4) free, student $4.00, senior $4.00
Attendance: 62,000
Established: 1982
Membership: Y
Wheelchair Accessible: P
Open: Grounds, Tuesday to Sunday, 9am-5:30pm; Visitors Gallery, Tuesday to Saturday, 9am-4pm; Sunday, 1pm-4pm; Closed: Legal holidays
Best Time(s) of Year to Visit: March to May (wildflowers)
Facilities: Auditorium (232 seats); Food Services Wild Flower Café; Gallery; Gardens (23); Grounds (42 acres); Library; Nature Center; Shop Wild Ideas: The Store (gifts, apparel, books)
Activities: Education Programs (adult & children); Guided Tours (groups 15+, schedule in advance, fee, x129); Lectures; Traveling Exhibitions

A non-profit educational organization, the Center is dedicated to preserving and re-establishing native wildflowers, grasses, vines, shrubs and trees in planned landscapes. Among its offering are a wildflower meadow, a nature trail, a seed court, a formal courtyard landscaped entirely in native plants, and 23 theme gardens showcasing the many uses and adaptations of native plants.

UMLAUF SCULPTURE GARDEN & MUSEUM

605 Robert E. Lee Road, Austin, TX 78704
Tel: (512) 445-5582; Fax: (512) 445-5583
Internet Address: http://www.umlaufsculpture.org

Admission: Fee: adult $3.50, child free, student $1.00, senior $2.50
Attendance: 27,000
Established: 1991
Membership: Y
Wheelchair Accessible: Y
Parking: Next to museum
Open: Wednesday to Friday, 10am-4:30pm; Saturday to Sunday, 1pm-4:30pm; Closed: New Year's Day, Independence Day, Thanksgiving Day, Christmas Eve Day, Christmas Day, New Year's Eve
Facilities: Archives; Exhibition Area (3,500 square feet); Gardens (native Texas plants, waterfall, xeriscape); Library; Sculpture Garden; Shop
Activities: Arts Festival; Education Programs (children); Guided Tours; Lectures; Performances; Temporary Exhibitions

In 1985 Charles Umlauf, professor emeritus of sculpture at the University of Texas, donated to the City of Austin nearly 200 pieces of sculpture he had created. In 1991 the Umlauf Sculpture Garden & Museum was completed to house the collection. The mission of the Sculpture Garden is to foster the appreciation of sculpture in a natural setting.

ZILKER BOTANICAL GARDENS

2220 Barton Springs Road, Austin, TX 78746-5737
Tel: (512) 477-8672
Internet Address: http://www.zilker-garden.org/
Admission: Free
Established: 1962
Open: Grounds, Daily, 7am-dark; Garden Center: January to February, Monday to Friday, 8:30am-4:30pm; Saturday to Sunday, 1pm-5pm; Garden Center: March to December, Monday to Friday, 8:30am-4:30pm; Saturday, 10am-5pm; Sunday, 1pm-5pm
Facilities: Gardens (azalea, butterfly, cactus/succulent, caladium, daylily, herb, Japanese, organic, perennial, rose, sensory, xeriscape); Grounds (22 acres); Visitor Center Austin Area Garden Center
Activities: Education Programs; Festival Zilker Garden Festival (1st week in May); Flower Shows; Guided Tours (Fall & Spring, Mon-Fri; arrange in advance; $2/person, $50 minimum; 443-8673); Plant Sales

Begun in 1962, Zilker Botanic Gardens is a joint effort of the City of Austin and the Austin Area Garden Council. Highlights include a butterfly garden and trail, filled with local flowers and plants that attract numerous butterflies; a cactus and succulent garden, containing plantings of mostly native West Texas cacti and succulents; the Hartman Prehistoric

Garden, featuring reproductions of dinosaur tracks in a setting composed of plants from the Cretaceous period; an herb garden, consisting of raised beds containing numerous varieties of culinary and fragrance plants; a rose garden with over 800 rose plants, including the All-American Rose Selections; the 3-acre Tanaguchi Oriental Garden, featuring koi filled ponds; waterfalls and an authentic tea house; and a xeriscape garden, displaying native and low-water use plants. Additionally, the Heritage Area offers a blacksmith shop, a 19th-century school building, a pioneer cabin, and the Pioneer Organic Garden, displaying economically important plants grown with traditional organic methods. The Austin Area Garden Center is the site of as many as 45 to 50 meetings each month, making the facility one of the most popular buildings in the city.

BEAUMONT

CITY OF BEAUMONT—BOTANICAL GARDENS AND WARREN LOOSE CONSERVATORY

5305 Tyrrell Park Road at Fannett Road, Beaumont, TX 77706
Tel: (409) 842-3135
Admission: Free
Attendance: 5,500
Established: 1971
Wheelchair Accessible: Y
Open: Daily, daylight hours
Best Time(s) of Year to Visit: May
Facilities: Auditorium (150 seats); Conservatory Warren Loose Conservatory (Wed-Fri, 10am-2pm; Sat, 10am-5pm; Sun, 1pm-5pm; small admission fee); Gardens (Japanese, sensory); Grounds (10 acres); Library (1,500 volumes); Nature Center
Activities: Education Programs (adults and children); Films; Flower Shows; Guided Tours; Lectures

Located just a short drive from the entrance to Tyrrell Park, the Botanical Gardens offers plants, shrubs, trees, and flowers. The gardens and trails offer good bird-watching opportunities. The conservatory is the second largest in Texas.

MCFADDIN-WARD HOUSE AND GARDENS

1906 McFadden Ave., Beaumont, TX 77701
Tel: (409) 832-2134; Fax: (409) 832-3483

Internet Address: http://www.mcfaddin-ward.org/
Admission: Fee (House Tour) $3.00; Fee (Carriage House only):
adult $1.00
Attendance: 9,000
Established: 1983
Membership: N
Wheelchair Accessible: P
Parking: Lot on site and on street
Open: Tuesday to Saturday, 10am-4pm; Sunday, 1pm-4pm; Closed:
Legal holidays
Best Time(s) of Year to Visit: Spring, Fall
Facilities: Architecture (Beaux-Arts Colonial style residence,
1905 design by Henry Conrad Mauer); Grounds, beds (½ acre),
lawn (1 acre)
Activities: Guided Tours (Tues-Sat, 10am-3pm; Sun, 1pm-3pm)

The site depicts the lifestyle of a wealthy southeast Texas family between 1907 and 1950. The grounds include a rose garden and a variety of
plants, shrubs and tree specimens, including twenty date palms. All tours
begin at the McFaddin-Ward House Visitor Center at the corner of
Calder and Third Street.

COLLEGE STATION

TEXAS A&M UNIVERSITY—HOLISTIC AND HERITAGE GARDENS

Next to Horticulture/Forestry Science Building (West Campus off
Raymond Stotzer Parkway/Route 60), College Station,
TX 77843-2133
Tel: (979) 845-3915; Fax: (979) 845-0627
Internet Address: http://aggie-horticulture.tamu.edu/holisticgarden/
index.htm
Admission: Free
Wheelchair Accessible: Y
Facilities: Gardens (butterfly, flower, herb, heritage, vegetable)

Located adjacent to the Horticulture/Forestry Science Building on the
Texas A&M west campus, the Warren and Margaret Barham Texas Heritage Garden features ornamentals, vegetables, fruit and herbs common in
the 1800s plus some modern varieties for comparison. The holistic gardens include an adaptive garden, children's garden, culinary/medicinal
herb garden, vegetable gardens, flower gardens, fruit plantings, butterfly
garden, and areas of wildlife habitat.

Nursery/Floral Crops Research & Education Center, Hensel Drive & North St. (off Texas Ave.), College Station, TX 77843
Tel: (979) 845-3658; Fax: (979) 845-3649
Internet Address: http://aggie-horticulture.tamu.edu/greenhouse/hortgardens/index.html
Membership: Y
Parking: Free on site.
Open: Daily, dawn-dusk
Facilities: Gardens (children's, cottage, native plant, ornamental grasses, perennial, trellis, water/bog, xeriscape); Greenhouse; Grounds
Activities: Education Programs; Guided Tours Groups (max 40 persons, $3/person, reserve in advance, (979) 458-4434); Plant Sales; Self-Guided Tours

A student-managed and maintained facility, TAMU Horticultural Gardens conducts a broad range of teaching, research and training programs for horticultural professionals, as well as home gardeners. The site contains over 1,000 specimens in 30 different beds and planting areas representing a wide range of habitats from bog and wetlands to desert southwest. Highlights include the Lou Cashion Memorial Garden, a Texas-style cottage garden; a trellis garden, containing annual and perennials with special emphasis on vining plant species; a water and bog garden, containing a small pond that is home to over 30 aquatic plant species, as well as several large koi; the West Texas Garden, consisting of over 50 desert dwelling species set in an appropriate landscape; and a xeriscape, displaying drought-tolerant and native Texas plants in beds designed to optimize water conservation.

CORPUS CHRISTI

CORPUS CHRISTI BOTANICAL GARDENS AND NATURE CENTER (CCBG/NC) (AHS RAP)

8545 S. Staples St., Corpus Christi, TX 78413-5901
Tel: (361) 852-2100; Fax: (361) 852-7875
Internet Address: http://www.ccbotanicalgardens.org/
Admission: Fee: adult $4.00, child (<5) free, child (5-12) $1.50, senior $3.50
Attendance: 40,000
Established: 1996

Membership: Y
Wheelchair Accessible: Y
Parking: Free on site
Open: Tuesday to Sunday, 9am-5pm; Closed: New Year's Day,
Thanksgiving Day, Christmas Day
Best Time(s) of Year to Visit: March to June, September to November
Facilities: Gallery; Gardens (arid, hibiscus, hummingbird, rose, sensory,
tree demo, water); Grounds (180 acres); Nature Trail; Picnic Area;
Shop; Special Collections (hibiscus, orchid, plumeria)
Activities: Education Programs; Guided Tours (school groups); Plant
Sales (April & October); Self-Guided Tours; Workshops

Located along Oso Creek, the Gardens combine nature tourism and
eco-education with colorful, exotic floral exhibits. Major floral exhibits
include an orchid house, plumeria collection, hibiscus garden, sensory
garden, hummingbird garden, arid garden, and rose garden. A "walk on
the wild side" features the shaded Bird and Butterfly Trail, Birding
Tower, and Palapa Grande on Gator Lake, as well as Wetland Awareness Boardwalk.

DALLAS

DALLAS ARBORETUM AND BOTANICAL GARDEN (AHS RAP)

8525 Garland Road at Lakeland Drive, Dallas, TX 75218
Tel: (214) 327-8263; Fax: (214) 319-8052
Internet Address: http://www.dallasarboretum.org/
Admission: Fee: adult $7.00, child (<3) free, child (3-12) $4.00,
senior $6.00; Discounts for groups of 20 or more
Attendance: 300,000
Established: 1974
Membership: Y
Wheelchair Accessible: Y
Parking: On site, $4.00
Open: Daily, 10am-5pm; Closed: New Year's Day, Thanksgiving Day,
Christmas Day
Facilities: Arboretum; Architecture Camp House (1938), DeGolyer
House (Spanish colonial Revival residence, 1939-40); Gardens (blue,
color, fern dell, herb, rose, shade, sunken, trial, water, white); Grounds
(66 acres); Reading Room; Shop
Activities: Concerts Cool Thursdays (Jun-Aug, Thurs, 7pm-8:30pm);
Education Programs (adults, student and children); Festivals Autumn at

the Arboretum (Oct), Dallas Blooms (Mar-early Apr), Holiday at the Arboretum (Thanksgiving-New Year's), Summer at the Arboretum (early Jun-early Sept); Guided Tours; Lectures; Temporary Exhibitions

Situated on the eastern shore of White Rock Lake in sight of downtown Dallas, the Arboretum is a joint project of the City of Dallas and the Dallas Arboretum and Botanical Society, a private non-profit organization. The site, composed of the formerly private DeGolyer and Camp estates, contains several formal gardens, mature trees, lawns, and landscaped grounds, as well as fountains, sculpture and the two historic residences. Highlights include the original 4½ acres of gardens surrounding DeGolyer House, consisting of a magnolia allée, a sunken garden, a rose garden, a wisteria arbor, and hundred of annuals and perennials; the Hunt Paseo de Flores, the central walkway of the Arboretum and a linear garden composed of flowering trees and seasonal plantings; the Jonsson Color Garden, 6½ acres planted with over 2,000 varieties of azaleas and 15,000 chrysanthemums, as well as spring bulbs and flowering trees; the Palmer Fern Dell, a one-acre mini garden located within the Jonsson Color Garden that displays over 90 types of ferns, camellias, witch hazels, and azaleas; the Woman's Garden, a 1.8-acre formal garden featuring a Mediterranean-style balustrade enclosing seven theme gardens celebrating the spirit and essence of woman; and the Lay Ornamental Garden, 2.2 acres showcasing native and adapted perennial plants of the North Central Texas region, as well as shaded areas featuring white and blue flower collections, an antique rose garden, aquatic plants displayed in a multi-level pond/water curtain, and a fern grotto.

TEXAS DISCOVERY GARDENS

State Fair Park, 3601 M. L. King Blvd. at Robert B. Cullum, Dallas, TX 75210
Tel: (214) 428-7476; Fax: (214) 428-5338
Internet Address: http://www.texasdiscoverygardens.org/
Admission: Fee: adult $3.00, child $1.50, senior $2.00; Free: Tuesdays
Attendance: 275,000
Established: 1941
Membership: Y
Wheelchair Accessible: Y
Parking: Free on site
Open: Tuesday to Sunday, 10am-5pm; Sunday, 1pm-5pm; Closed: Legal holidays
Facilities: Architecture (Centennial Home, 1936); Conservatory William Douglas Blachly Conservatory (two-story, tropical plants);

Gardens (butterfly, herb, native plant, perennial, rose, sensory, xeriscape); Grounds (7½ acres); Visitors Center
Activities: Education Programs (children); Flower Shows; Lectures; Performances; Temporary Exhibitions

Formerly the Dallas Horticulture Center, the Texas Discovery Garden features the Benny J. Simpson Texas Native Plant Collection (native plants selected for their aesthetic qualities, as well as their natural tolerance of Texas climate and soils), a sensory garden, a rose garden, an iris garden, and a variety of other floral display gardens. The Blachly Conservatory houses an African plant collection, including aloes, euphorbias, eavenala madagascariensis, and ferns and exotic orchids.

EL PASO

CITY OF EL PASO—MUNICIPAL ROSE GARDEN

1702 N. Copia St. at Aurora St., El Paso, TX 79930
Tel: (915) 598-4170
Internet Address: http://www.zianet.com/adminspt/eprs/page4.html
Admission: Free
Established: 1958
Open: Tuesday to Saturday, 8am-1pm
Best Time(s) of Year to Visit: April to early May (roses bloom)
Facilities: Garden (rose)
Activities: Open Gardens (Spring & Fall)

A joint project of the City of El Paso and the El Paso Rose Society, the Municipal Rose Garden contains almost 1,500 roses, representing approximately 200 varieties. A number of "Open Garden" days with Rose Society members in attendance are held each spring and fall.

UNIVERSITY OF TEXAS AT EL PASO—CHIHUAHUAN DESERT GARDENS

Centennial Museum (UTEP Campus, corner of University & Wiggins), El Paso, TX 79968
Tel: (915) 747-5565; Fax: (915) 747-5411
Internet Address: http://www.utep.edu/~museum/home.html
Facilities: Amphitheater; Gardens (15; native plant, ornamental grass, patio, sand, sensory, shrub, succulent, wall, water)

Located on the grounds of the Centennial Museum (a cultural and natural history museum focusing on the Southwest and Mexico), the Chihuahuan Desert Gardens offer of a variety of gardens designed to show the attractiveness of native desert plants for landscaping, to demonstrate landscaping techniques that conserve water in this desert region, and to serve as a resource for both formal and informal botanical and environmental teaching. Display areas and habitats include arroyo, contemplative, desert shrub, succulent, ornamental grass, patio, sand, sensory, short grass prairie, sierra, terrace, wall, and water gardens.

FORT DAVIS

CHIHUAHUAN DESERT NATURE CENTER AND BOTANICAL GARDENS

Route 118 (4 miles south of Ft. Davis), Fort Davis, TX 79734
Tel: (432) 364-2499; Fax: (432) 364-2686
Internet Address: http://www.cdri.org
Admission: Fee: adult $2.00, child (<12) free
Attendance: 7,500
Established: 1974
Membership: Y
Wheelchair Accessible: P
Open: Monday to Friday, 9am-5pm; Saturday, 9am-3pm; Closed: New Year's Day, Independence Day, Thanksgiving Day, Christmas Day
Best Time(s) of Year to Visit: April (cacti bloom), September (wildflowers & woody plants bloom)
Facilities: Gardens (20 acres); Greenhouse (1,400 square feet); Grounds (507 acres); Shop Leapin' Lizards Nature Shop (gifts, books); Trails (3 miles); Visitor Center
Activities: Education Programs; Guided Hikes (Tues, 10am, $5 includes admission); Guided Tours Gardens & Greenhouse (Thurs, 10am, $5 includes admission); Native Plant Sale (annual, last weekend in Apr); Self-Guided Tours (brochure available); Workshops (monthly, usually 3rd Sat in month)

The Chihuahuan Desert Nature Center and Botanical Gardens is the headquarters of the Chihuahuan Desert Research Institute (CDRI), an organization that promotes public awareness, appreciation, and concern for the natural diversity of the Chihuahuan Desert Region through research and educational programs. The Nature Center and Botanical Gardens is a 507-acre expanse of rolling grassland and igneous rock outcrops. Visitors are encouraged to check in at the Visitor Center for admission to interpretive exhibits, a wildscape demonstration garden, a geologic timeline, and a desert mining exhibit. The botanical garden features over 250 species of trees, shrubs, and perennials native to the Chihuahuan Desert region. Garden strengths include plants within the rose and legume families as well as a diverse collection of salvias. The greenhouse contains approximately 200 species of cacti and succulents, one of the largest publicly accessible collections of Chihuahuan Desert cacti in the world.

FORT WORTH

FORT WORTH BOTANIC GARDEN (AHS RAP)

Fort Worth Botanic Garden, Fort Worth, TX. Pete Vollenweider photograph.

3220 Botanic Garden Blvd., at University. Drive & I-30, Fort Worth, TX 76107
Tel: (817) 871-7686;
Fax: (817) 871-7638
Internet Address: http://www.fwbg.org
Admission: Free (Grounds); Fee (Conservatory): adult $1.00, child $0.50, senior $0.50; Fee (Japanese Garden): adult $3.00, senior $2.50
Attendance: 600,000
Established: 1933
Membership: Y
Wheelchair Accessible: Y
Parking: Free on site
Open: Grounds, Daily, 8am-dusk; Visitor Center, Monday to Friday, 10am-9pm; Saturday, 10am-6pm; Sunday, 1pm-6pm; Closed: Thanksgiving Day, Christmas Day
Best Time(s) of Year to Visit: Spring to Fall
Facilities: Conservatory (10,000 square feet); Food Services (restaurant); Garden Center; Gardens (21; cactus, daylily, four seasons, iris, Japanese, perennial, rose); Grounds (109 acres); Library (5,000 volumes); Special Collections (begonia, cactus, chrysanthemum, daylily, iris); Visitors Center
Activities: Concerts; Education Programs; Flower Shows; Guided Tours; Self-Guided Tours

The oldest botanic garden in Texas, the gardens offer sweeping vistas, pathways through forests, ponds, waterfalls, and 21 specialty gardens. Highlights include European-style, miniature, and Texas heritage rose gardens (over 3,400 roses) and a 7½-acre Japanese stroll garden with several small sub-gardens (Suzuki, meditation) designed by Kingsley Wu. The conservatory features tropical plants, including an extensive species begonia collection and birds. The gardens are owned and managed by the Fort Worth Parks and Community Services Department.

FORT WORTH WATER GARDENS

W. Lancaster (between Commerce at Houston Sts.),
Fort Worth, TX 76102
Tel: (817) 871-7698
Admission: Free
Established: 1974
Open: Daily, 24 hours
Facilities: Grounds (4½ acres, 1974 design by New York architects Philip Johnson and John Burgee)

Located just south of the Tarrant County Convention Center, the Water Gardens are given over mainly to concrete forms and water. The Gardens feature three pools: the aerating pool, the quiet pool, and the active pool with water tumbling down a series of terraces down to a small pit. The grounds also include approximately 500 species of plants and trees. A gift from the Amon G. Carter Foundation to the City of Fort Worth, the Park is maintained by the Fort Worth Parks and Community Services Department.

FREDERICKSBURG

THE NATIONAL MUSEUM OF THE PACIFIC WAR— JAPANESE GARDEN OF PEACE

340 East Main Street, Fredericksburg, TX 78624
Tel: (830) 997-4379 Ext: 228; Fax: (830) 997-8220
Internet Address: http://www.nimitz-museum.org/
Admission: Fee: adult $5.00, child (<6) free, student $3.00
Established: 1976
Parking: Adjacent to site
Open: Daily, 10am-5pm; Closed: Christmas Day
Best Time(s) of Year to Visit: Fall to Spring
Facilities: Garden (Japanese)

Focusing exclusively on the Pacific Theater of World War II, the museum's exhibits include a traditional Japanese garden in which the three basic elements are represented: stone, plants and water. Donated to the people of the United States by the military leaders of Japan in honor of Fleet Admiral Chester W. Nimitz, the garden is similar to the private meditation garden of Admiral Togo (1846-1934), founder of the modern Japanese navy. Situated in the garden is an exact replica of Admiral Togo's study, which was crafted in Japan, disassembled, shipped to Fredericksburg, and then reassembled (without nails) by the same craftsmen who originally built it. The museum is a unit of Texas Parks and Wildlife.

GALVESTON ISLAND

MOODY GARDENS

1 Hope Blvd., Galveston Island, TX 77554-8928
Tel: (409) 744-1745
Internet Address: http://www.moodygardens.com/
Admission: Fee, call or view website
Open: Sunday to Friday, 10am-6pm; 10am-8pm
Facilities: Grounds (242 acres); Rainforest Pyramid

Attractions at Moody Gardens include the Rainforest Pyramid, a ten-story glass enclosure containing thousands of species of tropical plants, exotic butterflies, birds and fish native to the rain forests of Africa, Asia and the Americas. Moody Gardens also offers an aquarium, a discovery museum with IMAX theater, and a white sand beach. Outdoor plantings are primarily devoted to tropical and subtropical flora.

GLADEWATER

HELEN LEE FOUNDATION—MRS. LEE'S GARDEN

County Road 3103 (off CR 3104, 7 miles N of junction Route 271 & I 20), Gladewater, TX 75647
Tel: (903) 845-5780
Internet Address: http://www.daffodilgarden.com/
Admission: Free
Attendance: 4,500
Open: mid-February to March, Daily, 10am-4:30pm
Facilities: Architecture (reconstructed one-room pioneer log cabin); Garden (daffodil); Grounds (918 acres), Daffodil Gardens (20 acres); Trail (4 miles)

A wildlife/nature reserve, the site contains hundreds of thousands, perhaps millions, of golden daffodils scattered along a four-mile trail that meanders through the estate. The reserve, originally the private estate of oil businessman T. W. Lee and his wife Helen, is maintained by the Helen Lee Foundation. The garden is open only during the daffodil blooming period (around the middle of February through sometime in March). Wishing not to detract from its natural setting, the site offers few amenities. Please note that as there are no paved roads, the garden closes when the roads are wet. For road conditions and predicted blooming schedule, contact Mrs. Lee's Daffodil Garden at the number above.

HALE CENTER

CITY OF HALE CENTER—HERSHELL BELL PARK CACTI GARDEN

Avenue K and Cleveland St. (FM 1424 and FN 1914), Hale Center, TX 79041
Tel: (806) 839-2411
Admission: Free
Attendance: 2,500
Established: 1964
Membership: N
Wheelchair Accessible: P
Open: Daily, dawn-dusk
Best Time(s) of Year to Visit: May to September
Facilities: Garden (cactus); Picnic Area

Established in honor of agronomist and ranger management authority Hershell Bell, the garden contains more than 350 specimens representing 15 different species of cacti.

HEMPSTEAD

PECKERWOOD GARDENS

FM-359 (1.7 miles S of intersection with Route 290), Hempstead, TX 77445
Tel: (979) 826-3232; Fax: (979) 826-0522
Internet Address: http://www.peckerwoodgarden.com/
Admission: Minimum contribution: adult $5.00, student free
Open: Open Days: March to June, Saturday to Sunday, 1pm-5pm; call for dates; Open Days: Oct, Saturday to Sunday, 1pm-5pm; call for dates
Facilities: Garden (design by architect John G. Fairey); Grounds (19 acres); Shop Yucca Do Nursery

Activities: Education Programs; Guided Tours Groups (anytime, arrange in advance, $60 minimum)

Laid out in a rustic setting along a creek, the Gardens make use of a wide variety of plant material in compositions that flow into one another. The Gardens contain more than 3,000 plants, mostly native to west Texas and northern Mexico. Please note children under 12, strollers, and pets are not admitted. Established to preserve the plant collection of professor of architecture, painter, and plantsman John Gaston Fairey, the Peckerwood Gardens Foundation operates the Gardens. Many of the plants are offered for sale at the adjacent Yucca Do Nursery. Also managed by the Foundation, proceeds from the Nursery support the Gardens.

HOUSTON

BAYOU BEND COLLECTION AND GARDENS

1 Wescott St., Houston, TX 77007-7009
Tel: (713) 639-7750; Fax: (713) 639-7770
Internet Address: http://www.bayoubend.uh.edu/
Admission: Fee (Gardens): $3.00; Fee (House & Gardens): adult $10, child (<11) free, child (11-18) $5.00, student $8.50, senior $8.50
Attendance: 62,000
Established: 1956
Membership: Y
Wheelchair Accessible: Y
Open: Garden: Tuesday to Saturday, 10am-5pm; Sunday, 1pm-5pm; Home: September to August, Saturday to Sunday, 1pm-5pm; Home: August, Tuesday to Saturday, 10am-5pm, Sunday, 1pm-5pm
Facilities: Gardens (formal, azalea, boxwood, butterfly, ornamental, topiary, white, woodland); Grounds (14 acres)
Activities: Education Program; Guided Tours Home (Tues-Fri, 10am-11.30am & 1pm-2:45pm; Sat, 10am-11:15am; reservations recommended); Lectures

Originally the home of Miss Ima Hogg, daughter of former Texas Governor James S. Hogg, Bayou Bend is a subsidiary institution of the Museum of Fine Arts, Houston. It exhibits a remarkable collection of American fine and decorative arts, tracing the evolution of style from 1620 to 1870. Masterworks of painting are on view, including portraits by John Singleton Copley and Charles Willson Peale. Most of the essential elements of the gardens evolved over six decades in collaborations between Miss Hogg and professional landscape architects, including the partnership of Pat Fleming and Albert Sheppard. Bounded on two sides by a marshy creek known as Buffalo Bayou, the grounds consist of eight formal garden compositions set against natural woodlands featuring native trees and shrubs. The gardens are noted for rare Duchess De Caze Pink Camellias and Kurume hybrid azaleas, along with varieties of other azaleas, camellias, gardenias, antique roses and seasonal plantings. Since 1961, the grounds have been supervised by the River Oaks Garden Club, which offers garden tours.

HARRIS COUNTY EXTENSION—DISPLAY GARDENS

Bear Creek Park, 3033 Bear Creek Drive, Houston, TX 77084
Tel: (281) 855-5600; Fax: (281) 855-5638
Internet Address: http://urbantaex.tamu.edu/Harris
Admission: Free
Best Time(s) of Year to Visit: Spring, Fall
Facilities: Gardens (flower, herb, orchard, vegetable); Grounds (1 acre)
Activities: Plant Sales Fall Plant Sale (September, last Saturday), Fruit Tree Sale (January, last Saturday), Spring Plant Sale (April, last Saturday), Tomato Pepper Sale (February, last Saturday)

The Extension's Master Gardener program maintains a variety of demonstration gardens including an All-America Selections display garden. The program also maintains a satellite location, the Genoa Friendship Garden, at the Genoa-Red Bluff Maintenance Camp (1202 Genoa Red-Bluff Road) in southeast Harris County.

HOUSTON ARBORETUM AND NATURE CENTER

4501 Woodway Drive (next to Memorial Park), Houston, TX 77024
Tel: (713) 681-8433; Fax: (713) 681-1191
Internet Address: http://www.houstonarboretum.org
Admission: Free
Attendance: 250,000
Established: 1951
Membership: Y
Parking: Free on site
Open: Grounds, Daily, 8:30am-6pm; Nature Center, Daily, 9am-5pm
Facilities: Arboretum; Gardens (butterfly/hummingbird, sensory); Grounds (155 acres); Nature Center; Shop
Activities: Education Programs (adults and children); Guided Tours (Sat-Sun, 2pm & 3pm); Lectures Urban Nature Series (Sun, 1pm)

The Houston Arboretum contains three major habitats: forest, consisting of pines and hardwoods such as oaks and hickories; meadow, a demonstration grassland habitat dominated by herbaceous plants such as grasses, sedges, and wildflowers (including sunflowers, asters, coreopsis, gaillardia, and basketflowers); and pond. There are also a wildlife garden, demonstrating plantings that are appropriate for attracting hummingbirds, butterflies and other wildlife to an urban backyard, and a sensory garden, featuring native plants that are attractive to the senses.

HOUSTON GARDEN CENTER AND J.M. STROUD ROSE GARDEN

Hermann Park (north edge), 1500 Hermann Park Drive,
Houston, TX 77004
Tel: (713) 284-1989
Open: Grounds, Monday to Friday, 8am-6pm; Garden Center,
Monday to Friday, 8am-5pm
Facilities: Garden (rose); Garden Center; Grounds Hermann Park (455 acres, 1916 design by landscape architect George E. Kessler)
Activities: Education Programs

Located on the north edge of Hermann Park, the Garden Center offers rose, bulb, fragrant and perennial gardens, an international sculpture garden and a Chinese pavilion. The J. M. Stroud Rose Garden is an All-American Rose Selections accredited garden. Japanese Garden in Hermann Park is listed separately.

JAPANESE GARDEN IN HERMANN PARK

1500 Hermann Drive (Main St. and Sunset Blvd.), Houston, TX 77004
Tel: (713) 284-1914; Fax: (713) 466-8735
Internet Address: http://www.japanesegarden.org
Admission: Fee: adult-$1.50, child (<3)-free, child (3-12)-$0.25, senior-$1.00.
Established: 1992
Open: April to September, Daily, 10am-6pm; October to March,
Daily, 10am-5pm
Facilities: Garden (Japanese, designed by Ken Nakajima); Tea Room
Activities: Events Japan Festival (Apr); Guided Tours and Tea Ceremonies (by arrangement with Japanese Garden Society of Houston, (713) 466-1690)

A gift to the city from the Japanese-American community, the Japanese Garden in Hermann Park is located near Rice University, a few minutes from downtown Houston. The copper-roofed teahouse, constructed in Japan and reassembled on the site without the use of nails, was donated by Japan after the World Economic Summit in 1990. The garden is designed in the daimyo style, and includes a tea garden, a kaiyushiki stroll garden, and a dry landscape garden. The garden is maintained by the City of Houston, Parks and Recreation Department.

HUMBLE

MERCER ARBORETUM AND BOTANIC GARDENS

22306 Aldine Westfield Road (just north of Intercontinental Airport), Humble, TX 77338-1071
Tel: (281) 443-8731; Fax: (281) 209-9767
Internet Address: http://www.cp4.hctx.net/mercer/
Admission: Free
Attendance: 75,000
Established: 1974
Membership: Y
Wheelchair Accessible: Y
Parking: Free on site
Open: Summer, Monday to Saturday, 8am-7pm; Sunday, 10am-7pm; Winter, Daily, 8am-5pm; Closed: New Year's Day, Thanksgiving Day, Christmas Eve to Christmas Day
Facilities: Arboretum; Gardens (azalea, bamboo, bog, butterfly, color, conservation, day lily, endangered species, fern, ginger, herb, iris, maze, native plant, perennial, rock, rose, tropical, vine, water, xeriscape); Grounds (250 acres); Herbarium; Library (non-circulating); Picnic Area; Special Collections (bamboo, day lily, fern, ginger, Louisiana iris, perennial, salvia, tropical); Trails (5 miles)
Activities: Education Programs; Events Ginger Workshop & Sale (Aug), Tropical Summer Sale (Jun), Tropical Workshop & Sale (Jul); Festival Arbor Day (annual, January); Guided Tours (reserve 3 weeks in advance); Plant Sales (annual, March); Self-Guided Tours

Situated in the East Texas piney woods, Mercer Arboretum contains the Houston area's largest display of native and cultivated plants. The Aldine Westfield Road divides the facility into two special use areas. To the east are the Botanic Gardens with over 20 acres of developed gardens and horticultural facilities, including herb, ginger, fern, day lily, tropical, bamboo and endangered species collections, color displays and extensive walking trails. On the west side is the Arboretum, including outdoor classrooms, picnic area, a barbecue pavilion and three miles of walking trails that wind through beautifully preserved woodlands and a prairie display area with environmental interpretation. The site is operated by Harris County.

KERRVILLE

RIVERSIDE NATURE CENTER (AHS RAP)

150 Francisco Lemos St., Kerrville, TX 78028
Tel: (830) 257-4837 ,
Internet Address: http://www.riversidenaturecenter.org
Admission: Suggested contribution: adult $3.00, student $1.00, family $5.00
Attendance: 3,000
Established: 1989
Membership: Y
Wheelchair Accessible: Y
Parking: On site, gravel lot
Open: Tree Trail, Daily, dawn-dusk; Office, Monday to Friday, 9am-4pm; Saturday to Sunday, 10am-3pm
Best Time(s) of Year to Visit: February to May, September to October
Facilities: Gardens (annual, butterfly, native plant, perennial, wildflower, xeriscape); Grounds; Shop; Trail (.7 miles); Visitors Center
Activities: Education Programs; Self-Guided Tour (Tree Trail)

The Nature Center is a botanical garden that features native plants of the Texas Hill Country, including more than 100 species of trees and shrubs, 200 species of native wildflowers and grasses, and a xeric garden with cacti and succulents.

LANGTRY

JUDGE ROY BEAN VISITOR CENTER—GARDEN

Northeast corner of Loop 25 and Torres Ave., Langtry, TX 78871
Tel: (432) 291-3340; Fax: (432) 291-3366
Admission: Free
Attendance: 85,545
Established: 1968
Membership: N
Wheelchair Accessible: Y

Open: Labor Day to Memorial Day, Daily, 8am-5pm; Closed: New Year's Day, Easter Sunday, Thanksgiving Day, Christmas Eve to Christmas Day
Best Time(s) of Year to Visit: April to October; Memorial Day to Labor Day, 8am-6pm
Facilities: Gardens (2 acres)

Little remains today of the town of Langtry other than the Judge Roy Bean Visitor Center, which preserves the second of two buildings that housed Roy Bean's saloon, billiard parlor, and courtroom. The site also includes a cactus garden with walking trail and labeled specimens.

LUBBOCK

TEXAS TECH UNIVERSITY—HORTICULTURAL GARDEN AND GREENHOUSES

Brownfield Highway & Indiana Ave., Lubbock, TX 79409
Tel: (806) 742-2838; Fax: (806) 742-0775
Internet Address: http://www.pssc.ttu.edu/vgarden
Admission: Free
Established: 1982
Open: Daily, dawn-dusk
Facilities: Gardens (annual, ornamental grass, iris, perennial, rock, vegetable, vineyard, native plant xeriscape); Greenhouses (8; Mon-Fri, 8am-4pm; 742-2856); Special Collections (day lily, ornamental grass, iris)

Begun in 1982, the Horticultural Gardens have evolved into a rich demonstration area providing an outdoor laboratory to test potential ornamental plants for adaptation to semiarid conditions. The gardens display thousands of annual and perennial species, as well as extensive collections of ornamental grasses, iris, and day lilies. The formal gardens include a demonstration vineyard, a water-conserving native plant garden, two rock gardens, a perennial demonstration garden, a vegetable demonstration garden, a paving materials collection, and a constantly changing annual display garden.

MINERAL WELLS

CLARK GARDENS

567 Maddux Road (off route 180, 5 miles east of Mineral Wells), Mineral Wells, TX 76068

Tel: (940) 682-4856; Fax: (940) 682-4078
Internet Address: http://www.clarkgardens.com
Admission: Fee: adult $6.00, child $4.00, senior $4.00
Attendance: 5,000
Established: 1977
Membership: Y
Wheelchair Accessible: Y
Parking: Private parking lot
Open: Monday to Saturday, 7:30am-6pm; Sunday, 10pm-5pm;
Closed: New Year's Day, Christmas Day
Best Time(s) of Year to Visit: late April to early May (irises & roses)
Facilities: Gardens (50; azalea, children's, conifer, formal, heirloom iris,
lily, native plant, orchard, oriental, rose, sensory, white, woodland);
Grounds (30 acres)
Activities: Events Plant Fair (Fall), Rose Cutting Day (late June)

Begun as a private garden, Clark Gardens now offers a wide variety of
plantings containing more than 1,200 types of iris, 500 varieties of day
lilies, more than 500 antique and hybrid tea roses, and hundreds of deciduous and evergreen trees and shrubs. It is an All-American Rose Selections test garden.

NACOGDOCHES

STEPHEN F. AUSTIN STATE UNIVERSITY—MAST ARBORETUM (SFA MAST ARBORETUM)

Wilson Drive (between College Ave. & Starr St.), Nacogdoches,
TX 75962-3000
Tel: (936) 468-3705; Fax: (936) 468-4047
Internet Address: http://arboretum@sfasu.edu
Admission: Free
Attendance: 20,000
Established: 1985
Membership: Y
Wheelchair Accessible: Y
Open: Daily, dawn-dusk
Facilities: Arboretum (rare trees, vines, shrubs, ground covers,
herbaceous perennials); Climatic Areas (Asian valley); Greenhouse
(468-4404); Grounds (19 acres; 7,000 taxa in many theme gardens);
Special Collections (azalea)
Activities: Guided Tours (schedule in advance); Lecture Series Les
Reeves Arboretum Lectures; Plant Sales (semi-annual)

Developed and maintained by students in the horticultural program, the Mast Arboretum displays native plants of Texas, adapted landscape plant materials, and habitat collections. Theme gardens include bog, containing many rare wetland plants of the south; children's, including a model butterfly garden; day lily, including the Stout Medal winners; native plant; rock, featuring heat and sun-loving species; shade, displaying plants adapted to dry and moist shade; Texas heritage, featuring plants used by early Texas pioneers; and a one-acre, full-sun vegetable. Other plantings include an Asian valley exhibit, containing many unusual plants of China, Japan, Korea and the Himalayas (including 200 different azaleas and 50 Japanese maple cultivars) and a conifer and holly collection that includes many unusual forms and cultivars. An additional site (connected to the rest of the Arboretum by the Lanana Creek Trail), the Ruby M. Mize Azalea Garden, is located just south of the W. R. Johnson Coliseum. The Mize Garden features 6,500 azaleas in 46 beds complemented by camellias, hydrangeas, ornamental trees and shrubs, and Japanese maples displayed beneath patriarch pines, sweetgums, oaks and pecans in an eight-acre naturalistic woodland setting. The arboretum is also the beneficiary of the Sam B. and Penelope Hayter Mill Creek Garden and Plant Sanctuary Endowment. Located six miles west of the University, Mill Creek Gardens is a 119-acre natural area offering a unique mix of wetland, mesic mid-slopes, and xeric uplands. The endowment funds research and development activities on that property: projects that promote the conservation, selection and use of the native plants of Texas and the testing of new plant materials for Texas. Also connected to the arboretum by the Lanana Creek Trail, the SFASU Pineywoods Native Plant Center Wildflower Demonstration Garden is listed separately.

STEPHEN F. AUSTIN STATE UNIVERSITY— PINEYWOODS NATIVE PLANT CENTER

2900 N Raguet St., Stephen F. Austin State University, Nacogdoches, TX 75962
Tel: (936) 468-4104; Fax: (936) 468-4047
Internet Address: http://pnpc.sfasu.edu/default.htm
Admission: Free
Attendance: 5,000
Established: 1999
Membership: Y
Wheelchair Accessible: N
Parking: Parking At Tucker House
Open: Daily, dawn-dusk

Best Time(s) of Year to Visit: Spring to Fall
Facilities: Grounds Center (40 acres), Garden (Demonstration—dry upland, mesic mid-slope, riparian, bog, prairie plant)
Activities: Guided Tours (by reservation; 936-468-1832)

A cooperative project of the SFASU Mast Arboretum (see separate listing) and the College of Forestry's Forest Resource Institute (FRI), Pineywoods Native Plant Center (PNPC) consists of the grounds, including a remnant of east Texas forest surrounding FRI's headquarters, Tucker House. The front six acres of this 40-acre estate have been developed as the Lady Bird Johnson Wildflower Demonstration Garden. A footpath, the Lanana Creek Trail, connects PNPC with the Mast Arboretum. The mission of the center is to promote education regarding conservation and use of native plants of the southern forest.

ROSENBERG

FORT BEND COUNTY EXTENSION DEMONSTRATION GARDENS

1436 Band Road, Rosenberg, TX 77471
Tel: (281) 341-7068; Fax: (281) 342-8658
Internet Address: http://www.fbmg.com
Admission: Free
Established: 1995
Wheelchair Accessible: P
Parking: Parking at Agricultural Center lot
Open: dawn to dusk
Best Time(s) of Year to Visit: Spring to Fall
Facilities: Demonstration Gardens (2 acres)

The gardens include circle perennial gardens; butterfly habitat; children's, vegetable, water, Japanese, yardwise, rose, and herb knot gardens; a citrus orchard; and a grape vineyard.

SAN ANGELO

CITY OF SAN ANGELO—INTERNATIONAL WATER LILY GARDEN AND MUNICIPAL ROSE GARDEN

Civic League Park, W. Beauregard & Park Sts., San Angelo, TX 78900
Tel: (325) 657-4279; Fax: (325) 481-2712

Internet Address: http://sanangelotexas.org/parks/gardens.shtml
Admission: Free
Attendance: 10,000
Established: 1907
Membership: N
Wheelchair Accessible: P
Parking: On street; free public parking close by
Open: Daily, 6am-11pm
Best Time(s) of Year to Visit: late April to late October
Facilities: Gardens (annual, bulb, native plant, perennial, rose, water);
Grounds Civic League Park (11 acres)
Activities: Guided Tours (arrange in advance)

Established in 1907, Civic League Park is the city's unofficial botanical gardens. Extensive development of the site was undertaken in the early years of the Great Depression; stone walls, tree rings, bridges, and walkways were constructed employing Dallas architects and Works Progress Administration labor. Most of this original work remains and in some areas has been supplemented with more recent construction. In the 1980s Kenneth Langdon, a resident water lily expert, in partnership with the San Angelo Council of Garden Clubs was given authorization to adopt the large reflecting pool. Quickly expanding beyond this initial display area, the International Water Lily Garden has gained recognition for both the number and significance of the lilies displayed. The collection includes rare species lilies (most notably those of the Australian species nymphea gigantea), tropical and hardy lilies of many varieties, Victoria Longwood water lilies, numerous hybrid lilies, and various other water and bog plants. The Municipal Rose Garden, features approximately 950 plants representing 75 different cultivars or varieties. There are also plantings of seasonal annuals, perennials, and bulbous plants of many kinds, as well as lot of attractive native trees and shrubs.

CITY OF SAN ANGELO—RIO CONCHO PARK GARDENS

400 Block of Rio Concho Drive, San Angelo, TX 78900
Tel: (325) 657-4279; Fax: (325) 481-2712
Internet Address: http://sanangelotexas.org/parks/gardens.shtml
Admission: Free
 Attendance: 15,000
Membership: N
Wheelchair Accessible: P
Parking: Limited off-street parking, ample at nearby Convention Center
Open: Daily, 6am-11pm

Best Time(s) of Year to Visit: late April to late October
Facilities: Gardens (3); Grounds Rio Concho Park (26 acres)

This entry represent a collection of three large gardens a within a ½-mile stretch along the North Rio Concho River Trail. The James M. Rigers Gazebo Gardens presents a somewhat formal display of roses, perennials, bulbs, and annuals selected to produce a succession of bloom through ten months of the year. The informal Terrace Garden features terraced beds containing grasses, bulbs, and perennials that offer changing areas of texture, color, form and bloom throughout the year. The Rio Concho Garden presents native and adapted plants in a natural setting.

CITY OF SAN ANGELO—SUNKEN GARDEN PARK (CANNA GARDENS)

S. Abe St & W. Avenue D, San Angelo, TX 78900
Tel: (325) 657-4279; Fax: (325) 481-2712
Internet Address: http://sanangelotexas.org/parks/gardens.shtml
Admission: Free
Attendance: 8,000
Established: 1917
Wheelchair Accessible: P
Parking: On street and adjacent to Visitor Center
Open: Daily, 6am-11pm
Best Time(s) of Year to Visit: May to October.
Facilities: Grounds Garden (½ acre), Park (7 acres);
Special Collections (canna)
Activities: Guided Tours (arrange in advance)

The garden contains an extensive collection of cannas (approximately 40 cultivars), as well as native plants, annuals, perennials, and bulbous material. The rock walls and terraces were built during the depression with Works Progress Administration labor.

SAN ANTONIO

CITY OF SAN ANTONIO—JAPANESE TEA GARDEN

Brackenridge Park, 3853 N. St. Mary's St. (adjacent to San Antonio Zoo), San Antonio, TX 78212-3172
Tel: (210) 821-3120
Internet Address: http://www.sanantonio.gov/sapar/japanhis.asp

Admission: Free
Established: 1918
Open: Daily, 8am-dusk
Facilities: Garden (Japanese, water); Grounds Brackenridge Park
(343 acres)

Located at the northwestern edge of Brackenridge Park in an old rock quarry, which produced the limestone used in building the State Capitol in Austin, the Japanese Tea Garden was originally constructed in 1917-18 using prison labor. The garden features a wide variety of plants, shaded winding walkways, stone bridges, waterfalls, and ponds. Listed on the National Register of Historic Places, the site is designated a Texas Civil Engineering Landmark and a Registered Texas Historic Landmark.

CITY OF SAN ANTONIO—RIVER WALK (PASEO DEL RIO)

Downtown (S. St. Marys to Lexington Sts.), San Antonio, TX 78205
Tel: (210) 227-4262
Internet Address: http://www.sanantonio.gov/parksand rec
Admission: Free
Attendance: 7,000,000
Established: 1941
Membership: N
Wheelchair Accessible: P
Parking: Surface and garage parking
Open: always open
Best Time(s) of Year to Visit: March to November
Facilities: Grounds (30 acres—20 varieties of plants); Restaurants,
bars, shops

A linear walkway constructed below street level along the banks of the San Antonio River, River Walk winds through the downtown business district. Subtropical vegetation, cypress trees, oaks, palms, and flower gardens border the walks. River Walk is maintained by the Parks and Recreation Department.

SAN ANTONIO BOTANICAL GARDENS (AHS RAP)

555 Funston Place (off N. New Braunfels), San Antonio, TX 78209-6635
Tel: (210) 207-3250; Fax: (210) 820-3528; TDDY: (210) 821-5143
Internet Address: http://www.sabot.org/
Admission: Fee: adult $4.00, child $2.00, student $3.00,

senior $3.00; Discounts available for groups of 15 or more
Attendance: 99,000
Established: 1977
Membership: Y
Wheelchair Accessible: Y
Open: 9am-5pm; Closed: New Year's Day, Christmas Day
Facilities: Architecture (2 southwest Texas adobe structures, 19th
century; East Texas house and dependencies, late 19th-century), Auld
House (Hill County settler's house, 1870), Schumacher House
(German settler's house, 1849), Sullivan Carriage House (1896, design
by architect Alfred Giles); Climatic Areas (Texas hill country, east
Texas pineywoods, southwest Texas); Conservatory; Food Services
Carriage House Kitchen (Tues-Sun, 11am-2pm); Gardens (azalea,
Biblical, butterfly, children's, day lily, herb, heritage, Japanese, rose,
sensory, wisteria arbor, xeriscape); Grounds (33 acres); Shop (botanical
books, gifts and accessories)
Activities: Classes; Concerts; Education Programs (adult and
children's); Guided Tours (groups 20+, adult-$3.00/child-$0.50);
Lectures; Plant Sales

The gardens, divided into several distinct areas, offer a wide variety
of horticultural experiences. The Formal Areas contain specialized and
thematic landscapes combining decorative and native plants for educational and/or aesthetic purposes. Gardens in the Formal Area include
an azalea garden, also displaying other acid-loving plants such as
camellias, hollies, dogwoods, and gardenia; a day lily garden; a biblical
garden, consisting of a landscape of plants mentioned in the Bible or
cultivated in biblical times; the Garden for the Blind, featuring plants
chosen for their fragrance and texture; a Japanese Garden (Kumamoto-
En), providing examples of many styles and techniques of Japanese
Garden construction; a rose garden, offering old fashioned and antique roses as well as the popular hybrid teas, grandifloras, florabundas, climbers, miniatures and tree roses; an herb garden, containing
both medicinal and culinary herbs from all over the world; the Old
Fashioned Garden, combining traditional annuals and perennials with
some of the new hybrids in colorful displays; and a wisteria arbor. The
Native Areas consist of plant communities characteristic of the Hill
Country or Edwards Plateau; East Texas Pineywoods; and Southwest
Texas, three distinctive and diverse ecological regions of Texas varying
in soil, plant life, topography, and weather. In addition to the different
plantings in each habitat, characteristic dwellings of early Texas residents have been relocated from their original sites to illustrate the in-
terrelationship between habitat, materials, and building techniques
utilized by these early pioneers. The Lucile Halsell Conservatory

houses specialty collections including alpine plants, epiphytes, desert plants, equatorial tropicals, palms and cycads, tropical fruits, ferns and aroids, insectivores, and aquatic plants. Each group is displayed in its own climate-controlled environment. There is also an extensive children's garden program. The San Antonio Parks and Recreation Department operates the site in cooperation with the San Antonio Botanical Society.

TYLER

TYLER MUNICIPAL ROSE GARDEN AND ROSE MUSEUM

420 Rose Park Drive, Tyler, TX 75702
Tel: (903) 531-1211
Internet Address: http://www.cityoftyler.org/264437216bbb46ad
b523b3af20a785d8/default.ht
Admission: Free
Established: 1952
Open: Gardens, Daily, dawn-dark; Museum, Tuesday to Friday,
9am-4:30pm; Saturday, 10am-4:30pm; Sunday, 1:30pm-4:30pm
Best Time(s) of Year to Visit: Spring, mid-October
Facilities: Gardens (rose); Grounds (14 acres); Museum
((903) 597-3130); Shop (gifts).
Activities: Festival Texas Rose Festival (mid-October)

The Tyler Municipal Rose Garden, the nation's largest, contains over 38,000 rose bushes representing 500 varieties. As well as being an All-America Rose Selections test garden, the rose gardens include heritage and sensory areas, and a special section displaying 300 David Austin roses. While roses are the main attraction at the site, there are a variety of other gardens and exhibits to compliment the roses. Created by the Smith County Master Gardeners, the IDEA demonstration garden features new and under-utilized plants for East Texas, a water-garden and bog area, an area devoted to teaching composting, displays of various mulching materials, ground cover plants for sloping areas, and water-wise landscaping techniques. Other plantings include a camellia garden, a meditation garden, a day lily collection and a hosta trail. The Rose Museum interprets the history of Tyler's rose industry (Tyler produces about 20% of America's commercial rose crop) and the Texas Rose Festival. Note: September is the least desirable time to visit the garden, as the roses are pruned in preparation for the annual Texas Rose Festival.

VICTORIA

CITY OF VICTORIA—MEMORIAL ROSE GARDEN

Riverside Park, McCright Drive (next to Parks Administration Building), Victoria, TX 77902
Tel: (361) 572-2767; Fax: (361) 572-6636
Internet Address: http://www.victoriatx.org
Admission: Free
Membership: N
Wheelchair Accessible: Y
Parking: On site, limited
Open: Daily, 6am-11pm
Best Time(s) of Year to Visit: March to June (peak rose bloom)
Facilities: Garden (rose); Grounds Garden (1 acre), Riverside Park (562 acres)
Activities: Workshops (rose pruning classes, late Jan-early Feb)

Accredited by All-American Rose Selections, the garden contains over 1,300 rose bushes representing over 100 varieties, including hybrid teas, grandiflora, floribunda, climber, shrub, miniature, and tree roses. A final addition to the garden is scheduled for completion in early 2005, adding an additional 300 roses including a selection of antique roses. The Memorial Stolz Fountain is the centerpiece of the southern section of the garden, while a gazebo is the focal point of the northern section.

WEATHERFORD

CHANDOR GARDENS

711 W. Lee St., Weatherford, TX 76086-4121
Tel: (817) 613-1700
Internet Address: http://www.chandorgardens.com/
Admission: Fee: adult $6.00, child (<3) free, child (3-11) $4.00
Membership: Y
Open: 1st Sat in April to mid-November, Saturday, 9am-4pm; Sunday, 1pm-4pm
Facilities: Gardens; Grounds (3.5 acres)
Activities: Guided Tours group (schedule in advance)

Begun in 1936, the garden was the creation of English portraitist, Douglas Chandor and his wife, Ina Kuteman Hill. Over the next 16 years until his death, Chandor created a series of well-defined garden rooms described as having "the style and ambience of a Chinese garden as well as subtle hints of English accents." Features include rock sculptures, fountains, grottos, and a 40 foot man-made waterfall. The garden fell into disrepair after Chandor's wife's death in 1973. A private restoration effort was begun in 1994 and the city acquired the property in 2002.

WESLACO

LOWER RIO GRANDE VALLEY NATURE CENTER

301 S. Border Street, Gibson Park, Weslaco, TX 78586
Tel: (956) 969-2475; Fax: (956) 969-9915
Internet Address: http://www.valleynaturecenter.org
Admission: Fee: adult $2.50, child $1.00
Attendance: 10,000
Established: 1984
Membership: Y
Wheelchair Accessible: Y
Open: Tuesday to Friday, 9am-5pm; 8am-5pm; 1pm-5pm
Best Time(s) of Year to Visit: Fall to Spring
Facilities: Environmental Education Center (plants and animals);
Gardens (butterfly, cactus, native plant, ponds with aquatic
vegetation); Grounds (6 acres); Trails (3/4 miles; signs identify plant species).
Activities: Education Programs; Guided Tours (arrange in advance);
Self-Guided Tours

The center offers a subtropical habitat containing ten distinct plant community ecosystems, as well as cactus and butterfly gardens. It is home to over 300 plant species native to the Rio Grande Valley and features Tamaulipan Thorn Forest.

WEST COLUMBIA

VARNER-HOGG PLANTATION STATE HISTORIC SITE—GARDEN

FM 2852 (2 miles north of West Columbia), West Columbia, TX 77486
Tel: (979) 345-4656; Fax: (979) 345-4412
Internet Address: http://www.tpwd.state.tx.us/park/varner

Admission: Fee (House Tour): adult $6.00, child (<12) free, student $2.00; Free (Grounds)
Attendance: 78,000
Established: 1958
Membership: Y
Best Time(s) of Year to Visit: Spring, Fall
Facilities: Architecture (Antebellum mansion, ca. 1835 with Colonial Revival alterations, 1920); Grounds (65 acres)
Activities: Guided Tours House (Wed-Sat, 9-4pm; Sun, 1pm-4pm, fee)

Located on an 1824 Mexican Land Grant issued to Martin Varner, the site consists of an extensive 19th-century decorative arts collection as well as an antebellum home and other historical buildings. The grounds include modern and plantation-era flora as well as pecan orchards, containing over 27 varieties of pecans. Donated to the state in 1957 by Miss Ima Hogg, Varner-Hogg is listed on the National Register of Historic Places.

WOODWAY

CARLEEN BRIGHT ARBORETUM

9001 Bosque Blvd. (across from City Hall), Woodway, TX 76712
Tel: (254) 399-9204; Fax: (254) 399-9216
Internet Address: http://www.woodway-texas.com
Admission: Free
Attendance: 15,000
Established: 1999
Membership: Y
Wheelchair Accessible: Y
Parking: On site, 70 spaces including handicapped parking
Open: Grounds, Daily, 9am-dark; Visitor Center, Monday to Friday, 9am-5pm; Saturday, 10am-2pm; Closed: City holidays
Facilities: Arboretum; Art Center Whitehall Center; Garden (cactus, demonstration, meditation, succulent, veterans memorial); Grounds Gardens (5½ acres), Woodland (11 acres); Nature Trail; Visitor Center
Activities: Events Gardeners Gathering (3rd Sun in Mar, 1pm-4pm); Temporary Exhibitions Artworks (Jan-Nov)

Maintained by the City of Woodway, the Arboretum offers a variety of plantings and natural forest.

UTAH

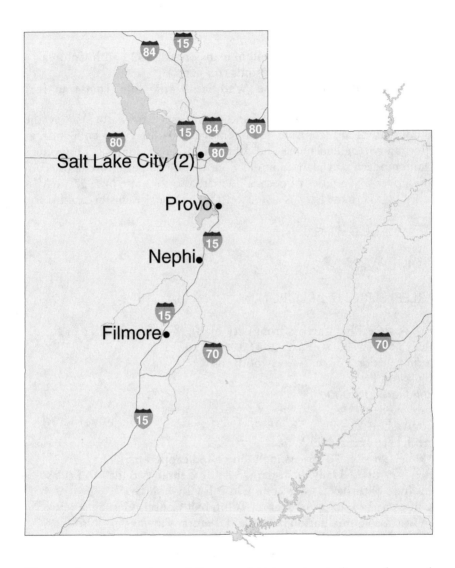

The number in parentheses following the city name indicates the number of gardens/arboreta in that municipality. If there is no number, one is understood. For example, in the text two listings would be found under Salt Lake City and one under Provo.

FILLMORE

TERRITORIAL STATE HOUSE STATE PARK—ROSE GARDEN

50 West Capitol Avenue, Fillmore, UT 84631
Tel: (801) 743-5316
Admission: Fee (Museum): adult $2.00, child (<16) $1.00, family
$5.00; Free (Grounds)
Established: 1930
Membership: N
Open: Daily, dawn-dusk
Best Time(s) of Year to Visit: Spring, Fall
Facilities: Garden (rose); Grounds Garden (1,440 square feet); Picnic
Area

Fillmore was the capital of the Utah Territory until the government
was moved to Salt Lake City in 1858. The park includes an All-American
Rose Selection rose garden adjacent to a museum housed in the sole constructed wing of the planned state house. The Garden contains approximately 330 roses representing 33 varieties.

NEPHI

NEPHI FEDERATED WOMEN'S CLUB ROSE GARDEN

100 East 100 North (one block east of Main), Nephi, UT 84648
Tel: (801) 623-0822
Open: Daily, dawn-dusk
Facilities: Garden (rose); Grounds Garden (½ acre); Picnic Area

Dedicated in remembrance of those soldiers who gave their lives in
World War II, the garden is an accredited All-American Rose Selection
garden. The site contains approximately 1,000 roses.

PROVO

BRIGHAM YOUNG UNIVERSITY—HARRISON ARBORETUM

Benjamin Cluff, Jr. Botanical Laboratory, 8 North St. (between 4th &
5th East), Provo, UT 84602
Tel: (801) 422-2582
Internet Address: http://www.byu.edu
Admission: Free
Established: 1945
Parking: Parking pass from booths on campus
Open: Daily, 24 hours
Facilities: Arboretum; Grounds Arboretum (small—1 block x 2 blocks)

Located on the Provo campus, the Harrison Arboretum contains
trees from the eastern and western United States. There is a wide variety of additional plantings throughout the campus; the grounds department maintains a campus tree tour website (http://bioag.byu.edu/aghort/
tree_tour) that provides a map and specific information on 114 trees on
campus. About a block from the Arboretum on the south hillside of the
campus is a range garden displaying a variety of range plants in a setting
that makes it possible to follow paths with pavers to study the plants in
the various beds.

SALT LAKE CITY

CHURCH OF JESUS CHRIST OF LATTER DAY SAINTS—
GARDENS AT TEMPLE SQUARE

50 W. North Temple St., Salt Lake City, UT 84150
Tel: (800) 537-9703
Admission: Free
Open: Daily, 9am-9pm
Facilities: Gardens (annuals, bulbs, formal); Grounds Gardens (10 acres)
Activities: Concerts; Guided Tours (originate in southwest lobby of
Chruch Office Building; summer every 10 minutes, winter every 15
minutes)

Temple Square is a beautifully landscaped 10-acre plot surrounded by
granite walls in the heart of downtown Salt Lake City. In summer the
grounds are home to beautiful flowers, and in winter there is a "Lighting
of Temple Square."

UNIVERSITY OF UTAH—RED BUTTE
GARDEN AND ARBORETUM (AHS RAP)

300 Wakara Way, Salt Lake City, UT 84112
Tel: (801) 581-4747; Fax: (801) 585-8454
Internet Address:
http://209.61.176.91/index.html
Admission: Fee: adult $5.00, child (<2) free,
child (3-17) $3.00, senior $3.00
Attendance: 140,000
Established: 1961
Membership: Y
Wheelchair Accessible: Y
Parking: 136 parking spaces

University of Utah—Red
Butte Garden and Arbore-
tum, Salt Lake City, UT

Open: May to September, Monday to Saturday, 9am-9pm; Sunday,
9am-5pm; October to April, 10am-5pm
Facilities: Amphitheater (2,500 seat); Arboretum; Gardens (Children's,
courtyard, four seasons, fragrance, herb, medicinal, rose, terrace,
water); Grounds Campus Arboretum (1,500 acres), Red Butte: Gardens
(13 acres), Red Butte: Natural Areas (140 acres); Library; Shop
Activities: Concerts (hotline 801-587-9939); Education Programs
(801-581-7230); Guided Tours (groups, arrange in advance, 801-585-
5688); Lectures; Performances; Temporary Exhibitions

Situated in the east foothills of the Salt Lake Valley (south of the University of Utah campus and east of University of Utah Research Park),
Red Butte Garden displays and interprets regional horticulture. A combination of display gardens (including an American Hemerocallis society
display garden), an orangerie indoor garden and special events space, and
natural habitat, the site features over 20,000 individual plants representing 1,500 different species. Additionally, the 1,500-acre University of
Utah campus, officially designated the State Arboretum of Utah, contains
over 9,000 specimens of trees and shrubs from around the globe.

WASHINGTON

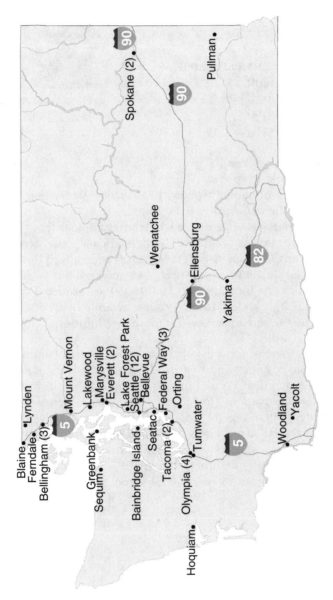

The number in parentheses following the city name indicates the number of gardens/arboreta in that municipality. If there is no number, one is understood. For example, in the text two listings would be found under Tacoma and one listing under Greenbank.

BAINBRIDGE ISLAND

THE BLOEDEL RESERVE

7571 N.E. Dolphin Drive, Bainbridge Island, WA 98110-1097
Tel: (206) 842-7631; Fax: (206) 842-8970; TDDY: (206) 842-7631
Internet Address: http://www.bloedelreserve.org/
Admission: Fee (Reservation Required): adult $10.00, child (<5) free,
child (5-12) $6.00, senior $8.00
Attendance: 26,000
Established: 1974
Membership: Y
Parking: Ample parking available
Open: Wednesday to Sunday, 10am-4pm, reservation required;
Closed: Legal holidays
Facilities: Arboretum (second growth trees); Architecture (French-style
country house, 1931); Bird Refuge; Gardens (moss, perennials,
reflection, rhododendrons, Japanese, Zen); Grounds Arboretum (84
acres), Gardens, Ponds, Meadows (66 acres)
Activities: Guided Tours (arrange in advance)

Once the home of the Bloedel Family, the site consists of a French-inspired country house (now the visitor's center), gardens, a formal European-style park, and woodlands. The gardens include a Japanese pond garden designed by Fujitaro Kubota, dry Zen gardens designed by Dr. Koichi Kawana, a moss garden, and a formal reflecting garden. The rhododendron glen displays thousands of perennials, bulbs, and wildflowers set among the rhododendrons, including more than 15,000 cyclamen plants, one of the largest plantings in the world. Approximately 300 varieties of tree grow in the reserve. The site is also a bird refuge.

BELLEVUE

BELLEVUE BOTANICAL GARDEN (AHS RAP)

Wilburton Hill Park, 12001 Main St., Bellevue, WA 98005-3522
Tel: (425) 452-2749
Internet Address: http://www.bellevuebotanical.com/
Admission: Free
Membership: Y
Open: Grounds, Daily, dawn-dusk; Visitor Center, Daily, 9am-4pm
Facilities: Gardens (alpine rock, fuchsia, ground cover, Japanese, knot, native plants, perennial border, rock, water conservation); Grounds Bellevue Botanical Garden (36 acres), Wilburton Hill Park (105 acres); Picnic Area; Shop (daily, 10am-3:30pm); Special Collections (dahlia, fuchsia); Visitor Center
Activities: Classes; Concerts; Education Programs; Events Garden d'Lights (illuminated display, winter); Guided Tours General (Apr-Oct, Sat-Sun, 2pm at visitor center; Groups (Apr-Oct, maximum size 50, schedule in advance, 451-3755); Plant Sales

Bellevue Botanical Garden contains display gardens, woodlands, meadows and wetlands. Highlights include the perennial border, designed and maintained by the Northwest Perennial Alliance; the Waterwise Garden, designed to demonstrate water-conserving plants and design; the Yao Japanese Garden, a stroll garden combining the use of some northwest plants with those that are native to Japan; an alpine rock garden; and summer displays of dahlias and fuchsias. There is also a Botanical Reserve consisting of 19 acres of natural woodlands, wetlands and meadows. The garden is owned and maintained by the Parks and Community Services Department of the City of Bellevue.

BELLINGHAM

CITY OF BELLINGHAM—BIG ROCK GARDEN PARK

2900 Sylvan St. at Illinois Lane, Bellingham, WA 98226
Tel: (360) 676-6985; TDDY: (360) 738-7366
Internet Address: http://www.cob.org/Parks
Admission: Free
Membership: N
Parking: Parking adjacent to park entrance
Open: April to October, Daily, 10am-5pm

Facilities: Gardens (oriental); Grounds Garden, Park (14 acres);
Special Collections (azalea, rhododendron, Japanese maple)
Activities: Concerts (Summer)

Situated above Lake Whatcom, Big Rock Garden Park was originally a
nursery and outdoor gallery. It contains an oriental-style garden featuring
sculptures and works of art placed among plantings of azaleas, rhododendrons, and Japanese maples.

CITY OF BELLINGHAM—CORNWALL PARK ROSE GARDEN

2800 Cornwall Avenue at W. Illinois Ave., Bellingham, WA 98225
Tel: (360) 676-6985; Fax: (360) 647-6367; TDDY: (360) 738-7366
Admission: Free on-street parking
Open: dawn-dusk
Facilities: Garden (rose); Grounds Park (65 acres)

The garden contains over 100 varieties of roses.

CITY OF BELLINGHAM—SEHOME HILL ARBORETUM

25th St. & Bill McDonald Parkway (adjacent to Western Washington
University), Bellingham, WA 98225
Tel: (360) 676-6985
Internet Address: http://www.cob.org/Parks
Admission: Free
Established: 1979
Parking: Parking at top and bottom of arboretum
Open: Daily, 6am-sunset
Facilities: Arboretum (second growth trees); Grounds (180 acres);
Trails (6 miles)

Bounded by Western Washington University and residential neighborhoods, Sehome Hill Arboretum features a natural forest habitat containing a diverse collection of native plants. The Arboretum is a cooperative
project of the City of Bellingham and Western Washington University.

BLAINE

PEACE ARCH STATE PARK

19 A St., Blaine, WA 98231
Tel: (360) 332-8221

Internet Address: http://www.parks.wa.gov/parkpage.asp?selectedpark=
Peace%20Arch
Admission: Fee: $5.00/auto
Parking: Lot on site, 20 spaces
Open: Daily, 8am-dusk
Best Time(s) of Year to Visit: April to May (azalea & rhododendron),
July to August (bloom).
Facilities: Concrete Arch; Greenhouses; Grounds Park (20 acres);
Picnic Area

Situated on the international boundary between Canada and the United States and jointly maintained, the Park features lawns, gardens planted with 18,000-20,000 annuals, and a concrete arch spanning the border. Gardens include a rose garden containing 30 named varieties, a dahlia garden offering 50 named varieties, a large tuberous begonia bed, and 20-year-old fuchsia trees. Other highlights include a summer outdoor sculpture display and an American flag rendered in 3,500 annuals. The Peace Arch commemorates the signing of the Treaty of Ghent in 1814 and the Rush-Bagot Agreement in 1817 establishing the longest demilitarized border in the world and is dedicated to the lasting peace between the two countries.

ELLENSBURG

CENTRAL WASHINGTON UNIVERSITY—
DONALD L. GARRITY JAPANESE GARDEN

Walnut & 11th Ave., Ellensburg, WA 98926
Tel: (509) 963-1111
Admission: Free
Established: 1992
Open: Spring to Fall, Daily, 7am-dusk
Facilities: Garden (Japanese); Grounds (design by Masa Mizuno of
Masa & Associates [Tualatin, Oregon])

Located off the Walnut Mall walkway near the center of the CWU campus, the Garden employs two traditional Japanese landscape styles, the stroll garden and the rock and sand meditation garden (karesansui). It features a number of Japanese stone lanterns and dozens of types of plants, including cherry trees donated by the Japanese Consulate General. Masa Mizuno, the landscape architect who designed the garden, returns annually to consult with the University's staff concerning the ongoing maintenance of the Garden.

EVERETT

EVERETT COMMUNITY COLLEGE—NISHIYAMA GARDEN

NBI Japanese Cultural & Resource Center, 905 Wetmore Ave., Everett,
WA 98201
Tel: (425) 388-9380
Internet Address: http://evcc.ctc.edu/template.cfm/doc_id=114
Established: 2003
Parking: On campus, obtain parking pass in Park Building
Open: Monday to Friday, 10am-3pm
Facilities: Garden (Japanese)

Located at the Nippon Business Institute's Japanese Cultural and Resource Center, the site serves as a buffer between the surrounding campus and neighborhood and the Japanese environment of the NBI center. Constructed using Japanese traditional methods, the Garden incorporates many classical Japanese garden elements, including a formal entry gate, waterfall and stream, tea garden, rock garden, tsubo garden, stone bridge, earthen bridge, and wooden bridge, and is enclosed by a tiled roof and earthen wall. The centerpiece of the garden is the wooden bridge built with lumber salvaged from the restoration of a much larger bridge originally constructed in the 1670s in Everett's sister city, Iwakuni, Japan.

EVERGREEN AREA ARBORETUM

144 Alverson Blvd. at West Marine View Drive, Legion Memorial
Park, Everett, WA 98203
Tel: (425) 259-0300
Internet Address: http://www.evergreenarboretum.com/
Admission: Free
Parking: Free on site
Open: dawn-10pm
Facilities: Arboretum; Gardens (dahlia, dwarf conifer, Japanese maple grove, native plant, perennial border, water conservation, woodland)
Activities: Education Programs; Lectures

Located on the west side of the Legion Memorial Park near the Parks Department's Horticulture Center, the Arboretum offers a variety of theme gardens, including a woodland garden, water conservation garden, perennial border, dwarf conifer garden, dahlia garden, and Japanese maple grove.

FEDERAL WAY

LAKEHAVEN UTILITY DISTRICT WATER CONSERVATION GARDEN

French Lake Park, 31531 1st Avenue South, Federal Way, WA 98003
Tel: (253) 946-1426; Fax: (253) 839-9738
Internet Address: http://www.lakehaven.org/conservation.htm
Admission: Free
Established: 1994
Parking: Parking available adjacent to garden
Open: 8am-5pm
Facilities: Garden (water conservation)
Activities: Self-Guided Tours

The site contains a demonstration garden promoting outdoor water conservation. Brochures on conservation gardening, soil preparation and plant lists are available at the site.

RHODODENDRON SPECIES BOTANICAL GARDEN

2525 South 336th St., Federal Way, WA 98003-9996
Tel: (253) 838-4646; Fax: (253) 838-4686
Internet Address: http://www.rhodygarden.org/index.html
Admission: Fee (March-October): adult-$3.50, child (<12)-free, student-$2.50, senior-$2.50; Free (November-February)
Attendance: 16,557
Established: 1964
Membership: Y
Wheelchair Accessible: Y
Open: March to May, Friday to Wednesday, 10am-4pm; June to February, Saturday to Wednesday, 11am-4pm
Best Time(s) of Year to Visit: mid-March to mid-May, Fall (foliage)
Facilities: Classrooms; Garden (alpine, pond, rhododendron, woodland, hardy fern); Greenhouse; Grounds (22 acres); Library; Reading Room; Shops Gift, Plants Sales Pavilion; Special Collections (species rhododendron)
Activities: Classes/Workshops; Docent Program; Education Program (adults); Gallery Talks; Guided Tours Groups (reserve in advance, 661-9377); Lectures; Plant Sales (Spring & Fall)

Located next to the Weyerhaeuser Company world headquarters on land leased from the company at no cost, the Rhododendron Species Botanical Garden contains one of the largest and most diverse collections of rhododendron species in the world. The collection consists of over 10,000 rhododendrons representing over 2,100 forms of approximately 450 species native to the temperate regions of North America, Europe, and Asia, as well as the tropical regions of southeast Asia and northern Australia. Complementing the rhododendrons are numerous companion plantings of ferns, primroses, iris, heathers, maples, magnolias, conifers, and many other exotic and unusual plants. The Garden is a project of the Rhododendron Species Foundation, a nonprofit organization dedicated to the conservation, research, acquisition, evaluation, cultivation, public display, and distribution of rhododendron species.

WEYERHAEUSER CORPORATE HEADQUARTERS— PACIFIC RIM BONSAI COLLECTION

33663 Weyerhaeuser Way S., Federal Way, WA 98003
Tel: (253) 924-5206; Fax: (253) 924-3837
Internet Address: http://www.weyerhaeuser.com/aboutus/wherewe operate/worldheadquarters/b
Admission: Free
Attendance: 34,000
Established: 1989
Membership: N
Wheelchair Accessible: Y
Parking: Signed bonsai garden parking area in company lot
Open: March to May, Friday to Wednesday, 10am-4pm; June to February, Saturday to Wednesday, 11am-4pm; Closed: New Year's Day, Thanksgiving Day, Christmas Eve to Christmas Day
Best Time(s) of Year to Visit: Summer
Facilities: Conservatory; Grounds Corporate Headquarters (500 acres,), Outdoor Bonsai Conservatory (1 acre); Special Collections (bonsai)
Activities: Education Programs; Guided Tours (Sun, noon; groups, schedule in advance, 924-3153); Lectures (May-Sept, alternate Sundays, 1pm); Self-Guided Tour (complimentary visitor guidebook available); Temporary Exhibit (1/year)

Situated in a landscaped woodland setting, the collection includes over 100 bonsai (60 displayed at any one time) from Canada, China, Japan, Korea, Taiwan and the United States elegantly displayed in a tropical conservatory and outdoor exhibit area. The grounds of the Weyerhaeuser Corporate Headquarters offer public access walking trails through a mostly wooded environment with a stream and small lake. For information on the neighboring Rhododendron Species Garden see separate listing.

FERNDALE

WHATCOM COUNTY—HOVANDER/TENNANT LAKE COMPLEX

Hovander Homstead Park: 5299 Nielsen Road, Tennant Lake: 5236
Nielsen Road, Ferndale, WA 98248
Tel: Hovander Park (360) 384-3444, Tennant Lake (360) 384-3064
Internet Address: http://www.co.whatcom.wa.us/parks/parklist
Admission: Free
Established: 1971
Open: Grounds, Daily, 8am-dusk; Hovander Farmhouse: May,
Saturday to Sunday, noon-4:30pm; June to Labor Day, Thursday to
Sunday, noon-4:30pm
Facilities: Architecture (farmhouse, 1903); Garden Hovander Park
(flower, vegetable, orchard), Tennant Lake (children's, sensory);
Grounds Hovander Park (60 acres), Tennant Lake (624 acres); Picnic
Area; Trails (3; Tennant Lake Boardwalk, open mid-Jan-early Oct);
Visitor Center Tennant Lake Interpretive Center (mid-June-Labor Day,
Thurs-Sun, noon-5pm)
Activities: Education Programs; Guided Tours (schedule in advance)

Operated by the Whatcom County Parks and Recreation Department,
the complex consists of the Hovander Homestead Park and the Tennant
Lake Wildlife Area. Hovander Homestead Park, situated along the Nook-
sack River, features the restored home of Swedish architect Hokan Hovander, a mammoth barn, and outbuildings. Flower and vegetable gardens and a
fruit orchard surround the farmhouse. The site is listed on the National Register of Historic Places. The adjacent Nielsen Farm (now the Tennant Lake
Wildlife Area) offers an environmental education center with wildlife displays and special programs. The site includes a fragrance garden with Braille
signs and raised beds containing over 200 hundred varieties of flowers and
herbs and a children's garden, as well as walking trails and an elevated
boardwalk that meanders through the marsh surrounding Tennant Lake.

GREENBANK

MEERKERK RHODODENDRON GARDENS

3531 S. Meerkerk Lane, Whidbey Island (at Highway 525 and Resort
Road), Greenbank, WA 98253
Tel: (360) 678-1912
Internet Address: http://www.meerkerkgardens.org/

Admission: Fee: adult $5.00, child (<16) free
Membership: Y
Wheelchair Accessible: P
Parking: Free on site
Open: Daily, 9am-4pm
Best Time(s) of Year to Visit: late March to mid-May (peak bloom)
Facilities: Arboretum 43 acres (cedar, hemlock, fir); Gardens (azalea, rhododendron, spring bulb); Grounds Gardens (10 acres), Woodland Preserve (43 acres); Nursery; Test Garden
Activities: Concerts; Guided Tours Groups 15+ (schedule 2 weeks in advance); Plant Sales

Situated on Whidbey Island overlooking the Saratoga passage of Puget Sound, the Gardens were begun by hybridizers Ann and Max Meerkerk for the purpose of developing and maintaining a horticultural test garden for rhododendrons and companion plants. The site contains a variety of display gardens, a test garden, naturalized areas, and a woodland preserve. Plantings include mature rhododendron hybrids, rare and unusual rhododendron species, azaleas, spring bulbs displays, and naturalized companion plants.

HOQUIAM

POLSON MUSEUM—BURTON ROSS MEMORIAL ROSE GARDENS

1611 Riverside Ave., Hoquiam, WA 98550
Tel: (360) 533-5862
Internet Address: http://www.polsonmuseum.org
Admission: Free (Grounds), Fee (Museum): adult $4.00, child (<12) $1.00, student $2.00, family $10.00
Attendance: 3,000
Membership: Y
Open: Grounds, Daily, dawn-dusk; Museum: January to March, Saturday, 11am-4pm; Sunday, noon-4pm; Museum: April to Christmas, Wednesday to Saturday, 11am-4pm; Sunday, noon-4pm
Best Time(s) of Year to Visit: June to September (roses)
Facilities: Architecture Museum (1926, 6,500-square-foot residence); Garden (rose); Grounds (2½ acres); Picnic Area

Situated along the banks of the Hoquiam River, the Park contains a rose garden and Hoquiam's only standing old-growth Douglas fir tree, as well as the 26-room mansion of lumberman Arnold Polson, now a regional museum focusing on the history of Grays Harbor County.

LAKE FOREST PARK

CITY OF LAKE FOREST PARK—BLUE HERON GARDEN

Blue Heron Park, Brookside Blvd. & NE 170th St., Lake Forest Park,
WA 98155
Tel: (206) 368-5440 Ext: 110
Admission: Free
Open: dawn to dusk
Best Time(s) of Year to Visit: Spring to Fall (spawning salmon)
Facilities: Garden (native plant)

The park includes a demonstration garden with native plants.

LAKEWOOD

LAKEWOLD GARDENS

12317 Gravelly Lake Drive S.W., Lakewood, WA 98498
Tel: (888) 858-4106; Fax: (253) 584-3021
Internet Address: http://www.lakewold.org
Admission: Fee: adult $5.00, child (<12) free, student $3.00, senior $3.00
Attendance: 12,000
Established: 1989
Membership: Y
Wheelchair Accessible: P
Parking: Free on site
Open: April to September, Wednesday to Sunday, 10am-4pm
October to March, Friday to Sunday, 10am-3pm
Facilities: Architecture (neo-Georgian residence); Champion trees;
Gardens (alpine scree, boxwood parterre, ferns, Elizabethan knot,
Japanese maple, rhododendron, rock, rose, topiary); Grounds (10
acres, 1958 design by landscape architect Thomas Church); Library;
Shop; Special Collections (Japanese maple, rhododendron); Waterfall
Activities: Guided Tours (April-Sept, with reservation in advance)

Located on the west side of Gravelly Lake, Lakewold was originally a
private estate. It boasts one of the Northwest's largest collections of rhododendrons and Japanese maples. Other plantings include a rose garden, Elizabethan knot garden, alpine (scree) garden, fern garden, boxwood parterres
and topiary, and woodland garden. The gardens and Lakewold are sophisticated and elegant in design and richly reward the attentive visitor.

LYNDEN

BERTHUSEN PARK AND GARDEN

8837 Berthusen Road, Lynden, WA 98264
Tel: (360) 354-2424
Admission: Free
Wheelchair Accessible: P
Open: Daily, dawn-dusk
Facilities: Arboretum; Garden (dahlia); Grounds Park (236 acres);
Museum Barn (ca. 1913, antique farm machinery)
Activities: Camping (Apr-Oct)

Situated in a stand of old growth Douglas fir one mile northwest of
town, the Park, best known for an enormous barn that houses a collection
of antique farming artifacts, also contains a dahlia garden.

MARYSVILLE

WASHINGTON STATE UNIVERSITY EXTENSION—
MASTER GARDENERS DEMONSTRATION GARDEN

Jennings Park, 6915 Armar Road, Marysville, WA 98270
Tel: (425) 338-2400; Fax: (425) 338-3994
Internet Address: http://snohomish.wsu.edu/gardemo.htm
Established: 1993
Facilities: Compost Demonstration Site; Gardens (butterfly, cottage,
enabling, fruit, grass, medicinal herb, medieval knot, Northwest Native
American, rose, vegetable, water conservation)
Activities: Demonstrations; Guided Tours (Summer, arrange in advance,
(425) 338-2400); Lectures; Self-Guided Tours (brochure available);
Staff (on site, May-Sept, Mon/Tues/Friday/Sat, 10am to 2pm)

The WSU Extension Master Gardeners program maintains an extensive demonstration garden in Jennings Park. The garden features both
permanent and annual garden beds, showcasing a wide variety of ornamentals, flowers, vegetables, herbs, and fruits. There are a variety of permanent theme gardens, including a mature English cottage garden, a medieval knot garden, a medicinal herb garden, an enabling garden, a rose
garden, a Northwest Native American garden, an extensive grass garden,
a waterwise (drought tolerant) garden, an All-America Selections display
garden, and several other beds of seasonal interest.

MOUNT VERNON

WASHINGTON STATE UNIVERSITY EXTENSION— SKAGIT DISPLAY GARDENS

WSU Mount Vernon Research & Extension Unit, 16650 Memorial Highway (Star Route 536), Mount Vernon, WA 98273-4768
Tel: (360) 426-4270; Fax: (360) 848-6159
Internet Address: http://mtvernon.wsu.edu/frt_hort/display_garden.htm
Admission: Free
Established: 1996
Membership: N
Wheelchair Accessible: P
Parking: Free on site
Open: Daily, dawn-dusk
Facilities: Gardens (children's, enabling, fruit, herb, native plant, perennial border, rose, vegetable); Greenhouse; Grounds (10 acres); Picnic Area
Activities: Education Programs; Self-Guided Tours; Workshops/Clinics

A demonstration site for innovative ideas about home ornamental and vegetable gardening, the Gardens are being developed by the Mount Vernon Unit in cooperation with a number of volunteer garden-oriented organizations. The WSU/Skagit County Cooperative Extension Master Gardeners created the WSU Discovery Garden, illustrating a variety of planting and landscaping techniques, including an enabling garden, a naturescaping garden, a children's garden, an herb garden, and a vegetable/small fruit garden, as well as an ornamental area offering a shade garden, cool and hot color borders, an easy-care garden, a fall/winter garden, a cottage garden, and a Japanese garden. Other participant organization gardens include the Skagit Valley Rose Society Demonstration Garden containing over 400 roses, including rugosa hedges, ten beds of hybrid tea roses, and a special selection of old garden and shrub roses; the Washington Native Plant Society Salal Chapter Garden, a one-acre garden promoting the appreciation and conservation of Washington's native plants; and the Western Washington Fruit Research Foundation Garden, displaying fruit varieties suitable for Western Washington, edible landscaping, small fruit, unusual fruit, a grape arbor, a kiwi arbor, nut trees, and a demonstration orchard.

OLYMPIA

CITY OF OLYMPIA—PRIEST POINT PARK ROSE GARDEN

2600 East Bay Drive, Olympia, WA 98501
Tel: (360) 753-8024; Fax: (360) 753-8267
Admission: Free.
Parking: Parking for 25 cars
Open: Summer, 7am-10pm; Winter, 7am-7pm
Facilities: Garden (roses mixed with perennials and annuals, rhododendrons, magnolias); Grounds Park (282 acres; hiking trails)

The park contains a small, but well-maintained rose garden.

CITY OF OLYMPIA— YASHIRO JAPANESE GARDEN

900 Plum St. at 9th St. SE, Olympia,
WA 98501
Tel: (360) 753-8380; Fax: (360) 753-8267
Admission: Free
Parking: Parking in City Hall lot
Open: Summer, Daily, 7am-10pm; Winter,
Daily, 7am-7pm
Facilities: Garden (Japanese)

City of Olympia—Yashiro Japanese Garden, Olympia, WA.

Located across from the Olympia City Hall, the Garden is designed in the hill and pond style, a naturalized landscape featuring a stream, waterfall, and pool. Featured plantings include a timber bamboo grove, azaleas and rhododendrons, and flowering cherry tree. Created to honor Olympia's Japanese sister city, it also contains four Keyake (zelkova) trees, the official tree of Yashiro, as well as two cut-stone lanterns and a 13-tier granite pagoda, which were gifts from the people of Yashiro.

WASHINGTON STATE CAPITOL CAMPUS—CONSERVATORY AND GARDENS

Between 11th & 14th & Capitol Way & Cherry Lane, Olympia, WA 98504
Tel: (360) 586-8687
Internet Address: http://www.ga.wa.gov/visitor/#campus

Admission: Free
Established: 1939
Parking: Metered state lots
Open: Grounds, Daily; Conservatory, Monday to Friday, 8am-3pm
Facilities: Conservatory (753-5689); Gardens (cottage, native plant, pioneer herb, rose, sunken); Grounds (54 acres, 1928 design by Olmsted Brothers landscape architecture firm); Visitor Center State Capitol Visitor Center
Activities: Guided Tours

Constructed by the Work Projects Administration in 1939, the Capitol Conservatory houses 500 varieties of tropical and desert plants and seasonal displays of flowers and produces bedding plants for the Capitol Campus. The campus grounds contain the state rose garden, a sunken garden, an English cottage garden, and over 120 different varieties of trees (15 of which are indigenous to Washington). Also on the campus, the Washington State Capitol Museum maintains a native plant garden and a pioneer herb garden.

ZABEL'S RHODODENDRON AND AZALEA PARK

2432 N. Bethel, Olympia, WA 98506
Tel: (360) 357-6977
Admission: Free
Attendance: 2,500
Established: 1960
Membership: Y
Wheelchair Accessible: Y
Parking: Free on street
Open: May, Daily, 9am-8pm
Facilities: Garden (azalea, rhododendron); Grounds (3 acres)

A private park, the site consists of woodlands planted with hundreds of varieties of rhododendrons and azaleas. If enough flowers are in bloom the season is extended through the first two weeks in June.

ORTING

THE CHASE GARDEN

16015 264th St. E., Orting, WA 98198
Tel: (206) 242-4040
Internet Address: http://www.chasegarden.org/
Admission: fee (by appointment only): adult $5.00, child free

Membership: Y
Wheelchair Accessible: P
Parking: Next to house or short walk down driveway
Open: mid-April to June, by appointment only
Best Time(s) of Year to Visit: April to June
Facilities: Gardens (Japanese-style, rock, alpine meadow, native plant, perennial beds, rhododendron, woodland); Grounds (4½ acres, area around house designed by landscape architect Rex Zumwalt; Ione & Emmot Chase created the remainder)
Activities: Guided Tours (10:30am-noon or 1:30pm-3pm, by appointment only); Plant Sales

Situated on a bluff overlooking the Puyallup River Valley, the site commands a spectacular view of Mount Ranier. The Garden has a naturalistic style derived from the owners' love of their native mountains; non-native plants are chosen for their ability to blend well into the local landscape. The central garden, surrounding a contemporary house, was inspired by Japanese design principles. Subsequently the owners added a ground cover meadow inspired by the alpine meadows of Mt. Ranier, containing large beds accented by Japanese maples, rhododendrons and conifers, and paths through the primarily second growth woodland. A private garden assisted by the Garden Conservancy's Preservation Projects Program, the Chase Garden is open by appointment only, with a limited number of reservations available.

PULLMAN

CITY OF PULLMAN—LAWSON GARDENS

750 S.E. Derby St., Pullman, WA 99163
Tel: (509) 338-3285
Internet Address: http://www.pullman-wa.com/rec/lawson/
Admission: Free
Attendance: 5,000
Established: 1987
Wheelchair Accessible: Y
Parking: Free on site.
Open: March to November, Daily, dawn-dusk
Best Time(s) of Year to Visit: April to October
Facilities: Gardens (annual, perennial, peony, rose, xeriscape); Grounds (15 acres)

Mr. Gerald Lawson, a local farmer, purchased fifteen acres, developed the central core of the gardens, and established an endowment to cover operating expenses and future development. The garden is oriented around a large reflecting pool and gazebo, and seasonal planting of colorful annuals accent the walkways and terraced lawns. Ever since his generous donation, the garden has expanded yearly to include a rose garden containing 600 roses representing a variety of types; a perennial garden designed for year-round interest; a peony bed with over 80 varieties; and a xeriscape garden containing a variety of trees shrubs, perennials, grasses, and bulbs that are drought resistant. Plans for future development of the gardens include a conservatory for tropical and indoor plants, as well as theme gardens.

SEATAC

HIGHLINE SEATAC BOTANICAL GARDEN

S. 138th and 24th Ave. S. (next to North SeaTac Park Community Center), Seatac, WA 98168
Tel: (206) 391-4003
Internet Address: http://www.highlinegarden.org/
Admission: Free
Established: 2000
Membership: Y
Parking: Free on site
Open: Daily, 7am-dusk
Facilities: Garden (English cottage); Grounds (10½ acres)
Activities: Education Programs; Guided Tours (arrange in advance, (206) 391-4003.); Plant Sales; Workshops

The currently developed 2 acres feature plants relocated from the 35 year-old garden of SeaTac resident Elda Behm, a display bed planted by the King County Iris Society, and seasonal displays of spring bulbs and dahlias. The potential destruction of Ms. Behm's "Paradise Garden," which was located in the crash zone for the Port of Seattle's third runway project, provided the impetus for the establishment of this community-owned garden. The Garden is a joint project of the Highline Botanical Garden Foundation, a non-profit organization established to develop and maintain the garden, and the City of SeaTac.

SEATTLE

THE BELLTOWN P-PATCH

2520 Elliott Ave. at Vine St. (Downtown), Seattle, WA 98121
Tel: (206) 441-7702; Fax: (206) 233-5142
Internet Address: http://www.speakeasy.org/ppatch

Admission: Free
Parking: Metered on street
Open: Daily, dawn-dusk
Best Time(s) of Year to Visit: Spring to Summer
Facilities: Grounds (35 garden plots)

Located in an area that has long been home to artists and creative people, the Belltown P-Patch is a community garden containing 35 garden plots as well as artistic installations, including a garden implement iron fence, a twelve-foot tall mosaic retaining wall, and solar powered water fountain. P-Patch, a city program administered by the Department of Neighborhoods in conjunction with the not-for-profit Friends of P-Patch, provides community garden space for residents of 44 Seattle neighborhoods.

BURKE MUSEUM OF NATURAL HISTORY AND CULTURE—ERNA GUNTHER ETHNOBOTANICAL GARDEN (BURKE MUSEUM)

17th Ave. NE and NE 45th St., Seattle, WA 98195
Tel: (206) 543-5590; Fax: (206) 685-3039
Internet Address: http://www.washington.edu/burkemuseum/
Admission: Fee: adult $6.50, child $5.00, student $4.00, senior $5.00; Free: First Thursday of the month
Established: 1984
Membership: Y
Wheelchair Accessible: Y
Parking: Pay parking on campus
Open: museum, Monday to Wednesday, 10am-5pm; Thursday, 10am-8pm; Friday to Sunday, 10am-5pm; Closed: New Year's Day, Independence Day, Thanksgiving Day, Christmas Day
Facilities: Garden .25 acre (basketry plants; open every day); Museum (natural and cultural history)

Located on the campus of the University of Washington, the Museum is the State museum of natural and cultural history, and the only major natural history museum in the Northwest. Established with the support of the Seattle Garden Club, the garden features plants grown or used by Native Americans for ethnobotanical purposes.

CITY OF SEATTLE—FREEWAY PARK

700 Seneca St., Seattle, WA 98101
Tel: (206) 684-4075

Internet Address: http://www.seattle.gov/parks/parkspaces/
FreewayPark.htm
Admission: Free
Established: 1976
Membership: N
Wheelchair Accessible: P
Parking: On-street parking; also paid garage
Open: 6am-11:30pm
Facilities: Grounds (5 acres, design by landscape Lawrence Halprin)

Located in downtown Seattle, Freeway Park is an award-winning urban landscape, designed to unite city neighborhoods separated by Interstate 5. Weaving over a garage and under a street the 1,300-foot-long, multi-level site offers grass lawns, mature trees, beds of flowers, water features, and public art installations. The park is unique in that it is the first in the United States to have been created from airspace.

CITY OF SEATTLE—JAPANESE GARDEN

Washington Park, 1075 Lake Washington Blvd. E., Seattle, WA 98112
Tel: (206) 684-4725
Internet Address: http://www.cityofseattle.net/parks
Admission: Fee: adult $3.00, child (<6) free, child (6-18) $2.00, student $2.00, senior $2.00
Established: 1960
Membership: Y
Parking: Free on site
Open: March 2 to April 3, Tuesday to Sunday, 10am-6pm; April 4 to May 9, Tuesday to Sunday, 10am-7pm; May 30 to September 5, Tuesday to Sunday, 10am-8pm; September 7 to October 30, Tuesday to Sunday, 10am-6pm; October 31 to November 30, Tuesday to Sunday, 10am-4pm
Best Time(s) of Year to Visit: April to March (Spring bloom), October (Fall color)
Facilities: Architecture Tea House (206) 324-1483); Gardens (Japanese); Grounds (3½ acres, 1960 design by Juki Iida)
Activities: Demonstrations Tea Ceremony (3rd Sat in month, 1:30pm); Education Programs; Events Tanabata Festival (early July); Guided Tours (Apr-Oct, Sat-Sun, noon & 1pm); Performances; Workshops

Located with the Washington Park Arboretum (see separate listing), this Japanese stroll garden features two streams, a pond with koi, lanterns, teahouse, and twin "mountains," situated within a park of conifers, maples and ornamental trees. In 2000, the *Journal of Japanese Gar-*

dening ranked the Garden as one of the ten highest-quality Japanese gardens outside of Japan, out of 300 sites surveyed.

CITY OF SEATTLE—VOLUNTEER PARK CONSERVATORY

1400 E. Galer St., Seattle, WA 98112-2834
Tel: (206) 684-4743; Fax: (206) 684-4304
Internet Address: http://www.seattle.gov
Admission: Suggested Contribution $2.00
Attendance: 200,000
Established: 1912
Membership: Y
Parking: Free parking
Open: Conservatory: Summer, Daily, 10am-7pm; Conservatory: Fall to Spring, Daily, 10am-4pm; Park, Daily, 4am-11:30pm
Facilities: Conservatory 5 houses (1912; 8,000 square feet; palm, seasonal display, cactus, fern, bromeliad); Greenhouses (not open to public; 20,000 square feet); Grounds Volunteer Park (44½ acres, 1904-09 design by Olmsted Brothers landscape architecture firm); Special Collections (orchids, cacti, bromeliads)
Activities: Guided Tours (on request)

Located in the Capitol Hill district of Seattle, the Conservatory is composed of five houses, each with a different climate and unique collections of plants. Displays include cacti and succulents in the Cactus House; palms and orchids in the Palm House; ferns, cycads and palms in the Fern House; and epiphytes in the Bromeliad house. The orchid collection contains approximately 600 varieties. The Seasonal House features changing seasonal displays of annuals and perennials. The Conservatory is an official plant rescue center of the Department of Agriculture.

E. B. DUNN HISTORIC GARDEN TRUST

Broadview Neighborhood (just south of The Highlands), Seattle, WA 98177
Tel: (206) 362-0933; Fax: (206) 367-2318
Internet Address: http://www.dunngardens.org
Admission: Fee: adult $10.00, senior $7.00
Established: 1993
Open: April to September, Thursday to Friday, 10am & 2pm, by appointment only; Saturday, 10am, by appointment only
Facilities: Grounds (10 acres, 1915 design by Olmsted Brothers; restoration by Jones & Jones Architects and Landscape Architects [Seattle])
Activities: Guided Tours (by appointment only)

The property was originally purchased in 1915 by Seattle business-man Arthur Dunn for his country residence. Later his son Edward B. Dunn, prolific garden writer and authority on Pacific Northwest native plants, used a portion of the grounds for growing prized rhododendrons. Listed on the National Register of Historic Places, it is the only private garden in Seattle designed by the firm of Olmsted Brothers that is accessible to the public. The site is open to the public for guided tours only. Reservations must be made in advance. Children under 12 and pets are not admitted.

KUBOTA GARDENS

9817 55th Ave. S. at Renton Ave. S., Seattle, WA 98118
Tel: (206) 684-4584
Internet Address: http://www.kubota.org/
Admission: Free
Established: 1987
Parking: Parking lot off 55th Ave. S
Closed: Daily, sunrise-sunset
Best Time(s) of Year to Visit: Spring (blossoms), Fall (foliage)
Facilities: Garden (Japanese American); Grounds (20 acres, 1927-87 design by Fujitaro Kubota); Picnic Area; Visitor Center (Mon-Fri, 7am-3:30pm)
Activities: Guided Tours General (Apr-Oct, 4th Sat & Sun in month, 10am, originate in parking lot), Groups 8+ (schedule two weeks in advance, (206) 725-5060); Plant Sales (May & Sept); Self-Guided Tours (map and guide located in metal box near kiosk)

Located in the Rainier Beach neighborhood of South Seattle, the gardens were originally the residence, demonstration gardens, and nursery of Seattle landscape designer Fujitaro Kubota. A horticultural pioneer, Kubota combined traditional Japanese techniques, innovative site-specific design, and North American materials. The resulting site features a rich array of plant materials set among hills and valleys, interlaced with streams, waterfalls, ponds, bridges, rock outcrops, and expansive lawns. The garden is now owned by the city of Seattle and cared for by the Kubota Garden Foundation, a private non-profit organization.

SOUTH SEATTLE COMMUNITY COLLEGE ARBORETUM

6000 16th Ave. S.W., Seattle, WA 98106-1499
Tel: (206) 764-5396

Internet Address: http://department.seattlecolleges.com/arboretum
Admission: Free
Established: 1978
Open: Daily, dawn-dusk
Best Time(s) of Year to Visit: Spring
Facilities: Arboretum; Gardens (dwarf conifer (2), fern, heather/birch, maple, native plant, perennial, rhododendron, rose, sensory, sequoia grove, water conservation); Grounds (6 acres); Shop Garden Center (April-June, Tues-Sat, 10:30am-3:30pm; 764-5323)
Activities: Education Programs; Events Arboretum in Bloom (mid-Summer), Tour & Tea (early June); Guided Tours Groups (by appointment); Plant Sales; Workshops

Located at the north end of campus on a bluff over looking the City of Seattle and Elliott Bay, the Arboretum offers walking paths, multiple specialty gardens, a reflecting pool and a large gazebo in a park-like setting. Gardens include an entry garden, featuring a formal display of ornamental grasses, herbaceous perennials, bulbs, and annuals; a sensory garden, showcasing fragrant, textural and edible plants in raised beds surrounding a reflecting pond; a rose garden, containing more than 100 varieties of hybrid tea, floribunda, grandifloras, and English roses; a rhododendron garden, offering species rhododendron and hybrids interplanted with native companion plants, a fern garden with a collection of 20 different ferns and a variety of companion plants; two conifer gardens, one highlighting an extensive collection of conifer species and cultivars suited for small urban gardens, the other displaying conifers in a rocky environment; a sequoia grove, displaying specimens of giant sequoia, coast redwood and dawn redwood; an acer (maple) garden, offering forty different maples with an emphasis on Asiatic species; and an old-fashioned perennial garden. Adjacent to the Arboretum, the Seattle Chinese Garden is scheduled for completion in 2009.

U.S. ARMY CORPS OF ENGINEERS—CARL S. ENGLISH, JR. BOTANICAL GARDENS

Hiram M. Chittenden Locks, 3015 54th Ave. NW, Seattle, WA 98107
Tel: (206) 783-7059 Ext: 310
Internet Address: http://www.nws.usace.army.mil/opdiv/lwsc/
Attendance: 1,500,000
Established: 1931
Membership: N
Wheelchair Accessible: Y
Parking: Free two-hour parking

Open: Grounds, Daily, 7am-9pm
Facilities: Fish Ladder; Gardens (573 species; 277 varieties; English style); Visitor Center (May-Sept, daily, 10am-6pm; Oct-April, Thurs-Mon, 10am-4pm)
Activities: Self-Guided Tour (plant identification map available at Visitor Center)

Situated on the bank overlooking the Hiram M. Chittenden Locks, the garden is a tribute to the devotion of Carl English, who spent 43 years working for the Corps of Engineers transforming a barren construction site into a botanical garden, combining the elegant lines and vistas of the romantic English landscape style with the original character of more than 573 species and 1,500 varieties of plants from around the world. Plantings include pines, palms, oaks, dawn redwood, swamp flowers and trees, a hardy fuschia test garden, and a great collection of rhododendrons. The Locks have been designated a National Historic Place.

UNIVERSITY OF WASHINGTON—MEDICINAL HERB GARDEN

Stevens Way (south of Chemistry Building), Seattle, WA 98195
Tel: (206) 543-1126
Internet Address: http://nnlm.gov/pnr/uwmhg/
Admission: Free
Established: 1911
Wheelchair Accessible: P
Parking: On campus. Parking free after noon Saturday and all day Sunday
Open: Daily, 24 hours
Best Time(s) of Year to Visit: June to September
Facilities: Garden (medicinal herb); Grounds (2½ acres)

Located in the heart of the University of Washington campus on Stevens Way, the Medicinal Herb Garden was begun in 1911 by the School of Pharmacy. The garden, containing 600 species of medical herbs and useful plants, is a resource for herbalists and botanists of all levels.

UNIVERSITY OF WASHINGTON—WASHINGTON PARK ARBORETUM (AHS RAP)

2300 Arboretum Drive East (E. Madison and Lake Washington Blvd. E.), Seattle, WA 98112

Tel: (206) 543-8800; Fax: (206) 325-8893
Internet Address: http://depts.washington.edu/wpa/
Admission: Free
Attendance: 400,000
Established: 1934
Membership: Y
Open: Daily, dawn-dusk; Closed: New Year's Day, Thanksgiving Day, Christmas Day
Best Time(s) of Year to Visit: December to March (Winter Garden), February to June (Rhododendron Glen), September to October (Japanese maples, foliage)
Facilities: Classroom (outside); Climatic Areas (Mediterranean, Sino-Himalayan, Chilean, New Zealand); Greenhouse; Grounds (230 acres, 1930s design by landscape architect James Dawson of Olmsted Brothers); Lecture Room; Reading Room; Shop (543-8801); Special Collections (mountain ash, azalea, camellia, cedar, drought tolerant, fir, crab apple, holly, magnolia, pine, spruce, Japanese maple, oak, rhododendron, woodland); Visitor Center (daily, 10am-4pm)
Activities: Docent Program; Education Program (adults); Films; Gallery Talks; Lectures

Located on the shores of Lake Washington just east of downtown Seattle and south of the University of Washington, the Washington Park Arboretum is a living plant museum emphasizing trees and shrubs hardy in the maritime Pacific Northwest. The Arboretum contains approximately 40,000 trees, shrubs and vines of which more than 10,000 are catalogued in collections representing 4,600 different species cultivated varieties from around the world and 750 taxa collected in the wild. Its collections of oaks, conifers, camellias, Japanese maples and hollies are known internationally and are among our nation's largest. Current ecogeographic collections include Mediterranean, Sino-Himalayan, Chilean, and New Zealand plants. There are also three functional landscape displays: the Winter Garden, containing a variety of fragrant flowers, colorful foliage, showy fruit, and striking twigs and bark; the Rhododendron Glen, featuring rhododendrons along with companion plants that thrive under similar conditions; and the Woodland Garden, exhibiting the Arboretum's extensive Japanese maple collection complemented by a native overstory and a range of small trees and shrubs appropriate for the woodland setting, including Cornus kousa, lindera obtusiloba and kalmia latifoli. The University of Washington manages the Arboretum and its plant collections through the Center for Urban Horticulture. The City of Seattle's Department of Parks and Recreation holds title to the land and cooperates in its management. The Japanese Tea Garden, located within the Arboretum, charges an admission fee and is listed separately.

WOODLAND PARK ROSE GARDEN

700 North 50th St. at Fremont Ave. N., Seattle, WA 98103
Tel: (206) 684-4863
Internet Address: http://www.pan.ci.seattle.wa.us/seattle/parks/
parkspaces/Gardens.htm#w
Admission: Free
Attendance: 200,000
Established: 1924
Membership: N
Wheelchair Accessible: Y
Parking: Parking available—$3.50, 9:30-6:00; otherwise free
Open: Daily, 7am-dusk
Best Time(s) of Year to Visit: May to September
Facilities: Grounds Rose Garden (2½ acres)
Activities: Guided Tours groups of 10 or more (reserve 3 weeks in
advance; donations encouraged)

Located just outside the Woodland Park Zoo's south entrance, the
Rose Garden is one of only two dozen certified All-America Rose Selection Test Gardens in the United States. The garden contains approximately 5,000 roses representing 290 varieties of hybrid teas, miniatures,
climbers, tree roses, floribundas, and David Austins. The garden is managed by the Woodland Park Zoological Society.

SEQUIM

OLYMPIC PENINSULA MASTER GARDENER
DEMONSTRATION GARDEN

2711 Woodcock Road, Sequim, WA 98382
Tel: (360) 417-2279; Fax: (360) 417-2414
Internet Address: http://clallam.wsu.edu/mg/demo_gardens.html
Established: 1987
Open: May to September, Thursday, 9am-1pm; Saturday, 9am-1pm
Facilities: Gardens (cottage, formal, small fruit, grass, herb, mixed
border, orchard, rose, shade, shrub, vegetable); Grounds (2½ acres)
Activities: Plant Sales; Staff (on site, Thurs & Sat, 9am-1pm)

Focusing on the home garden, the site features native and imported
plants that thrive on the North Olympic Peninsula. Demonstration areas
include a traditional cottage-style garden, formal garden, mixed border
garden, grass garden, culinary and medicinal herb garden, native plant

shade garden, rose garden, native shrub garden, orchard, small fruit garden, and vegetable garden. Master Gardeners is a volunteer program of the Washington State University Cooperative Extension.

SPOKANE

CITY OF SPOKANE—JOHN A. FINCH ARBORETUM

3404 Woodland Blvd. at Sunset Blvd., Spokane, WA 99201
Tel: (509) 625-6657; Fax: (509) 625-6958
Internet Address: http://www.spokaneparks.org/parks/
Admission: Voluntary contribution
Established: 1947
Open: Winter, Daily, 5am-10pm; Summer, Daily, 4am-11pm
Facilities: Arboretum; Grounds (65 acres); Library (600 volumes); Reading Room
Activities: Guided Tours

Located along Garden Springs Creek, the Arboretum features a collection of over 2,000 native inland northwest trees and shrubs labeled for field study. In addition, a wide variety of cultivated plants from around the world, compatible with Spokane's growing conditions, has been planted throughout the wooded hills. Highlights include a native pine forest and extensive rhododendron plantings.

CITY OF SPOKANE—MANITO PARK CONSERVATORY AND GARDENS

Grand Boulevard between 17th and 25th Aves., Spokane, WA 99203
Tel: (509) 665-6622
Admission: Free
Established: 1912
Parking: Free on site
Open: Daily, dawn to dusk; Closed: New Year's Day, Thanksgiving Day, Christmas Day
Facilities: Conservatory; Fountain; Gardens (European formal, Japanese, lilac, perennial, rock, rose); Greenhouses; Grounds (90 acres, design by Olmsted Brothers)
Activities: Education Programs; Events Holiday Open House; Workshops

Manito Park contains a conservatory and several formal gardens. The Gaiser Conservatory houses seasonal displays of colorful flowers and tropical plants all year round. Just south of the conservatory, Duncan Garden is a three-acre European Renaissance-style design featuring a large granite fountain, expanses of lawn, and symmetrical planting beds containing 70,000 annuals. Just to the north of the conservatory, the Joel E. Ferris Perennial Garden provides an extensive collection of perennials. Northwest of the conservatory, Rose Hill, a cooperative project of the Parks Department and the Spokane Rose Society and an All-American Rose Selections display garden, offers over 1,500 roses representing 150 varieties in formal beds, as well as informal plantings of older rose varieties. Farther afield at Bernard and 21st Streets, is Nishinomiya Garden, a Japanese stroll garden constructed as a symbol of the friendship between Spokane and its sister city, Nishinomiya, Japan.

TACOMA

METRO PARKS TACOMA—POINT DEFIANCE PARK

5400 N. Pearl St. at North 54th St., Tacoma, WA 98407-3218
Tel: (253) 305-1016; Fax: (253) 591-1908
Internet Address: http://www.tacomaparks.com
Established: 1905
Open: sunrise-sunset
Best Time(s) of Year to Visit: Spring (Japanese Garden & rhododendron bloom), June to September (roses), August (dahlias)
Facilities: Gardens (dahlia, herb, iris, Japanese, native plant, rhododendron, rose); Grounds Park (696 acres); Picnic Area

Point Defiance Park offers a variety of gardens, most maintained with volunteer support from horticultural societies and clubs. The focus of the Park is more than an acre of roses, totaling over 1,500 plants. The garden, accredited by the American Rose Society as an All-American Rose Selection display garden, includes miniature roses, arbors of climbing roses, a picturesque wishing well and quaint gazebos. A Japanese garden, built as part of Tacoma's Sister City relationship with Kitakyushu, Japan, contains azaleas, rhododendrons, Japanese cherry trees, crab apples, and large and small pines, as well as an oriental footbridge, waterfall, Japanese lanterns and a small teahouse. Other gardens include an herb garden, containing more than 150 perennial plants that thrive in the Puget Sound area; a native plant garden, exhibiting examples of plant life found in all six geographic and climatic zones of the Pacific Northwest; an official trial garden of the American Dahlia Society; an iris garden, containing 101 tall bearded iris, 80 Pacific Cost iris hybrids and 26 iris tectorum; and a 5-acre rhododendron garden, containing more than 160 plants, 115 cultivated varieties and 29 species of rhododendrons.

METRO PARKS TACOMA—W. W. SEYMOUR BOTANICAL
CONSERVATORY AND WRIGHT PARK ARBORETUM

Wright Park, 316 South G St., Tacoma, WA 98405-4733
Tel: (206) 591-5330; Fax: (206) 305-1005
Internet Address: http://www.tacomaparks.com
Admission: No charge/donations accepted
Attendance: 85,000
Established: 1908
Wheelchair Accessible: Y
Open: Conservatory, Tuesday to Sunday, 10am-4:30pm; Wright Park,
Daily, sunrise-½ hour after sunset; Closed: Thanksgiving Day,
November 30 to December 3, Christmas Day, New Year's Day
Facilities: Arboretum; Conservatory (Victorian-style, 1908; on
National Register); Gardens; Grounds Wright Park (27 acres, 1890
design by landscape architect E. O. Schwageral); Picnic Area; Shop
Activities: Education Program (adults and children); Gallery Talks

Located in Wright Park, the Victorian-style Conservatory, featuring a
twelve-sided central dome and over 12,000 panes of glass, houses a permanent collection of over 200 species of exotic tropical plants and
changing seasonal floral displays. The tropical collection includes such
plants as bird of paradise, ornamental figs, tropical fruit trees, orchids,
palms, bromeliads and ferns. Seasonal exhibits feature azaleas, Easter
lilies, hydrangeas, begonias, caladiums, chrysanthemums and a brilliant
holiday display of red, white and pink poinsettias. During the summer,
the Conservatory offers an All-American Selections display garden featuring award-winning annuals. The Wright Park Arboretum contains a collection of more than 700 mature trees representing over 100 species. Both
Wright Park and the Seymour Conservatory are on the Tacoma, Washington State, and National Registers of Historic Places.

TUMWATER

OLYMPIA ROSE SOCIETY—CENTENNIAL ROSE GARDEN

330 Schmidt Place (off I-5, Exit 102, near Olympia Brewery),
Tumwater, WA 98501
Tel: (360) 357-5153
Internet Address: http://www.olyrose.org/centennial.htm
Admission: Free
Established: 1989
Membership: Y

Wheelchair Accessible: Y
Parking: Large parking lot close to garden
Open: Daily, 8am-4:30pm
Best Time(s) of Year to Visit: May to October
Facilities: Garden (rose)

Located on the grounds of the Schmidt Mansion in Tumwater, the Centennial Rose Garden was constructed and is maintained by the Olympia Rose Society in cooperation with the Olympia Tumwater Foundation. The garden displays over 300 modern and antique roses, including many historical varieties grown by early settlers. The mansion, built by members of the Schmidt family, founders and operators of the nearby Olympia Brewery, sits on a hill overlooking the scenic Tumwater Falls Park.

WENATCHEE

OHME GARDENS

3327 Ohme Road (near the junction of Routes 2 & 97A),
Wenatchee, WA 98801
Tel: (509) 662-5785
Internet Address: http://www.ohmegardens.com/
Admission: Fee: adult $6.00, child (<7) free, child (7-17) $3.00
Established: 1939
Wheelchair Accessible: N
Parking: Free on site
Open: April 15 to Memorial Day, Daily, 9am-6pm; Memorial Day to Labor Day, Daily, 9am-7pm; Labor Day to October 15, Daily, 9am-6pm
Facilities: Gardens (alpine, rock); Grounds (9 acres); Picnic Area; Trail (1 mile)
Activities: Plant Sales; Self-Guided Tour (map available)

Situated on a rocky bluff overlooking the Wenatchee Valley and Columbia River, Ohme Gardens features naturalistic alpine plantings, particularly evergreens and low-growing plants, set among rock formations. Ohme was begun in 1929 by Herman Ohme as a private family retreat. The gardens were officially opened to the public in 1939 and since 1991 have been a state-owned park maintained by Chelan County. Note: Due to the steep and rugged nature of the grounds, the gardens are not recommended for those with physical limitations or health problems.

WOODLAND

HULDA KLAGER LILAC GARDENS

115 S. Pekin Road, Woodland, WA 98674-9532
Tel: (360) 225-8996
Internet Address: http://www.lilacgardens.com/
Admission: Voluntary contribution: adult $2.00, child (<12) free
Membership: Y
Open: Grounds, Daily, 10am-dusk; Farmhouse: Lilac Days, 10am-4pm
Best Time(s) of Year to Visit: April to May
Facilities: Architecture (Victorian frame farmhouse, ca. 1880); Gardens
(hybrid lilacs, Victorian); Shop (open only during Lilac Days Festival)
Activities: Events Lilac Days (mid-April—Mothers Day); Guided Tours
(groups, schedule 6 weeks in advance during Lilac Days); Plant Sales

A National Historic Site, lilac hybridizer Hulda Klager founded the
gardens in the early 1900s. The site contains over 150 varieties of lilacs,
as well as many rare and unusual trees, shrubs, perennials and flowering
bulbs.

YACOLT

POMEROY LIVING HISTORY FARM—GARDENS

20902 N.E. Lucia Falls Road, Yacolt, WA 98675
Tel: (360) 686-3537; Fax: (360) 686-8111
Internet Address: http://home.pacifier.com/~pomeroy
Admission: Fee: adult $5.00, child (3-11) $3.00; Free during
historic events
Attendance: 12,000
Membership: Y
Wheelchair Accessible: Y
Parking: Parking available nearby
Open: June to September, 1st full weekend in month
Facilities: Architecture (log house, 1920); Gardens (1/4 acre; herb and
vegetable gardens); Grounds (4 acres); Shop; Tea room (Wed-Sat,
11am-3pm)
Activities: Education Programs; Events Herb Festival (mid-May), Open
Farm Weekends, Pumpkin Festival (early Oct)

Listed on the National Register of Historic Properties, the Farm is a
living history museum interpreting agrarian life in southwest Washington

State during the 1920s. The site includes the Pomeroy's log home, a working blacksmith shop, barn, extensive herb and vegetable gardens, pastures and woodlot.

YAKIMA

YAKIMA AREA ARBORETUM

1401 Arboretum Drive (corner of I-82 & Nob Hill Boulevard),
Yakima, WA 98901
Tel: (509) 248-7337
Internet Address: http://www.ahtrees.org/
Admission: Free
Membership: Y
Open: Daily, dawn to dusk
Facilities: Arboretum; Gardens (Japanese); Grounds (46 acres); Herbarium; Library Walker Horticultural Library; Shop; Trail (wetland); Visitor Center Jewett Visitor & Interpretive Center (Tues-Sat, 9am-5pm; Sat, 9am-4pm)
Activities: Plant Sales (fall)

Adjoining the riparian habitat of the Yakima River, the Arboretum contains over 2,000 native and exotic plant species. Exhibits include a Japanese garden, "Trees of Washington," and a wetland trail.

WYOMING

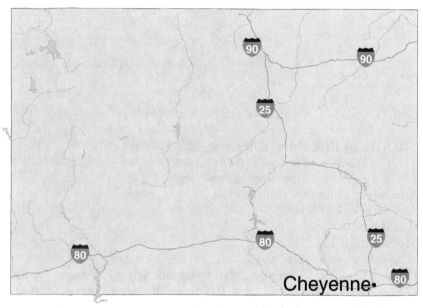

The number in parentheses following the city name indicates the number of gardens/arboreta in that municipality. If there is no number, one is understood. For example, in the text one listing would be found under Cheyenne.

CHEYENNE

CHEYENNE BOTANIC GARDENS (AHS RAP)

710 S. Lions Park Drive, Cheyenne, WY 82001
Tel: (307) 637-6458; Fax: (307) 637-6453
Internet Address: http://www.botanic.org
Admission: Voluntary contribution
Attendance: 30,000
Established: 1976
Membership: Y
Wheelchair Accessible: Y
Parking: On site; 33 regular, 3 handicapped, and 2 RV spaces
Open: Gardens, daylight hours; Building, Monday to Friday, 8am-4:30pm; Saturday to Sunday, 11am-3:30pm
Facilities: Conservatory (Mon-Fri, 8am-4:30pm; Sat-Sun, 11am-3:30pm); Gardens (conifer, cactus, cottage, herb, labrynth, perennial, rose, sensory, woodland, xeriscape); Greenhouses 6,800 square feet; Grounds (8+ acres); Library
Activities: Concerts; Events Summer Cultural Arts (Jul-Aug), Stained Glass Art Celebration); Lectures (Mar-Apr)

The solar conservatory features an herb garden, waterfall, exotic vines, and tropical trees. In summer exterior displays include annual, perennial, xeriscape, and rose gardens; an insprational Peace Garden; a medicinal herb garden; a high plains native plant garden; and a wetlands discovery area.

APPENDIX:
COMMERCIAL NURSERIES
WITH DISPLAY GARDENS

Hawaii

Hilo

Hilo Tropical Gardens
1477 Kalanianaole Ave., Hilo, HI 96720
Tel: (800) 278-8005
Internet Address:
http://www.hilotropicalgardens.com/

Nani Mau Gardens
421 Makalika St. (Highway 11, 3 miles south of Hilo Airport), Hilo, HI 96720-9999
Tel: (808) 959-3500
Fax: (808) 959-3501
Internet Address:
http://www.nanimau.com/

Wailuku

Maui Tropical Plantation—Display Gardens
1670 Honoapilani Hwy. (between Maalaea Wharf & Wailuku), Wailuku, HI 96793
Tel: (808) 244-7643
Internet Address:
http://www.mauitropicalplantation.com

Tropical Gardens of Maui—Display Gardens
200 Iao Valley Road, Wailuku, HI 96793
Tel: (808) 244-3085
Fax: (808) 242-6152
Internet Address:
http://www.tropicalgardensof maui.com

Iowa

Farmington

Wildthings Flower Farm and Learning Center—Gardens
31309 W. Highway 2 (1½ miles west of Farmington), Farmington, IA 52626
Tel: (319) 878-3324

Muscatine

Pearlcity Perennial Plantation & Karkosh Korners— Display Gardens
2820 Highway 22 (1 mile east of Muscatine on Route 22), Muscatine, IA 52761
Tel: (319) 264-3116

Odebolt

Prairie Pedlar—Display Gardens
1609—270th Street, Odebolt, IA 51458
Tel: (712) 668-4840
Internet Address:
http://showcase.netins.net/web/ppgarden/

Montana

Kila

Full Circle Herb Farm
1230 Truman Creek Road (12 miles west of Kalispell), Kila, MT 59920
Tel: (406) 257-8133
Internet Address:
http://digisys.net/~herbfarm

Nebraska

Clarkson

Bluebird Nursery, Inc.
519 Bryan St., Clarkson, NE 68629
Tel: (800) 356-9164
Fax: (402) 892-3738
Internet Address:
http://www.bluebirdnursery.com/

New Hampshire

Mason

Pickity Place
248 Nutting Hill Road, Mason, NH 03048
Tel: (603) 878-1151

Internet Address:
http://www.pickityplace.com/

New Mexico

Santa Fe

Salman's Santa Fe Greenhouses— Display Gardens
2904 Rufina Street, Santa Fe, NM 87507-2929
Tel: (505) 473-2700
Internet Address:
http://www.santafegreenhouses.com/

Oregon

Albany

Nichols Garden Nursery— Display Gardens
1190 Old Salem Road NE, Albany, OR 97321-4580
Tel: (541) 928-9280
Fax: (541) 967-8406
Internet Address:
http://www.nicholsgarden nursery.com/

Eugene

Greer Gardens—Display Gardens
1280 Goodpasture Island Road (off Delta Highway), Eugene, OR 97401-1794
Tel: (541) 686-8266
Internet Address:
http://www.greergardens.com/

Medford

Jackson and Perkins Test and Display Garden
1310 Center Drive, Medford, OR 97501
Tel: (800) 292-4769
Internet Address:
http://www.jacksonandperkins.com

Salem

**Schreiner's Iris Gardens—
Display Gardens**
3625 Quinaby Road N.E., Salem,
OR 97303
Tel: (800) 525-2367
Internet Address:
http://www.schreinersgardens.com

Texas

Alamo

**Sunderland's Cactus Garden—
Display Gardens**
North FM 907 at FM 495 (0.7 miles
north of Alamo), Alamo, TX
78516
Tel: (210) 787-2040

Brenham

Ellison's Greenhouses
2107 E Stone St., Brenham,
TX 77833-5131
Tel: (979) 836-6011
Admission: Tour Fee: adult-$2.00,
child-$0.50.
Internet Address:
http://www.ellisonsgreenhouses.com

Brookshire

Lilypons Water Gardens
839 FM 1489 Koomey Road,
Brookshire, TX 77423-8804
Tel: (713) 391-0076

Fort Worth

**Weston Gardens—Demonstration
Gardens**
8101 Anglin Drive, Fort Worth,
TX 76140
Tel: (817) 572-0549
Fax: (817) 572-1628
Internet Address:
http://www.westongardens.com

Fredericksburg

Fredericksburg Herb Farm
407 Whitney St., Fredericksburg,
TX 78624-3613
Tel: (800) 259-4372
Fax: (830) 997-5069
Internet Address:
http://www.fredericksburgherb
farm.com

Independence

**Antique Rose Emporium—
Display Gardens**
10,000 Highway 50, Independence, TX 77833
Tel: (979) 836-5548
Fax: (979) 836-7236
Internet Address:
http://www.antiqueroseemporium
.com

Washington

Bainbridge Island

**Bainbridge Gardens—Display
Gardens**
9415 Miller Road N.E., Bainbridge
Island, WA 98110-3420
Tel: (206) 842-5888
Fax: (206) 842-7645
Internet Address:
http://www.bainbridgegardens.com/

Brinnon

**Whitney Gardens and Nursery—
Display Gardens**
306264 U.S. Highway 101, Brinnon, WA 98320
Tel: (360) 796-4411
Internet Address:
http://www.whitneygardens
.com

Clinton

Maxwelton Valley Gardens—
Display Gardens
3443 E. French Road (Whidbey Island), Clinton, WA 98236
Tel: (360) 579-1770

Internet Address:
http://www.whidbey.com/mvg/

Kingston

Heronswood Nursery, Ltd.—
Display Garden
7530 NE 288th Street, Kingston,
WA 98346
Tel: (360) 297-4172
Fax: (360) 297-8321

Internet Address:
http://www.heronswood.com

Mount Vernon

Roozengaarde Display Garden
and Retail Center
15867 Beaver Marsh Road, Mount
Vernon, WA 98273
Tel: (360) 424-8531
Fax: (360) 424-3113

Internet Address:
http://www.roozengaarde.com

West Shore Acres Display Garden
956 Downey Road, Mount Vernon,
WA 98273
Tel: (360) 466-3158

Port Orchard

Elandan Gardens—
Display Gardens
3050 W. State Highway 16
(east of Gorst), Bremerton,
WA 98312
Tel: (360) 373-8260
Fax: (360) 373-8260

Internet Address:
http://elandangardens.com

Puyallup

VanLierop Bulb Farm—
Display Gardens
13407 80th St. E., Puyallup,
WA 98372
Tel: (253) 848-7272

Internet Address:
http://ohwy.com/wa/v/vanliero.htm

Redmond

Bamboo Gardens of Washington—
Display Gardens
196th Ave. & Redmond-Fall City
Road (Rte 202), Redmond, WA
98053
Tel: (425) 868-5166
Fax: (425) 868-5360

Internet Address:
http://www.bamboogardenswa.com/

Tumwater

Faerie Herb Gardens—
Display Gardens
6236 Elm St. SE, Tumwater,
WA 98501
Tel: (360) 754-9249

Vancouver

Aitken's Salmon Creek Gardens—
Display Gardens
608 NW 119th St., Vancouver,
WA 98685
Tel: (360) 573-4472
Fax: (360) 576-7012

Internet Address:
http://www.flowerfantasy.net

17th Ave. NE and NE 45th St.,
Seattle, WA 98195
Tel: (206) 543-5590
Fax: (206) 685-3039

Internet Address:
http://www.washington.edu/burke
museum/

Vashon Island

The Country Store—
  Demonstration Gardens
20211 Vashon Highway S.W.,
  Vashon Island, WA 98070

Tel: (206) 463-3655
Internet Address:
http://www.tcsag.com

INDEX

Page numbers refer to the page upon which a garden's entry begins.